LEGAL HELL

Angus M Brown

Pen Press

First published in Great Britain by Pen Press

All paper used in the printing of this book has been made from wood grown in managed, sustainable forests.

ISBN13: 978-1-907499-22-7

Printed and bound in the UK
Pen Press is an imprint of Indepenpress Publishing Limited
25 Eastern Place
Brighton
BN2 1GJ

A catalogue record of this book is available from
the British Library

Cover design by Tin Racer Design Ltd

This book is dedicated to the people of the country I love – Scotland – and to true democracy.

Democracy is so precious – it simply must prevail. It is too important to ignore, let alone to be taken for granted. There are many countries in this world who are crying out for the freedoms we enjoy. So let us value those freedoms and nurture them. Let us not allow them to be eroded within our own land.

Many thousands of people have found, or currently find, themselves in a similar position to me, suffering at the hands of a self-regulated, non-accountable, undemocratic legal profession. This book is also dedicated to these people. My message – you are not alone. There is hope. Be strong and know that I will continue to strive ceaselessly on your behalf – to bring about a more democratically accountable legal profession, and true justice for genuine complainants.

Contents

Acknowledgements

I wish to thank all those who have helped me to get this True Story completed and published. With their help I am now in a position to finally rid myself of the dreadful helpless feeling of "there is nothing I can do about it". With their help I am proud to have been able to prove that anything is possible when common sense is reinforced with a positive mental attitude and good people are behind me, all committed to ensuring that democracy shall prevail.

I would like to thank my good friend Aidan Duff, and his wife Beth, for their support over the past years. Aidan always believed me. What is more, he believed in me and encouraged me to embark on this challenging project. He committed much of his time to help me with the fine tuning of the book. I am aware of his other commitments, as a coach and facilitator and also as an author of three amazing books. So I am fortunate to have had his help, and the support of Beth in releasing Aidan from their business commitments, especially those relating to their work with people and horses. Their **red horse speaks** programme is a great example of a modern and enlightened approach to personal and team development.

I am particularly grateful to Pauline Brough for her constant encouragement and especially for her care and attention to me at times in my life when I needed it most. I have been through a series of health problems over the past years and she has always been there for me. Everyone who knows this wonderful lady will understand what I mean when I refer to her patience, understanding and care.

I wish to extend special thanks to the medical profession for their care and their complete understanding of my situation.

Finally I want my family to know how special they are to me. My wife, Kathleen, my son Alan and my daughters Maureen (Moe) and Lynda have shared my nightmare. Nor will I forget the help I was given by Moe's former husband, Doug Bruce, who through his support did more for me than I could have expected. This has been as hard on them as it has been for me. Yet, through it all they have shown patience, perseverance and support in the face of horrendous challenges – health and financial strains – throughout this whole 25 year saga.

Preface

This story is entirely true. The facts that are included are supported by documented proof and concrete evidence throughout. Any opinion, or subjective judgement based on the circumstances described herein, is identified in context as such. It is crucial for me that this principle is accepted by my readers because the purpose of this book is simply to serve those who may be experiencing similar circumstances, to prevent a similar nightmare from occurring in their lives, and to outline my own ideas of how the legal profession could be better monitored and made accountable to the ordinary, decent folk it is meant to serve. If you are one of these people, please understand that my intention is to help you, and not to embark on a personal crusade against the legal profession, where I know there are many decent human beings.

In *The Heartmath Solution* Doc Childre makes a beautiful point, that in the long run it's not a question of whether (others) deserve to be forgiven. One is not forgiving them for their sake. One is doing it for one's own sake. This is true for me. It is a place to which I have come after many years of turmoil and unnecessary pain that had torn away my peace of mind and brought me to ill health and unhappiness.

I have at last learned to release what has controlled me for so long. I no longer let the legal profession live rent-free in my head. I no longer hold a grudge. I am now free from the toxicity of torment. This may not appear to be the case within the book. In it, I have tried to capture the emotions that gripped me at the time – an accurate reflection of how I was being affected by the experience. If you are reading this story because you are facing a similar experience, I hope that I am able to help you, even if it is simply to say "You are not alone. I understand." It is in your power to be free of torment too.

Oscar Wilde said "Always forgive your enemies – nothing annoys them so much". If you are in the clutch of those to whom you are simply a unit of monetary gain, or of those who are prepared to go to any lengths to avoid taking responsibility for their own actions and incompetence, or if you feel controlled by a system that is self-serving, complacent and impersonal, please read this story. Release, if only for a moment, your own feelings of hatred. Instead read this story, relate to it if it is what you too are experiencing, and know that there is a voice here speaking on your behalf, a voice that reflects the many, many thousands who have lived a similar nightmare. Know that you are not alone and that one day, with inevitability, the British (Scottish) legal profession will change. Do not hold a grudge that you may not live to see that change, for holding that grudge is like drinking a poison and expecting the other person to die.

Forgive yourself for the times that you gave way to anger in the face of torment, and now read this book with an open heart and mind. If you choose to take this course of action, your challenges with the legal profession will not be solved magically, but you will regain control of your own thoughts and actions. What you may then do is see the traps into which you are walking, ask the right questions of those who represent you, refuse to accept that the profession holds a monopoly over competence and rectitude, and then challenge; insist on being the focus of your lawyer's actions, demand written justification of legal decisions and advice, record your experience and be vigilant. Let the profession know that its ethics and competence are under scrutiny and that your legal representatives are duty-bound to put your interests above their own.

"Who will guard the guardians?" In this world, right now, the legal profession is self-regulating. In purporting to be fair and open in its self-regulation, it has become **self-serving**. That is why as you embark on your relationship with the profession you can become the guardian of those who have no guardians. Let this book be your strength and your source of wisdom. In your discussions with them, let the legal profession be aware that you have read this book, that you are aware of the standards that they are obliged to work to, but that you have knowledge of what might happen when they are faced with a challenge to their professional ethics and practices. And then...

...embark on your journey with that profession without malice, without rancour and without ever finding cause to hold a grudge. Be polite but firm. Be gentle but strong. Be insistent but Courteous. Be unremitting in your resolution to prevail, but open to listening. That way, you will find clarity and peace of mind.

Finally, here is something to remember at all times – with reference to standards of ethics and practice, always have in mind:

1. **Professional Ethics and Practice for Scottish Solicitors 1984**

    DUTIES TO THE CLIENT. You owe a duty of care to your clients, and negligence may not only render you liable to compensate the client, but also may be of such a character and so aggravated as to constitute professional misconduct. Similarly, delay can also amount to professional misconduct.

    References to fact and law. You must not give to Court any information, which to your knowledge is contrary to the facts. You must investigate a case properly before raising an action.

2. There are First Division rulings stating that:

    A cardinal principle is that a solicitor should put his client's interest first and not his own.

    Failure to advise as to Legal Aid may lead to a claim for professional negligence.

3. *In Scotland where a conflict of interest either arises or seems at all likely to arise, a solicitor should immediately cease acting for one party, if not for both, advising him or them to seek independent legal advice.*

Note: All the above professional practice rules, ethics, and duties to the client can also be found in *Greens Solicitors Professional Handbook*

As you read through my True Story you will find the legal profession, within its system of self-regulation, makes a mockery of the above Ethics and Practices.

The legal profession is governed by a statute of law: **Solicitors (Scotland) Act 1980**, in which it is stated:

(1) The Law Society of Scotland (referred to in this Act as "the Society") shall continue to exist and shall exercise the functions conferred upon it by this Act.

(2) The object of the Society shall include the promotion of

(a) *The interests of the solicitors' profession in Scotland; and*

(b) *The interests of the public in relation to that profession.*

(3) The Society may do anything that is incidental or conducive to the exercise of these functions or the attainment of those objects.

Just look at these words again! It is my experience that a self-regulated legal profession – which is what we currently have – has looked after its own interests, in perfect accord with (2a), but has done so at the expense of complainants whose needs have been ignored. Thus the balance offered by (2b) has been nullified. Add to this the potentially sinister emphasis of the word "anything" in (3). When you read my story you will see how the legal profession is able to go to "any" lengths whatsoever to protect its interests. In a purportedly democratic society, this has been the sinister and perhaps inevitable consequence of self-regulation. Certainly, the needs of society have not been met.

And a final note:

Some readers may get a sense of repetitiveness in parts of the book. Please bear with me, recognising that I am reflecting the horrendous cycle of repetition that I experienced at the hands of a profession for which duplication of effort carries with it a very lucrative silver lining.

Chapter 1

The Man Who Had A Dream

My name is Angus McIntyre Brown. In 1979 I had a dream. It was to extend my business by starting a project that would provide for the future security of myself, my wife and my children. Surely I am just as entitled to have such a dream as the grandest and most powerful politician dreams of changing a country, or an actor dreams of stardom, or a saint of working towards a better world? This is my dream.

After five years of running a guest house in Aberdeen, my wife Kathleen and I decided to convert and extend our guest house, providing additional rooms, showers, and toilets. I was certain that, with a greater capacity, we would be able to better serve the higher demand that existed in Aberdeen at that time. Aberdeen was riding an economic boom as a result of North Sea oil. There was a need to accommodate offshore workers in transit between the oil rigs and their homes across Britain.

This conversion and extension project was put on hold for a short time when the hotel next door to us was put up for sale and we put in a bid to buy that hotel with the intention of saving ourselves the inconvenience of having to close down our own guest house for eight weeks whilst the conversion and extension were completed. Unfortunately we failed to secure the hotel; we were outbid.

After this setback, I concentrated once again on the conversion and extension project. We had already secured the services of our First Solicitor who had previously worked for us, successfully, when we purchased a country home. We looked upon him as a family solicitor, and asked him if he could now recommend an architect to do the necessary drawings and warrants for our guest house. I followed through with his recommendation and met with this First Architect. So began a nightmare that was to lead to over 20 years of hell.

As this story unfolds it will become clear why mention is made of a "first" Solicitor and a "first" Architect. Both were trusted as so-called "professional" gentlemen and I quite naturally assumed that they would act within the rules and ethics of their respective professions. How wrong I was! By being taken in by them I was soon to be engulfed by the machinations of a legal profession that, within the confines of a self-regulated hierarchy, was both crooked and incompetent. The words "crooked" and "incompetent" can only be deemed libellous if they are untrue. Let this story show their truth.

This True Story is told chronologically. By going through it year by year, it will be easier to read and more simple to follow.

Chapter 2

The First Architect

1979

When I was given the name of the Architect by my Solicitor (hereafter referred to as "[First Solicitor]") I arranged to have a meeting at the guest house to brief the Architect on all the details needed to obtain the conversion and extension. After going over these details and viewing the building, the Architect suggested a further meeting at his own house to sign an Agreement for the appointment of an Architect. This Memorandum of Agreement, under the RIBA book of engagement through to stage "H", namely the issuing of a Completion Certificate, was signed by the Architect (hereafter referred to as "[First Architect]") and myself, together with the agreed costs.

It was now the first architect's role to draw up the plans and obtain the necessary warrants. The drawings were duly completed and the warrants granted. During this process, [First Architect] was informed by the City of Aberdeen Department of Planning and Building Control that the guest house was in the list of buildings of Special Architectural Interest as a category B building. The permissions were granted, and carried with listed consent after going through all the necessary proceedings.

Any future changes to the scope of work would be required to go through the same procedure. [First Architect] was now fully aware of the situation before the construction began. It only remained for myself to select a building contractor.

While [First Architect] was making the drawings and warrants available, the selection of a contractor was put on hold because of a chance meeting with an officer from the Aberdeen Planning and Environmental Department who suggested that a grant would be available if I was to change the straight dormer windows already drawn up by [First Architect] back to the original bay type. This information was passed to [First Architect] who made the necessary changes (in 1980). The required documents, i.e. building warrants and planning permission, were now received from the Aberdeen Building and Planning Department, and [First Architect] was paid in full. We were now in possession of the necessary documents to proceed with the works.

1980

On 29th April (File 12-1), I received a letter from [First Architect] stating that he had joined another company as senior architect. He informed me that they operated from Glasgow and Aberdeen as a partnership and he wished to ask formally that the project commission for which he was originally appointed be transferred to the company he had now joined. In his capacity as a senior architect with this firm, he gave assurances that he would continue to give the commission his full personal attention and that his professional services would now be supported by the broader-based services offered by his new company. These services would include Town Planning, Landscaping, Design, and Interior Design, together with many years of experience as architects both in the UK and abroad. I was impressed and thanked him for the letter.

I then arranged a meeting with my accountant to calculate projected accounts. This was followed by a meeting with my bank manager for the purpose of raising a loan. There then followed meetings with the Scottish Tourist Board, to discuss grant funding and, finally, I interviewed a potential building contractor. The bank manager who granted the loan suggested that the conversion phase of the project be completed first, then to pause the building work for a further six months to trade normally and review the situation before continuing with the extension work. This approach was agreed.

Unfortunately, the Scottish Tourist Board refused any form of grants to help with the conversion or extension.

1981

With the avenues for any further assistance now fully explored, I asked [First Architect] to send me sets of drawings so that I could, in turn, issue these to building contractors for quotations for both the conversion and extension work.

[First Architect]'s reply (File 13) dated 15th May stated:

> *Please find enclosed the sets of drawings you requested. Should you wish to proceed with the works and would like me to supervise the construction, an essential factor in such a complex alteration, my fee would be in the region of £360. I trust this will be of interest to you.*

This sum was duly paid by me. I now had the services of an architect who would not only carry out the designs, but was also committed to **supervising** the construction work. After receipt of the drawings I then sent them out for tenders to seven building contractors. I then visited two of the contractors and also visited previous projects they had completed. I also contacted the owners of these projects who stated they were very happy with the builders, testimonials which helped me to make my choice of Contractor.

1982

After visiting the guest house and approving the plans for the conversion and extension, I received a letter from the Department of Planning and Building Control, in July 1982 (File 23) confirming the approval of a £3,000 grant towards the cost of restoration of our guest house. The grant was conditional on the work being completed to my satisfaction by March 1983. This letter was signed by the Director of Planning and Building Control.

On August 13ᵗʰ 1982 a meeting was held in the offices of [First Solicitor]. Present at that meeting were [First Solicitor], the Director of the construction company (hereafter referred to as "[Contractor]") that I had chosen, [First Architect], and myself. This meeting was called to sign the contract drawings and the contract between the builder and the employer, Mr Angus M Brown. At the conclusion of the meeting, after the contracts had been signed, I asked [First Solicitor] a vital question, "What do these documents do for me?"

His answer was "If either [First Architect] or [Contractor] invalidates the contract, this will be the document to constitute legal proceedings against either or both parties."

The signed Building Contract (File 19/20) referred to [First Architect] as "the Architect/supervising officer". The contract also stated that [Contractor] offered to carry out and complete the works (i.e. the conversion) for the sum of £14,500. On page 2 the contract stated that the work would commence on 23ʳᵈ August and would be completed by 18ᵗʰ October. Specific reference was made in this six-page contract to the fact that both [Contractor] and [First Architect] should adhere to these stipulations. That is why I asked the specific vital question at the above meeting in the Solicitor's office.

Everything now seemed to be in order, and it looked like my dream was finally in the process of being fulfilled. Or so I thought.

My architect, who was in complete control of the project, informed the Aberdeen Building and Planning Department that the building contract would commence on the 23ʳᵈ of August (File 24). It was now very important that, at the end of the conversion work, a Completion Certificate should be issued. This was under the control of [First Architect]. A Completion Certificate is essential for the following reasons:

1) To allow me to trade legally for a further six-month period in order that the bank would issue the loan for Phase 2 of the contract – the extension work

2) To release the £3,000 grant from Aberdeen District Council

3) To ensure that the £350 per week Liquidated Damages clause could be applied according to the building contract (the penalty for late completion).

Phase 1 – the conversion work – started on 23rd August, and seemed to be going quite well. The Contractor sealed off the upstairs of the guest house to minimise the noise and contain dust particles. My **supervising** [First Architect] must also have been happy with the way things were going because he wrote to me (File 25) on the 21st September stating:

> *Please find enclosed first interim payment certificate for £6175.00 to the Contractor for the conversion at the guest house…the sum is reasonable and should be made direct to the Contractor within 14 days of the above date.*

This was duly paid on time.

Because of all the pressures my wife and I had been under, we decided to take a holiday to our static holiday caravan, and leave the guest house in the hands of two friends with whom we would keep in touch by phone. It was early October. We had been gone four days when we got an emergency call from our friends. The rain in Aberdeen at that time was horrific and water penetration had come down the stairs from the conversion upstairs and caused substantial damage. This was due to both the severe weather conditions and the poor tarpaulin cover over the roof. I was furious and called [First Architect] to get this rectified as soon as possible. Unfortunately, we had to abandon our holiday although we were also fortunate inasmuch as our insurance covered some of the repair costs.

With the first £6,175 bill duly paid, just over three weeks into the contract, and with time now moving into October, I began to get a little concerned because things seemed to be taking a downturn. The pace of construction was slowing down and it was becoming quite obvious that things were radically wrong; firstly because of the attitude of the workers and secondly the standard of the work was poor. The agreed date of completion (18th October) was fast approaching.

My fears were exacerbated after talking to Council Planning Department inspectors on site. I followed this up with a request for a meeting at the guest house between [Contractor] and [First Architect] in an attempt to find out the current situation and future progress in relation to the Completion Certificate.

At the start of the meeting there was obvious discontentment between [Contractor] and [First Architect]. When I started to ask pertinent questions clear answers were not given because of the state of agitation between [First Architect] and [Contractor]. So heated was the meeting that [First Architect], without any apologies, simply got up and walked out. [Contractor] followed and, in passing, turned to me and said: "Where did you find that Mickey Mouse architect?"

I now ask the readers of this book what would you do in this kind of situation? Your questions have been ignored, you feel completely in the dark, and yet you must cooperate, stay calm, and get your priorities correct. How do you feel? Needless to say, I was utterly demoralised.

The completion date was now well past. In fact, it was Christmas time and the Contractor was still working at the guest house. We had to take things as they came and make the best of it, little knowing what lay in store for us – the unbelievable problems that I was going to face in the future. At the time, all we could do was soldier on regardless, bearing in mind again our key priorities – to keep running the guest house, regrettably at a reduced rate.

Remember, [First Architect] was in charge at all times. He had been hired to inform his employers (namely myself) of the progress of the contract all the way through to the award of the Completion Certificate.

It transpired that on 6th October (File 30) [First Architect] had written to the town planning officers. It was apparent that there was insufficient headroom, within the existing roof void, to take the five water storage tanks, so they had therefore been relocated in an insulated housing above the rear dormer window roof. I think I can fairly use the term "incompetent" to describe [First Architect]. How could his design have missed this basic element? He then compounded this error by removing the five water tanks from inside the apex at the front of the building and replacing them with a large water tank, with a capacity of 1,139 litres, on top of the roof **outside** at the rear of the guest house. This would require extra support plus various changes to other layouts. The main wall at the rear of the building had to be moved back to further support this large water tank.

This was a clear case of incompetent initial design resulting in a change to the scope of work approved by the Planning Department. [First Architect] attempted to cover his incompetence by writing to the Planning Department stating (untruthfully) that the wall at the rear had been moved because of "*demands made by my bankers for increased capacity of the guest house*"! This statement is an insult to the intelligence of any reasonable person.

On 21st December 1982 (File 43) [First Architect] wrote to me enclosing a copy of an undated letter he had sent to [Contractor] (File 42) regarding the works, in which he stated:

Following our recent meeting prior to Christmas I enclose a copy of outstanding items intimated to me by Aberdeen District Council still requiring your attention on the above project. You will therefore return to site and attend to all items on the enclosed list and inform me in writing as to the exact position regarding the complete rectification of all outstanding items.

Until such time as the items on the attached list are completed and the Certificate of Completion is issued by the Local Authority no further monies will be issued to you on the contract. Your failure to comply with this instruction will necessitate the termination of your contract under the terms of the standard form of building contract and the matter will be referred to Mr Brown's lawyers for the recompense of compensation under the terms of the building contract previously agreed and signed by yourselves. It will therefore be in the interest of both yourself and Mr Brown to achieve an amicable and efficient conclusion to this contract without further delay. Please acknowledge receipt of this letter and your willingness to comply noted.

I was very impressed with this conclusive, detailed letter, and wondered if there had been a positive knock-on effect from the pre-Christmas meeting that I had asked for. As I say, I was impressed with the letter, but I was also becoming very suspicious. The letter was undated. The contract had been due to be completed on the 18th October and there had been no correspondence from [First Architect] prior to that date. That in itself was strange given that [First Architect] and the builders had taken over the guest house and [First Architect] was in full charge, having been hired until the Completion Certificate had been issued, and having signed the contract to this effect.

Irrespective of what was going on in the background, I had to step carefully, balancing the need to keep things moving, whilst at the same time holding back further payments to [Contractor] until the Completion Certificate was forthcoming and in the hands of [First Architect].

I think at this point in time it is important for the readers to feel comfortable with the fact that this is a True Story by seeing evidence concerning the reported behaviour by the people who I had hired (and paid) to honour the signed contracts with integrity and honesty, following the rules of their profession. I think that by giving you the evidence against each individual, as it happened, I can best show you the type of people I was dealing with – people who lied, cheated, used corrupt practices, and took monies fraudulently.

As stated above, I was most impressed with the letter I received from [First Architect], however, I was at the time still ignorant of the fact that this architect had no morals. Strong words indeed! Here is the reason I use them: the Completion Certificate could not possibly be issued because of the undermentioned.

1) As already mentioned, his incompetence with the original design, as witnessed by his letter dated 6th October (File 30), asking for extensive amendments to the original plans 12 days before the contract was due to be completed.

Note: He was fully aware, by previous correspondence from the Council, that any amendments would require Listed Building Consent as my guest house was included in the list of Buildings of Special Architectural or Historical Interest as a category "B" (Group) building.

2) His inability to be truthful as witnessed by his letter to the District Council dated 8th November (File 32), making an Application for Amendment of Warrant, whilst on the same date (File 34) requesting a Completion Certificate for the works, which he stated were completed in November *on schedule*.

Note: The contract was supposed to be completed by 18th October 1982. How, therefore, could [First Architect] deem a November completion to be on schedule?

If I had been aware of the above details at the time I would have been alerted to the possibility of collusion between [First Architect] and someone in the Planning Department because of the suspicious nature of the correspondence.

[First Architect], already shown to be incompetent, is now seen to have no morals. His recourse to lies is unbelievable. His undated letter, copied to me, instructing the contractor to return to my guest house, had been very carefully written with the intention of trying to pass the blame on to the contractors. I was being misled. There is more evidence against this architect:

On 9th November (File 39) the District Council (Building Control) responded to [First Architect]'s Application for Amendment of Warrant stating that the Amended Plan was incorrect.

On 18th November (File 40) [First Architect] received a further letter from Planning Department, stating that:

1) The rear elevation did not relate to what was on site.

2) It was anticipated that enforcement action would be taken against the owner by planning *to secure the removal of (certain) works at the rear.*

Prior to the above correspondence (i.e. **evidence**) being sent to [First Architect], he had received a letter from the Contractor dated 13th October stating:

> *Due to the extremely bad weather of late, and the **ADDITIONAL** works to the contract, we would ask you to grant our company an extension of time. We trust you will grant us this additional time.*

At the time of all this correspondence, I was completely ignorant of the above facts. But I was not alone. [First Architect] had kept all incriminating evidence to himself, even to the extent that he failed to tell the Contractor of the enforcement action against me and the refusal of the Completion Certificate by the Planning Department.

It is important to note here the existence of the £350 per week liquidated damages clause for late completion. [First Architect] did not grant them an extension of time, for the obvious reason that he would have had to tell me the reason for the extra time and the necessary additions to the scope of work, all of which changed the contract price from £14,500 to approximately £18,000. This amounted to an increase of 25% to the contract price and, by keeping me in the dark regarding the changes to the scope of work and the delays, both parties had violated their contracts. Furthermore, by ignoring a reasonable request for extra time, [First Architect] had prejudiced any likelihood of my making any claims for late completion.

But that is not all. Further evidence started to mount against [First Architect] in that:

1983

On January 6th (File 52), [First Architect] wrote to me stating:

> *In view of the fact that your Phase 1 conversion is almost complete, I am now submitting my interim fee account for the works to the value of £175.00. I look forward to receiving your cheque as soon as convenient.*

My Phase 1 conversion was supposed to have been completed by 18th October 1982. I faced the dilemma – what could I do? I still had no Completion Certificate. I needed to pay this interim bill to keep things moving, and yet I had not received value from him for the money he sought. Furthermore, in 1980 I had already paid [First Architect] the amount of

£948 to cover the fees involved in drawing up the plans and obtaining the warrants. I had his signature to a contract with me agreeing to supervise the contract through to the awarding of a Completion Certificate (scheduled for 18th October 1982 and not yet received). And up to this moment I had received no apologies, let alone notification of reasons for the delays. I had to contain my anger. After much consideration, I decided to hold back the payment. After all, I had no Completion Certificate, and I now had a copy of the letter he had sent to the builders indicating that no monies would be paid to them until the work was satisfactorily completed.

On 7th February (File 50), [Contractor], still working at the guest house, wrote to [First Architect]:

> *Reference your letter of 21st December 1982. We have attended to all works noted as outstanding and completed same. The building inspector...has passed the works on 7th February 1983...*
>
> *We therefore ask that you make final inspection of the works and issue a valuation certificate, forthwith, to cover outstanding monies, less retention, all as detailed in our letter of 13th December 1982...*

The building inspector had indeed passed the works, but only in respect of the details that were listed, not the complete works or the completion of the building contract. I still had no Completion Certificate.

It is worth noting the time scale of the above correspondence – [First Architect] had sent his (undated) letter to [Contractor] in December 1982 (File 42) and copied to myself (File 43) on 21st December 1982, and [Contractor] had responded on 7th February 1983.

The pressure was really building. Furthermore, the standard of the work was still not to my liking. Now I simply **had** to let [Contractor] know about my concerns. I was furious with them, and blamed them for causing all the upheaval and the hassle in letting out the new bedrooms that were not quite finished. At the time I kept blaming them for everything – I had to keep moving guests from room to room. This dreadful situation continued for several months.

In late October I was at my wit's end. I simply had to get straight answers to what was going on and find out who was to blame for the Completion Certificate still not being issued. I decided to call [First Solicitor], hoping that with the authority of a legal practice supporting his presence, he would be well placed to ask straight questions and obtain straight answers. A meeting was arranged in their offices where all the above details were discussed. They were not entirely unaware of the agreement; after all, the original contracts had been signed in their office. I considered that it was better to leave it to them to find out why [first Architect] was evading his duties.

On 1st November 1983, (File 56) I received a letter from [First Solicitor]:

> *I refer to your recent meeting with myself and [fellow Solicitor] of this office. Following upon the meeting I duly wrote to [First Architect]* (File 58), *asking him to proceed with the certification of non-completion and defective works. I have now received the reply from [First Architect]* (File 58-1) *who states that he is not prepared at this stage to carry out the certification required. He gives as his reason for this: "I was outstanding a considerable sum in back fee" and "I am not prepared to continue to expend a considerable amount of time on this job unless fees are agreed in advance".*

Note: The true reason that he did not carry out the certification required is that he had tried on several occasions to get a Completion Certificate from the Planning Department and had been refused on every occasion. The reason for the delays is now quite obvious,

namely that he was still trying to hide the fact that he could not possibly get a Completion Certificate because of the unauthorised work, and the now impending enforcement order.

[First Solicitor]'s letter continues:

> *Obviously this is the first intimation of this I have had. In the past [First Architect] has indicated that he would be prepared to carry out the works and as you will recall a meeting was arranged but for certain reasons it did not take place. [First Architect]'s position will require to be clarified and I would be obliged by your telephoning me to discuss this.*
>
> *I would however indicate that matters are reaching a stage at which a positive decision must be taken. It is clear that you contend that [Contractor] are not entitled to any further payment due to the fact that they have (1) failed to complete the contract and (2) the works which they have undertaken to date are faulty and require rectification. If this can be established then [Contractor] would be in breach of the contract and this would give rise to certain remedies to you. These remedies would allow you to set off any sum which you were due to [Contractor] against any expenses incurred in connection with their breach of contract. These expenses would include extra interest, the cost of putting the defective works right and any extra costs in completion of their contract. Indeed given the terms of the contract there is also provision for damages for late completion at the rate of £350 per week. Having stated this, there is however a doctrine which the Court will apply and this is basically known as mitigation of loss, i.e. where one party is in breach of contract the other party must take all reasonable steps to minimise the loss incurred by him. It is clear therefore that any further delay in having the defective works certified, and obtaining a new builder to complete the works may fall outwith this doctrine of mitigation loss.*

Whilst it appears from correspondence that [First Architect] had not certified that [Contractor] are due any sums there is certainly a claim by them outstanding against you in the sum of £7,552.69 and it is against this sum which you are seeking to set off your losses. There has already been a delay in having the remedial works carried out and the work of which [Contractor] were contracted completed and I believe that any further delay would be held by the Court to be a delay not occasioned by [Contractor]'s breach in contract but by a failure on the part of yourself or [First Architect] to have the necessary works carried out as soon as reasonably possible. I certainly feel that the Court would not allow any further claim for the liquidated damages and may restrict claims for further elements. Obviously therefore it is essential that steps are taken to bring matters to a head. It is unfortunate that [First Architect] has taken the attitude that he is not prepared to carry out any further works but if the position is truly as stated in his letter then I see no alternative but that of your paying his fees so that we obtain from him as quickly as possible the necessary certification and thereafter having the remedial works carried out and the contract completed. This would then allow us to establish the amount of counter claim to which you would be entitled and enter into the necessary negotiations. In the circumstances I suggest that you consider matters and let me have your instructions as soon as possible. I look forward to hearing from you.

I called the Solicitor's office as requested, thanked them for the above letter, and in our phone discussion regarding fees to be paid to [First Architect], I reminded him that the contracted fees were payable to [First Architect] only on the completion of the contract and the awarding of the Completion Certificate. I should not have to pay him to return to our guest house to certify the non-completion and defective works. I reminded him of the earlier letter, now a whole year past, sent by [First Architect] to [Contractor] in December 1982 (File 42) and copied to me on 21st December 1982 (File 43). However, after further discussions I had to relent and pay the amount that was detailed in [First Architect]'s reply to the above Solicitor's letter (File 56), dated 1st November 1983.

1984

That reply was dated 31st January 1984 (File 58-1) where he detailed the amount of time it would take and the cost per hour, which would amount to a total of £371 and which included £20 of out-of-pocket expenses! He stated that the costs were in accord with the RIBA conditions of engagement.

Imagine the fury and anger inside me! It was making me feel ill. But, and I ask my readers to recognise how big a "but" this was, I simply had to comply with [First Solicitor]'s advice. It must be noted (for future reference) the date of [First Solicitor]'s letter to [First Architect] – 1st November 1983 (File 58) – and [First Architect]'s reply dated 31st January 1984 (File 58-1), a space of two whole months.

The fees, for [First Architect] to return to the guest house to complete the necessary works, were paid to the solicitor in advance. I was now waiting for [First Architect] to return to the guest house. The question kept raising its head: "What can I do about it?" The answer – nothing, except wait.

I received a letter from [First Solicitor], dated 6th September 1984 (File 66):

> *I refer to previous correspondence with regard to the guest house. I note that it has been some time since I heard either from yourself or [First Architect]. The last notification I have in the File is when you were to be on holiday and arrange a meeting on your return so that the issuing of the final certificate could be completed.*

> *I have not heard from [First Architect] either and I wonder whether or not the meeting has taken place. As I advised you in the past there is provision for liquidated damages amounting to £350.00 per week. However, I believe that the certification has dragged on for so long that only a small proportion of the time for which it has taken to certify the finalisation of the contract will be allowable for the purposes of calculation of liquidated damages. Obviously also until such time as certification has taken place, it is virtually impossible for you to instruct an alternative contractor. Perhaps in the circumstances you could advise me whether or not you have met with [Contractor] and if a final certificate has been issued.*

I could not believe this letter. I had done everything that had been asked of me, none of which had been enough to force [First Architect] back to the guest house. He simply kept coming up with excuses. All I could do was refer the Solicitor to all the past correspondence and the contracts, signed in front of the Solicitor in their offices, and rely on the Solicitor, now that he had been paid [First Architect]'s fees in advance, to press [First Architect] to return to the works at the guest house. I ask my readers to consider – surely that is what he has been paid to do? It is interesting to note the statement in the earlier letter of 1st November 1983 (File 56):

> *I see no alternative but that of paying his fees so that we obtain from him as QUICKLY AS POSSIBLE the necessary certification and thereafter having the remedial works carried out and the contract completed.*

I was becoming increasingly suspicious that there was collusion between [First Solicitor] and [First Architect]. After all, who was now holding up the proceedings with these exceptional delays?

I was furious with [First Solicitor]. He knew I had paid [First Architect] in full for his services which included – I repeat yet again – the completion of the contract through to the awarding of a Completion Certificate. But what could I do? I had been misled when I had to comply and pay the extra fee. It was perfectly reasonable to then expect things would move on quickly. But, of course, at the time I did not know how evasive and crooked [First Architect] was going to be. At least I thought, with the help from [First Solicitor], things would change, and change they did! But not for the better, as I was now discovering through the actions of [First Solicitor].

Given the knowledge that [First Solicitor] now had following my meeting in their offices in October 1983, his most recent correspondence to both [First Architect] and myself, where they mentioned remedial works and the Completion Certificate, and his possession of the contracts signed in his office with all the pertinent information including the start date of the contract and the date of completion, the obvious next step, even for a simple-minded solicitor, would have been to communicate with the Building and Planning Department and gather all the important information that could be found in the correspondence between [First Architect] and the Planning Department, starting as far back as 6th October 1982 when [First Architect] wrote (File 30) asking for amendments which he knew could not be accepted for various reasons including the fact it was a listed building in a conservation area. If [First Solicitor] had set up a simple meeting with the Planning Department, he could quite easily have gathered enough evidence to issue a writ against both [First Architect] and [Contractor].

According to the **Professional Ethics and Practice for Scottish Solicitors 1984**, any solicitor who is being paid by his client should put his client's needs before anything else, including his own. If he had followed through with all this information, and having asked me to pay [First Architect] an additional £371, he would have discovered the following list of important details, had he simply met with the Planning Department:

1) The Completion Certificate could not possibly be issued because of the undermentioned.

2) Certain works at the rear had to be removed (costs not known at this time).

3) Enforcement action against the owner.

The above further payment of £371 would have been avoided. The time-wasting could also have been avoided, although that is nothing compared to what I would face in the future regarding additional costs, and further unimaginable delays.

After many calls to [First Solicitor] and also to [First Architect], who I could not contact even after paying him the additional fees, I wrote [First Solicitor] a four-page letter (File 62). Because of my ignorance at the time in thinking that the blame lay primarily at the door of the Building Contractor, this letter detailed a list of defects which I had raised against [Contractor], who I was crucifying for all the mistakes and delays, unaware that [First Architect] had made massive changes to the original plans, resulting in an additional £4,000 to the contract price. I now know that, no matter who [Contractor] was, there would always have been unavoidable delays.

Along with my family, I was succumbing to the continuous pressures that had been put on us. I was now going to the doctor for help, describing to him the reasons for my symptoms. I was prescribed tranquillisers to help relieve me of the continuous pressures. I truly thought I had done everything correct in order to safeguard against any problems during the "eight-week" contract. In summary, I had:

1) Hired a reputable solicitor (or so I thought)

2) Hired and signed a contract with a listed architect, recommended by [First Solicitor]

3) Obtained seven contractors' quotes and assessed some of their previous work

4) Secured a bank loan

5) Secured a £3,000 grant

6) Signed a contract in [First Solicitor]'s office, (along with the Solicitors themselves, [First Architect], and [Contractor]).

1985

It was now nearing 1985 and I was not even close to receiving a Completion Certificate. Who was to blame? In thinking at first it was [Contractor], I had a rude awakening – discovering that my incompetent [First Architect] had been going behind my back, pretending he was an honest, forthright and first-class architect with qualifications after his name (DA, RIBA, ARIAS).

Here is a letter [First Solicitor] received from [First Architect], dated 8th February 1985 (File 68). This letter is in answer to [First Solicitor] asking [First Architect] to return to the guest house after I had paid the fees in November 1983.

Note: It had taken him all this time supposedly to correct the mistakes and certify the contract.

> *As **REQUESTED**, please find enclosed a statement of the final sum due by Mr Brown on the (guest house) contract. With retentions, outstanding payments and agreed additions this comes to £5,245.00.*
>
> *However, as you will see from the attached schedule of defects, I would not advise Mr Brown to settle any monies without first receiving satisfaction and reimbursement for his considerable additional financial outlay and personal inconvenience.*

> *Due to the exceptionally poor state of the workmanship and the fact that to this date [Contractor] or their agents have failed to complete the works, Mr Brown in theory at least, would be entitled to enforce the liquidated and ascertained damages clause in the contract at the rate of £350/week from 18th October 1982.*

It had now become quite apparent to me who the liar and cheat was, who had been hiding behind a cloak of deceit and corruption. Here is further evidence:

1) First of all he mentions in the first paragraph of his letter *agreed additions*. Nobody agreed to any additions. What additions? Here was a violation of his contract. He was simply covering up for his original mistakes and incompetent designs.

2) Some of the details and contents of his letter bear close similarity to the details and contents of [First Solicitor]'s letter to me (above) dated 1st November 1983 (File 56).

3) The attached schedule of defects **and** the words "due to the exceptionally poor state of the workmanship" are **alarmingly similar to the four-page detailed letter I wrote to [First Solicitor] in 1984 (File 62 mentioned above) where I listed the defects and lambasted aspects of the builder's workmanship**, at the time not knowing the reason they were rushing the contract.

The Architect had forced long delays in attempting to get a Completion Certificate. The question arises, therefore, why had [First Architect] indicated his satisfaction with progress and, after only three weeks, asked me to pay [Contractor] the sum of £6,175?

Now the corruption can be exposed. I can now go into his lies, deceit, incompetence and going behind my back in his communication with the Town Planning Department and [Contractor], and the collusions with [First Solicitor].

The Case Against [First Architect]

This incompetent [First Architect] knew beyond any shadow of a doubt that a Completion Certificate would never be granted. He was very clever and kept this fact to himself. He corresponded with the Department of Planning and Building asking for a Completion Certificate, but was refused on every request. Here are the details:

Note: With my readers' forbearance, and at the risk of repetition, I will now go back in time and revisit evidence that had not been in my possession at the time:

1. 6th October 1982 (File 30), [First Architect] wrote to Aberdeen District Council:

    Please find enclosed amended plans to take account of the following amendments:

    1) *The alteration to the front dormers was made following a request from the Planning Department to construct dormers and windows in line with the aspirations within the area of Mr Brown's guest house conservation area and for which my client was offered a grant. Planning consent has already been obtained for the dormers as previously designed.*

    2) *The rear dormer has been moved back 500mm to maximise the available floor area on the upper floor area and in order to give my client a higher financial return on his investment and as demanded by his bankers.*

    3) *There proved to be insufficient headroom within the existing roof void to take the water storage tanks and to still comply with Water Board regulations for access and headroom etc. Tanks have therefore been located in an insulated housing above the rear dormer window roof. Provision is also to be made within Phase 1 for an access door and stairway*

off the top landing on to the roof of Phase 2 in order to provide the households with an external clothes drying area. This door will remain locked, at all times, until Phase 2 is complete, but is to be constructed now in order to allow the stairwell to be fully and completely decorated.

Regarding item 2 above, I could not believe how far [First Architect] would go with his lies and deceit. If he had told the truth he would have had to admit that he moved the wall back to support the single large water tank that was to be constructed on the roof as a result of his own faulty design in failing to see that there was insufficient headroom to accommodate the five storage tanks he had originally catered for. Then he brings my bank manager into the fray! I could not believe the duplicity of this man.

Before submitting his request for the above amendments, he had been fully informed by previous correspondence that any amendments would require Listed Building Consent as my guest house was included in the list of buildings of Special Architectural or Historical Interest as a category 'B' (Group) building.

2. He was so clever – telling me in his letter dated 8th February 1985 all the items I could claim back from [Contractor], including the £350 per week liquidated damages for late completion, which in reality would be impossible to claim. Impossible, because he did not grant an extension of time in response to [Contractor]'s written request on 13th October 1982 stating:

    Due to the extremely bad weather of late, and the ADDITIONAL WORKS [£4,000 worth, which was kept hidden from me], we would ask you to grant our company an extension of time.

3. What follows is mind-boggling to say the least. I discovered much later that the Director of Planning and Building Control had written to [First Architect] on the 29th October 1982 (File 31):

I refer to the meeting on site 28ᵗʰ October 1982 with regards to The Browns' guest house and would confirm that certain matters which were discussed on site require some attention.

1) *The new stairway, which has been formed to give access to the upper floor bedrooms, is defective in a number of aspects.*

   (a)   *The clear headroom is inadequate at the top section of the stairway.*

   (b)   *The width of the Stair is not as per approved plan.*

   (c)   *The width of the half-landing between ground and first floors is not as approved plan*

2) *The exit passage and stairway are in the process of being covered with a wood laminate type of board. This must give a 'Surface Spread of Flame' rating of Class 'O'.*

3) *The new Dormer Windows to the front of the building do not comply with the necessary criteria for escape purposes.*

4) *There does not appear to be any secondary ventilation to the bedrooms. In addition to the above items it will also be necessary to apply for an Amendment to Warrant, for the changes to layout.*

I trust you will put these matters in hand at your earliest convenience.

Let me remind my readers, the above letter was dated 29ᵗʰ October 1982. Ten days later the following were submitted by [First Architect]:

8ᵗʰ November 1982 (File 32) – Application for Amendment to Warrant

8th November 1982 (File 34) – Application for Certificate of Completion for works at The Brown's guest house, which was completed in November 1982 *on schedule*

Both of the above were signed and dated by [First Architect]. I am sure the readers of this book will agree that this is unbelievable. Here we have a so-called "qualified architect" who, having been given the above precise details in the letter dated 29th October 1982 (File 31), could ask for an amendment and a Completion Certificate at the same time in a space of 10 days.

Remember, all this came to light in 1985. Had I been aware of the above details at the time I would have suspected some sort of collusion, conniving, or conspiring between the Planning Department and [First Architect]. Further information then came to light:

4. On 9th November 1982 (File 39) the Planning Department sent a reply to [First Architect] stating A*mended plan incorrect*, followed by a further letter dated 18th November 1982 (File 40) which states the following:

1) *The rear elevation does not relate to what is on site.*

2) *It is anticipated that enforcement action will be taken against the owner by Planning, to secure the removal of certain works at the rear.*

The above letter is crucial because of the enforcement order (2) and the further costs that would be imposed on me to remove the works at the rear.

All the above correspondence between [First Architect] and the Building and Planning Control had been cleverly concealed from me in 1982. I could now (in 1985) see that I had employed an incompetent architect who had sought all along to escape this situation. He had cleverly sent me the letter dated 21st December 1982 (File 43) – which is a copy of a letter he sent to [Contractor] – referring to the Aberdeen District Council's list of defects for [Contractor] to correct, but failing to mention the unauthorised works and the pending enforcement action. The rest of that letter had been cleverly worded to take the pressure off himself by not disclosing to me the full list of defects and by intimating that only one further item (a fire coat certificate) needed to be resolved for a Completion Certificate. I was therefore under the impression that [Contractor] was the cause of the delays. [First Architect] was fully aware that he had kept me in the dark and completely ignorant of the true facts. He was trying to buy time. Another more sinister explanation existed. Was he colluding with a member of the Planning Department to get rid of the enforcement order of the unauthorised works, for which he and he alone was responsible? Why else would he persist in applying for a Completion Certificate when it was confirmed that both [First Architect] and [Contractor] had built unauthorised works.

5. Two weeks later (6th January 1983) he submitted his invoice stating *in view of the fact your Phase 1 conversion is almost complete I enclose my fee for* [supervision and drawings].

Note: This is important for future reference.

It must again be noted that [First Architect], who was in complete charge, should have kept me informed regarding everything related to the signed contract. I had put my full trust in [First Architect], who himself had been recommended by [First Solicitor], to keep me fully informed.

6. On 7th January 1983 (File 45) [First Architect] received a further list of defects, from the Planning Department, and also informing him that, if a Completion Certificate was not received, this could cause trouble obtaining further approvals and with any future attempts to sell the property. This was not all. Further defects came to light:

7. On 9th January 1983 (File 47) another letter was submitted to [First Architect] from the Planning Department itemising building and plumbing works to be completed by amended warrant.

8. On 26th August 1983 (File 48) the draining inspector informed [First Architect] that the first floor bedrooms required to be connected to the draining system.

I think it is important for the readers of this book to try to understand the predicament [Contractor] found themselves in as a result of the massive changes to the conversion work after starting the contract. [First Architect] kept receiving letters from the Planning Department requiring him to correct his own errors, thereby putting strain on [Contractor] because the completion date of 18th October 1982 still pertained and mainly because of his stupidity and incompetence in writing to the Planning Department on 6th October 1982, 12 days before the completion date, requesting an amendment with massive changes (increasing the contract price from £14,500 to over £18,000), and leading to an enforcement order being prepared against myself, who was completely ignorant of all the above.

9. On 7th February 1983 (File No 50) [Contractor] wrote to [First Architect] saying:

> *Reference your letter dated 21st December 1982 (File 42) we have attended to all works noted as outstanding, and completed same. We therefore ask you make final inspection of the works and issue a valuation certificate (this amount comes to £7,552).*

Again it is very important to note the above dates. With no correspondence from [First Architect] in relation to the Completion Certificate, I was furious but at that time could do nothing about it because of my ignorance of the true facts. For example, I was not aware of further correspondence from the Planning and Building Control Department to [First Architect], regarding Completion Certificate.

10. From Department of Planning and Building Control 12ᵗʰ July 1983 (File 53):

> **Building Scotland Acts 1959-70**
>
> *With reference to the notification of completion certification submitted for The Browns' guest house, I wrote to you on 7ᵗʰ January 1983 and 28ᵗʰ March 1983 stating a list of defects requiring attention before a Completion Certificate can be granted. Unless a reply is received indicating that these matters have been dealt with it may be necessary for me to commence legal proceedings under section 10 of the above Act. Should you wish to discuss this matter I would be pleased if you could contact a member of my building control section.*

The following remedial action was also listed:

> *1) An earth bond in an accessible position must be provided at the gas service.*
>
> *2) The gas supply must be bonded on the customer side of the meter.*
>
> *3) All plumbing pipe work has to be installed as per the approved plan.*
>
> *4) A final test is required on the plumbing works. Please contact my district drainage inspector before 10am Monday to Friday to have this test carried out.*
>
> *5) All permanent ventilation must be fitted a minimum of 2 meters above floor level.*
>
> *6) The wall finish to the stair enclosures must be completed to achieve a class 'O' wall finish.*

It is interesting to note here that no mention is made of the unauthorised works or the enforcement order.

11. Further lies then flowed from [First Architect]. On 24th August 1983 (File 55) he wrote to Planning and Building Control stating that he had been informed by his client (myself) that:

> *All outstanding works noted in your enclosed letter have been concluded. We would therefore be obliged if you could arrange an inspection and issue a Completion Certificate.*

He was cleverly lying, telling the Planning Department that I was involved in this scam. How far would this perpetual liar go? Was he colluding with someone in the Planning Department?

This was his final attempt to gain a Completion Certificate. He was in the full knowledge, along with [Contractor], that they had both violated and breached their contract. To reiterate:

1) [First Architect] had been paid to supervise the contract through to the awarding of a Completion Certificate under the signed conditions of the RIBA rules of engagement.

2) No additions or amendments to the contract could be applied without the employer's (my) permission.

3) [First Architect] must work to the drawings signed in [First Solicitor]'s office.

4) [First Architect] and [Contractor] both violated their signed contracts by not working to the drawings along with the warrants after they started the contract.

5) They both further violated and breached their contracts by **not** informing me of the massive changes without quotations, and of the increase to the original agreed cost of £14,500.

With all his guile, in keeping the correspondence between him and the Planning and Building Department to himself, and his failure to get a

Completion Certificate after three separate attempts, he could not escape the fact that his continuous lies and incompetence would eventually catch up with him.

He knew from the outset that the mistakes he had made with the drawings and the design of the conversion and the extension should not have been made by any reasonably informed architect.

From the time he asked for the amendments (6th October 1982 – File 30) up to 24th August 1983 (File 55), 10 months had passed with three different attempts to gain a Completion Certificate resulting in three refusals. He was fully aware he would never get a Completion Certificate because of the correspondence he received from building control as far back as 18th November 1982 telling him:

> *The rear elevation does not relate to what is on site and it is anticipated that enforcement action will be taken against the owner by planning to secure the removal of certain works at the rear.*

This enforcement action would inevitably cause further grief and added expense to the ongoing rising costs.

The reason that I had I continued to trust [First Architect], until I had received no further communication regarding the contract, was because of the letter he wrote to [Contractor] on 21st December 1982 telling them to return to the guest house to rectify the list he sent (which they apparently did according to their letter on 7th February 1983 – File 50) and because he had written to me about one more item that required attention for a Completion Certificate, namely the fire coat certificate, giving the impression that he had everything in hand. In 1985, when all the facts became known to me, I was furious with [First Solicitor], who knew I had paid [First Architect] in full for his services, which included payment for the completion of the contract with the awarding of the Completion Certificate, which had not yet been issued.

I had been misled. I'd had to comply and agreed to pay the extra fee to [First Architect]. I had fairly expected things to move on quickly. But I had not known how evasive and crooked this architect was going to be! I had thought with the help from [First Solicitor] things would change. They did change, though certainly not for the better. I had yet to find out that further troubles lay ahead from the actions of [First Solicitor].

Chapter 3

The First Solicitor

Any solicitor who is being paid by his client should put his client's needs first before anything else, including his own interests. If [First Solicitor] had followed through with all the information relating to the remedial works and the Completion Certificate mentioned in his letter after asking me to pay [First Architect] an additional £371, all the wasted time and costs which will be revealed as we go through this incredible saga could have been avoided. He would have discovered the following important details if he had met with the Planning Department.

1) [First Architect] had attempted to vary the contract to compensate for his original faulty design, resulting in:

2) The Completion Certificate could not possibly have been issued, because of the undermentioned:

   a) Certain works at the rear were required to be removed.

   b) Enforcement action was threatened against myself, as the owner.

After many calls to [First Solicitor], and also to [First Architect] who I could not get hold of after paying him the additional fees, I wrote a four-page letter to [First Solicitor], dated May 1984 (File 62). Because of my ignorance this letter detailed a list of defects which I had been taking against [Contractor] who I was crucifying for all the mistakes and delays. When I wrote the letter I did not know that [First Architect] had made massive changes to the original plans, adding £4,000 to the contract. Irrespective of who the contractor was, there was always going to be unavoidable delays. I had been misled.

[Contractor] went into liquidation in 1983 and appointed receivers who tried to get monies from me for the unfinished contract. They wrote to [First Solicitor] in April 1985 stating that, according to their records, the delays on the project were not of [Contractor]'s making but were due to other trades, variations and in particular (as discussed) the need for adequate planning approvals to be obtained to allow for the issue of an adequate habitation certificate. They had clearly rumbled the incompetence of [First Architect]. This further evidence was now in [First Solicitor]'s possession and raised the obvious question – where were the writs that should have be issued against both [Contractor] and [First Architect] back in 1983?

By writing the above four-page letter to [First Solicitor] I had unwittingly played into the hands of both [First Solicitor] and [First Architect], bearing in mind I had no knowledge of the correspondence between the Planning Department and [First Architect] regarding unauthorised works, the enforcement order, and the Completion Certificate that would never be granted.

I received a letter from [First Solicitor] on 6th September 1984 (note the date) (File 66), saying:

> *I refer to further correspondence with regards to the works to the guest house. I tried to contact your architect but he was away on holiday. I have not heard from him. Was there a meeting between you and your architect when he returned from holiday?*

My frustrations and anger were growing. The additional fee was paid to [First Architect] using the funds held by [First Solicitor] when, as factor, he collected rental for my country home. I had not, nor should I have had to, give instructions to anyone. That was up to [First Solicitor] who was being paid to act in my interests.

As further evidence against [First Architect], it is important to note that the letter from [First Architect] to [First Solicitor] dated 8th February 1985 (File 68) starts off by stating *as requested.* Also the bottom of the letter it showed *cc Mr Brown.*

A postscript included the words *"my appointment as architect for Mr Brown extended only to the production of drawings and obtaining planning permission and building warrant (site supervision was not requested)."*

It does not require a high degree of intellect to cross reference all the aforementioned correspondence (for example, an invoice dated 6th January 1983 (File 44) – "Fee for supervision and drawings") and to come to the conclusion that a so-called professional architect could stoop as low and resort to writing the above postscript. Further examples of his taking on a "supervision" role are in his attendance at site meetings with the Planning Department to discuss the unauthorised works.

As I have stated before, all of the above correspondence between [First Architect] and the Building and Planning Department was kept from me. Any suspicions I had in regards to [First Architect] had remained as suspicions, until now. My fears were verified by the above postscript. And also by the concrete evidence in my possession at that particular time. It was also becoming clear that the further suspicions I had about [First Solicitor] were reaching a point where I did not trust him – because of the above File 68 starting with *as requested.* [First Solicitor] must have made the request!

Here is the concrete evidence I had in my possession prior to the above letter dated 8th February 1985 (File 68):

1) Agreement for the appointment of an Architect under the RIBA conditions of agreement to stage "H", i.e. to the issuing of a final certificate of completion. On the issue of the final certificate the final instalment of all fees and other charges would then be due for payment.

2) Building contract to be carried out under the direction of [First Architect] referred to as the "Supervising/Architect".

3) After three weeks into the contract (21st September 1982) the supervising architect asks me to pay [Contractor] the sum of £6,500 (a supervisory activity).

4) His instructions to [Contractor] in December 1982 (File 42). He must have forgotten that he sent me a copy of this letter – (File 43) on 21st December 1982 – which is clearly supervisory.

5) Invoice from [First Architect] to me dated 6th January 1983 (File 44) – fee for **supervision and drawings**.

With all of the above details/evidence in my possession I now knew for certain that [First Architect] was both cunning and crooked, with no morals. I felt that he was in collusion with [First Solicitor] and, if that was indeed the case, where and to whom could I turn after having paid all the fees to [First Architect] (a total of £1,308)? I still did not have a Completion Certificate and I was facing an enforcement order because of this architect, with unknown further costs.

First and foremost I had to deal with the above letter dated 8th February 1985 (File 68). Had [First Solicitor] suggested to [First Architect] that he write the above very clever letter, with copy to me, both parties knowing full well that I could not get a Completion Certificate? [First Solicitor] had in his possession the signed contracts relating to [First Architect] supervising the contract. What was he going to do about it, bearing in mind the rules and regulations set by the legal profession?

In many discussions with [First Solicitor] I kept asking him the same question over and over again. Why have you not researched this case properly with all the evidence in your possession when you stated at the signing of the contracts that, if either or both violate the contracts, they could be taken to Court? On every occasion, I was brushed off by his replies.

I am sure the readers of this book, like me, will not believe what is coming next. I received a letter from [First Solicitor] dated 22nd February 1985 (File 73), saying:

> *My firm of Solicitors are splitting up and moving to set up a new partnership.*

I retained my original Solicitor and gave instruction to leave my papers there. Of course I was dubious and would eventually learn at my cost all about solicitors, the legal profession and the Law Society.

After the split the bubble finally burst on [First Architect]. On 14th March 1985 a newspaper article carried the story: **City guest house owner may be facing legal action for allegedly carrying out unauthorised building improvements.**

After reading the local newspaper I was extremely upset and angry, even depressed. What could I do? Surely, at least, I would now get the whole truth (or so I thought).

I wrote a lengthy letter to [First Solicitor] regarding the newspaper article and let him know my feelings. It was now up to him to issue the writs and bring both [Contractor] and [First Architect] to Court.

He wrote to me on 21st March 1985 (File 75):

> *I have read the file in connection with the above. It surprises me that this matter has been going on for such a long period of time without anybody taking the bull by the horns and getting the matter resolved. I must say that I would have handled things differently and would have got things sorted out by now. I will do my best to resolve matters as quickly as possible.*

> *As regards the article, at the moment of dictation I have still to do more research, but I doubt if there is much we can do if it is fair reporting. The difficulty regarding the works seems to be one of some confusion. I hope to be able to clarify matters in very early course.*

I was impressed with some of the details in this letter. However, I also wondered if I was at last going to see some positive quick progress, or whether it was just a con. Was I going to be misled once again? It was not long before I found out. The following communications may give some indication that matters continued to decline:

On 12th August 1985 (File 76), the receivers acting for [Contractor] wrote to [First Solicitor] regarding "monies due".

On the same date (File 77), the Council's Department of Law and Administration wrote to [First Solicitor], saying:

> *I am in receipt of your letter of 30th July 1985 and am disappointed that a misunderstanding appears to have risen in relation to the payment of the Grant i.e. £3,000 from the Council's Conservation Fund. Although the Council had previously decided not to make payment of the Grant in the light of the unauthorised works which had been carried out, the Director of Planning and Building Control in a recent report on the Conservation Fund for the current financial year suggested, and the Council have accepted his suggestion, that payment of a grant possibly at a reduced level be made.*

> *I understand the relevant members of the Planning Department would be willing to participate in the joint meeting which you have suggested with a view to resolving the outstanding matters to the satisfaction of all concerned and I await your suggestion of possible dates. The best time for me would be the week commencing 26th August 1985.*

So, it had taken five full months for [First Solicitor] to finally get back to me, on 14th August 1985 (File 79), by sending me a copy of the above report, and suggesting that 27th August would be a suitable date for the meeting with the Department of Law and Administration. Further, in this letter he suggested that only he and I attend this meeting, at which he would do all the talking. He then had the gall and the audacity to tell me to find another architect – he did not want [First Architect] to attend this meeting.

I was furious, but I knew that it would be ludicrous to approach another architect at this moment in time. I was trapped, forced to continue. However, it was becoming quite obvious who he was protecting – certainly not The Browns. He knew full well what was going on and was possibly waiting for a vehement reaction from me. Fortunately, I had more sense.

Included with his letter was a copy of a letter he received from the receivers acting for [Contractor], in which it was stated that the receivers blamed [First Architect] for all the contract problems.

What had happened since the newspaper article in March up to 14th August 1985 (five months since he told me he would have sorted things) was that he had been meeting with [First Architect] to plan various cunning ways to avoid actions against him. Could this have been the reason he wished to avoid taking him to the planned meeting with the Department of Law and Administration?

One does not need to be a solicitor, nor does it require any great intellect, simply common sense, to make sure that [First Architect] should have been required to attend the meeting. After all, it was he who had drawn up the plans, got the building warrants, stated in writing when the contract would start and finish, made all the amendments, including carrying them out without permission, thus resulting in the unauthorised works enforcement order against his employer, namely myself. Of course [First Architect] should have been present at the meeting, prepared to answer for his actions and quantify everything in relation to both [Contractor] and himself. This would have been the very opportunity for all of the details of the correspondence between the Planning and Building Control Department, together with that between [Contractor] and [First Architect], to be aired. We could then have moved forward very quickly.

But [First Solicitor] asked me to find another architect! I approached two other firms of architects telling them the truth and what was going on. They both declined, aware of the possible legal action against [First Architect].

I also followed [First Solicitor]'s instructions to keep quiet at the arranged meeting. Without [First Architect] present, [First Solicitor] made several attempts to get the unauthorised works order removed but the Planning Department stood firm and the enforcement order still pertained.

I would now like to make two comments to allow my readers to understand how impotent I felt:

1) As you read this True Story you will learn, as I have done, that one of the biggest ploys used by the legal profession is to agitate a potentially difficult complainer/complainant. This gets rid of them easily and quickly for the simple reason that, if you react violently you then have no hope of progressing your case. I have found through discussion with many others that this very tactic has been played on them, resulting in an adverse and costly outcome.

2) I have received many communications with people in similar circumstances to my own. All have said the same thing – that the thought, *"What can I do about this?"*, constantly comes to mind. Sadly, the answer is *"Nothing"*. Nothing, that is, unless you have read this book and the advice it contains.

Solicitors garner information from many different sources, including through discussion with their client. It becomes second nature for them to read what is on the mind of the client. With all the concrete evidence in his possession against [First Architect], it was becoming clear that [First Solicitor] was far from inept. He was actually cunning. Was he soon going to have two clients from whom he could collect monies (in legal terms – a conflict of interest, frowned upon by the Law Society) now that he had all of the details from the meeting? He had certainly done an efficient job in protecting [First Architect] thus far – especially by making sure he was not exposed at the arranged meeting.

[First Solicitor] then called me to say that he had been in touch with another firm of architects who would soon contact me with a view to helping with the unauthorised works, and to once again try for a Completion Certificate. I then asked him about the signed contracts in his possession regarding both [Contractor] and [First Architect], and asked what action he was going to take. His first remark was that we had to concentrate on getting rid of the pending enforcement notice and keep the Planning Department happy. In this respect I had to agree. However, he was playing a clever game, avoiding further obvious questions. He then asked me if I would provide him with all the evidence I had against [First Architect]. This I did, furnishing him with 17 pages of documents.

Surely now, with the concrete evidence in his possession from various people, [First Solicitor] could at last act accordingly in the best interests of his client – myself – and find me the justice I deserved? After all, I had done nothing wrong and had followed the rule of law. It was now up to [First Solicitor].

What did he now do? Is it possible he colluded with [First Architect] and passed all the details to him? Could this be a true conflict of interest? I ask my readers to wait and see!

On 3rd September 1985 (File 80) I received a letter from a firm of architects (now identified as "[Second Architect]"), saying:

I have been asked by your Solicitor to look into the possibility of acting on your behalf in resolving difficulties which you are presently encountering with the Disctict Council. Prior to becoming involved it is clearly essential for me to isolate the problem to be overcome, specify that problem precisely and propose a method by which I would expect to resolve it.

Accordingly I refer to our telephone conversation yesterday when you summarised the situation and your understanding of it. Following that conversation I spoke to two members of Disctict Council's Planning Department

It appears that the matter can be resolved by the following method.

1) A plan should be prepared showing the building elevations as they have been constructed.

2) With reference to the above plan a revised proposal should be designed to show compliance with the requests of Disctict Council in order that such a plan may be returned to the planning committee for their further consideration and, if appropriate, works carried out bringing out the current building form into line with an agreed form.

I understand that if the above proposal is followed then, upon re-consideration of the matter, the District Council's Planning Committee may release all or part of those funds, which were previously to be paid to you by way of a Conservation Grant. Alternatively, I understand that you presently have planning permission for an extension utilising a mansard roof arrangement.

I am advised that if this permission were acted upon then it might well be the case that point (2) as mentioned above, could be superseded. It would be necessary for you to return to the

Planning Committee with a clear statement of your intent in respect of your proposal to carry out further works for which you presently have planning consent in such a manner as to overcome the presently unauthorised works.

If your proposal to construct four additional bedrooms, etc, exceeds the proposal for which you currently have planning consent then I understand from the gentleman I spoke to in Planning, that this may well be considered over-development of the site (my own investigation of the site does tend to suggest that the congested area of the back "garden" area may well be construed as over-development).

Whilst I am not totally acquainted with the situation I did understand from the gentleman, that your proposed roof garden/ drying area was not altogether out of the question if it were placed at first floor level. He seemed to believe that your proposal was that it be constructed at second floor level.

In consideration of accepting a commission to resolve your problems I spoke to [First Architect] as a matter of Courtesy. I understand he has been paid in full for his services and accordingly there are no difficulties in that respect.

You will appreciate that it is impossible for me to assess the amount of work which will be required to resolve this problem. The Planning Department's requirements have not yet been fully specified and I also have a distinct impression that you will oppose certain of their proposals and equally certain that your proposals may be wholly unacceptable to them. It is not my intention to act as mediator in this matter but merely to resolve the problem of unauthorised work and obtain a settlement with the Planning Authority, which will avoid you facing enforcement action. On this basis I can but suggest that my appointment be based upon fees charged at a quantum merit rate.

Fees charged for my own involvement amount to £25 per hour and time spent by my assistants, in preparing plans etc. are charged at £18 per hour. To this must be added a charge for expenses which may be incurred in printing/duplicating, etc. plus VAT at the normal rate. Fee accounts would be raised on a monthly basis with a statement indicating the number of hours expended along with a statement of progress. I would also wish your account, with me, to be placed in credit to the value of £250 as a gesture of good faith.

Finally, should we agree on this matter, I would require that my appointment be confirmed by you in writing.

Should the above conditions be agreeable to you I would be pleased to meet and discuss the matter further.

I had no choice but to agree to the above appointment. I met with [Second Architect] and agreed to the contract fees and the deposit of £250. I felt I had no choice but to agree – because of the unauthorised works and the pending enforcement order.

Once more I was in a state of shock, gutted! I had to contain myself and act accordingly but the same thoughts kept nagging in my head, namely:

1) I had signed contracts with both [Contractor] and [First Architect] in front of [First Solicitor] to complete a simple conversion in eight weeks. That was in August/October 1982!

2) The original signed contract seemed worthless given the seemingly endless monies lost – the fact that we couldn't rent out the rooms, the changes to the contract, i.e. the £4,000 additions, the loss of the £3,000 grant, monies already paid to [Contractor] and [First Architect] (£7,669), what I was losing as a result of the nonexistence, now, of the second project (extension) which should have been started six months after the conversion, and whereby

my banker was to have given me a loan of £6,000 on completion of the conversion.

But I simply had to soldier on irrespective of the situation.

A meeting dated 1st October 1985 was set up at the Council offices where I met with a member of the Council and [Second Architect]. This meeting did clarify many details in regards to planning applications, specific drawings acted on throughout the contract, and we started making headway with the new applications, as required by the Council.

[Second Architect], also on the same day (File 82) wrote to [First Solicitor] giving him the specific details of the meeting, and informing him that Mr Brown had agreed that:

I ask you to provide me with all correspondence relative to this project which you may hold on File including drawings, sketches, and the like. When I have used these, I will copy those of interest to me and return the principal copies as soon as possible. I have asked Mr Brown to do likewise.

In the meantime it may be appropriate to ask [First Architect] to surrender all drawings and documents pertaining to the Local Authority approvals, which he may hold on File. Again if these were made available to me they would be of great help.

On 7th October 1985 (File 85) [Second Architect] wrote to [First Solicitor] thanking him for sending the files, and saying:

Having read both files I have extracted those items, which are of particular interest in resolving the current planning difficulties. Needless to say much of the file pertains to contractual difficulties, which although of interest, are of no relevance to my appointment.

> *Sadly, there were only two drawings in the files. It will therefore be necessary to obtain further information from [First Architect].*
>
> *I have promised Mr Brown I will handle this matter in the most economical form possible and since I am aware of the substantial quantity of drawings/information being available it would seem fruitless for me to have my staff resurvey the building at some considerable cost.*
>
> *I would be obliged if you would contact [First Architect] and arrange for me to be provided with the relevant information. For your information I have, as a matter of Courtesy, advised [First Architect] of my appointment and he seems content to relinquish responsibilities for resolving the difficulties to my practice.*

With regard to the last sentence, it goes without saying that [First Architect] would be more than content to hand over **his** responsibilities after all the difficulty and torment he had caused me, not to mention the added expenses, the impending enforcement order, and the unauthorised works he had negligently introduced. Also, he would have had to incur the same further additional costs for the work that [Second Architect] was now charging for, and finally, he could only be delighted that all the unknown costs needed to restore the conversion to an acceptable conclusion for the Building and Planning Department to finally issue a Completion Certificate no longer lay at his door!

[First Solicitor] wrote to [First Architect] on 8th October 1985 (File 86):

> *We should be pleased if you would forward to us copies of the relevant plans in connection with The Browns' guest house. We understand that [Second Architect] has contacted you in this respect.*

[Second Architect] wrote to [First Solicitor] on 22nd October 1985 (File 87):

I would be obliged if you exert all pressure for [First Architect] to release drawings for The Browns' guest house.

I have promised Mr Brown prompt action on this matter especially whilst it is fresh in the mind of the District Council's Planning Department. There is also some considerable urgency in view of their delaying enforcement action on the promise of action from my office. I would not wish them to think that I am delaying matters in any way.

[First Solicitor] wrote to [First Architect] on 29th October 1985 (File 88):

We refer to The Browns' guest house. It is imperative to make progress with the Council in respect of endeavouring to remove the enforcement notice that we have the full set of plans. Could you please forward these without delay?

[Second Architect] wrote to the District Council on 30th October 1985 (File 89):

I refer to a meeting on Tuesday 1st October 1985 when my client, Mr Brown and I met with a member of the Council.

At that meeting a promise was made that my client would provide proposals to remedy the situation that you presently find unacceptable viz, unauthorised building works at The Browns' guest house.

I have been instructed by Mr Brown to prepare the information that you require but prior to doing so it has been necessary to obtain copies of the plans approved by the Disctict Council along with those from which the alterations works were carried out.

Unfortunately, my client's previous architect has failed to make these available hence the delay of one month since our last meeting. In this connection my client's agents are taking suitable legal action to recover the documents and I hope to be in a position to provide the promised information in early course.

Whilst sight, in your office, of the approved plans held by you is helpful, I would ask, if it is found possible to retrieve the original documentation, that those plans be released, under my personal guarantee of prompt return, for the purpose of photo-graphic copying.

This letter was copied to both me and [First Solicitor].

Meanwhile [Second Architect] kept up the pressure by writing to [First Solicitor] on 4th November 1985 (File 90):

Before we lose the "goodwill" of Aberdeen District Council's Planning Department I think it wise that you take action against [First Architect] for recovery of documents.

As you have been made aware these documents are fundamental to progressing the matter further. I have, as a contingency measure, asked the Director of Planning to release his own documentation to me, on a personal guarantee, in order that it may be duplicated and returned thereafter. However, I do not expect this request to be favourably received

In response to the above [First Solicitor] wrote to [First Architect] on 5th November 1985 (File 91):

Further to our letter dated 29th October to which we do not appear to have received a reply. We would advise that unless we receive the plans within the next seven days we shall have to raise an action for delivery of the plans. This will of course involve unnecessary expense.

This is the first time [First Solicitor] has threatened action. It is worth reminding readers here that [First Solicitor] wrote to me on 21st March 1985 (File 75) suggesting that the time had come for *taking the bull by the horns and getting the matter resolved as quickly as possible.*

Multiple requests for drawings had been made since [First Solicitor]'s first request on 8th October 1985 (File 86):

1) On four occasions, from 1st October 1985 through to 4th November 1985, [Second Architect] asked [First Solicitor] to acquire all the drawings from [First Architect].

2) On six occasions, from 8th October 1985 through to 5th November 1985, [First Solicitor] asked [First Architect] to surrender all the drawings in his possession.

Up to 5th November 1985 the drawings (which legally belonged to me), had still not been received. Thus, the obvious questions arose:

1) Why was [First Architect] reluctant to part with the plans/drawings?

2) Why was [First Solicitor] delaying the inevitable (i.e. issuing a writ) when he knew after meeting with the Council's Law Administration Department, along with the Building and Planning Department, that pressures were building against his client to remove the unauthorised works? Was there actually a conflict of interest situation and at that particular time was he protecting what he knew well enough to be an incompetent architect? The evidence in his possession against both [First Architect] and [Contractor] was overwhelming. So what was he waiting for?

When [First Solicitor] wrote to [First Architect] on the 29th October 1985 (File 88) he also sent me a four-page letter (File 92/95). The following extracts, taken from that letter, are most relevant:

*The works have never been completed to the satisfaction of either yourself or the **Supervising** officer [First Architect]*

The works were not completed by 18th October 1982, therefore (according to the provisions of the contract) liquidated damages "shall be payable".

Is there a definite date from which damages can run? You would argue that if the answer to this would be in the affirmative, the date would be 18th October 1982 as set out in the contract. However if by the operation of intervening circumstances the date fixed for completion in the contract has ceased to be operative the right to recover liquidated damages may be forfeit. If for example you ordered additional work to be carried out which was not specified in the contract (as I think you did) and [Contractor] agreed to carry out this extra work but not necessarily within the same time limit, the right to liquidated damages may be forfeit. (Could you confirm whether you did this)?

[Contractor]'s receivers state in a letter of 30th April 1985 that according to their records "the delays on the project were not of [Contractor]'s making but were due to other trades, variations and in particular as discussed adequate planning approvals had to be obtained to allow an adequate habitation certificate".

If either yourself or [First Architect] can be blamed to any extent for the delay, then the liquidated damages provision may not apply. It is unclear from the correspondence in my File, whether [First Architect] or yourself made changes to the contract drawings etc. as the project progressed. What is clear however is that (1) extras/additions were ordered (e.g. the Tank Room Boxing), the exit stair and door, the additional work to the wall.

Further, from the copies I have, one can see an obvious deviation between the plan relating to the rear elevation and what was

> *carried out in practice. Presumably these are the amendments to the warrant referred to in [First Architect]'s letter to the District Council dated 6th October 1982. It would appear therefore that additional work had indeed been instructed subsequent to the execution of the contract.*

[First Solicitor] continued this letter by giving me the details of the costs that I could claim against [Contractor] as an offset to the sum due to [Contractor] (certified by [First Architect] as £5,245).

Note: How could [First Architect] certify any monies due to [Contractor] when he has tried to avoid responsibility by asserting that he was not paid to *supervise*? Clearly he was responsible for supervision.

I replied on 11th November 1985 (File 96/99) to the above (File 92/95) in a four-page letter in which I again crucified [Contractor] for shoddy work and for trying to cut corners. Remember, this was before I became aware of the additions to the contract, i.e. approximately £4,000 and the request from [Contractor] for additional time due to the incredibly time-consuming changes in the contract imposed by [First Architect].

In my ignorance, I had assumed that [First Architect] had refused any additional time on the basis of [Contractor]'s poor workmanship, thereby putting extra pressure on [Contractor] to speed up the work.

This four-page letter (File 96/99) crucifying [Contractor] **because of my ignorance** had played right into the hands of [First Architect] and [First Solicitor] (as will be seen later on).

On 11th November 1985 (File 100) [First Architect] wrote to [First Solicitor], stating:

> *With reference to your recent correspondence in relation to your demands for sets of plans for the above Mr Angus Brown, I am reluctant to provide these without first having prior knowledge of the requirement to fulfil this request. I would point out that it is my impression that your client has chosen to appoint other agencies to pursue the matter of his own involvement and negotiations with the Department of Planning and Grants in relation to grant assisting of conservation area properties and that it is not normal practice for architects' drawings to be provided for the use of other agencies.*
>
> *Unless I am absolutely satisfied that the request for drawings is in no way to prejudice my own position I will therefore be unable to provide them.*

This response is hardly consistent with the words of [Second Architect] on 7th October 1985 (File 85): *I have, as a matter of Courtesy, advised [First Architect] of my appointment and he seems content to relinquish responsibilities for resolving the difficulties to my practice.*

It seems incredible that a human being who purports to being a professional architect, could have been allowed by [First Solicitor] to wait, from the first request for the drawings/plans, i.e. 8th October 1985 (File 86) through to the above mentioned File 100. In the face of [First Solicitor]'s request for a reply within seven days, in fact it took [First Architect] a time span of over **four weeks** to respond.

On 15th November 1985 (File 101) [First Solicitor] replied as follows:

> *We thank you for your letter of 11th November 1985 and note what you write therein. We feel that we must insist that you make the plans available for collection within the next seven days, failing which we will have no alternative but to raise the appropriate action for delivery on behalf of our client. We would point out that all fees in this matter have been settled to date and we cannot understand why you should withhold the plans.*

> *P.S. We would suggest that you notify your Professional Indemnity insurers of this matter.*

Also on 15th November 1985 (File 102), [Second Architect] reported to [First Solicitor], copied to me:

> *As expected my avenue of research with the District Council has failed and it is now imperative that we obtain the drawings from Mr Brown's [First Architect].*

On 21st November 1985, in an attempt to succeed where [Second Architect] had failed, [First Solicitor] wrote to the Department of Planning and Building Control (File 103) hoping to get the drawings/plans from them:

> *We write to confirm that although copyright remains with [First Architect], it is licensed to the client so long as [First Architect]'s fees have been paid in full. We can confirm that all sums due to [First Architect] have now been paid and accordingly the client should be at liberty to copy any plans. In any event, as we understand it, any action relating to an alleged breach of copyright would be brought against our client and he is prepared, on our advice, to take the risk.*
>
> *Accordingly, please confirm that the plans may now be copied.*

On 21st November 1985 [First Solicitor] again wrote to [First Architect]:

> *I refer to our letter of 15th November 1985 and should be pleased if you would confirm that the plans are now available for collection without prejudice.*

This was followed by another letter dated 27th November 1985 (File 105) from [First Solicitor] to [First Architect]:

> *We refer to our telephone conversation and write to confirm that*
> *the plans are required in order to assist with the current application*
> *for Building warrant, possible planning permission and possible*
> *new planning permission for work to be carried out at the subject's*
> *guest house. Please forward copies as soon as possible.*

With the plans still not being released, an internal memo dated 7th
December 1985 from one solicitor to another in [First Solicitor]'s office
stated:

> *Please prepare action for delivery against The Browns' Architect*
> *for the plans. Please phone first.*

Action was now inevitable but, in a final attempt to avoid such a recourse,
[First Solicitor] wrote to [Second Architect] on 10th December 1985 (File
107) stating:

> *I refer to our telephone conversation this afternoon and enclose*
> *the only plans in my possession. One I know is a detailed floor*
> *plan but does not bear a warrant stamp, the other seems to be*
> *an elevation which does bear a warrant stamp 82-1777. Please*
> *confirm as soon as possible whether these are sufficient for*
> *your purposes or whether we should proceed with the action of*
> *delivery against Mr Brown's First Architect.*

As I have just stated, when [First Solicitor] made his second request for
the drawings to [First Architect] (File 88 dated 29th October 1985), he
also wrote to me on the same day (File 92-95), asking if I had ordered any
extras like moving a water tank and tank boxing room. With this letter he
referred to a letter he had received from the receivers dated 30th April 1985,
some six months earlier, in which the receiver asserted that the delays on
the project were not of [Contractor]'s making, but were due to *other trades*
variations and in particular, as discussed, adequate planning approvals
that had to be obtained to allow an adequate habitation certificate to be
issued. Further to this, [First Solicitor] stated:

> *...it is unclear from the correspondence in the File whether [First Architect] or yourself made changes to the Contract drawings etc as the project progressed".* [This is evidence of wilful deceit because [First Solicitor] knew that it was perfectly clear from the correspondence that [First Architect] was at fault.]

[First Solicitor] then went on to state the weaknesses of my case against the receivers. I had no weaknesses. In fact the evidence against both [First Architect] and [Contractor] was so clear from both [Second Architect], the Planning Department, and myself that, when added to that [First Architect]'s refusal to hand over the drawings, the case was incontrovertible. [First Solicitor] knew perfectly well where and who caused the problems. The question has to be asked:

Was this solicitor trying to agitate and irritate me to provoke an adverse reaction?

Remember, [First Solicitor] had received detailed evidence from [Second Architect] in his copied letter dated 10th October 1985 (File 89, referred to above) to the Aberdeen District Council, Director of Planning and Building Control.

Furthermore, on 13th December 1985 (File 108/10) [Second Architect] had written to [First Solicitor] stating:

> *Many thanks for your letter of 10th December and enclosed plans.*
>
> *Firstly, the plans which you enclosed are planning consent drawings duly stamped by the District Council. These are the plans based upon an application by [First Architect] on 6th August 1982. Contemporary correspondence shows that [First Architect] hoped to lodge the plan as an amendment to the original planning consent, which was approved by the Planning Committee on 15th November 1979. In a letter dated 24th August*

1982 the Director advised [First Architect] that such a course of action would not be possible and advised that the enquiry had been treated as a new application and would be advertised in the normal way.

On the 6ᵗʰ October 1982 [First Architect] wrote to "District Council" advising that the enclosed amended plans were "to take account of the following amendments". Those amendments included changes to the front dormers, (presumably referring to the changes evident on the planning consent, a change in the position of the rear dormer window, the formation of a tank room above roof level, small alterations to first floor wardrobes and the formation of external staircases to basement room in the front elevation.

It is important that we have sight of these plans as they do tend to suggest, along with later correspondence of 21ˢᵗ December 1982 that [First Architect] was aware that the changes had taken place and indeed was asking for certain works to be made good in connection with those changes.

In the meantime I can confirm having surveyed the building in some detail and now enclose copies of the resultant drawings.

Sadly, reference to the plans currently available indicating "Phase 1" and the proposed "Phase 2" shows a serious dimensional error whereby the height of a second floor, to be added to the building would be approximately 600mm higher that anticipated in the original plans. Thus, windows on the existing first floor would be partly covered by such an extension and the additional height would unquestionably rule out the very slim chance Mr Brown may currently have in achieving his ambition of having a roof garden and drying area. May I suggest you obtain from [First Architect] copies of the drawings referred to in his letter of 6ᵗʰ October 1982 to the "District Council"?

At the present moment my basic references are the plans, which you have now provided. These are the plans which the District Council refer to in claiming that unauthorised building works have been carried out (although it is fair to say that the work did not comply with the original consent in any event). The survey and record Photographs show considerable variance between the approved plan and the works carried out on site. Certain of the differences may be related to those plans referred to by [First Architect] in his letter of 6th October 1982.

[Second Architect] had thus made it quite clear to [First Solicitor] where and who was responsible for the unauthorised works and the refusal of the Completion Certificate.

I urge my readers to consider. With all of the evidence before him, and in his possession, it can only be reasonable to suggest that [First Solicitor] would act professionally, i.e. follow the rules and regulations and protect his client by starting to issue a writ against [First Architect], to secure the drawings in order to help me get rid of the unauthorised works and the pending enforcement order. Not only that, however, he should also have been issuing writs against both [Contractor] and [First Architect] for the unauthorised works outside the signed contract drawings signed in the First Solicitor's office three years previously, and against [First Architect], for additions to the contract without permission.

In fact, it would be fair to suggest that anyone with common sense, and in particular a professional solicitor protecting his clients interests, should have issued writs against both [First Architect] and [Contractor] as far back as 1982/83.

In response to the above (File No 108/9/10) [First Solicitor] wrote to [Second Architect] on 19th December 1985 (File No 111) undertaking to write to [First Architect] for the warrants and the drawings **again as requested.** This was [Second Architect]'s sixth request to [First Solicitor] for him to get the drawings.

Furthermore on 23rd December 1985 (File 112) [Second Architect] again wrote to [First Solicitor] saying:

> *You are completely wrong to think that the only problem at the rear of the of The Browns' guest house is the middle window at the rear elevation. Details have been already detailed by the Planning Department, and already explained to you in telephone conversation and correspondence, that the water tank on the roof at the rear of the house will definitely not be accepted. The middle window at the rear has got nothing to do with it.*

So, here again the crooked (a fair description) [First Solicitor], after talking to the Planning Department, was seemingly trying to get the crooked (by now self-evidently a fair description) [First Architect] off the hook. However, he had been told many times that the Planning Department would not accept the large water tank in its present position on the roof at the rear of the guest house. How many times can a crooked man continue to ignore the fact that the truth will always prevail?

Let the story continue to unfold…

On 28th December 1985 (File 113), I received the following from [First Solicitor]:

> *I have spoken to [Quantity Surveyor]… I am almost certain we will not have to pay anything to [Contractor] and in fact we can make a claim against [Contractor].*

The Department of Planning wrote to [Second Architect] 10th January 1986 (File 114):

> *Further to your letter of 23rd December1985 regarding the front elevation of The Browns' guest house, the Committee reluctantly*

> *granted Listed Building Consent and Planning Permission for the works which presently exist, despite the deviation from the approved plans. It should be noted however the Committee also decided at the meeting that the £3000 conservation Grant be withheld and enforcement proceedings be initiated with respect to the unauthorised works at the rear.*

This is what had triggered the Newspaper Article on 14th March 1985 (File 74) already mentioned above:

> **A city guest house owner may be facing legal action for allegedly carrying out unauthorised works.**

1986

After six requests from [Second Architect], [First Solicitor] **finally** issued a writ against [First Architect] for the long-awaited drawings which he would not release (File 115/116 dated 30th January 1986):

The writ for the drawings included a statement of claim whereby [First Solicitor] stated that the works at The Browns' guest house did not conform to the original plans and no Completion Certificate had ever been issued.

Note: The first request from [Second Architect] for the drawings was dated 1st October 1985 (File 82). It had taken [First Solicitor] four months (16 weeks) to issue a writ for drawings that had always belonged to me! Both [First Architect] and [First Solicitor] knew perfectly well the extent to which, after all this time, the pressures would bear down on the myself as a result of the delays. These delays limited the effectiveness of [Second Architect] in carrying out his brief – to complete the job of removing the unauthorised works and to satisfy the City of Aberdeen Planning Department that the pending enforcement order should be lifted.

With all this evidence against [First Architect] and [First Solicitor], surely it needs only common sense to see that these two gentlemen were colluding in the hope of getting that same architect off the hook by stating the only problem was on the rear elevation was the middle window. With concrete evidence in his possession to show otherwise, [First Solicitor] had no grounds whatsoever to allow [First Architect] a four-month delay before issuing a writ!

Furthermore, through correspondence and at the special meeting, [First Solicitor] had been in touch with the Aberdeen Building and Planning Department and must have been well informed about all the errors and incompetence of [First Architect]. It beggars belief why he had ever allowed [First Architect] to hold on to the drawings until now.

One would have thought that any decent solicitor would seek every opportunity to protect his client's interests. And, a final question: should not a writ have also been issued against [Contractor] as far back as 1982 when the contract was supposed to have been completed?

There then follows an incredible letter from [First Architect] to [First Solicitor] in answer to the summons for the drawings. This is dated 3rd February 1986 (File 117):

> *...it was a surprise for me to receive your summons for delivery on 1st Feb. May I remind you of our agreed terms of our last Telephone conversation and similar calls with your Assistant. I am now placing on record the terms of our last conversations and call upon you now to provide such a letter as agreed.*

I now ask – can you, the public, see the corruption gathering momentum? What terms have been agreed?

The next letter, dated 12th February 1986 (File 118), from [First Solicitor] to [First Architect] is equally unbelievable. Remember, I had to continue paying [First Solicitor], a man who was having conversations off the record and then producing letters to cover his tracks!

> *We thank you for your letter of 3ʳᵈ February 1986. We regret that we cannot enter into detailed correspondence with you. We can give no assurances regarding the delivery of plans in exchange for agreements not to consider action against you. Nobody in fact has mentioned actions against you other than yourself. The simple fact is the plans belong to our client and he is entitled to them, and we will have no alternative but to proceed with the Court action if you still refuse to hand the plans over.*

[First Solicitor] should have followed through with the Court action then and there. Given the above four letters, i.e. Files 115/116, 117 and 118 (particularly 115/116), the summons for the drawings should have commenced back in 1985 after [First Solicitor] had received [Second Architect]'s first request for the drawings. That date was 1ˢᵗ October 1985 (File 82) and, as already well established above, the drawings belonged to me.

On 17ᵗʰ February 1986 (File 119), [First Architect] replied to [First Solicitor] in answer to the above (File 118):

> *I enclose for your information all Drawings, Warrant and Planning Consent in my files which I trust will be of use to Mr Brown. Again, I must repeat this should have taken place one year previous.*

[First Solicitor] forwarded these to [Second Architect] (File 120) on 19ᵗʰ February 1986, saying:

> *At long last I enclose full set of plans received from [First Architect] after we had raised a Court action. I trust these will assist now in finalising matters with the Council. I would hope that the Conservation Grant of £3,000 would be available in early course. I understand that this would be on submission of an appropriate plan rather than actual completion of the work.*

[Second Architect] duly replied (File 121/122/123) on 25th February 1986, thanking [First Solicitor] for the above letter and the enclosed drawings. This particular letter also detailed to [First Solicitor] the many serious problems [Second Architect] had to overcome, including one in particular, whereby he discovered that the Planning Department's drawings had been removed from the Department by [First Architect] and had never been returned. [Second Architect] used the words *"fishy business"* in summing up. It seemed clear to me that there had been collusion involving [First Solicitor], [First Architect] and the Planning Department.

It was also mentioned in the letter that the Director of Planning was not happy with the delays.

On 10th June 1986 [First Solicitor] wrote to me (File 128) as follows:

> *I refer to our meeting on Monday 9th June and write to confirm I have spoken to the Town Council and have advised them it is not your intention to proceed with the extension project at the rear and accordingly you wish to obtain a Completion Certificate by submitting an application for amended Building Warrant to carry out works to bring the middle window into line with their requirements.*
>
> *As I understand them they are prepared to cooperate with this and they would like to meet with your Architect on site in order to discuss the best way of disposing of this matter. They tell me they will not be unreasonable to deal with. They will not insist on the dismantling of the Structure but have talked about the probability of having to change the position of the water tanks etc, However, they did not seem to be hard and fast on this.*
>
> *I will leave you to get in touch with [Second Architect] in order to dispose of this matter and obtain the grant.*

All seemed well. However, on 20th June 1986 [Second Architect] also wrote to me (File 128-1) to clarify the situation between [First Solicitor]'s opinion of the rear elevation and how he thought things could be disposed of in relation to the opinions of the Planning Department. Again it appeared that [First Solicitor] was colluding with the Planning Department. The real truth of the matter was once again clarified by [Second Architect], who contradicted [First Solicitor]'s constant reports about the middle window. This had nothing to do with the problems at the rear, and [First Solicitor] had been informed of this on many occasions.

The discussions with the Planning Department, detailed in [First Solicitor]'s letter, were simply hogwash. Here is the real truth, as specified in this letter from [Second Architect]:

> *He informs me that [First Solicitor]'s discussion with a member of the Planning Department – that they would accept the rear dormers in their current position (although they were by comparison to the approved drawing incorrectly placed relative to the wallhead) – is false. I have spoken with the same gentleman from the Planning Department, and he has made it abundantly clear that the tank room located above the level of the dormer roof is totally unacceptable and must be removed in its entirety.*

Note: Had [First Solicitor] been acting with a conflict of interest, a serious situation in the eyes of The Law Society? Had he been protecting [First Architect], by the months of delays, and had he been accepting monies for this protection, whilst also accepting monies from me?

Why had [First Solicitor] not issued a writ against [First Architect] to protect me? And why had he not issued a writ against [Contractor] when the contract was not completed on the specified date in October 1982 when no Completion Certificate had been issued?

On 22nd August 1986, I received another incredible letter (File 129) from this supposedly professional gentleman. He began with the words *I again wish to summarise the position with regards to various matters outstanding.*

This shows incompetence or disingenuousness. I had lost count of the number of meetings we had had, each one so repetitive they had become boring. Each time we met, I'd had to wait for half an hour before being seen. Each time, when I had asked a question or raised an issue, his reply had been by rote – and he would scrabble through the large pile of papers on the desk before stating that there was something in the papers about my issue, yet he could never find it!

His letter then addressed the issue of the claim by [Contractor] which he stated, should go to arbitration if no agreement could be reached, followed by:

> *Possible claim against [First Architect]*
>
> *With regards to this I would comment as follows:-*
>
> *In order to have any case we would have to prove that [First Architect] was negligent in his actions. We would have to establish that his standard of actings were far below that which could be expected of an Architect of his particular experience and standing. This criterion is a very objective one in that we require not simply to show that [First Architect] made an error but rather that the error made would be one that no reasonably skilled architect would make.*
>
> *Your argument is that you instructed [First Architect] to prepare plans that would be acceptable to the Local Authority and thereafter having done so and having obtained the appropriate Planning Permission and Building Warrant and permission from the Historic Building Council, he would then supervise the work until a satisfactory completion. As I understand it you alleged that the failure to obtain permission for the second storey at the middle window at the rear was his fault. Your view is you asked him to make plans to show the second storey so that could incorporate the second storey in the proposed second phase of the development.*

Note: This incompetent [First Solicitor] was still going on about the middle window even after having met with the Law Administration and Planning Department. How stupid can one be?

Work was started and completed without that permission being available and the permission which was eventually granted last year was in respect of the original drawings which showed the middle window at the back being at a lower level. You further alleged that as a result of this action which you claim is negligence on his part you have suffered loss in that you were due to get a conservation grant of £3,000 which will not be paid until remedial work is carried out, which is expected to cost £12,000. You would therefore be seeking to recover this from [First Architect].

Although on the face of it there would appear to be at least a prima facie case for [First Architect] to answer, professional negligence cases are notorious for being difficult to obtain a satisfactory result. This is partly due to the objective test, which I have described above, and also the conflict of evidence as regards what the professional advisor was instructed, or not instructed, to do. There can therefore be no guarantee of success and as you are aware litigation is generally a slow and expensive process. Regardless of the eventual outcome a great deal of expense will be incurred and, even if you are successful there would still be a distinct possibility of your own costs in the matter being in excess of £1,000.

Note: I ask my readers to look back at the evidence laid before them in this book. Surely it exposes professional negligence, at the very least, by [First Architect]? Would it not have been better for a competent solicitor to have acknowledged the wealth of evidence and been more upbeat about the likelihood of success?

I think it is appropriate to mention at this point that to date, despite the years of effort we have expended on your behalf no payment has been sought to date. The minimum expense due in connection with [Contractor]'s case is at least £500 (excluding VAT and outlays). If you wish to proceed with the case against [First Architect], I feel it appropriate that a payment of £1,500.00 be made to cover services and expenses already incurred and also a deposit for future service. You have mentioned that we have some monies of yours deposited from our dealings with your lease. I would advise that this amounts to £339.70 with a small amount of interest to be applied bringing the total to approximately £350. I trust this sets out the position clearly and I look forward to hearing from you.

It is worth reminding readers of a very clever ploy used by the members of the legal profession when it suits them. It is to irritate and agitate (especially if he/she is a high-risk complainant) to provoke an adverse reaction. This gets rid of a client, if he/she acts inappropriately, and it then makes it difficult to find another solicitor. Also, remember that you cannot get another solicitor until all fees are paid to your first one. And all this, by definition, is at a time one is challenging the competence of a solicitor and does not feel inclined to pay for inept services! It is a dilemma in every sense of the word.

I followed through with the above request for payments, i.e. £575 regarding [Contractor] and to fund any work in respect of a possible Court case against [First Architect]. I also arranged to pay [First Solicitor] £200 per week for six weeks commencing 29th September 1986.

[First Solicitor] wrote to [First Architect] on 8th October 1986 (File 132):

We have been instructed by Mr Brown who advises us that he instructed you in your professional capacity in 1982/1983 in connection with the alterations to be carried out at The Browns' guest house. We understand from our client that you were instructed to prepare plans that would be acceptable to the Local Authority to be carried out in two phases with the appropriate consents and permissions including that of the Historic Building Council. Our client advises us also that a conversion Grant was available if the design of the alterations were such that they satisfied the requirements for the Grant.

We understand that prior to all the necessary permissions being granted you allowed [Contractor] to commence work without approved plans and permissions being available. As a result of your doing this our client required to do extensive remedial works to conform to the plans which were ultimately approved.

Our client therefore takes the view that you were negligent in allowing such works to take place and accordingly he is holding you liable for the whole losses sustained by him as a result of your actions. This includes the loss of the Conservation Grant.

We would be grateful therefore to have your proposals or comments in connection with this and we should be grateful if you would confirm that you have passed this matter to your professional indemnity insurers. In the event that we do not hear from you or them within the next 14 days then our client will pursue the Legal remedies open to him.

This letter is written without prejudice to all rights and pleas competent to our client and is not to be founded upon or referred to in any Court Action except at the instance of our client.

To help the readers of this True Story and fellow complainants, I think it is important to reiterate crooked actions by the legal profession or what I sometimes call "ploys" used against clients. Take another look at the date of the above letter – 8th October 1986. [First Architect] is given 14 days to respond before *our client will pursue the legal remedies open to him.*

[First Solicitor] had taken all this time to threaten action, after many meetings, plus the evidence from different sources (all three years previous). Was he receiving monies from [First Architect] to delay the case and eventually get rid of the problems one way or another? Was he acting in a conflict of interest situation?

Remember, in March 1985 [First Solicitor] had written to me and in that letter made a very interesting comment given the date of File 132 above:

> *It surprises me that this matter has been going on for such a long period of time without anybody TAKING THE BULL BY THE HORNS. I must say I would have handled things differently and got things sorted out by now.*

On 24th October 1986 (File 135), [First Solicitor] informed me that [First Architect] *has gone to his solicitor about the matter. This is what we wanted.*

The big question then arises. Was [First Solicitor] going to stay incompetent or was he going to protect his client? We will just have to wait and see.

On 24th October 1986 (File 136/137) [First Architect]'s Solicitor wrote to [First Solicitor]. In this correspondence I discovered that [First Architect] had continued with his lies and deceit; e.g. before the start of the contract in August 1982 and without my knowledge, he had sent out three invitations to tender and had selected a contractor – a friend of his and, coincidentally, the one I had used in my country home and had previously rejected as unsuitable because of the quality of his work. This is simply another example of the way [First Architect] tended to take action behind my back.

I am sure the readers of this True Story will by now have gathered how I feel about solicitors and the legal profession. Now [First Architect] had appointed a firm of solicitors to assist with his lies and deceit. As if I didn't have enough trouble with my own solicitor! Would they both start to collude and further protect [First Architect]?

[First Architect]'s solicitor wrote to [First Solicitor] on 24th October 1986 (File 136/137). In this letter he obviously has to take as the truth whatever his client, [First Architect], tells him.

As mentioned above, the letter states that tenders were sent out to three contractors. [First Architect] had forgotten to tell his Solicitor that, at my request, he had sent me seven sets of drawings so that I could send them out for quotes. In the covering letter accompanying the drawings, he also wrote:

> *Please find enclosed the drawings you requested. Should you wish to proceed with the work and would like me to **supervise the construction**, an essential part in such a **complex alteration**, my fee would be in the region of £346.*

It is interesting to note here the comments *supervise the construction* and *complex alteration*. Later, you will read his own contradictions in relation to both comments, namely in his correspondence to the RIBA and secondly when he submitted his fee for supervision.

[First Architect]'s solicitor's letter also alleged that I had originally chosen an unsatisfactory contractor. With regard to these comments I now refer to the quotes received for this *complex alteration*.

The various quotes received ranged from £45,000 down to £8,000. It is interesting to note here that the cheapest quote came from [Contractor] that [First Architect] had chosen. My choice of contractor had quoted £14,500. Irrespective of whichever contractor was used at the start of the contract, the unauthorised works and the impending enforcement order had been brought about by this incompetent architect and his own mistakes, in particular errors associated with the taking of the simplest of measurements – mistakes that any reasonably informed architect would never make.

[First Architect] must have further lied to his solicitor because the letter now stated:

> *We must stress that our client was at no time instructed to supervise the construction work. He did, in the interests of your client and as a (gratuitous service) take a (cursory look) at the progress of the work from time to time.*

It appeared as though [First Architect] had forgotten to tell his solicitor of the following important details:

1) The Memorandum of agreement under the RIBA conditions of agreement between Mr Brown and his architect to stage "H", i.e. the issuing of a Completion Certificate.

2) With reference to the comment that The Browns were under pressure and had started the contract without permission, I now quote File 24 where [First Architect] wrote to Aberdeen Planning Department stating that the contract at The Browns' guest house will commence on 23rd August 1982 to be completed by 18th October 1982 under Mr Brown's Contractor.

3) With reference to the comment about [First Architect] at no time having been instructed to supervise, at the risk of being repetitive there now follows the absolute truth and evidence to refute these allegations.

   Aug/Sept 1982 (File 22/23) – Architect's instruction sheets to [Contractor]

   6th October 1982 (File 30) – [First Architect] asked Planning Department for approval of amendments.

   20th September 1982 (File 25) – [Contractor] submitted claim to [First Architect] for monies for work done to date.

21st September 1982 (File 26) – [First Architect] informed me that interim payment should be made direct to [Contractor].

21st September 1982 (File 27) employer's copy of [First Architect]'s interim certificate dated 21st September 1982, valuation date 20th September 1982, amounting to £6,175.00.

28th September 1982 (File 28/29) – [First Architect] wrote to [Contractor] saying:

> *After visiting site today I must emphasise that when I issue an instruction I expect it to be acted upon without undue delay.*

Note: It is interesting to note here that [First Architect] had, in August/September 1982, issued instruction sheets, which included adding £4,000 to the contract. Then, after issuing these instructions in September, he wrote to the Planning Department (6th October 1982 – File 30) asking for amendments to the contract. Two weeks previously he had just handed these changes to [Contractor].

28th October 1982 (File 31) – The Director of Building Control wrote as follows to [First Architect]:

> *I refer to a meeting on site in regards to The Browns' guest house and would confirm that certain matters, which were discussed on site require some attention*

8th November 1982 (File 34) – Application for Completion Certificate signed [First Architect]

29th November 1982 (File 37) – above application rejected

19th December 1982 (File 40) – Director of planning and building control wrote as follows to [First Architect]:

> *DRAINAGE and STRUCTURAL FAULTS*
>
> *1)   The rear elevation does not relate to what is on site*
>
> *2)   It is anticipated that enforcement action will be taken against the owner by Planning to secure the removal of certain works at the rear.*

6th January 1983 (File 44) – Fee (Invoice 31) from [First Architect] requesting interim payment for *(type of service supplied) Supervision and Drawings*

12th July 1983 (File 53) – Application for Completion Certificate (Rejected).

Note: The contract was for eight weeks (completion date of 18th October 1982). Note the date of this application!

24th August 1983 (File 55) – [First Architect] wrote to the Planning and Building Control Department stating: *All works have been completed we would be obliged if you can issue a Completion Certificate.* This was his third request for a Completion Certificate but, like the others, it was rejected. No matter how many times [First Architect] applies for a Completion Certificate it would always be rejected because of his incompetence, i.e. the unauthorised works at the rear of the project.

I would have thought that anyone reading the facts/evidence listed above could only agree that the point raised above, namely *We must stress that our client was at no time instructed to supervise the construction work* makes a complete mockery of the contents of that solicitor's letter and [First Architect].

Further correspondence between both solicitors continued. With all this information and concrete evidence in [First Solicitor]'s possession, he wrote to [First Architect]'s solicitor stipulating that Phase 2 (the extension work) would have been impossible to build *because of your client's incompetent drawings.*

The reply (File 142/3) stated: *We are informed that the work involved in Phase 2 extension was of a fairly standard nature, a type found all over Aberdeen.* Yet earlier he had stated that it was a complex alteration. A "separate professional opinion", in the form of [Second Architect], confirmed the inconsistency between these statements. It is interesting to note how [First Architect] kept contradicting himself. It becomes the trait of a perpetual liar – always complicate matters. Shakespeare uses the words "Oh what a tangled web we weave when first we practise to deceive". Even so, the truth always emerges!

1987, 1988, 1989

On 19th January 1987 (File 141) [First Solicitor] wrote to [First Architect]'s solicitor:

> *We refer to our recent letter and telephone conversation. We regret we do not appear to have heard further from you and if we do not hear from you within the next seven days we are under pressure from our client to raise a Court action without further notice.*

The response does not take long to arrive (26th January 1987, File 142/143):

> *You explained both in your letter and on the telephone that your client was anxious to raise a Court action against our client. You may be assured that the action will be strenuously defended.*

A writ was lodged on 11th August 1987 (File 149):

> *Mr and Mrs Brown –v– [First Architect]*
>
> *Sheriff Clerk*
>
> *Sheriff Court*

> *We herewith enclose initial writ for lodging together with our cheque for £21.00*
>
> *We look forward to receiving a warrant in due course.*

On 21st August 1987 (File 152) [First Architect]'s Solicitor wrote to [First Solicitor], stating:

> *We enclose a copy of the notice of intention to defend, which we have lodged with the Sheriff clerk and would advise that the case will be calling for tabling on 9th September 1987.*

Process was lodged on 4th September 1987 (File 153)

> *Mr and Mrs Brown –v– [First Architect]*
>
> *We herewith enclose process relative to the above case and should be obliged if you would lodge same in Court.*

It looked like [First Solicitor] had, at last, taken *"the bull by the horns"*. How long has it been since he first used those words, suggesting the need for such action?

Note: At this point in the story my readers should know that [First Solicitor] made no attempt to meet with me regarding this writ and its contents (nor the contents of the above three files (149/152/153). I was never informed of what was happening! Like [First Architect], [First Solicitor] kept things to himself. His reasons? We will all find out later!

On 10th September 1987 (File 154) an associate solicitor of [First Solicitor] wrote to [First Solicitor] as follows:

> *We write to advise when the above case was called in Court we tabled it on your behalf and thereafter moved that the action be sisted pending consideration of your client's application for Legal Aid. We enclose our fee note in connection with this appearance.*

At the risk of repetition, may I once more draw to my readers' attention the date of submission of the above writ (11th August 1987, File 149). This same writ could have, and should have, been issued in 1982/83. The contracts were signed in August 1982, with the work starting 23rd August 1982 and contracted to be completed by 18th October 1982. [First Architect], supervising the contract, should have honoured his contract and made sure that his employers were issued with a Completion Certificate to give them permission to continue with their business and to complete the extension, as agreed, six months later. Also, [First Solicitor] should have at that same time (1982/83) issued a writ against [Contractor] for failure to honour their contract by not completing the contracts by the agreed date (18th October 1982) and for building unauthorised works.

[First Solicitor], in fact any solicitor with any decency in him, with the signed contracts in his possession since August 1982 and having explained to his client that the contract represented his permit for legal action against either the contractor or architect if they did not honour their contracts, should have called a meeting after the contracted completion date had passed. The pressures, costs and ill health have been unbelievable to say the least and could have been avoided.

All the pertinent information had always been available to [First Solicitor]. If he had behaved in a proper professional manner, working to the guide rules and thereby protecting his client, all he need ever have done was to write to the relevant authorities and call a meeting with all the involved parties. His prevarication and inaction could only paint a picture of a crook with no morals, i.e. taking monies under false pretences and (planning) a conflict of interest situation to line his own pockets.

I hope my readers will be able to keep up with the twists and turns of this True Story as they happen.

As stated above the writ had been lodged and, according to the records, I was pursuing Legal Aid (supposedly).

This story so far has focused on me, quite rightly, seeking true justice against [First Architect], with the help (unfortunately) of [First Solicitor] who obviously knew the tricks of the trade within a self-regulated legal system. Through his wile had [First Solicitor] found the perfect conflict of interest situation, whereby he could manipulate taking monies under false pretences from both me, and [First Architect]?

When he issued the above writ, he immediately sisted it under the false pretence that he was applying for Legal Aid on my behalf. This turned out to be a real scam; one which I was to discover only later. The main reason he sisted the writ was that he was buying time. Unbeknown to me this scheming solicitor had, or was planning to get [First Architect] off the hook.

Here are the contents of the writ that he cleverly sisted, having no intention of acting on it:

> *The Pursuers Mr and Mrs Brown*
>
> *Crave the Court:-*
>
> *To grant decree against [Defender] for payment to the Pursuers to the sum of (£30,000.00) Sterling with interest thereon at the rate of 15% per annum from the date of citation to follow hereon until paid, and to find the Defender liable in the expenses meantime to grant warrant to arrest on the dependence.*
>
> *In or around August 1982 the Defender was contracted by the Pursuers to produce plans and obtain planning permission and building warrant for building works to be carried out at the Pursuer's guest house. The plans were to be for building works to provide inter alia the provision of additional bedrooms in the rear of the house, the provision of dormer windows and the re-siting of the water storage tanks. The initial plans submitted to the Department of Planning and Building Control of Aberdeen*

District Council required to be amended and the works were to be done in two phases. In addition the Defender was contracted to (supervise) the works and contractor on site and ensure the works were carried out to the specification of the plans and to the approval of the appropriate departments of the local Authority.

The Pursuers' said guest house was also a Listed Building and they were advised that a Conservation Grant would be made available on the Works being satisfactorily completed.

The Defender failed in his contractual duty to the Pursuers. The Defender failed to obtain the appropriate permissions and consents for the amended plans from the appropriate authorities. Notwithstanding there were no proper consents for the works the Defender on or around 16th September 1982 **[Note: this date is incorrect – it should have been the month of August]** *instructed contractor to commence the works. As a result of the Defender instructing the commencement of the works the Local Authority served an enforcement order on or around June 1985 requiring the works to be restored to the original specification in the plans. Until this point the Pursuers were unaware that the proper permissions had not been obtained by the Defender.*

As a result of the Defender's actions the Pursuers have suffered loss. The Pursuers required to instruct fresh Drawings in order to conform to the requirements of the Local authority. The Pursuers had to instruct further contractors to restore the unauthorised works to the satisfaction of the Local Authority. The conservation Grant, which was to be made available was refused by the Local Authority. In addition the Pursuers were deprived of a peaceable existence and were subject to a great amount of stress and anxiety. The costs of the preparation of the fresh plans and the fresh works are in the region of £25,000.00.

The Defender has refused or at least delayed to compensate the Pursuers and this action is accordingly necessary.

[First Solicitor] was informed in detail by [Second Architect] in 1986 that the second phase of the contract, which included four additional bedrooms and two bathrooms, could not be built because of the incompetence of [First Architect]'s dimensional mistakes on the drawings. This was not mentioned in the writ.

It is important to note here, in relation to the writ, that it is unfortunate that I had taken on this incompetent [First Architect] recommended by [First Solicitor]. In retrospect, after looking at the date of the above writ, the original plans I had for the guest house which, had they been properly drawn up and irrespective of who the contractor was, [Contractor] was obliged to adhere to these plans if they had the proper permissions. The contract was for a conversion and extension, which included the four additional bedrooms. If everything had gone according to the quoted time scale with proper drawings, by the end of 1983 I should have been operating an extended guest house with a total of 13 letting bedrooms.

Aberdeen is the oil capital of Europe. I do not think there is any need to elaborate to my readers upon the extent of the future potential of the guest house or upon its future value (a Listed Building), yet, as a result of lies, deceit and corruption, my dream for the future was completely shattered.

While all the above was going on, the receivers acting for [Contractor] had been negotiating with both me and [First Solicitor] for payment. I refused to pay because of the evidence against [Contractor], in particular the unauthorised works and lack of Completion Certificate. I continued to deal with them through [First Solicitor]. I wanted all the errors corrected to a high standard so I made up the list and passed it to [First Solicitor], not knowing that this list would backfire on me because of [First Solicitor]'s double standards. [First Solicitor] had not issued a writ against [Contractor] in 1982. He thereby left me wide open for the receivers to take me to Court.

Because of the incompetence of [First Solicitor], the receivers acting for [Contractor] issued a writ against me, dated 5th December 1986. Solicitors from Glasgow represented the Pursuers [Contractor] against the Defenders [Mr and Mrs Brown].

I would like the readers to try to imagine and understand how I felt at this time, constantly worrying about what lay ahead, and plagued with doubts about this solicitor. I certainly was not prepared for what would happen. Even before the case started an inhibition order was placed on me for £7,500. Then I was called to a meeting in [First Solicitor]'s office, with a member of the firm I had never met before and had had no contact of any kind with previously. What I heard was absolutely mind-blowing. As I have already said, I had to rely on [First Solicitor] to get me through this case against the receivers. What I was now about to find out at this meeting confirms for the first time what has been niggling my mind for so long – namely fears and suspicions about planned delays, collusion and corruption. He told me that they were going to use [First Architect] to give evidence in the case against the receivers. I was flabbergasted, speechless. I had to contain myself.

I reminded him that I had paid fees earlier for a Court action against [First Architect]. How could we now even consider using him against the receivers acting for [Contractor]?

This very clever solicitor had known without any shadow of a doubt that the aforementioned writ for £30,000 had never been copied to me. There had been no meetings about it. I had been intentionally kept me in the dark. The solicitor knew I could not mention the writ because of my ignorance of it! He had obviously been fishing. Because of the fees I had paid, maybe he was afraid I had found out.

When one is ignorant of the things that are going on behind one's back and what is being planned, one becomes impatient and demoralised. Confidence starts to waver. I have mentioned earlier that the legal profession will irritate and agitate a client when it suits them, especially after they have paid them monies (in my case £2,000). At this meeting I did not react adversely to suit them. I feel now that I must have disappointed them. However, the person sitting opposite me got a mouthful, controlled as it was with specifications. I told him I didn't need my incompetent [First Architect] to represent me in the forthcoming case. I reminded him of all the witnesses that were available, namely my Quantity Surveyor, the Building and Planning Department, and [Second Architect] who was well versed and very knowledgeable about the whole situation and would make a good witness.

I said, in no uncertain terms, that there was no need for the incompetent [First Architect] to represent me. If any more witnesses were required it would be up to [First Solicitor] to find them to protect his client in line with the requirements of the legal profession. That was what I paid him for. I further told him that I had paid good monies to take [First Architect] to Court. How could I then expect the man to be a good witness on my behalf?

Remember they had not yet told me about the writ being served. [First Architect] must have known about the writ. It is only reasonable to wonder now, in hindsight, given all the facts – was someone getting protection money?

The thing that most bothered me after the meeting was not knowing what they were planning next. What was now obvious was that there must have been meetings between [First Solicitor] and [First Architect]. To what purpose? Possibly that of making promises to protect him. Were they double dealing?

The Court case against [Contractor] began on 5th December 1986 and continued through to 18th October 1989, during which time there were 28 interlocutors where the Defenders, i.e. me, had to pay expenses on three occasions.

The readers will find interesting the details of this case. It will reveal further unbelievable planned corruption, even to the extent where I believe the Sheriff became involved. The full details of the case and the corruption will be revealed later in the story.

In the meantime, allow me to continue the story about [First Architect] and [First Solicitor]. As you read on, always hold in mind the question – why were there planned delays?

I received a letter from [First Solicitor], dated 25th July 1989 (File 160).

We enclose herewith the Sheriff's judgement in the case against [Contractor]. The Sheriff has decided that you are due to pay [Contractor] the sum of £3,741.84 with interest at the rate of 15% since the action began.

In the circumstances and in the light of the evidence produced, we do not think the result could have been any better. Indeed the figure that the Sheriff has decided upon equals to that which was reached by negotiations at the time that the first receiver was involved but which you ultimately declined to settle on. We shall be pleased to discuss this with you once you have read the contents.

When you come across crooked people, always know that you are in the presence of a perpetual liar. I simply could not believe how deceitful a so-called professional person could get:

1) He had forgotten about a phone call to me where he stated that he had in his office at that particular time a gentleman representing [Contractor] and if I was to come to his office and write out a cheque for £4,000 we could close out the whole case. Now that is what he called negotiation!

2) He had also forgotten about his letter dated 28th December 1985 (File 113):

> *I have spoken to [Quantity Surveyor]...* **I am almost certain we**
> **will not have to pay anything to [Contractor] and in fact we can**
> **make a claim against [Contractor].**

His next letter is dated 17th August 1989 (File 174 1-2). In it [First Solicitor] dwells on questions and answers about the ongoing case against [Contractor], complimenting his own so-called good work. We will soon find out the truth!

The contents of page two of this letter are incredible:

> *I will deal with [First Architect]'s Case separately.*
>
> *The Legal Aid Committee will bear the cost of the action against [Contractor] no matter what the decision on expenses is. I will advise you as soon as we hear on this.*
>
> *No Legal Aid was sought with your [First Architect]. This would have held up the case as you know for a considerable period and we decided that we would raise the action but in the circumstances have sisted it pending the resolution of [Contractor]'s case. I trust that this is in order.*

Note: The legal profession, under self-regulation in Scotland since 1980, has and is undermining standards. Is it possible certain solicitors think that because they pay their annual insurance fee (£3,000-£4,000) they can get away with ignoring the rules and code of practice?

With reference to standards and self-regulation, I now give you the next letter from [First Solicitor]. See what you think. The letter, dated 23rd August 1989 (File 184/5) was hand-delivered to me on a Saturday morning. It was left inside the front door and I only happened to find it. The reference at the top of the letter had never been used before.

You –v– [First Architect]

I have looked through the papers for this and the initial writ has been served and it was agreed that the action would be sisted because [First Architect]'s evidence was required in the case against [Contractor].

Note: I ask my readers to consider his words – *it was agreed that the action would be sisted*. How could it be possible for me to have agreed to the sisting of the writ when I was completely ignorant of its existence and its contents?

There seems to be a difference of opinion as to the sequence of events and [First Architect]'s responsibilities relating thereto. The main difference as I see it is that [First Architect] states that he was not involved with the Council in relation to amendments to the original plans for the conservation Grant. He says the work was to be done in accordance with the original Planning permission that he obtained.

You state that [First Architect] gave authority for the plans to be deviated from. [First Architect] is claiming no responsibility for the big normal window appearing nor the work being carried out towards the completion of Phase 2.

[First Architect] in correspondence, states that Phase 2 was feasible from a building point of view. It is not his place to be involved with the financial aspects of projects and whether they are viable after the event. [Second Architect]'s opinion came subsequently. The core of the case appears to be relying on the evidence of you and [First Architect] in relation to these matters and whose evidence would be the most credible.

As I indicated previously, the onus of proof in showing professional negligence is very high generally, particularly when there seems to be considerable doubt as to whether [First Architect] was responsible for supervising the work. Then I suspect there will be difficulties in showing that [First Architect] was professionally negligent.

In addition the corroboration of evidence is difficult in the absence of any one else who has an intimate knowledge of the detailed sequence of events.

I would like to point out finally that not only have we raised the action in [First Architect]'s case and not charged any fee but that over the years I have given various advice in relation to various matters and so far have not charged any fee. We have bent over backwards to try to accommodate you and to give your case a sympathetic approach.

I leave you to decide whether you wish to further the matter.

I would now ask the readers of this True Story to try and put themselves in my position after receipt of the above letter. I was absolutely gutted, furious, and completely demoralised. I really had to contain myself. Obviously, if you go over this letter again you will see it was carefully planned to frustrate me, and put me in a position of despair leading to a quick adverse reaction. That is why it was hand-delivered on a Saturday morning.

I did not fall in with their plans. I composed myself and hoped I could muster enough courage to face the future whatever it may hold. What kind of person would write such a letter to a client who has paid him £2,000 in advance? All the details in the letter were easy for me to contradict. For example:

He stated in paragraph (6): *In addition the corroboration of evidence is difficult in the absence of any one else who has an intimate knowledge of the detailed sequence of events.* How can he overlook the presence of [Second Architect], representatives from the Council's Planning Department and their Department of Law and Administration, and the Quantity Surveyor?

In paragraph (7): *I would like to point out finally that not only have we raised the action in [First Architect]'s case and not charged any fee…* He has conveniently forgotten the earlier correspondence, dated 22nd August 1986 (File 129/130) in which he asks for monies for dealing with [First Architect]. I had paid him £2,125. (Six weeks at £200 per week from 29th September 1986, plus £575 in connection with [Contractor], and £350 from monies held by him from a prior factoring agreement).

In the last paragraph he states: *I leave you to decide whether you wish to further the matter.* How could a competent solicitor end a letter in this way, showing such disregard for the human being that is his client, a person to whom he has lied (see comments above regarding paragraphs 6 and 7)? More irritation and agitation?

What an incredible position I had been forced into! How could a lay person with little knowledge of the law prevail against this incompetent representative from what I am now convinced to be a dubious profession?

It would be interesting to know what honest, decent, members of the legal profession reading this True Story would think of the professionalism of [First Solicitor], and what advice they would give me now after reading File 184/5 and all the detailed evidence therein and elsewhere within this whole saga. Remember, solicitors must, and do, follow their own rules and are governed under a system of self-regulation.

After receipt of the hand-delivered File 184/5 and having read the contents, my feelings were such that I had to visit my doctor. I was in despair and turmoil, barely able to comprehend such a devious well-planned letter. I decided to wait until I felt I could cope with whatever came next. It came in the form of a phone call.

Here are the details of that phone call, between myself and a supposedly professional solicitor. At first I spoke with a secretary who answered the phone. I asked to talk to [First Solicitor]. He "conveniently" was not available, so I was put through to the same solicitor I had met on the occasion it was suggested that we used [First Architect] as a witness against [Contractor]. You can imagine that this was a very difficult situation with an equally difficult phone call so I did not pursue the issue of the case regarding [Contractor]. I felt I'd had enough. There was now only one thing on my mind knowing that I had indeed paid the fees demanded of me to take [First Architect] to Court. To anyone who has read this far in the story, you simply will not believe the answer I got when I asked the obvious question: "When are we taking [First Architect] to Court?"

I was glad to be sitting at home when I got the answer, which was:

"Why are we taking him to Court and for what reason?"

There was only one thing I could do at the time – to just put the phone down. This solicitor must have been disappointed at my reaction, especially if the phone call was being recorded.

I had been dealing with the office of [First Solicitor] for the last seven years and I found myself in an indescribable and hopeless position.

I beg my readers to indulge me once again, and allow me to repeat this very important warning to any person dealing with the legal profession and experiencing similar circumstances: any complainants/complainers must be aware how solicitors will knowingly use an unethical tactic to agitate and irritate clients to provoke an adverse response. They know full well that a violent response will destroy that client's ability to pursue any current or future complaint against the legal profession.

Again I ask those decent honest members of the legal profession: What do you think of your so-called professional colleagues who stoop so low?

How was I now going to find a way forward and get justice in Scotland? We are supposed to be a democracy, underpinned by democratic principles offering recourse to natural justice within an ethical legal system. What a farce these words become! Under self-regulation, so-called professional people are free to behave in a manner consistent with the very pits of this Earth. When I was growing up I was always under the impression that only vermin could be found down in the sewers.

After the phone call I had discussions with my family to determine how we were going to proceed. We were upset, despondent and barely able to believe that this was happening to us in Scotland. After the discussions, we considered our options, deciding – perhaps naively – that justice would prevail in the end. We decided to look for the services of another well-known solicitor in Aberdeen. Prior to doing so I called my daughter and asked her to go to the offices of [First Solicitor] and pick up a copy of the complete file. The secretary at that time copied everything in front of my daughter and handed her the complete copied file. I had already warned my daughter to make sure it was a copy and not the originals.

We then made further copies. I asked my daughter to deliver one set to our new solicitor [Second Solicitor] and get a signature for receipt of same. This was duly done and a meeting was arranged. We were now hoping [Second Solicitor] would act professionally and seek for us the justice we deserved, hoping that, unlike [First Solicitor], he would adhere to the following:

Professional Ethics and Code of Practice – the Scottish Legal Profession

This indicates:

1) Rules of professional conduct are not designed simply to define obligations, a breach of which may involve disciplinary sanction, which is imposed only as a remedy of last resort and, in turn, can be regarded as an indication that the self-discipline of the profession has been unsuccessful.

2) Professional rules of conduct are designed through the willing acceptance by the Lawyers involved to ensure the proper performance by Lawyers of a function, which is essential, or supposedly so in all civilised societies.

3) A Lawyer's function in society does not begin and end with the faithful performance of what he is instructed to do so far as the Law permits. A lawyer must serve the interests of justice as well as of those that seek it and it is his duty not only to plead his client's cause but to be his advisor.

4) Relationships of trust cannot exist if a Lawyer's personal honour, honesty and integrity are open to doubt. For the Lawyer these traditional virtues are professional obligations. The corporate spirit of the profession ensures a relation of trust between honest lawyers for the benefit of their clients, and in order to avoid litigation. It can never justify setting the interests of the profession against those of justice or of those who seek it.

If we were to seek an example of guilt and dishonesty which can be found within the legal profession in Scotland the case of **Adams –v– Queen** (fraud through concealing information) is the prime example. Here it was found that a person was deemed to be guilty of fraud when he dishonestly concealed information from another which he was under a duty to disclose to that other, or which that other was entitled to require him to disclose.

Over the last 30 or more years, many books have been published in relation to the *Code of Ethics and Practice of the Scottish Legal Profession*, discussing both the pros and cons of self-regulation. One would have thought that those members of the profession who religiously stand by these Codes and Practices would speak out in protest against the rotten eggs within their own system – namely those who, by concealing their incompetent ways under cover of a self-regulated system, are bringing the overall profession and system into worldwide disrepute.

Question – Where are the lawyers out of the 8–10,000 practising in Scotland who abhor these crooks and the crooked system? When and where are they going to start protesting? Or is it a case that the present system suits everyone under self-regulation?

If any profession, such as the legal profession operating under a Statute, acts as if it is privileged and able to overstep boundaries with impunity, or worse still acts with abuse of power, a Complainant should **never** be suppressed or deterred from seeking justice – it is his right. His own lack of awareness of the law should **not** allow abuse of power by those lawyers that are incompetent.

Any reasonable lay person who is not well versed in legal matters would have come to the conclusion that any solicitor who is being paid by his client to take over a case should abide by the rules and take forward the case with honesty, and integrity. In my case, that means making sure I got the justice I deserved without the sort of undue delays experienced at the hands of [First Solicitor]. All I could do now, as a lay person, was provide the evidence to [Second Solicitor] and rely on his knowledge and professionalism to take the case forward.

After receiving the complete copy file from [First Solicitor]'s office, [Second Solicitor] had a short introductory meeting with me. Before the meeting concluded I asked him to give me an estimate of how long it would be before we could get our case against [First Architect] to Court. His answer was *nine months*. I thought it important to ascertain this information because of my experience of the well planned delays of [First Solicitor].

Chapter 4

The Second Solicitor

[Second Solicitor]'s first letter was dated 4th September 1989 (File 186/7):

Dispute with [First Architect]

I have had an opportunity of reading your File over the weekend. It really does not tell me a tremendous amount because apart from the squabbling in correspondence between [First Architect] and [First Solicitor] the only real meat in the File is the correspondence that passed between [First Architect]'s Solicitors and [First Solicitor], when the issues were being identified. In their letter of 24th October (1986) [First Architect]'s Solicitors give a rather different view of things than that put forward on your behalf and the matter becomes further discussed and it is clear that there are issues of fact between you which make it difficult to assess the prospects of success because success where facts are at issue is likely to lie on the side of whose version of events is acceptable as more probable and at this stage I don't have enough information to take a view.

However, what I have done is written to [First Architect]'s Solicitor telling him that I am now interested. I am off…the second week September and do not anticipate anything happening before then but that we are to get a Legal Aid application filed on your behalf…

> *... I am still waiting to get a look at the case quoted by the sheriff and will do so during this week and hope to write you another note telling you whether I think there is any prospect of your being successful in an appeal* (in the case of [Contractor]).
>
> *If the case referred to by the Sheriff says what he says it does (and I would expect the Sheriff to be right in this) then it does appear that your remedy is restricted in law, although it appears to be a very logical result. Anyway, I will write to you about this.*

[Second Solicitor] then wrote to [First Solicitor] on 6th November 1989 (File 210):

> *Mr Brown has consulted us following your completion of a case for him by [Contractor]. That matter has now ended as a result of disposal of the question of expenses and while Mr Brown was not greatly happy with the outcome, our own view for what it is worth is that there is nothing he can do about it, and he has to accept the position as final.*
>
> *He has asked me to take up with you the question of a claim against [First Architect] in this case, which he instructed you to follow out...if you would be kind enough to let us know what steps you have taken for Mr Brown against [First Architect].*

[First Solicitor] continued playing his usual game of delaying tactics. [Second Solicitor] had to send him a reminder. This was dated 8th December 1989 (File 209).

1990

On 14th February 1990 (File 207) I wrote to [Second Solicitor] asking for copies of the correspondence between him and [First Solicitor] to verify to the Law Society that we had asked the same questions in relation to the case (regarding [First Architect]) and what actions he had taken. I also asked him for an update on the application for Legal Aid.

I received the copies I requested but no positive answer on the question of Legal Aid.

On 11ᵗʰ April 1990 (File 243) [Second Solicitor] wrote as follows to [First Solicitor]:

> ### *Mr and Mrs Brown –v– [First Architect]*
>
> *We gather this case has been raised and has been sisted and is therefore capable of being awakened. We are told by Mr Brown that he paid you £2,000.00 as a pre-payment for the expenses in this case and we shall be pleased to receive the balance unexpended given how little has been done in the matter.*

[First Solicitor] replied on 19ᵗʰ April 1990 (File 244). For future reference it is important to note the heading in this reply. It refers to the case against [First Architect], fees for which I had reluctantly been obliged to pay to [First Solicitor] (refer File 129/130). Yet the reference within the letter to a repayment of £2,000 was, in fact, the refund of the balance of a £7,500 inhibition order – an issue that will be described shortly – and nothing at all to do with the pre-payment described in File 129/130. Yet again [First Solicitor] was being duplicitous, this time attempting to give the impression that the amount was a return of the advance fees I had paid and for which I had received so little value.

> ### *Mr and Mrs Brown –v– [First Architect]*
>
> *We thank you for your letter of 11ᵗʰ April and note all that you write.*
>
> *We had, in fact, already been in discussions with Mr Brown regarding sums to be repaid to him and, indeed, on 6ᵗʰ April we provided him with a cheque for £2,000.00 in this connection. There is a balance due, however, and in terms of your letter, we wonder whether this should be paid direct to Mr Brown, as we have agreed with him, or whether it is to be paid to yourselves on his behalf. We should be grateful to receive clarification.*

What I am about to tell you next was relayed to the Law Society, who in turn told me that if my solicitor had misled me in any way, they would certainly look into the matter. Here are the details of how [First Solicitor] used **my** money in different ways, i.e. using the same amount to prove payment of two different bills; [Contractor]'s case and my attempt to pursue [First Architect] for recompense for all his negligence.

Note: When an inhibition order was placed on me, requiring £7,500 to be paid to our solicitor's account (prior to [Contractor]'s case being heard), I expected this to be handled with integrity and honesty. [First Solicitor] sent us a Statement of Accounting detailing the principal sum of the £7,500 with deductions.

When [Second Solicitor] wrote to [First Solicitor] regarding the conclusion of [Contractor]'s case and the possibility of an appeal against the Sheriff's decision, he was unaware that I had already been told by [First Solicitor] not to appeal the decision – that I would have to accept whatever the decision was and forget my specific reasons for appealing, namely a counter claim (which should have been thoroughly investigated but was never done).

Prior to the case, the receivers acting for [Contractor] wrote to [First Solicitor] claiming that the delays on the project were not of [Contractor]'s making but of other trades variations and in particular, **as discussed**, planning approvals yet to be obtained. Approvals had not been obtained and no Completion Certificate had ever been issued. Is it possible that the three parties had got together, i.e. [First Architect], [First Solicitor] and the gentleman acting for the receivers to organise a plan before the case began. What an utterly incredible position for any lay person to find himself in!

Here we have a solicitor, supposedly protecting his client and who had previously issued a writ for £30,000 against [First Architect], and a gentleman acting for the receivers, who had previously blamed the self same architect for all the problems regarding the building contract, actually meeting! At that meeting, is it possible that they planned between them not to mention or to rule out the following:

1) The unauthorised works costs unknown

2) The £4,000 additions to the contract built by [Contractor] without permission

3) The loss of the £3,000 conservation grant because the person responsible for all the above was being used as a witness **against my wishes**

If the costs of the unauthorised works had been introduced into the case I would have had no expenses to pay. In fact, the counter claim, if it had been properly introduced in the case, would have exceeded any claim from [Contractor].

And yet [First Solicitor] had refused to appeal stating there were no grounds for an appeal and it would not be accepted. *What could I do about it? NOTHING!*

At that time that's exactly what I did, deciding instead to continue with my quest for justice through [Second Solicitor], with reservations.

It is now May 31st 1990. I received a letter from [Second Solicitor] (File 256):

> *Please find enclosed Statement of Accounting received from your First Solicitor. We have received from him the sum of £672.22 and have put this into a client's account here in your name. We look forward to receiving your observations.*

What could I say? The deal had already been completed. [First Solicitor] must have been upset because I had not responded adversely to his incompetence, so here he was trying to upset me further by passing the balance of the inhibition order, after accounting, i.e. £672.22, which should have been passed to **me**, now on to [Second Solicitor] instead.

After I decided to go to [Second Solicitor] to continue my case against [First Architect], I also decided to look for a **third** architect to support [Second Architect]'s findings, and give further evidence for [Second Solicitor] to act on. I wanted proof that [Second Architect]'s research against [First Architect] was just not an opinion, as claimed by [First Solicitor]. By doing this, I hoped to make my case as solid as it could be – namely determining the complete incompetence of [First Architect].

[Third Architect] wrote to me on 18th August 1989 (File 182):

> *I refer to our telephone conversation earlier this week and now enclose for your consideration two copies of my report with regard to the problems associated with the building works previously undertaken at your guest house.*
>
> *Close scrutiny of the drawings previously prepared and used for the building works and the applications for statutory consent may identify the fundamental reason or cause of this entire mess. However, as noted in my report, control over the building contractor during the course of construction seems to have been totally inadequate. In terms of potential professional liability two distinct areas must be considered. Firstly, the drawings prepared should have been accurate to a certain degree and secondly it must be established beyond reasonable doubt what role your previous architect played during the course of the construction. Once these two areas of concern have been more accurately defined you should be in a position to consider effective legal advice on the matter. In this regard I personally have no reservations of fully supporting you in any action deemed appropriate to cover any consequential loss.*
>
> *I would suggest that you consider the report over the next few days and then contact me to arrange an early meeting to progress matters further.*

I did study the report in detail and found it very interesting; and encouraging, particularly the evidence supporting the case against [First Architect], all of which should have greatly helped [Second Solicitor]. This report had been completely independent from [Second Architect]'s report and it had agreed with and confirmed the total incompetence of [First Architect]. Here are just some of the details of that **total incompetence**. There is not just one single instance of incompetence, negligence or misconduct but, rather, an appalling catalogue of wholly unacceptable professional actions. These are summarised below:

1) The architect failed to competently survey the existing building.

2) The architect failed to competently prepare accurate proposal drawings based on the actual physical dimensions of the property.

3) The architect failed to competently accommodate within his proposal drawings adequate provision for the required cold water storage tanks.

4) The architect failed to competently ensure that his first and second phase proposals were adequately designed and could reasonably be constructed.

5) The architect, during the course of construction instructed [Contractor] to make material and substantial alterations to the proposed works without the prior knowledge and consent of the client, to conceal the inadequacies of his proposal drawings.

6) The architect, during the course of construction, instructed [Contractor] to make material and substantial alterations to the works without first seeking and obtaining the requisite Listed Building Consent contrary to the provisions of the Town and Country Planning (Scotland) Act 1972 thus exposing his client

to Legal action and to the loss of a conservation grant previously awarded. This serious action was again an attempt to conceal the underlying inadequacies of his project drawings.

7) [First Architect]'s profound incompetence in relation to the inadequate project drawings compromised his professional ability to supervise the works during construction and to ensure that acceptable standards of construction were achieved.

8) By virtue of [First Architect]'s incompetence the building works were not timeously completed nor was a Certificate of Completion obtained from the Building Authority (which would have permitted the client to lawfully occupy their property).

In asking for the assistance of [Second Solicitor] and [Third Architect], I had hoped that, with the mounting evidence, I would have received further assistance from the Law Society in helping me to clarify the actions of solicitors in relation to the Law Society. I felt at the time the best way forward would be to visit their offices in Edinburgh, which I did on 5th March 1990. Their Deputy Secretary's reply was dated 9th March 1990 (File 220):

I refer to the statement, which you made at this office on 5th March 1990 and would advise that I am now investigating the position. I have to tell you that the Law Society is an administrative body and does not give legal advice. Their concern is as to the professional conduct of Solicitors and I am enclosing the pamphlet "Complaints Against Solicitors" from which you will see how the Law Society are involved and just what they can and cannot do.

I shall be in touch with you in due course.

You can see from the above that I had started my complaint against [First Solicitor] and, with the help of the Law Society, I hoped to at last find success in my fight for true justice.

Some of the concrete evidence I had gathered against [First Solicitor] had been sent to the Law Society, at their request. I fell into line with these requests hoping it would be to my benefit.

Now, both the second and third architects, independently of each other, both agreed on the incompetence of [First Architect], exposing a criminal offence (by allowing the building of unauthorised works without the proper consents and planning permission, knowing full well he had been fully informed that he was dealing with a protected listed building). Yet he had ploughed on, instructing [Contractor] to commence the contract. Then he had the audacity to blame me for starting the contract and notified the authorities accordingly. And to think that he was to have been used as a witness in the case! No wonder I had been led towards thinking there was a cover-up. We will soon find out.

The receivers issued a writ in November/December 1986 against me for monies they claimed to be due to [Contractor]. My counter claim was completely and incompetently quantified by [First Solicitor] who, at the hearing, criminally ignored the concrete evidence to support my case and further acted criminally by misrepresentation. Here are some of the details introduced at the hearing. I have highlighted significant comments:

No 3/3 and 4/3 of Process: The undated instruction sheets from [First Architect] to [Contractor] detailing 13 changes to the contract including additions without permission. **Note Supervisory Role**.

No 14/6 of Process: Interim Valuation Certificate dated 20th September 1982. Amount due for payment on this certificate £6,175, signed by [First Architect]. **Note Supervisory Role.**

No 3/6 of Process: Letter from [Contractor] to [First Architect] asking for extension of time due to bad weather and (**additional works**).

No 4/9 through to 9/9 of Process: Building Contract. Six pages, page one of which stating that [First Architect] is the supervising architect. Also on this page it states *[Contractor] shall carry out and complete the works for £14,450.* **This was increased to over £18,000 without me being informed.** Page 2 states the contract shall commence on 23rd August 1982 and be completed by 18th October 1982.

Note: It is incredible that [First Architect] informed the Aberdeen Building and Planning Department that I, Angus Brown, was in a hurry to get going and told [Contractor] to start the contract before the appointed date.

What I am about to reveal in the next No of Process (No 14/9) makes me think that certain people from both the legal profession and the RIBA suffer from some kind of professional sickness simply not found in normal people. This is a very clever document to be introduced into the case, for various reasons and double meanings. Only cheats and liars resort to these kind of tricks to get them off the hook.

How far will [First Solicitor] go in his conflict of interest? This particular number, believe it or not, is File 68 dated 8th February 1985 from [First Architect] to [First Solicitor], copied to me. This is the letter that begins:

> As **REQUESTED**, *please find enclosed a statement of the final sum due by Mr Brown on the [guest house] contract. With retentions, outstanding payments and agreed additions this comes to £5,245.00.*

Note: The additions were never agreed.

> *However, as you will see from the attached schedule of defects, I would not advise Mr Brown to settle any monies without first receiving satisfaction and reimbursement for his considerable additional financial outlay and personal inconvenience.*

> *Due to the exceptionally poor state of the workmanship and the fact that to this date [Contractor] or their agents have failed to complete the works, Mr Brown in theory at least, would be entitled to enforce the liquidated and ascertained damages clause in the contract at the rate of £350/week from 18th October 1982.*

As I said earlier, this was a very clever letter to have introduced at the hearing. He cleverly finishes off with a P.S:

> *My appointment as architect for Mr Brown extended only to the production of drawings and obtaining planning permission and building warrant. Site supervision was not requested.*

If he is not supervising, why has he told [First Solicitor] the amount of money above to be paid to [Contractor].

Anyone reading this story up to this point will by now, I am sure, only be able to agree with me when I say, this Mickey Mouse (using the words of the contractor) architect had produced drawings, as mentioned above, that were absolutely useless and created the fundamental cause for the unauthorised works. Also, to further claim planning permission as part of his appointment is truly rich! He did not even achieve that end. The reason for this whole mess was due to the dubious acts of one man (and one man only) and his creation.

This Mickey Mouse architect had been very fortunate in that he was being very well protected. As far back as 1985, [First Solicitor] had called a meeting with the Law Administration and Building and Planning Department and made it quite clear that the offending architect would not be there! Protection indeed! And now the reason has become crystal clear.

This protection had carried on throughout the case with [Contractor] where, through the research described above, I uncovered an incredible situation, namely all the pre-planning prior to the case starting. Now wait for this piece of incriminating evidence, perhaps the very icing on the cake: in 1988 [First Solicitor] had travelled from Aberdeen to [First Architect]'s home, some 15–20 miles from Aberdeen, to agree their nefarious strategy and would you believe he charged this to Legal Aid. This meeting had been planned prior to [Contractor]'s case, and possibly even before that.

Now what an interesting meeting that must have been! Could it have gone something like:

"Listen, Mr Architect, I want you to be a witness in the forthcoming [Contractor]'s case against The Browns."

"Mr Solicitor, why do you want me to do that?"

"You will recall I protected you back in 1985 when I made sure you were not present at the meeting with the Law Administration Department and the Building and Planning Department where we discussed the unauthorised works and the conservation grant. Bear in mind, if you had been there, you would have had to answer some awkward questions. I have also further protected you by delaying the problem of trying to get the drawings from you. Mr Brown's second architect had requested the drawings on six occasions but I held back for six to eight weeks until I was forced to issue requests for them, as you know – because of the writ. In one particular request to you I mentioned that we needed the drawings to remove the impending enforcement order."

"Yes. Go on."

"Remember also, you refused to pay the costs of raising the writ for the drawings so I charged Mr Brown instead."

"But, Mr Solicitor, there is something really worrying me. You have also issued a writ against me for £30,000. What am I going to do about that?"

"My dear Mr Architect, you have no worries about that because: (1) Mr Brown knows nothing about the writ. I have kept that fact from him. (2) For further protection I have sisted it and have put down the reason that we are seeking Legal Aid."

"Thank you".

"What's more, I could also say I need you as a witness in the case against [Contractor]. Now, back to you Mr Architect. What can you do for me? At the forthcoming hearing, I want you to make up a list of defects against the receivers, including other details. I will introduce the letter I received from you where you opened by saying *as requested* (File 68). This is a perfect letter to further protect you, especially taking the P.S. at the end where you state you were not paid to supervise. I know that the Sheriff will take particular note of this letter and whatever he says will further protect you."

Is it not a fair assumption to say that the above dialogue is a possible reflection of such a conversation? Whatever was discussed at the meeting between these two parasites it is just unbelievable that it ever took place at all. Can you for the moment picture the scene: [First Solicitor] sitting in the house of [First Architect] against whom he has issued a writ for £30,000! And to think I had paid money to both men.

As the case continued from 1986 through to 1989, I ask my readers to understand what a truly harrowing experience I was going through – more than three years at the hands of corrupt people, not even able to begin to comprehend how corrupt they were going to be. It was a terrible position to be in, made so much worse by the fact that it was not of my own making.

Now, a question. Did the Sheriff protect [First Architect]? If so, could we also say that he was an incompetent Sheriff? It would seem so when we look at the evidence before the Sheriff at the hearing regarding our [First Architect]. Look at his findings and see whether there are indeed grounds to suggest utter incompetence at best and double dealing as a more likely possibility:

1) The evidence shown by Nos 3/3 and 4/3 of Process: Architect's instruction sheets to [Contractor].

2) 14/6 of Process: Instructions from [First Architect] to pay [Contractor] an interim payment of £6,175.

3) 3/6 of Process: Letter from [Contractor] to architect asking for additional time.

4) 4/9 through to 9/9 of Process: Six pages of Building Contract signed by [First Architect], [Contractor] and myself.

All the above documentation, presented in front of the Sheriff, clearly shows the function of [First Architect]. He **was** paid to supervise the contract throughout.

Following on now to No 25/2 and 26/2 of Process:

The Sheriff refers to a case as far back as 1920 to justify the proposition that [First Architect]'s failure to extend the time would be fatal to the application of the liquidate damages clause. But he then concludes:

I find it unnecessary to comment on this except to say that the Architect here was not employed as a supervising architect.

Note: It was very important for my case against [First Architect] that the Sheriff ruled against him and found in my favour that he was supervising. In one fell swoop the Sheriff had destroyed any chance of success in my case against [First Architect].

With all this evidence, [First Solicitor] had ignored his duty of protecting his client in that he failed to challenge the Sheriff's ruling. I hope my readers understand why I became convinced that there was the rank smell of collusion in the air. What could I do about it? NOTHING.

I would again ask the members of the legal profession reading this True Story – has the Brown family found justice through our democratic system of justice, or have they found themselves at the mercy of a legal system that is corrupt? The story is only just beginning. Before describing the complaints procedure, and the machinations of the Law Society, I would remind them of the following Professional Ethics and Code of Practice:

1) A lawyer's function in society does not begin and end with the faithful performance of what he is instructed to do so far as the law permits. A lawyer must serve the interests of justice as well as of those that seek it and it is his duty not only to plead his client's cause but to be his advisor.

2) Adams –v– Queen (fraud through concealing information) is the prime example. A person can be found guilty of fraud when he dishonestly conceals information from another which he was under a duty to disclose to that other or which that other was entitled to require him to disclose.

After the findings of the dubious Sheriff that [First Architect] was not "supervising" I had no choice but to soldier on in my case against this [First Architect] now in full knowledge that the Sheriff's decision was not helping my cause. It was becoming clear to me at this point in time, much as I dreaded the idea, that the corruption was spreading. I was beginning to wonder how far it would spread.

Would it spread as far as [Second Solicitor]? Time will tell. Surely we would now move towards success, given the concrete evidence already in [Second Solicitor]'s file and now I had [Third Architect]'s further evidence.

[Second Solicitor] received the following letter, dated 27th April 1990, from [First Architect]'s solicitor (File 253):

> ***Mr and Mrs Angus M Brown –v– [First Architect]***
>
> *We have been advised by Mr Brown's [First Solicitor], that you are now acting for Mr and Mrs Brown. We act for the Defender in the above case which we note has been sisted since September 1987.*
>
> *We would be obliged, therefore, if you would advise us whether or not your client intends to pursue the action and, if not, can it now be disposed of? We look forward to hearing from you.*

[Second Solicitor] replied on 3rd May 1990 (File 254):

> ***Mr and Mrs A. M. Brown –v– [First Architect]***
>
> *We acknowledge receipt of your letter of 27th April and note the contents. Our instructions are to proceed with the action against [First Architect] and we recently have been perusing the file to see what steps (need) to be taken. We shall be in touch.*

You can imagine the pressures that were building on me. I now had to correspond with [Second] and [Third Solicitors], [Third Architect] and the Law Society.

When the case against the receivers acting for [Contractor] was concluded, I wrote to [First Solicitor] and charged him with unprofessional conduct and with a further charge of negligence. I listed the facts in relation to these charges and I then wrote to the Law Society to inform them of the charges. I asked them what they were going to, or could do, to help me in regards to the actions of [First Solicitor], starting from the time we signed the building contract in his office in 1982 through to the conclusion of the case in 1989.

Here is an interesting question for my readers and for any current or future complainers/complainants who have complained against a member of the legal profession: Will the Law Society support me through this ordeal or could it be a case of a crooked solicitors' club that sticks together under the umbrella of self-regulation and their Law Society.

Here is some advice to those finding themselves in a similar position:

Any time in the future when you have dealings with anyone in the legal profession, always be cautious and have reservations.

In my case, and I am sure everyone will agree, after the last eight years of misery and high costs which should and could have been avoided, I wish I had heeded my own advice and found both a professional, decent, honest, solicitor and a professional, decent, honest and competent architect. Hindsight is so easy!

After the accusations and charges against [First Solicitor], which I copied to the Law Society, I received the following response from the Deputy Secretary of the Law Society, dated 20th March 1990 (File 221):

> *I thank you for your letter of 14th March and the various copy correspondence enclosed.*
>
> *This is most useful. I am still awaiting a response from [First Solicitor], and when I receive it, of course I will copy it to you.*
>
> *In the meantime, I think it would perhaps be useful if you send me copies of your letter to [First Solicitor] dated 14th February and his response of 23rd February. I look forward to hearing from you.*

I also received a response from [First Solicitor] dated 22nd March 1990 (File 223), saying:

> *We are in receipt of your letter of 14th March. We have also received a letter from the Law Society relative to this matter.*
>
> *In light of the fact that the Law Society has now become involved, we shall correspond with them relative to this matter.*

Accordingly, it would not be our intention to answer your letter of 14th March and we have advised the Law Society.

I then received a further letter from the Law Society, dated 28th March 1990 (File 237) headed *Complaint against [First Solicitor].*

I refer to the above and now enclose for your attention a copy of a response I have received from [First Solicitor] in relation to your complaint.

I would at the outset remind you that the Law Society is an administrative body whose concern is with the professional conduct of Solicitors. The Society cannot give legal advice nor will it comment upon how any Court action has been conducted. I would refer you to the pamphlet "Complaints Against Solicitors" which you already have a copy of, and would point out that if you regard the actings of a Solicitor as being negligent then it would clearly be in your interests to consult another agent to see if any other recourse is open to you.

In light of these comments, I would ask you to carefully consider the letter from [First Solicitor]. It does appear to me that they narrate a history of events upon which you will wish to comment and, as you will see they have not replied to your letter of 14th March on the grounds that this office is now involved.

I have to say that I have asked them for clarification of a couple of matters and I will contact you once I hear further from them.

In the meantime, perhaps you would let me have your comments on the copy letter enclosed.

I responded to the Law Society on 28th March 1990 (File 241) enclosing copies of letters I had written to [First Solicitor]. They had asked me to do this in their letter dated 20th March 1990 (File 221).

In response I received the following letter dated 2nd April 1990 (File 242):

> *I refer to my recent telephone call with you and thank you for your letter of 28th March 1990 and the documentation enclosed therewith.*
>
> *I have read the correspondence with interest and feel it appropriate at this stage to remind you of what I said in my letter of 28th March, which you will by now have received. If you think [First Solicitor] has been negligent then you should consult with a Solicitor regarding the action you might take against him. I can assure you that the question of the professional conduct of the Solicitor will be looked at but it is normal practice where a negligence claim is considered for the professional conduct aspect to be dealt with once the negligence case has been disposed of.*
>
> *It does also appear to me that you have instructed new agents to act for you and in that respect [First Solicitor] is technically correct in stating that they should really respond to your new agents, and should not have direct dealings with yourself. I look forward to hearing your further comments in due course.*

Further correspondence was received from the Law Society, dated 18th April 1990 (File 245):

> *I...now enclose a copy of a further letter received from [First Solicitor] together with enclosures.*
>
> *Doubtless you will wish to consider these and respond to me.*
>
> *I would again however reiterate the point, which I have previously made to you, namely that the Law Society is only in a position to consider the professional conduct of the Solicitor and that you should seek separate advice relating to negligence which you think has occurred.*

With regard to the many enclosures being sent back and forth and also to the Deputy Secretary asking me to respond to these enclosures, I think it is fair to ask – how on Earth can a lay person, on his own, take on the might of the legal profession and its 8–10,000 members. Membership of a club that is self-regulating can only result in that club closing ranks in times of difficulty. The club member I had been dealing with for the last seven to eight years, was now about to garner the support of his fellow members and the Law Society itself.

I would advise any future complainant/complainer to take particular note of the significance of the correspondence between myself and the Law Society – a society whose purpose is clearly to protect its own kind. They do so with what I can only describe as ploys. Ploys resulting in cover-up or misrepresentation.

On the face of it, in the short time I had been dealing with the Law Society, the general public might fairly be under the impression that they were being cooperative by sending to me the correspondence between themselves and [First Solicitor]. This was a clever ploy, giving the impression that there was no cover-up. What is more, in his letters, the Deputy Secretary always asked me to give my comments regarding the correspondence within the enclosures. Another seemingly fair and balanced approach hiding another ploy – an information-gathering exercise to ascertain my thoughts, to elicit evidence and any arguments that I may have, and what I intended to do in the future.

Furthermore, I had always thought that negligence would come under professional misconduct. But I had been informed by the Law Society that this was not the case, that I had an argument with my solicitor – or what they called a "difference of opinion" – about an end result. They made every effort to inform me that their definition of negligence and the public meaning of the word are completely different. Another ploy perhaps?

In his correspondence the Deputy Secretary kept telling me that he would look at the professional conduct of the solicitor but that I should seek separate advice relating to any negligence and find another solicitor to act for me.

Again this was another clever ploy. This time, the tactic was to encourage me to find another solicitor to take [First Solicitor] to Court. All the time spent on such a negligence case is time saved by the Law Society in addressing the issue of professional misconduct of one of their own – a fellow solicitor. Why on Earth could the two issues not be dealt with in parallel? In fact, why could they not be dealt with by the same body? On nearly every occasion, there will always be a causal link between negligence and professional misconduct.

Please bear with me. Here is a genuine question for my readers, the general public and, in particular, members of the legal profession: after reading the next three paragraphs, do we have a fair, democratic system under self-regulation in Scotland?

I put to the Law Society the following question: if you were to investigate the professional misconduct of my solicitor and found, through your own investigation that you agreed with my own allegations, then surely that would be of benefit to my case against him when, and if, I chose to proceed to Court and charge him with negligence?

The Law Society had repeatedly told me that they would not look at a negligence case. I was told to find another solicitor to act for me against [First Solicitor]. With the solid evidence in my possession against [First Solicitor], it would take a monkey to conclude that charge of unprofessional misconduct was valid.

So why delay? Yet here I find the Law Society, supposedly within a democratic accountable society, using self-regulation in full knowledge that they are acting against the rules of law, using a pre-planned system to undermine a complainer/complainant. The Law Society is perfectly aware that nobody has been successful in getting the services of one solicitor to act against another in a civil action involving negligence. This Deputy Secretary was knowingly telling me to follow the same steps that others had taken, and failed. If I decided to follow this road, I would be praying and hoping to find someone in the legal profession with honesty and integrity. There must be some good ones!

So it looked like I was in for a rough ride! Even so, at the time I kept faith that, by continuing with our legal system, I would find a successful conclusion and true justice. Remember too how costly this experience had been in terms of time and finances.

The case against [First Architect], taken forward with the assistance of [Second Solicitor], was beginning to concern me because of his correspondence with [First Architect]'s solicitor in May 1990 (File 254) where he informed him: *our instructions are to proceed with the action against [First Architect].*

The reason for my concern was, when I first met with [Second Solicitor] in August 1989 and asked him how soon it would be before we reached Court, I was informed that it would be nine months. Eight months had already passed. My further concern was the possibility now of contact between the two solicitors and their own contact with the Law Society now that I had raised the possibility of an action against [First Solicitor].

Any client who feels that he has been unfairly treated by one solicitor and intends to raise an action against him will find that he will have to contend with the full might of the legal profession. In other words he will be black-listed. That was how I felt at that moment, wondering how they would now con me with more delays, and further costs. The following correspondence is relevant:

Letter from [Second Solicitor] dated 9th August 1990 (File 264):

Dispute with [First Architect]

I see that I never sent you as requested in your letter some time ago, a copy of my letter of 11th April to [First Solicitor] but I am sending you this now. I am awaiting the return of [name supplied] from holiday for completion of your Legal Aid Forms and lodgement of the same in your case against [First Architect] because she deals with progress of Legal Aid matters here.

However, that is not stopping the case going ahead and I have got it enrolled for further procedure and shall keep you advised of developments.

Letter from Law Society, dated 11th May 1990 (File 255)

Complaint against [First Solicitor]

I refer to various, previous correspondence with you, and would advise you that I have now had the opportunity of briefly looking at the files of [First Solicitor].

I feel it appropriate at this point to make comments on two matters. In the first instance your case in relation to [Contractor] has been before the Sheriff's Court and a decision pronounced. You were advised after the decision was pronounced of the possibility of making an appeal and the likelihood of its success. I have to say that the Law Society will not comment on this matter at this time as it does appear that you were properly advised.

Of more interest to you, I think, will be the fact that according to the files an action was raised against [First Architect] on your behalf. After the action had been raised it was sisted. That means that it is still held in Court and recent correspondence suggests this is still the case. I would strongly recommend that you discuss this matter with your current agents in an attempt to take matters forward.

> *I would ask you to confirm in writing to me what you propose to do in this connection as I would not wish to consider any aspects of professional conduct until I am clear of what courses of action you are following.*

It is interesting to note in the above letter that he states he *briefly looked at the files of [First Solicitor].* Is it possible that these files could have been tampered with, by which I mean certain letters had been left out, to hide selective evidence, and some added to enhance [First Solicitor]'s actions.

If the file had not been tampered with, when he had seen that my case against [First Architect] was still held in Court, he would also have noticed the writ in the file and the reason that it had been sisted, i.e. Legal Aid. The letter above is dated 11th May 1990 and the writ was issued 11th August 1987 – a truly considerable time to wait. What is more, is it possible that the writ was approaching a time bar? It was never confirmed to me that I was to receive Legal Aid. In fact, through my research with representatives of Legal Aid with whom I had become familiar, I was informed that the Legal Aid had never been applied for. This is a fundamental rule in the eyes of the Law Society – a solicitor failing to apply for justifiable Legal Aid. Professional misconduct? Why had the Law Society missed this point, instead of suggesting that I had been correctly advised?

This is a grave offence under the rules of the Law Society. If I had been properly advised in the case against [Contractor] why did [First Solicitor] not challenge the Sheriff on his findings? And if it had been in the files given to the Law Society, he would also have discovered that [First Solicitor] was going to sue [First Architect] for £30,000 but prior to that he was going to use him as a witness supposedly in my favour against [Contractor].

I apologise to my readers for repeating these details, but I feel I must remind them that the Law Society and, everyone employed therein, are all parts of a crooked self-regulated system.

The details of my charge of fraud is based on the following:

1) [First Solicitor] instructed me to place funds to the amount of £7,500 into his firm's bank, because of the inhibition order placed on me by the receiver acting for [Contractor]. This was to ensure any monies being sought by the receiver would be guaranteed.

2) At the conclusion of the case there was a balance of £2,675. From this balance he sent me a cheque for £2,000. He then sent the remainder, i.e. £675.00, to [Second Solicitor]. I had no complaints about that.

3) [First Solicitor] had told me earlier he had not charged me any fees for all his hard work in the past, i.e. the case against both [First Architect] and [Contractor]. I reminded him with the written evidence I had paid him over £2,000 fees to take [First Architect] to Court and additional monies for the case against [Contractor].

4) He then had the audacity to write to [Second Solicitor] claiming he had repaid me a cheque for £2,000 in regards the case against [First Architect]. This sum was actually a refund of the balance of the deposit I had made as a result of the inhibition order.

All this information was, or should have been, in the files. [First Solicitor] would have wanted the Law Society to read what a wonderful solicitor he was by returning his client's fees. In actual fact, he still owed me £2,000. The Law Society seemed unaware of this professional misconduct when the Deputy Secretary wrote, on 14th June 1990 (File 258):

> **Complaint against [First Solicitor]**
>
> *I refer to my telephone conversation with you on Thursday, 7th June, and as promised write to confirm the views, which I expressed to you.*

The Society is, as I have previously said, an administrative body whose primary concern is with the professional conduct of Solicitors. It has no power to pay compensation or to adjudicate on any damages, which you may be due on the grounds of negligence.

Negligence is a matter for a Court of law and it is a matter on which you should seek legal advice. The Society's policy is quite simple, if a negligence claim is intimated and a Court action is to follow then the question of examination of professional conduct will be deferred until such time as the negligence action is determined. Whilst I accept what you said on the phone, the Courts have superior jurisdiction to the Society and the view is therefore that a matter to be decided in that form should be dealt with first. I would add that any finding in relation to professional conduct would not assist any case that you might have as it is an entirely separate matter.

As I have said to you previously your interests in relation to [First Architect] do now appear to be protected in that your Court action is up and running and, having examined my file and notes of the conversations which I have had with you, there has already been some consideration given to the fact that you might consider raising a negligence action against [First Solicitor].

Obviously, this is a matter on which you would be seeking legal advice and I would be grateful if you would confirm to me, yourself in writing, what you intend to do.

Rest assured that the question of professional conduct will be considered but, in the first instance, I do need to know what you are intending to do in relation to possible negligence.

So, the Law Society is an administrative body whose *primary concern is the professional conduct of solicitors.* Clearly they had done an excellent job of protecting that concern!

It staggers me that a professional body of people could stoop so low and insult the intelligence of the Scottish people. By telling us on one hand they will not look at negligence in the form of a complaint – that it must go through the Courts – when all the time they are aware of the length of time it takes for cases to go through the Courts. Just look at my own case against an architect. Can you imagine how long it would take for a negligence case against a solicitor to go through Court?

The first thing you would have to do is find another solicitor, one with integrity, to take on your case, and, not to be forgotten, you would then face huge legal costs.

But the main point I wish to make here is that for however long it takes for a negligence case to go through Court, any charges of professional misconduct against the same solicitor will not be considered by the Law Society for that same period of time. And during that time, the solicitor is free to carry on with business as normal. It would be interesting to know many are getting away with this planned corruption. What can clients do about it? Nothing.

On 20th July 1990, the Law Society continued to correspond in the same vein (File 262):

> *Complaint against [First Solicitor]*
>
> *I refer to my letter to you of 14th June and note that I have not heard further from you.*
>
> *I have to say that I have not heard from [Second Solicitor] in connection with this matter either.*
>
> *Perhaps you would be good enough to write to me and let me know if a negligence action is being pursued.*

The readers who have progressed this far in the story will by now know that [First Solicitor] raised an action against [First Architect]. After raising this writ he sisted it, declaring that he was applying for Legal Aid. This information was contained in files, and was now with [Second Solicitor], who was supposed to take the case forward, including Legal Aid cover. However, first it was necessary for me to ask, on two separate occasions, whether he had done so. The first occasion was at a meeting, the second by correspondence.

At last, [Second Solicitor] wrote to me letting me know that he had the necessary forms ready to apply for Legal Aid. All that was needed was for me to complete these forms. He also informed me, in the same letter, that he had enrolled the case for further procedure.

Note: An important question to pose here is: did [Second Solicitor] have a meeting with me before he enrolled the case for further procedure? The answer is a resounding no! Instead he told me on the phone there was no need for me to be at the debates. I responded that I felt it was indeed up to me to decide whether or not I attended. That way I could see for myself what progress had been made.

It is important to those readers who are using this book as a source of advice, and it is absolutely crucial for any complainer/complainant, to ensure that your solicitor applies for Legal Aid if you are proposing to take Court action. It is then the solicitor's duty to follow the appropriate rules.

When applying for Legal Aid, [First Solicitor] had made a complete mess of it (in respect of the case against [Contractor]). At one hearing he had asked for a cancellation because of his incompetence and we then had to rush through an emergency application, which finally came through. This had resulted in my having to pay £413 towards the costs. Another point of interest in relation to costs – [First Architect] had received £460 expenses for his trouble in appearing at the hearing against [Contractor]!

Of further importance in relation to Legal Aid, always remember that complainants have a right to an effective remedy in Law pursued through a democratic process, namely the right to a fair unbiased hearing, and a right to justice through proper representation with financial assistance (namely Legal Aid), all without undue delays. An effective remedy should not be blocked by any individual or group of people using unethical methods or deterrents for their own benefit, for example financial gain or self-promotion (as is currently possible within our self-regulated system).

An important member of the legal profession stated in a speech to newly-qualified solicitors at Parliament House in Edinburgh:

> *There are a huge number of members of the public who could not afford to contemplate going to Court without the protection of some form of Legal Aid or other financial contribution. I know I could not face up to a major proof in the Court of session with the prospect of expenses being awarded against me. How much more for the ordinary man or woman in the street... I believe the Government speaks with forked tongue on these issues; it pays lip service to citizens' rights to get to Court but effectively puts so many barriers in their way, of a financial nature, that it is quite unrealistic for the ordinary man/woman ever to cross the threshold of the Court.*

Effectively puts barriers in the way. An interesting quote indeed! What effective barriers and deterrents does the Law Society use against complainants who, incidentally, are fellow human beings simply trying to get access to justice?

What effective barriers and deterrents can an offending solicitor put in front of clients, especially if that particular client intends taking a fellow solicitor to Court? Time will tell.

The first correspondence I received from [Second Solicitor] was dated 4th September 1989 (File 186) and the most recent was dated 9th August 1990 (File 264). At the first meeting in 1989 he had promised: *We will be in Court in nine months*. This was obviously out the window now.

Remember the solicitor is always in control and clients, especially those in my position, had to be careful. I couldn't voice my opinions and say exactly what was on my mind. The result of such an action might well be: *find yourself another solicitor*.

After many discussions with [Third Architect] he was fully appraised of my financial position and the costs to date. He was very sympathetic to my position knowing further heavy costs would be forthcoming. He wrote to me on 16th August 1990 (File 265):

> *Further to our meeting on Monday morning this week I enclose for your consideration and comment a copy of my opinion with specific regard to [First Architect]'s role in the matter under discussion. I would propose to contact you early next week to discuss details prior to forwarding a copy to [Second Solicitor] for his detailed consideration.*

As promised, [Third Architect] wrote to [Second Solicitor] on 27th August 1990 (File 266):

> *Further to our recent meeting I enclose for your consideration and comment a copy of my formal opinion with regard to [First Architect]'s professional activities undertaken on behalf of Angus Brown in respect of his guest house.*
>
> *I forwarded a copy of same to Angus and met with him last week to discuss the contents thereof, with particular reference to his earlier statements to the effect that he had clear proof of [First Architect]'s supervisory role during the construction period...the Solicitor acting for [First Architect] has I understand, previously denied that he was so retained.*
>
> *I was pleased to note that Angus has retained a range of documents including a copy of an architect's instruction issued by him to [Contractor] requiring the re-location of the cold water tanks to*

their existing and unacceptable position. There can clearly be no doubt that [First Architect] did act in a supervisory capacity on behalf of Angus Brown in this matter.

I have responded to the other matters raised during our meeting in a separate letter. Please do not hesitate to contact me with regard to any aspect of this matter.

There were six pages of incredible concrete evidence enclosed with this letter – evidence that would stand up in any Court of law, particularly when taken in conjunction with my own evidence.

[Second Solicitor]'s response to the above was dated 3rd September 1990 (File 276):

Many thanks for your letter of 27th August 1990 the contents of which are noted.

I am obliged to you for your report and shall keep you advised of developments.

I received the following from [Second Solicitor] dated 18th September 1990 (File 276-1):

We enclose form L20 which now requires to be completed for the Scottish Legal Aid Board. You should be able to complete the whole of this form yourself, sign the declaration on the final page and return it to us in the S.A.E. We also enclose the application form, which requires to be signed by you on page 8 where marked signature of applicant.

At long last it was possible to live in expectation that I would receive Legal Aid in relation to the case against [First Architect]. Two days later these forms were hand-delivered by me personally to [Second Solicitor]'s office.

Note: As a matter of interest, and what has been mentioned many times, and will be continued to be mentioned throughout this True Story, is the matter of delays. These are important to a solicitor – a circumstance that helps to swell their bank account, and one well known throughout the profession.

I then received further correspondence from [Third Architect], dated 27th December 1990 (File 278):

> *I enclose for your information a copy of a letter I have dispatched today to [Second Solicitor] regarding the current status of the litigation between yourself and [First Architect] the contents of which are self-explanatory.*
>
> *Given the nature of the written information you have on file and at your disposal to support your claim for damages against [First Architect] I am considerably surprised that this entire matter has not been resolved long before now.*
>
> *In the circumstances I am sure we would both now welcome an early resolution to the entire matter. Accordingly I would recommend that you contact [Second Solicitor] without fail during week beginning 7th January to arrange an urgent meeting to ascertain the current status of the litigation. I should be obliged to hear from you once the meeting has been arranged to enable me to ensure that I can attend.*

The copy of the letter he enclosed – the one he had sent to [Second Solicitor], dated 27th December 1990 (File 279/280), stated:

> *You may recollect our telephone conversation some weeks ago when I enquired as to the current status of the litigation between Angus Brown and [First Architect] during which I expressed my increasing concern with regard to two aspects of the matter. I recall that you undertook to investigate the current situation and advise accordingly.*

As I have not heard further from you I would now confirm the specific nature of my concerns as these may ultimately have some bearing on the litigation in hand.

*Having regard to the nature of the litigation and the substantial material available to support Angus Brown's position I had anticipated progress to a satisfactory conclusion within a reasonable time scale. On that basis estimated costs in respect of the required remedial works at [The Browns' guest house] were **forwarded to you some four months ago**. Obviously as time passes these estimated construction costs will come under increasing pressure as a result of inflationary trends.*

*Apart from the cost implications associated with the **continuing delay** in reaching a conclusion to the litigation, we face, on the 1st April 1991, the introduction of a completely new set of Building Regulations which will be applicable to any warrant application submitted after that date. In the case of [The Browns' guest house] the works previously undertaken under the auspices of [First Architect] were the subject of a Certificate of Completion and accordingly the entire works are currently unauthorised in terms of the Building Standard (Scotland) Regulations.*

It follows that, apart from the required remedial works previously detailed, all the other works undertaken on site approximately 10 years ago will have to be the subject of a retrospective building warrant application which will, by necessity, have to indicate compliance with current standards rather than those applicable at the time of the original warrant application.

As my initial investigations into this entire matter were undertaken some 15 months ago it was not possible to anticipate the potential impact of the introduction of a complete revision of the building regulations on either the proposed remedial works or the other existing unauthorised works.

From our mutual client's point of view, there would seem to be a clear necessity to satisfactorily resolve the litigation as funds are unavailable to underwrite the professional servicing of the situation, in the interim.

I would therefore welcome in the circumstances early receipt of your advices regarding the status of the litigation to enable me to ascertain whether a warrant application prior to the introduction of the revised legislation is now considered likely.

While time had passed and all the above correspondence had been exchanged, it had become ever more clear to me that there was a possibility that [Second Solicitor] was no more reliable than the first. My reasons for this were:

1) The delays in pursuing the case

2) The length of time it had taken to ensure I receive Legal Aid

Was he expecting me to quit? Would he even force me to quit? Why? Was it possible that such a tactic would fall in with his own agenda? Conflict of interest? The questions flooded in.

Meanwhile the Law Society had been getting anxious. Look at the following series of correspondence:

26th July 1990 (File 263):

I refer to our telephone conversation on Tuesday. I note that you are pursuing [First Architect] in Court and thereafter you intend to raise proceedings against [First Solicitor].

30th October 1990 (File 277):

Complaint against [First Solicitor]

I refer to previous correspondence and your conversation with my colleague.

Perhaps you might like to write to me to confirm whether your actions are up and running in Court or, alternatively, perhaps you would like to ask [Second Solicitor] to confirm the position to me. In any event I look forward to hearing from you.

1991

29th January 1991 (File 281):

Complaint against [First Solicitor]

I see from the file that I last spoke to you on 20th November and wonder if progress is being made.

I would ask, so I can keep a record of matters complete, if either you or your Solicitor would write to me to confirm the current position.

I phoned [Second Solicitor] regarding the above and asked him to contact the Law Society.

1st February 1991 (File 282):

Complaint against [First Solicitor]

I am sorry I was not available when you called this afternoon.

I understand from my Secretary that you are not prepared to write to the Society, but would wish to discuss matters with me.

In my letter of 29th January I asked you for details of the progress being made in the Court actions. With due respect I do not feel that I should become involved in a discussion with you regarding the mechanics of these actions.

> *What I need to know from you is quite simply, how the actions that*
> *[Second Solicitor] has raised on your behalf are progressing, As*
> *I have said previously once these matters have been dealt with*
> *by the Court I will be in a position to consider the question of*
> *professional conduct.*
>
> *I look forward therefore to receiving your written confirmation*
> *of the position.*

This was very interesting. He was claiming that he wanted to know the position and expected me to believe he had no information at all of what is going on! All he need have done was call either [First] or [Second Solicitor]s for updates at any time.

I wondered what he thought of the following information, already in his files, and was it possible that he was testing me to see what information I had on file?

Interlocutors

Start of my case against [First Architect]:

9th September 1987 (File 392)

Cause Tabled

The Sheriff, on Pursuer's motion, sisted the Cause to Enable the Pursuer to apply for Legal Aid.

12th December 1990 (File 392 continued)

The Sheriff, on Defender's motion, continued the Cause Simplicitor to the roll of 9th January, 1991.

9th January 1991 (File 392 continued)

The Sheriff, on Pursuer's motion No 6 of Process Consent, recalled sist of 9th September 1987.

Appointed defences to be lodged within 14 days from today's date and continued the Cause to the Adjustment roll of 6th February 1991.

6th February 1991 (File 392 continued)

The Sheriff, on Defender's motion, allowed defences to be received, though late. Form No 7 of Process continued the Cause to the Adjustment roll of 6th March.

6th March 1991 (File 392 continued)

The Sheriff, on Pursuer's motion of consent, continued the Cause to the Adjustment roll of 20th March 1991.

20th March 1991 (File 392 continued)

The Sheriff, on Pursuer's motion of consent, continued the Cause to the Adjustment roll of 1st May 1991.

Ignoring the legal terminology, which may be confusing my readers, I have simply chosen the above six interlocutors out of a total of 28 for various reasons:

1) To remind readers of the date of the writ against [First Architect] and the reason it was sisted, i.e.Legal Aid.

2) To take special note when the sist was recalled by [Second Solicitor], i.e. 9th January 1991, and to acknowledge the irony that I was still awaiting Legal Aid.

3) To allow readers to note that both the Pursuer's and the Defender's Solicitors were delaying the progress of this case, and to pose the question: can self-regulation really help the client? Delaying tactics certainly do not.

I just cannot believe, let alone come to terms with, the fact that anyone in the profession with any modicum of intellect or decency, can stoop to the depths that solicitors knowingly do and still be able to accept monies from their clients with a straight face.

As you can see from the above correspondence between [Third Architect] and [Second Solicitor], now at the end of the year (1990), that the most prominent feature which had upset [Third Architect] was the delayed response from [Second Solicitor]. It has taken four months to deal with simple questions such as costs, the remedial works and the status of the litigation.

The story now continues with further correspondence from [Third Architect] to [Second Solicitor], 12th February 1991 (File 284):

Angus has kindly forwarded to me a copy of your letter and enclosures dated 4th February 1991 regarding the above litigation for my consideration and comment.

The Defences would seem to be somewhat confused and inadequate in a number of important respects. At the bottom of page 2 reference is made to two separate elements of construction defined as the alterations to the main roof of the house and a first floor extension at the rear of the main part of the premises. It is noted that the Defender understood that both elements were proposed to be constructed at the same time.

In fact, as I have previously reported, the dimensional inaccuracies found within [First Architect]'s original drawings effectively precluded construction of the rear first floor extension.

The serious inadequacies of the original drawings insofar as they relate to the location of the cold water storage tanks is also fundamental to the resultant problem.

With regard to the denial that supervisory services were undertaken by [First Architect] during construction I understand that Angus Brown retains a fee note and encashed cheque specifically in respect of such services together with an architect's instruction signed by [First Architect] specifically requiring the re-positioning of the cold water storage tanks. In addition that same Architect's drawings, reference 79/02/04 also specifically makes reference to the relocation of the tanks.

I understand from Angus that we are to meet on the 26th February 1991 to discuss matters further and look forward to seeing you at that tine.

Further correspondence from [Second Solicitor] to myself, dated 29th April 1991 (File 286):

Further to our recent telephone call I am enclosing a copy of the First Adjustments done for you in the case and a copy of the inventory of Productions that has been lodged. I also enclose a copy of the writ and the defences so that you can see where these matters fit in.

As I said to you on the phone I am anxious to get details of the losses that you will sustain during the 6 week period or so when the place will not be capable of use while remedial works are being carried out. I am also going to need a very detailed quotation for the cost of the works but have written to [Third Architect] about this separately.

Letter from [Third Architect] dated 13th May 1991 (File 287/8):

I return herewith the copy of the inventory of productions and associated documents relative to [First Architect]'s litigation.

Taken with [Second Solicitor]'s comments to me last week we are now awaiting a formal response by [First Architect] to our productions, which certainly undermine his entire defences. Your Second Solicitor is attempting to secure informal guidance from the opposition's Solicitor as to the likely response to our productions.

The situation may now develop along one of two distinct routes. Firstly [First Architect] will accept that his position is untenable in terms of the litigation and discussions will proceed with a view to securing a negotiated out of Court settlement. Alternatively the litigation will continue with the prospect of an out of Court settlement being tendered at some later date.

It is my opinion, and I think it is shared by [Second Solicitor] that [First Architect] does not carry an indemnity insurance. Accordingly, it is possible that he will continue to attempt to delay the inevitable outcome of the litigation for as long as possible.

If this is the case we shall be forced to support our position by providing the detailed information required by [Second Solicitor] and as noted in the enclosed copy of his most recent letter to me. Given that it will take around 12 weeks to obtain the necessary information it would seem appropriate to make an early start to submitting the planning application and completing all warrant and tender documentation. I feel it would be beneficial to ensure that we do not assist [First Architect] in his endeavours to prolong this matter further.

In terms of the cost of this exercise you will appreciate that I have refrained from issuing a fee note in respect of the planning application stage of my services which were completed prior to the end of 1989 pending a resolution of the litigation. This amount is £700 plus VAT, i.e. £822.50 gross, with a further £900 plus VAT, i.e. £1057.50 gross, payable on submission of the building warrant.

Continued correspondence from [Third Architect], dated 14th May 1991 (File 289):

> *Further to our telephone conversation this morning, I am pleased to note that you agree that we should now take the initiative with regard to progressing matters with a view to being able to furnish [Second Solicitor] with the information necessary to support our litigation to the bitter end if need be. In this regard I enclose for your attention my agreed fee note in respect of the planning application stage of my service relative to this matter. While I am unable to progress the submission of the planning submission until the beginning of next week I have allocated the required time in anticipation of receipt of your remittance in respect of the enclosed fee note. I propose we meet next week to discuss the situation in detail and to investigate the magnitude of the remedial works required to the property including the resolution of the drainage problems.*

This letter that follows is a prime example of the delaying ploy. I invite my readers to take particular note of the ongoing problems that I had to deal with. Exactly these problems beset **many** complainers/complainants. The next correspondence, dated 19th April 1991 (File 292) between [Second Solicitor] and [Third Architect] is so very typical:

> *I refer to previous correspondence. Your letter of 27th August 1990 gave me an idea of figures. Is it possible that we can get a proper quotation done to illustrate exactly what the remedial works are and what they will cost. I have asked Mr Brown to provide details of the losses he anticipates he will sustain as far as his loss of the use of the subject's business commercially is concerned. A full and detailed list of the costs incurred by the remedial work will need to be done, made out including professional fees and tradesmen's estimates and I wonder if you could make arrangements towards obtaining these for me because our case will otherwise be lacking in specification.*

It is beyond belief what I had to put up with from the legal profession. I now find [Second Solicitor]'s incompetence is indeed beyond belief – look at his letter (above) where it is quite evident, by the date, that he is answering a letter he received nine months earlier, coincidentally exactly the same time as he gave me back in August 1989 for our case to reach Court. As a matter of record, I freely acknowledge that [Second Solicitor] did give a quick answer (3rd September) to the letter he received on 27th August. However, it is easy to respond timeously to what is innocuous – giving thanks to [Third Architect] for his report and offering to *keep him informed*. But the delay of nine months is utterly unacceptable. Even so, what could I do about it? Nothing!

Prior to the above, [Third Architect] had raised his concerns to [Second Solicitor] (back in 1990, File 279/80) about a further delay of four months waiting for important answers.

Meanwhile, the Law Society continued to communicate – 21st May 1991 (File 294):

> *I refer to my telephone conversation with you in February and note at that stage it was hoped that the first action you have raised, namely the action against [First Architect] was to go into Court. Has there been any further progress in relation to this? I look forward to hearing from you.*

Further correspondence from [Third Architect], dated 24th May 1991 (File 295):

> *I refer to our meeting earlier this week. I can now confirm that the Planning and Listed Building consent applications are completed ready for submission.*
>
> *The planning application fee has been established as £39, with the subsequent building warrant application fee set at £157.*

As Monday is a bank holiday, would it be possible to contact you on Tuesday next week to arrange to pick up a cheque made payable to Aberdeen City District Council in the amount of the planning application fee of £39?

I also enclose a copy of my letter to [Second Solicitor] advising that we are now progressing matters for your information.

Here are the details (from the "copy letter" referred to above) of the letter from [Third Architect] to [Second Solicitor], dated 24th May 1991 (File 296).

I refer to our recent telephone conversation regarding the above Litigation and to your advices that you would contact me once you had spoken to [First Architect]'s agent to ascertain, informally, what response could be anticipated in light of our recent submissions which discredits [First Architect]'s defence.

Notwithstanding the absence of your advices I have given the matter further consideration with specific regard to your most recent letter to me. I have concluded that if we do not proceed to obtain the information required to justify our claim we may potentially assist [First Architect] in delaying the inevitable outcome of the litigation.

Accordingly our mutual client has accepted my recommendation to proceed apace and the information required and as specified within your most recent letter should be available in around 12 weeks' time.

I shall keep you fully informed of progress. In the interim I await your advices regarding [First Architect]'s response to our last submissions.

Following on with his investigations, [Third Architect] contacted the Planning Officer on 28th May 1991 (File 297):

Proposed Alterations to Rear Dormer at [The Browns' guest house]

*During September 1989 discussions were held between one of your members and the writer with regard to the above property and in particular to **unauthorised works** to the rear dormer undertaken under the instruction of our client's first architect.*

At that time an agreement was reached with regard to the nature and scope of the remedial works necessary to accord with your Department's requirements. Unfortunately Litigation, initiated by our client against [First Architect], has only progressed to a point where a satisfactory outcome is now anticipated.

Accordingly we enclose for your consideration a detailed planning and listed building consent application covering the remedial works previously discussed and agreed.

We look forward to receipt of the consent document in due course.

[Second Solicitor] wrote to me on 3rd June 1991 (File 298):

I enclose, for your information, copy letter from [Third Architect] dated 24th May 1991 (File 296) together with a copy of my reply (File 299).

This reply (File 299) stated:

Many thanks for your letter of 24th May, the contents of which are noted. I look forward to hearing from you as matters progress on the ingathering of the relevant information that is required. In the meantime the case [was] called again on 29th May and was continued for 2 weeks for adjustment and for the Defender's agents to advise me on the existence or otherwise of any Indemnity Policy. I have made it clear to them that I require this knowledge immediately in order that I may put in place any diligence by way of Inhibition Arrestment etc. I am sending Angus a copy of this letter and will, of course, keep him advised.

On 5th June 1991 (File 301) [Second Solicitor] wrote again, informing me of a change.

I refer to the copy letter sent to you on 3rd June and write to advise that in fact rather than two weeks the case was continued until 26th June. On that date I trust that a hearing will be fixed.

On 27th June 1991 (File 302) [Third Architect] wrote to me, as follows. I ask my readers to share with me the refreshing nature of his upbeat and Courteous communication style, so different to the sombre tone of many of the other parties' communications reflected in this story:

Alterations to your guest house

I have been attempting to contact you by telephone this afternoon with regard to progress on the above project but unfortunately I have not managed to speak with you. I can, however, confirm that our planning application lodged on the 28th May 1991 is progressing to a satisfactory conclusion. As you may be aware planning applications are required to be advertised in the press when they involve works to a listed building. In this regard the expiry date following the press advert for receipt of any observations or objections is 3rd July 1991. Thereafter the Planning Authority can complete consideration of the application and issue the required consents. I am advised, that no difficulty in this regard is anticipated by the Planning Authority.

With regard to the warrant application I am pleased to advise that following detailed discussions with the appropriate officers of the Building Authority it has been agreed that the proposed warrant application will now only be required to cover the remedial warrant application will now only be required to cover

> *the remedial works required by the Planning Authority rather than the entire works covered by the warrant obtained by [First Architect]. Both the drainage and building inspectors have advised that they are satisfied in the circumstances that the works previously undertaken, except those without planning consent, are acceptable in terms of the Building Regulation then in force. I am also advised that once the warrant application in respect of the remedial works has been approved and the works completed a 'letter of comfort' may be obtained from the Building Authority confirming that the original works were satisfactorily completed and that no enforcement action will be taken **due to [First Architect]'s failure to obtain a Certificate of Completion.***
>
> *Accordingly I would now wish to submit the warrant application without delay and would request payment from you in the amount of £528,75 inclusive of VAT and as agreed, together with a payment to Aberdeen City District Council in the amount of £113.50 relative to the building warrant application fee.*
>
> *You will note that the warrant application fee is somewhat less than previously advised due to the restricted extent of the work which is now being applied for.*
>
> *As I am to be on holiday during the course of next week I would welcome the opportunity of collecting the required funds from you during the course of tomorrow afternoon.*

I paid both of above amounts (£642.25 in total) that following afternoon.

On 30th July 1991 (File 304) [Third Architect] wrote to me regarding the proposed works.

> *I have pleasure in enclosing for your attention and safe keeping the detailed planning and listed building consent relative to the above works received from the Planning Department this morning.*

While the building warrant application's progress through the system will inevitably be delayed by the holiday period I would expect to have, and thereafter tenders for the works can be obtained, it cleared within the next 21 days.

[Second Solicitor] wrote to me on 21st August 1991 (File 305):

We write to advise that a Diet of Debate has been arranged in the above case for 16th October 1991 within the Sheriff Court. A Diet of Debate is purely a legal argument and accordingly there will be no need for you to attend Court that day.

Meantime, the Law Society continued to sing their favourite tune. On August 23rd 1991 (File 306) they wrote, under the heading *Complaint against [First Solicitor]*:

I refer to my telephone discussion with you on 22nd May and would be grateful if you could write to me and confirm that progress is being made.

I note the next Court date is set down for next month and I would be grateful if you would confirm to me whether any other progress has been made in the meantime.

[Second Solicitor] informed me, on 6th September 1991 (File 308):

Just a note to confirm that I have effectively served letters of inhibition on your [First Architect].

The above inhibition order cost me £100.

This was followed by another letter, dated 24th September 1991 (File 309):

As you know a debate has been fixed for 16th October in your case.
I am still short of much detail on how your claim is made up

and that will cause difficulties on 16th October. I also need the information being provided by [Third Architect] and have written to him today to the same effect.

[Third Architect] wrote to me on 10th October 1991 (File 311):

*I enclose for your information a copy of the building warrant relative to the remedial works at your guest house together with a copy of recent correspondence to [Second Solicitor] **(providing all outstanding information as previously requested)**.*

I have also spoken with your Accountant and he is to advise [Second Solicitor] directly of the calculated loss of profit during construction. Hopefully, armed with this information he will be able to bring this protracted matter to a rapid and satisfactory conclusion.

You will recollect from previous correspondence that the Buildings Authority now only require us to undertake the remedial works as defined by the Planning Authority. This, accordingly, has reduced the cost of the works from that originally anticipated to a tendered figure of £7,258.74 inclusive of VAT Within the tender we have included a £500.00 provisional sum to cover any unforeseen works to the existing plumbing system and £750.00 to cover consequential redecoration of the stairway/landing etc. An additional non-specific contingency sum of £410.48 has also been included in the tender figure in common with prudent practice in this type of construction project. Given that we do not know exactly when these works may commence, I have also ensured that an inflation allowance covering a start of the works up to six months from now has also been allowed for within the gross tender figure.

In accordance with the terms of my letter to you dated 13th May 1991 I enclose my restricted fee note as agreed and look forward to receipt of your remittance in respect of same, in early course

[Third Architect] then wrote to [Second Solicitor] on 10th October 1991 (File 313), another example of professional competence expressed with businesslike Courtesy:

I refer to previous correspondence with regard to the above litigation.

As you may recollect the original advices received from the Building Authority indicated that a comprehensive and retrospective building warrant application covering all proposed remedial works together with all works previously undertaken under the direction of [First Architect] was to be required. Given that building regulations have significantly changed since [First Architect]'s original warrant application was submitted, I was anticipating considerable consequential improvement works throughout the building.

However as a result of negotiations, the Building Authorities subsequently agreed to accept a restricted warrant application covering only those remedial works required by the Planning Department once these works are completed and a Certificate of Completion obtained the Building Authority has agreed to issue a 'letter of comfort' with regard to the original works.

The restriction of the required works has had an impact on the costs of the construction and I can now confirm that the total tendered construction cost inclusive of VAT will be £7,258,74. As these works will presumably commence once the litigation has reached a satisfactory conclusion, an allowance of £294.17 is included within the tender to accommodate a site start within the next six months.

I have advised Angus Brown's accountant that the construction works can be comfortably completed within six weeks but that an additional two weeks be allowed to permit close down and start up activities to be undertaken with ease. The accountant will write to you directly with regard to the estimated loss of profit during this period.

I have advised Angus Brown's accountant that the construction works can be comfortably completed within six weeks but that an additional two weeks be allowed to permit close down and start up activities to be undertaken with ease. The accountant will write to you directly with regard to the estimated loss of profit during this period.

In terms of my own fees and expenses relative to this matter since my retention on the 5th May 1989, I enclose a detailed schedule herewith.

The *detailed schedule* of fees and expenses enclosed with the above letter amounted to a total of £3,177.13 inclusive of VAT

On 29th October 1991 File 315, [Third Architect] wrote to me:

I refer to our recent meeting, with [Second Solicitor] and our subsequent telephone conversation, regarding the litigation (i.e. between me and [First Architect]).

In my further endeavours to progress this matter I have, earlier today, discussed the current situation with [Second Solicitor].

As a result of our discussion I can confirm to you that the information provided by myself to [Second Solicitor] with regard to the reconstruction costs and associated professional fees is completely adequate for the purposes of the litigation.

During the course of our meeting I was somewhat concerned that a single package of information covering all other aspects of your claim was not to hand and that reliance was being placed on individual items of information being previously held in the files of [Second Solicitor]. To avoid any further confusion and delay I would recommend that one single information package covering all items in the enclosed list be prepared as soon as possible. While I spoke with your accountant immediately on return to my office after our meeting, I feel that a specific instruction to your accountant to prepare all the required information may be necessary to cover all aspects of the claim, effectively.

While the magnitude of the stress that this matter continues to place you under was readily evident during our meeting with [Second Solicitor] we have to ensure that our claim is competently supported as was suggested. While there is no doubt in my mind as to [First Architect]'s responsibility for this entire mess, our claim for compensation must be progressed within the constraints of the Scottish legal system which dictate that the claim must be specific, i.e. we must be able to demonstrate to the Court the precise nature of the loss.

If we can provide, as suggested, all the information in one package, [Second Solicitor] will readily be able to progress the situation. If you wish any further assistance please do not hesitate to contact me. In the interim I would welcome early receipt of your remittance in respect of my recently issued fee note.

On 5th December 1991 (File 317-1), I wrote to [Second Solicitor]:

I feel that both [First Architect] and his Solicitor will continue to delay the outcome of the above case by continually bringing up items which will require our response, and therefore many weeks' delay (as we have experienced in the past).

I thought it might be advantageous to summarise for you the main points in this litigation.

The enclosed document is a simple guide to answer all pertinent questions.

I would be most grateful if you spare a few minutes to read it.

This package, in addition to the summary of the financial claims and support documents already in your possession, should assist you on January 8th 1992 (which I have been informed is the next calling to Court).

I would also be very appreciative of your response to the following questions:

1) *Do you feel you now have absolutely everything you require to succeed against [First Architect]?*

2) *What was Edinburgh's response to our financial claims documents?*

3) *In layman's terms, what are the next steps after Court on 8.1.92?*

4) *When do you think this case will be finalised?*

5) *Could you kindly respond to the areas in the Financial Claims summary that require your input (as [Accountant] has written to me saying he is waiting your response)?*

[Accountant] had written to [Second Solicitor] as far back as 5th July 1991 (File 340) in response to the solicitor's request for written accounts. No reply was received. Here is the letter:

We have now gone over our client's invoices for the last four months and can confirm that an average month's income from letting would be £2,600. As food costs are minimal we would be of the opinion that loss of earnings per week could be fairly stated as being £600.00. If you wish any further information phone and let us know.

The Law Society wrote to me on 11th December 1991 (File 347):

I thank you for your letter of 28th November 1991 and enclose for your information a further copy of the pamphlet 'Complaints against Solicitors' which explains on the forth page the position if you perceive your Solicitor has been negligent.

As I said to you in my telephone discussion, I would be more than happy to try to arrange an appointment for you with a Solicitor to discuss the negligence question to see if there is anything that can be done.

Troubleshooters would be available in Edinburgh, Glasgow, Perth, Dundee, or possibly Elgin, and perhaps you would indicate to me which centre would be more suitable for you.

I should point out that the Law Society will pay for the initial interview and possibly a further interview but, thereafter, if the Solicitor is to take the matter on it would be under the normal Solicitor/client relationship.

Perhaps you would be good enough to write to me and confirm where you would wish to meet a Troubleshooter.

On 16th December 1991 (File 348), I responded as follows:

I thank you for your letter of the 11th December 1991 and the list of Troubleshooters and their respective areas.

I think Glasgow would be the most suitable, and appreciate the fact that the first interview, and possibly the second, would be paid for by the Law Society.

I await your further information as to which Solicitor will handle the complaint.

1992

The Law Society responded on 22nd January 1992 (File 360):

I refer to your letter of 16ᵗʰ December 1991 and apologise for the delay in acknowledging receipt. You will doubtless recall that we spoke by telephone on 13ᵗʰ January, and I would confirm at this stage that I have passed the file to a Member of the Troubleshooter Panel in Glasgow for consideration.

He will then contact you/me to confirm that he is prepared to meet you and I will thereafter, write to you.

*I would advise you that under the terms of the Troubleshooter Scheme the Law Society will pay for the first two interviews which you have with the Solicitor. Thereafter, if the matter is to continue, it will be for you to discuss the position with the Solicitor, although if the Solicitor is to continue to act it will usually be on the normal agent and client basis. Clearly, if that is to happen **you may wish to advise the Solicitor of your full financial circumstances.**

Chapter 5

The Third Solicitor – Troubleshooter

On 4th February 1992 (File 361), the Law Society confirmed that a solicitor on the Troubleshooter panel had agreed to meet with me to discuss matters regarding my assertion of negligence by [First Solicitor].

Matters "seemed" to be moving apace, with all the appearance of cooperation, including the offer of two free consultations with the prospective Troubleshooter. I wish to remind my readers of my earlier references to the legal profession's "ploys". Be prepared for another one to be revealed shortly! But first, consider the following. I did meet with a Troubleshooter. On 26th February 1992 (File 367) he wrote to me, as follows:

> *Further to our recent meeting and our recent telephone discussion, I confirm that I will issue, as soon as I am authorised by the Law Society, a copy of the letters of 22nd March and 9th April 1990 from [First Solicitor] to the Law Society.*

The relevance of the above will soon become apparent. For just a moment, however, let us return now to the case against [First Architect], an event running in parallel with the matter of [First Solicitor]. On 12th February 1992 (File 362) [Second Solicitor] confirmed that a *consultation has now been arranged with an Advocate for 10.30am on Thursday 20th February within our offices.*

On 17th February 1992 (File 363) [Second Solicitor] had to write to inform me:

> *...the Advocate is unable to come to Aberdeen during the week.*
> *Your consultation has now been arranged for noon on Saturday*
> *22nd February 1992 at our offices. You will of course require to*
> *be personally present on Saturday.*

I duly attended the meeting, during which it came apparent that [Second Solicitor] did not have to hand all the information required by the Advocate. So, in March 1992 (File 364) it fell upon me to provide information to [Second Solicitor]:

> *The enclosed (Files 365/366) 2 pages of answers that the QC*
> *required are in response to our meeting with the QC on 22nd*
> *February 1992. This information is obviously also of interest to*
> *you. Could you please forward this to the QC immediately.*

At this point in the story I think it is important to inform my readers about the incompetence of some members of the legal profession in Scotland, and the resulting suffering they put their clients through. Here now is just one example, of prime importance to me in particular, and it regards Legal Aid, the cause of ongoing suffering at the hands of [Second Solicitor]:

Back on 4th September 1987 (File 153) [First Solicitor] lodged in Court the case against [First Architect]. Six days later, on 10th September (File 154) he sisted the case, stating as the reason that his client was applying for Legal Aid. The facts find him to be a **liar** because Legal Aid was never applied for.

Earlier in this True Story I mentioned that a copy of my complete file had been passed to [Second Solicitor], which contained the above information. It was now up to [Second Solicitor] to follow through with Legal Aid, as discussed at our first meeting. The incompetence that follows can only come from members of the legal profession! On 9th August 1990, [Second Solicitor] wrote to me stating one of his staff was on holiday and he was awaiting her return for completion of my Legal Aid forms and lodgement of same in respect of my case against [First Architect]. It was therefore not until 18th September 1990 (File 276-1) that he had come the point of sending me the forms to complete!!

The forms were completed and returned (hand-delivered) within two days.

Almost 18 months later (28th February 1992) I wrote to [Second Solicitor] (File 368), referring to his letter dated 9th August 1990 and asking for progress regarding Legal Aid. Our first meeting had been in September 1989. It was now February 1992 and I was still waiting!

I know of no other profession on this Earth that is as incompetent and uncaring. I cannot bring myself to use the word "stupid", for they, in fact, are all too clever. Sly is a more appropriate word! They continuously come up with ploys included in which are **planned delays**. And, within a system of self-regulation, it is all too simple for them to perpetuate these ploys, oblivious to the fact that they are ignoring their established duty to ensure that their clients' – members of the general public – needs are paramount. They are duty-bound under law to offer clients a proper service. But what hope of ensuring that happens when the system is self-regulating?

I have also used the word 'uncaring' and that really is what they are. Please excuse the emotional nature of these words when I say it makes me sick to the stomach when I hear stories of people losing their homes, of others losing their businesses, the rewards of lifelong toil, simply snatched from them by incompetent solicitors – those who care not a jot about destroyed lives and morale sapped to the point of ill-health and depression. In my opinion you can contrast all this with the example of a medical profession – dedicated to save lives and rebuild morale.

Contrast this too with the professional people in our armed forces, putting their lives at risk all over this earth to secure us the democracy and rule of law that we all ought to enjoy. Instead we have a legal profession, backed by government, lying, cheating and using fraudulent ploys to "screw" money from their clients.

These are strong words. Even so, I challenge the legal profession and its members in Court, listen to these words and do not allow yourself to become a part of a system that destroys lives so "carelessly". Even if you are not one of those who knowingly perpetuate some of the ploys mentioned in this book, do not turn a blind eye to them. Allow the ordinary person to get back to democracy, and a proper democratic process supporting all clients in their right to progress their challenge in Court, without a myriad of ploys and blockages. Unfortunately, the very people who are knowingly aware and support the crooked members and crooked ways of this profession are the very people who work in the Law Society and related public organisations that need the presence of the legal profession.

Can you imagine, and it is possible, these same people could be sitting next to you in restaurants or theatres? They could possibly even be your next-door neighbour, outwardly respectable, yet knowingly "screwing" the public out of their well-earned livelihood. Is it possible these so-called professional people could be married with children? Is it also possible their children might one day follow in their parents' footsteps? I personally know where this has happened.

Through the media, the press and television, we are crying out asking that our children grow up respecting basic standards of decent behaviour. If you, as a parent, are a part of the legal profession, actively involved in crooked manipulation of a self-serving system, or even if simply passively benefiting from it, I now say to each one of you – lead by a better example.

Through this book I have tried, through the correspondence contained herein, to give my readers some idea how the legal system works and how a complainer like myself, and a multitude of others, suffer from such a crooked system. I have tried to expose to you, I hope successfully, the details of the lies, the cheating, the fraud, and in particular the planned long delays. I hope I have fairly exposed misrepresentation and professional misconduct.

After three architects, and now with [Second Solicitor], I still could not find justice. I am an innocent party. I have not embarked on this journey in search of justice vexatiously. I have been forced into it. Without a shadow of doubt, both of my solicitors knew full well that this was, and has always been, the case. In terms of personal responsibility, I accept that my biggest problem has been that I have always trusted people – too much perhaps, naively expecting that justice would prevail. I have kept telling myself so, that here in Scotland we have a true sense of fair play, supported by the best legal system in the world.

I have since learned, and am continuing to learn through friends and the stories of hundreds of fellow complainers/complainants, that my vision of a just and wholesome system has yet to become reality. I have also learned, from the same people, that our legal system is in a real mess – and not just in Scotland but throughout Britain as a whole – and the number of complaints has reached many thousands per year.

I know the above details help neither me nor my own case. This book is about opening up eyes and protecting others. It is about (re)creating the best legal system in the democratic world, a foolproof system wherein complaints against solicitors are dealt with fairly – for all parties concerned – in other words a system which has been perfected for the benefit of both the complainer and the solicitor. I challenge the Government on this very issue. It has been in the power of governments, over many years, to deal with this mess. And governments have turned a blind eye, possibly, dare I suggest, because they have always reflected within their ranks a large number of the legal profession?

So, back to the story! I had no choice but to continue to hope for the best and put my faith in the Law Society and their Troubleshooter scheme.

On 28th February 1992 (File 369) the Troubleshooter wrote to me:

> *One of the documents which you asked me to let you have a copy*
> *of was the judgement in the action against the receivers acting*
> *for [Contractor] –v– yourself and others. I enclose a photocopy*
> *herewith.*

On 3rd March 1992 (File 370) [Second Solicitor] wrote to me regarding
the case against [First Architect]:

> *Further to your recent letter I have had information from [Third*
> *Architect] which has been passed off to Counsel… I shall*
> *hear from him in early course with his final Amendments. In*
> *the meantime, because there was lack of information before*
> *the debate was fixed, **you are liable for the expenses of that***
> ***debate** and we will need to have a chat about this as soon as*
> *convenient.*

On the same day [Second Solicitor] also wrote (File 371):

> *We enclose for your information copy further Minute of*
> *Amendment, which has been prepared by Counsel and lodged at*
> *Court on your behalf.*

**Note: Prior to the above Minute of Amendment, the main purpose
of which was to increase the sum sued for to £100,000, I had asked
[Second Solicitor] for the services of a QC because of his lack of
progress and his further incompetence. Believe it or not, that was one
year previous. Now we have proof of this incompetence, including
that of [First Solicitor], who had initiated a writ for a paltry £30,000
without even having a meeting with his client – clear evidence that
my legal representatives had no grasp of the details behind my claim
for money, nor of the gravity of that claim.**

Further to my requests for a QC, we met with him on Saturday 22nd February 1992, a four-hour meeting in the offices of [Second Solicitor] attended by the QC, [Third Architect], myself and a member of [Second Solicitor]'s practice. This turned out to be a very interesting and informative meeting, a point agreed by all the attendees.

The following reflects the QC's opinion of the Minute of Amendment, lodged with the Court:

Following upon a lengthy consultation with Mr Brown and a number of interested parties, I prepared a lengthy Minute of Amendment in this case. In doing so, I appreciated that its terms could well be considered to alter much of the existing basis of the action. Nonetheless, having heard the facts narrated to me, I for my part could see no realistic alternative. What has to be said is that it is certainly regrettable that it took so many years for the issues properly to be explored. In all the circumstances, while one might have hoped for a happier outcome at debate, I fear that the Sheriff's exercise of what is after all his discretion will prove to be unimpeachable. Accordingly in view of the passage of time I can see only two possible courses open to the Pursuers, about neither of which I am particularly sanguine:

1) The Pursuers could proceed with the present action as it stands.

2) The Pursuers could seek recourse from such of their legal advisors as they deem to be responsible for the failure of their action properly to reflect their situation.

May I say, since my involvement was restricted to the said Minute of Amendment and proceeded upon the foundation of the existing pleadings, that I think it inappropriate for me to be involved in any further proceedings should there be any.

As a matter of interest the increased claim, from the original £30,000 to £100,000, was much more in keeping with my true losses between 1982 and 1987 when the writ was issued. This more realistic amount should have been quantified at the very beginning, reflecting the seriousness of not obtaining a valid Completion Certificate back in 1982, to lawfully permit me to operate my guest house at its planned levels of occupancy with increased bedrooms. The QC came to this conclusion at his summation of the four-hour meeting. Surely any competent solicitor, with all the facts at his disposal at the time, could have come to a similar conclusion and more vigorously pursued [First Architect] for what was blatantly negligence? Instead, [First Solicitor] – initially – and latterly [Second Solicitor] had complicated my case for so long that, what a child could have averted, had turned into a nightmare of ineptitude cloaked by deviousness and crookedness of unbelievable proportions. Only a system that was self-serving could oversee such a dreadful outcome. Why do lawyers overcomplicate matters? I think we have the answer, reflected perfectly in the following words – some lawyers are quite simply incompetent, and are able to get away with it under the protection of self-regulation.

I have just used word "overcomplicate". This is an understatement when you progress through the story. Let's carry on!

On 6th March 1992 (File 394) the Troubleshooter wrote to me, enclosing a letter he had in his possession from [First Solicitor], written on 22nd March 1990 (File 395/6/7) to the Law Society. This letter reflects the double standards that are continuously used by the legal profession.

> *We are in receipt of your letter of 9th March… We received a letter from Mr Brown dated 14th March, a copy of which we understand was enclosed to yourselves. We considered the terms in Mr Brown's letter and we decided that in view of your involvement with this matter that we would not answer that letter and correspond with yourselves regarding this matter. We have advised Mr Brown that this is our intention.*

In 1982 Mr Brown entered into a contract with building contractors to carry out certain works to his guest house. The parties entered into Building Contract, notwithstanding the fact that the contract price was only in the region of £14,500 and we understand the reason for this was [First Architect] who drew up the plans had expressed concern regarding the credibility and stature of the company.

It subsequently transpired that these fears were well founded as the company did an extremely poor job for Mr Brown leaving the job unfinished and eventually went into receivership in 1983.

At that time Mr A. Brown had paid some £10,000 towards the costs of the works, which were subsequently quantified at £18,000 for the purposes of a subsequent Court Action.

It is important that I interject here to let my readers know my view that here again we have this crooked solicitor perpetuating his lies and cunning ways. Is he trying to impress the Law Society and get himself off the hook, to wheedle the Law Society into ignoring my claims against him?

The true facts regarding the £14,500 contract price mentioned above are that the contract price that [First Architect] had recommended for the contract was £7,500 – the cheapest of **seven** quotations. Why hadn't [First Solicitor] mentioned that in his letter? Also, why had he not told the Law Society that the drawings that were used to get the quotations drawn up were those produced by the self same architect he had been trying to protect? Why had he not told the Law Society these were the same drawings that were so totally useless that even a high school student could have done better? And why had he further told the Law Society that [Contractor] had been paid between £6,000 and £7,000 **authorised by that same architect after only a few weeks on the job**?

When this solicitor had mentioned the £18,000 above he had carefully **not** informed the Law Society where this figure had really come from – a consequence of the horrific mistakes in the drawings of my incompetent

[First Architect], so many of which that it required massive changes to the contract. Hence the figure of £18,000. Hence, too, all the added alterations for which he had refused to grant [Contractor] additional time in which to complete.

The remainder of this three-page letter to the Law Society, so fully endowed as it was with lies and deceit, will be continued later.

Conflict of interest situations are ostensibly frowned upon by the Law Society. Heavy fines can be issued. [First Solicitor] had found perfect ground for conflict of interest. Here are the facts:

1) He had a client who owned a guest house, owned a big home in the country for which the solicitor was collecting monthly rent and whose monthly income he knew.

2) When his client had hired [First Architect], it had been at the recommendation of [First Solicitor]. Surely this had been a vote of confidence in [First Architect]'s ability to draw up the plans for the conversion and extension at their guest house and to make sure that the necessary warrants were granted before the contract started. I personally was ignorant of the rulings and penalties, including the possibility of a prison sentence, that could be imposed on anyone who contracted works to a listed building without the necessary papers.

3) I now realised why [First Solicitor] had told me to find another architect to attend the meeting with the law administration and building Planning Department. The way I see it is that there was now a possibility that [First Architect], having blighted my guest house, faced a possible prison sentence.

4) If this was the case, could [First Solicitor] have used this situation to bolster his own bank account? He had been in a position to

control the whole situation and turn it to his benefit. For example: he had issued a writ against [First Architect] for the sum of £30,000, and had avoided any meetings with his client, which could have pushed this amount upwards. He had never activated this writ, and never informed his client about it. He had been aware of everything that was going on but had kept it to himself. Why? Was he using the situation to gain monies from both parties – myself and [First Architect]? When I had asked his colleague, via a phone call, when were we taking [First Architect] to Court? his answer had been: "Why are we taking him to Court and for what reason?"

5) I think it would be prudent at this time to ask the following question of everyone, and in particular the Law Society and the legal profession: if a solicitor knows full well that he is acting for two clients, then even if there is only a remote possibility of conflict of interest, should he not warn the clients, even the Law Society, before taking any further action? This man had walked far more dubious ground. He had knowingly kept one of his clients in the dark and, in so doing, had manipulated the situation to his advantage, and later covered his tracks.

The principle in Scotland is that where a conflict of interest either arises or seems at all likely to arise a solicitor should immediately cease acting for one party, if not for both, advising him, or them, to seek independent legal advice. Similarly, one firm of solicitors cannot represent two competing clients in a Court case.

On 18th March 1992 (File 404) [Second Solicitor] wrote to me:

I refer to the above and now enclose herewith copy of Advocate Opinion and a copy of my reply. I am sending copies of these to [Third Architect].

On the same date (File 405) he wrote to the Advocate. This is the copy of his reply, mentioned above.

> *Thank you for your note regarding the above case. There seem to be separate matters to consider here.*
>
> a) *What is the worth of [First Architect] in the event that we do get a sizeable Decree against him?*
>
> b) *What is the likely value of Mr and Mrs Brown's claim in the event the amendment is not allowed?*
>
> c) *If the amendment is not allowed, is there a potential claim against [First Solicitor] who acted for Mr and Mrs Brown in raising the action and who by 1988 (i.e. 5 years after the incident giving rise to the claim) should have had all relevant claims included in the Court action instead of leaving it sisted?*
>
> *Your observations on the latter aspect would be appreciated before we advise Mr and Mrs Brown further.*

The revelations contained in the next correspondence are momentous and all but destroyed me and my family, and left my confidence in tatters. It placed us in dire straits financially, with a future that looked dreadfully bleak.

Note: Bear in mind this nightmare had been plaguing me for the last 10 years, and the costs had been unbelievable. It was very hard to take, trying all the time to stay sane. I ask my readers to try to comprehend what my family had been going through, and how they felt at this time. To those members of the legal profession for whom the shoe fits, I say this – you are the very pits of this Earth.

On 16th March 1992 (File 406/7/8), my Advocate, i.e. Counsel for the Pursuer, drafted the following note:

I refer to the opposed motion heard today in the Sheriff Court for the Pursuer's further Minute of Amendment to be received. I enclose a copy of the Minute, as adjusted by me, that I tendered at the Bar.

As I mentioned to the Pursuers, and his Agent, the Defender's Counsel indicated to me that his client is willing to attempt settlement of the case. I detected that the litigation is resting rather heavily on the Defender as it is on the first Pursuer, and that the Defender is suffering from some strain likewise. In my view agents should attempt to capitalise on the willingness of the Defender to settle the case, and such an attempt should be made as soon as practicable.

The type of figure indicated by the Defender's Counsel that I understood he would be willing to offer was in the middle single figure thousands (£5,000) probably with expenses. I noted all that the Pursuer said to me after the hearing to the effect that the restoration alone, regardless of other heads of damages would absorb a five-figure sum.

I would suggest that in the course of the meeting with agents scheduled for Saturday, a concise indication of what is required to bring the property into a level where it complies with planning standards is arrived at, or at least instructed from [Third Architect], the Pursuers expert. In short, what precisely is the District Council requiring to be done in order that the enforcement notice be discharged.

Once these details are prepared in a concise form agents can then approach their counterparts with a view to a more realistic counter offer being made. If it was possible to settle the action on this basis then settlement would not encompass all that the Pursuers seek either on the existing or amended pleadings, should the minute be allowed. Against that disadvantage is the certainty of obtaining some award, without the risk of obtaining after proof, in which situation the Pursuers would be required, in all likelihood to pay both sides' expenses.

Whilst one can never be certain about such matters, I would anticipate a higher offer from the Defender, although it has been made clear to me that a five-figure sum is unlikely to be offered. That situation may change of course, should the Defender's circumstances provide for it.

The concern about whether or not [First Architect] is insured, and therefore perhaps likely to be in financial difficulties should his defence fail, should not be overlooked. It does appear that he is funding the defence to the action himself, which suggests the absence of any insurer. Consequently, even if the Pursuer does succeed in total what prospects of success of recovery can be reasonably anticipated?

Finally, it appears to me that one of the principal problems facing the Pursuers is that the property, as a result of the order from the Local Authority, is rather blighted. The possibility of reaching some accommodation with the Local Authority in this regard should be perhaps considered. Agreement from them not to enforce the order/notice, given the difficulties that he Pursuer has experienced, coupled with a letter of comfort or the like from the authority regarding the absence of a Completion Certificate might be worth considering.

Anyone reading the above Counsel's notes will most probably, like myself, wonder – who was he acting for? Was he truly protecting the person that was paying him? Two things immediately emerge to the forefront when reading his notes:

1) He was introducing details that were irrelevant at this time and, furthermore, in reference to insurance – had the Counsel carried out proper research with [Second Solicitor] to discover the all-important fact that an architect under RIBA rules cannot operate without insurance? [First Architect] had registered with the RIBA, and was therefore subject to their rules. Also, did the Counsel know that an inhibition order had been placed on [First Architect]?

I had paid these two gentlemen from the legal profession the necessary fees. In turn, I could fairly have expected them to do the necessary groundwork on my behalf. Had they done so, they would have discovered, as I did almost two years later, that architects are governed in the UK by three main bodies, of which RIBA is one. Each of these three bodies has a committee with specific responsibility for maintaining professional standards and dealing with complaints of professional negligence, incompetence and misconduct. All architects have to be registered with the Architects' Registration Council of the United Kingdom and it is a criminal offence to use the description "architect" if one's name does not appear on the register of architects.

2) [First Architect] owned a house in the country. My legal team should have taken account of this, and acted accordingly. It may seem hard-hearted to some readers who may find crossing their minds – why do I not show any pangs of remorse in forcing a man to remortgage, or even to have to sell his home? If such a thought is crossing your mind, please remember that this architect had been "remorse-less" in his determination to shun responsibility for his own negligent actions, preferring to play hardball when the scent of escape had been in the air, and utterly "care-less" of my own dire straits – loss of livelihood and impending financial ruin. My legal team should have protected their own client at all times and not, under the guise of pragmatic common sense, engineered a conflict of interest situation.

Here is an often asked big question for my Counsel and for all those in the legal profession – why is it that it is the ordinary innocent man who always seems to pay/suffer at the hands of the legal profession whilst the well-connected, guilty ones slither successfully out of harm's way? Look what happens to the innocent. We live in a sick world under the sway of a crooked legal profession.

On 6th April 1992 (File 409) [Second Solicitor] wrote to me:

> *I have got outlays of about £750. It would be helpful if you could*
> *put me in funds in this respect. In the meantime I have still not*
> *had the Court's Decision following the recent Debate.*

It would be interesting to search through this True Story, and find a single situation where there had been a quick positive action in my favour, where the "legal eagles" could be seen working expeditiously on my behalf, responding crisply and effectively to any given situation and, dare I dream, bringing my case to a quick resounding financial victory! Here I was, 10 years later, with those same people asking me for money as time drags ever onwards. I have worked hard all my life, sometimes offering my services for a job done, not for hours spent. Is it too much to ask the legal profession to unwrap the warm cloth of comfortable working conditions and live in a real world, just occasionally? I live in hope. But, and it is a big "but", they still have time to show me how good, honest, and caring they really are. For I am sure that some of them are.

On 7th April 1992 (File 409-1) I wrote to the Troubleshooter regarding the case against [First Solicitor]:

> *Sorry for the delay in sending you this package. My family and*
> *I have been working hard to organise the enclosed information*
> *into the most effective format for your perusal.*
>
> *Although we have highlighted the most important parts of each*
> *document we hope you find the time, and enthusiasm, to give*
> *this case your full attention, as it has been a long slog since*
> *1982.*
>
> *The family eagerly await your comments on the likelihood of a*
> *successful case against [First Solicitor].*

The burden of legal correspondence continued to live with me. The next day – 8th April 1991 – I wrote to [Second Solicitor] (File 409-2-3)

Subject: **Diet Debate**

In the diet debate on 11th March there were many points brought up by the defence that I could have answered given the chance. However I feel it is necessary to make you aware of two points in particular.

1) Diet debate

2) Was [First Architect] covered by insurance?

1) *At the diet debate [First Architect]'s solicitor stated that after 1979, when [First Architect] completed the drawings for both phases at [The Browns' guest house] there was no further correspondence between Mr Brown and [First Architect] until the meeting at [First Solicitor]'s office to sign the contract.*

I have enclosed two letters from [First Architect], one dated 29th April 1980 type-written contained in an envelope with a letterhead of [the company in Glasgow that [First Architect] had joined as their chief architect – I was not aware that any firm in Scotland hired Mickey Mouse architects!] *and a second, hand-written by [First Architect] referring to the issue of supervision – (see pages 1 and 2 attached).*

He also commented that they had never before been made aware in 12 years that Phase 2 was not feasible. This is a blatant lie. I have enclosed a letter dated 14th November 1986 (File 139-40) when this point was raised by [First Solicitor] and responded to by [First Architect]'s solicitor (see highlighted parts of pages 3-6 attached).

**Note: If my legal representatives had done their research properly –
that's what they are paid to do – they would have discovered that on
15th May 1981 (File 13) [First Architect] sent me a letter enclosing
the drawings that I had requested. In that same letter he offered his
services to supervise the contract at a cost of £346. It is now becoming
more and more apparent the incompetence is spreading.**

2) Was [First Architect] covered by insurance?

Together with my letter I enclosed copies of two cashed cheques that I had
made out to [First Architect]. The back of one of the cheques contained the
words *"agents for [First Architect]"*. This implied that [First Architect]
was working under the umbrella of the Glasgow firm of architects that he
had joined just before I commissioned him to work for me. I raised this
possibility in my letter – was [First Architect] insured under the policy
carried by these *agents*?

**Note: This is an area my legal representatives should have properly
researched, by contacting the appropriate governing bodies.**

On 15th April 1992 (File 409-4-5) [Second Solicitor] replied, as follows.
Some of his grammar leaves much to be desired – showing all the signs of
a sloppily constructed letter by an overworked and ineffective mind. Such
was the calibre of the man on whom my livelihood depended:

> *Many thanks for your letter of 8th April 1992 about your case.
> When a Debate is heard the Statements made are not given in
> evidence by witnesses but by Solicitors or Counsel acting for
> the parties on their instructions. If a party provides his Solicitor
> with a wrong piece of information that can result in the Court
> being a little misled. However where a Debate has taken place
> this is usually not concerned with the facts of the case but the
> law relating to the case as applied to the pleadings. The criticism
> will either be that the pleadings are irrelevant because they seek
> a remedy that the law does not allow on the facts stated or that*

they are lacking in specification in that not enough information has been given to the other side to understand how the claim is made up. A third possibility and the one with which we are concerned here is that there has been considerable delay by the claimant in furthering his case to the point that the other side has been prejudiced by that delay. Furthermore given that any action for damages of a non personal injury nature will normally require to be raised within five years of the incident giving rise to the claim then any attempt to amend the pleadings after five years will be very carefully scrutinised by the Court and will probably be the subject of objection by the other side.

As you know the Debate took place in your case principally in relation to the last matter because [First Solicitor] had not advanced your case after raising the original action as a result of which, by 1988 the five-year period from the act of which you complained had expired. There is little point in commenting at this stage on matters which might have affected the position because the Debate has been heard and we must now await the Sheriff's Decision. It has not yet been issued but you can be sure that as soon as it comes to hand I will let you have a copy. Meantime I have retained the documents, which you kindly sent to me.

Meanwhile, on 29th April 1992 (File 409-6/7/8/9/10) the Troubleshooter duly responded to my letter dated 7th April 1992.

With reference to your recent letter sending me a large file of papers and correspondence, I confirm that I have now been through this file in detail and raise a number of points on what I have read therein.

I note that in the Amendment to Condescendence 4 in the latest Amendment to your action against [First Architect] that Amendment does not appear to fit well with that part of Condescendence 4, which remains from the original pleadings.

My further comment is that there would also appear to me to be a lack of specification of quantum of damages being claimed on your behalf, having said that the pleadings are now clear in so far as they relate to the grounds of negligence alleged against [First Architect]. When I turn however to relate those pleadings and those allegations of negligence against [First Architect] to any claim for negligence against [First Solicitor] the main points which arise from such consideration continue to be the unusual omission of [First Architect]'s supervisory role from the evidence which was led in the action against [Contractor].

The only aspect of all the correspondence from [First Solicitor] which tends to infer that he questioned [First Architect]'s position in that whole Contract is to be found in his letter of 14th August 1985 when he suggested a different architect should meet with the Director of Law and Administration in respect of the Grant etc. However, I am bound to say that as late as November 1985 I can find no evidence to support your contention that you were pressing [First Solicitor] to claim or sue [First Architect]. All correspondence to this point in time was directed it seems to me, to completing the work, and to not paying [Contractor].

The second possible area of negligence against [First Solicitor] relates to the matter of delay in pursuing [First Architect] to produce the requested plans for the remedial work. Despite your letter of 19th February 1986 the first mention of a claim being pursued against [First Architect] is from [First Solicitor] in his letter of 22nd August 1986. I am bound to say that I consider [First Solicitor]'s letter of 22 August 1986 to be a very reasonable resume of the Law and risks attendant on pursuing a professional negligence case. It is interesting to note further that the first intimation of a claim from [First Solicitor] against [First Architect] is 8th October 1986 and in reply thereto [First Architect]'s Solicitors specifically argue there was no supervisory function on the part of [First Architect].

You have asserted on a number of occasions that [First Architect] advised you that he had all necessary permissions for the rear work to the building. I can find no correspondence or writing in support of that assertion. Do you have any?

You refer in your preliminary points to there being an agreement between [First Architect] and yourselves in relation to the basis of his work. I cannot find any such document. Can you let me have a copy of this?

At our meeting I pointed out to you that the Sheriff in the case against [Contractor] had held that [First Architect] was not supervising. I indicated that I was extremely puzzled by this, standing the documentation you produced to me to consider and I remain of the view that the omission of anything which would amount to evidence in that respect comes close to negligence in the circumstances of your dispute with [First Architect]. The raising of the action against [First Architect] in August 1987, you advised, was also done without your knowledge or authority and you advised you would not have acquiesced in the level of the sum craved in the writ. I do not consider that that is in itself a basis for negligence as obviously the amount sued for can be amended as it has been and it may well have been that the Solicitor was justified in raising the proceedings, particularly as you maintain you had been pressing him to do so.

Reverting again to the matter of what you said [First Architect] had told you about Building Control approval having been given when it had not. I note [First Solicitor] also makes reference to this in his correspondence, but I also note that in the latest Amendment to the pleadings, that is not referred to. Did you have knowledge, which the Director of Planning is reported to have said you had neither Planning Permission nor Listed Building consent had been obtained or did you not? If you did not, was that because [First Architect] misled you, or because you made no enquiry?

At any rate whatever the answers to some of these comments which I raise are, in my opinion the only area where there could possibly be any negligence on the part of [First Solicitor] relates to the matter of evidence of the supervisory function of [First Architect] in the Action against [Contractor]. When I consider that matter it appears to me justifiable for the Solicitor conducting an action against [Contractor] to wish to underplay the role of [First Architect] in relation to unsatisfactory work. I have already indicated to you at our meeting that I thought it was understandable that [First Solicitor] did not wish to sue [First Architect] before suing [Contractor] because he needed [First Architect] to support the case against [Contractor]. In any event it appears to me from the correspondence you have shown me that all your efforts and [First Solicitor]'s efforts were aimed at recovery from [Contractor] rather than [First Architect] in the early years of this matter. There is, however, now a finding by the Sheriff in that case that [First Architect] did not exercise a supervisory role. That is a matter which may very well create difficulties for your current case against [First Architect] but it is an aspect which you will very properly be guided by [Second Solicitor] and your Counsel who will be able to advise on the prospect of looking in greater depth at [First Architect]'s duties and responsibilities, as this obviously forms the basis of the present proceedings which have been raised against [First Architect].

My conclusion therefore is that I do not consider that there is any real prospect of [First Solicitor] being found to have been negligent either in the matter of raising of proceedings against [First Architect] nor in failing to adequately produce evidence to show [First Architect]'s true responsibilities in the action against [Contractor] nor do I feel that the delay in obtaining the plans from [First Architect] of itself lays a basis for a claim against [First Solicitor]. Subject to there subsequently proving to be no assurance given to [First Architect] by [First Solicitor] that is adverse to your current proceedings against [First Architect].

Annexation referred to:-

Answers to your points regarding [First Solicitor]'s negligence.

In my view the course adopted by [First Solicitor] is supportable in seeking to obtain a Decree against [Contractor] before pursuing an action against [First Architect] that the case against [First Architect] would appear to be well founded and it is not therefore surprising that the professional indemnity Insurers have made an offer. They will no doubt in the normal way increase that offer before any hearing takes place and may further increase it at the door of the Court, in accordance with the practice of such Insurers. You can therefore anticipate increased offers in my opinion.

I do not perceive of any "unethical promises" made by [First Solicitor] to [First Architect], but as I have indicated should such information be found to exist as a result of your existing action against [First Architect] then that would give a possible basis for negligence against [First Solicitor] if it materially affects your claim against [First Architect].

I do not perceive [First Solicitor] has failed to pursue [First Architect], but rather that he has elected to follow a course against [Contractor] in the first instance. As I have indicated before, the matter is one, rather, of timing and methodology, and not negligence in my view.

It is never proper for a Solicitor to raise proceedings and deal with these proceedings without the client's specific authority and if he did not have your authority then that is the basis for a complaint against him to the Law Society. But I would not consider that you have sustained any loss as a result of such actings which you maintain were without your knowledge such as to found a basis for a claim for damages against [First Solicitor]. I do not read in the correspondence that [First Solicitor] is maintaining there is no case against [First Architect]. Indeed the raising of proceedings against [First Architect] would indicate quite the reverse.

There is no evidence before me to assess whether Legal Aid was mishandled or not. There is evidence that Legal Aid was granted.

Any offer of settlement from [First Architect] or his Insurers does not provide a basis for a claim against [First Solicitor] per se.

While I appreciate the considerable strain which you and your family have been under, for reasons I have indicated I do not see that [First Solicitor] can be held responsible for such stress, which essentially arose out of the issues which were required to be pursued. There would appear to me to be sufficient grounds to believe that compensation will be recoverable from [First Architect], or his insurers, as a result of the current measures which are being taken by your present Solicitors under Counsel's advice.

The contents of the above letter, in response to mine of 7th April (File 409-1) is very misleading, and confusing to say the least. I can, with confidence, demonstrate to my readers how a single profession is able to protect, even bolster, so many incompetent members within its "family". By ignoring incompetent practices, standards among these members can only go one way – down!

This Troubleshooter seems to have followed the same path as my previous solicitors, namely one of double standards. For example, he has made clear to me, at meetings and through correspondence, his opinion that [First Solicitor], in dealing with the case against [First Architect], has protected me by issuing a writ into Court even without my knowledge. He stated this same writ could be amended/altered any time later. He further stated that taking on [Contractor] first, and using [First Architect] as a "good witness", was the correct way forward. In other words he has intimated that it is perfectly in order to issue a writ and then put matters on hold, knowing that the writ can be withdrawn or amended some time in the future. And therein lies the double standard. If this is an acceptable approach, **then why does he not apply it to the case against [First Solicitor]**? Why has he refused to issue a writ against [First Solicitor]?

The reason he gave was that I should wait until the case against [First Architect] has concluded, to ascertain my true losses. I say, in turn, why can't we use the **same logic** adopted by [First Solicitor], and now supported by you, my dear Troubleshooter? Issue the writ against [First Solicitor] and, as you yourself contest, it can always be amended later.

Yet again, I felt let down by the legal profession. In my dismay at the time, I felt disgust, a sense of corruption, lack of consideration and support, and now I see with my own eyes an example of the profession not following its own advice to me. Once again, I was filled with despair, knowing now that I would have to put up with an incompetent Troubleshooter who was backing [First Solicitor], certainly in respect of his action, in going after [Contractor] first, being deemed correct.

I have never been trained in law. Therefore as a lay person I do not complicate matters, preferring to use **common sense**. Is it possible that this virtue is never used by members of the legal profession?

My common sense thinking tells me when things go wrong in a building contract one looks at the parties involved and analyses who could have been responsible for any problems that arose. One must obviously start with the person that drew up the plans because, if the plans are incorrect, one need look no further for the source of the problem. Irrespective of who the contractor is, the problem has already been created and will not go away. Furthermore, if one issues instructions to a contractor outwith of planning consent one has knowingly committed a criminal offence. If common sense had prevailed by the end of 1982, the "criminals" would have been exposed and the problems sorted out. Of course, all this requires common sense to prevail!

In any job or profession we all need, and must have, inspiration in our work to keep our morale going, to raise our standards and to engender a feeling of achievement. Imagine now this scene – certain members of the legal profession gathering together and praising each other over coffee or lunch, or a drink at the end of a week, all slapping each other on the backs, regaling each other with tales of clients "screwed", bank balances bulging with the fruits of Legal Aid, and standards ignored. I know I am offering a bleak image – one that may not ring true in many quarters. However, there are most certainly those who are, at the very least impervious to their clients' suffering, and there will, without doubt, be some who positively relish the dark and seedy world in which they live.

After receiving the above letter from the Troubleshooter I remained in a quandary, with my case in Court and its progress in doubt. So I wrote to [Second Solicitor], on 21st May 1992 (File 412):

> *Can you please give me an update on the amendment? We were promised an answer two weeks from 7th March.*

Here is his reply, dated 25th May 1992 (File 413):

> *I acknowledge receipt of your letter of 21st May. The Sheriff has not issued his judgement yet.*

And on 26th May 1992 (File 414) the Troubleshooter wrote:

> *Thank you for your letter of 20th Instant. I note that you would like a further meeting. I do not fully understand the last question of your second paragraph, but we can discuss that, and any other matters, you wish to make at our meeting.*
>
> *I note you wish a lengthy meeting. As you know The Law Society are responsible for my fees to date in this matter. However, any further meetings will require to be at your own expense and provided that is understood I am happy to meet with you. All that is required is for you to telephone my secretary and arrange a convenient time.*

On 2nd June 1992 (File 415), [Second Solicitor] wrote me regarding the case against [First Architect]:

The Sheriff's decision arrived today and rather as expected it is against us. We will need to have a chat about this. Please arrange with reception to see me. I am sending a copy of the decision to Counsel but I doubt that he would suggest an appeal. What we should now do is get on and fix a date for the hearing of the case, at the same time putting [First Solicitor] on notice as to any additional claim.

What I am about to reveal, believe me, is but nothing compared to what other unfortunate clients have had to endure. I have met and talked with many other complainers and listened to horrendous stories at the hands of the legal profession.

Here is what I have to reveal in connection with what happened at the Sheriff's Court on the 11th March 1992. The day before this hearing took place [Second Solicitor] tried to get hold of me by phone. I returned the call in the afternoon at 3.00pm, to find him somewhat annoyed that I had not made contact five hours earlier. He wished to inform me that he had taken it upon himself to send my file to an Advocate in Edinburgh – a man whom I had neither heard of nor seen before. I was furious because he told me that this Advocate would be representing me at the hearing the next morning, due to start 10am.

My daughter and I arrived at 9.45am the next day to find that Court 2 had been reserved for our hearing. [First Architect], with his agent, was already there and was clearly well prepared. My daughter and I patiently waited to meet our Advocate, for the first time ever! Five minutes before the appointed time this gentleman walked into Court. Following the usual pleasantries and introductions I asked him if he was representing me and if he was he familiar with my case. He responded in the following terms – "We had better go in; the case is about to start; I only got the briefing papers last night!" He mentioned the last sentence almost as a casual afterthought. What could I do? Here was someone I had never met before, and after less than 20 words of peremptory dialogue he was about to represent me in Court endeavouring to amend the writ from £30,000 to the correct amount of £100,000. **And** he gets my papers only the night before!

It was quite obvious from the start of the hearing, after listening to [First Architect]'s agent for 45 minutes followed by my own our agent for no more than 7-10 minutes, who had the best-prepared case. This was confirmed by my agent's apologies to the Sheriff, admitting that he had only received my papers the night before. I would think that the Law Society would call this incompetence. Needless to say the costs were awarded against us.

This next part of the story is even more incredible. On the September 24th hearing which had been specially arranged with this particular Sheriff to fit in with his heavy schedule, again my daughter and I attended in good time. Again the opposing parties were waiting. [Second Solicitor] did not appear for the 10am start. At 10.10am we were all patiently awaiting his arrival when the clerk of Court came to see me, in a somewhat confused state. She had called our solicitor's office to find out who was going to represent us for this hearing. As there was no one there at the time, she had been given two different names of lawyers who could step in to represent our case. Then, that plan was changed after a call from a local solicitor's office to say a solicitor was on his way to the Court. He arrived 15 minutes later in a flustered state and approached me to say that it would be he who would represent me in Court.

I asked this particular solicitor if he was fully conversant with my case and the amendments, and if he felt that he could represent me to the best of my interests. His answer was a simple: "**No.**" I then asked him if there was a quiet room where we could discuss the matter in private. I levelled all my anger and frustrations at him, refusing to allow him into the Court and making it perfectly clear that, in my opinion, if I had not been there to prevent his attendance, he would have gone into Court and utterly failed to fairly represent our case.

I left the Court house feeling very ill. I tried to find a doctor, but was unsuccessful, and I had to settle for a consultation with the local pharmacist, who gave me pills to try to relax me.

When I returned to Court the Sheriff was addressing the Court. He turned to me and said: "*Mr Brown you have been let down very badly, by [Second Solicitor].*"

After all these years of toil, and now shaken to edge of despair by the experience of the last two hearings leaving me still a long way short of justice, I ask my readers to agree with me, particularly after having complained to the Law Society about two incompetent solicitors: was it because I'd had the audacity to challenge the legal profession that everything was going against me. Had I been black-listed in some way? Why were they giving me such a hard time?

On 1st June 1992 (File 416/17) at Sheriff Court:

The Sheriff having resumed consideration of the cause, refuses to allow the Record to be amended in terms of Pursuers' Minute of Amendment No 17 of Process; finds the Pursuers Liable to the Defenders in the expenses occasioned by preparation for, and conduct, of the Hearing on 11th March 1992 as same may be taxed; continues the cause to the Procedure Roll of 17th June 1992 for further procedure.

This is a case which came before me for debate on 11th March 1992. At the outset I must apologise for the delay in issuing this interlocutor. At the debate the Pursuers, The Browns, were represented by their Counsel and the Defender [First Architect] by his Advocate. The parties jointly moved me to discharge the Diet of Debate but to allow a hearing to take place with regard to the Minute of Amendment and the amendments thereto proposed by the Pursuers.

By consent the Defender addressed me first and narrated the history of the action, the facts at issue, as per the Pursuer's pleadings and then contrasted the pleadings as they stood with the proposed Minute of Amendment. The Browns' Counsel similarly went through the procedural history and the terms of the Record at present and with regard to the proposed amendments. Both parties then had an opportunity to address me further. Both parties agreed that it was a matter of discretion in terms of the Sheriff Court rules, as to whether or not to allow the amendment and that it should be granted if it was necessary to bring the true matter in dispute between the parties.

The history of this action is that in September 1987 the Pursuer raised an action against [First Architect] for work apparently done in terms of a contract apparently entered into in 1982. The action being raised was sisted for over three years and has then wound its way along through adjustments and procedure roll Hearings, Minutes of Amendment and debates being discharged. The proposed Minute of Amendment coming as it does nearly five years since the action was raised and more than 10 years since the work was carried out, must put the Defender at a very considerable disadvantage. The Minute of Amendment increases the sum sued for from £30,000 to £100,000 and also puts in new grounds of action thus changing to some extent the basis of the case. Counsel for [First Architect] argued after putting forward a case in history that the amendments were well outside the prescription. They were matters which were well known to the Pursuers, that the basis of the action was being changed, the delay was unpardonable with no explanation being given as to why there was a delay of so many years before the amendment; that in any event the amendment to a great extent was irrelevant; that the Defender would suffer real and substantial prejudice trying to defend an action on new grounds 13 years after the events occurred. His submission was that it would be unreasonable for the Court to exercise the discretion in favour of the Pursuers to allow the Minute of Amendment and quoted various cases to me.

Representative for the Pursuers accepted many of the arguments which were put forward by [First Architect]'s Advocate that there had been unacceptable delays, no Motion to recall the sist; that sum sued for was being increased three-fold with no apparent explanation that some financial claims were new and an averment of new duties on the Defender. It appeared to me that [First Architect]'s Advocate was well founded and that this was one of the cases where discretion to allow the Minute of Amendment should not be exercised. It appeared to me that there were additional and substantial new grounds of action, the sum being sued for was substantial. The Pursuer was averring new grounds of duty on the Defender. The Defender in my opinion would suffer substantial prejudice in that this was the first notice he had had of such matters and it would be difficult if not impossible for him to recollect what had happened some 12 years or so previously and to produce witnesses who could similarly recollect those matters were or should all have been within the Pursuer's knowledge at the time that he raised the Court action in 1987.

I have therefore refused to allow the minute of amendment; I find the Pursuer liable to the Defender in the expenses of the preparation and conduct of the Hearing on 11th March and propose to put the matter on to the next procedure roll for further procedure.

In the Sheriff's ruling, it had been clearly pointed out exactly who was to blame for the mess. The Law Society should surely crucify [First Solicitor] in the face of such concrete evidence. But, as they had already explained to me on several occasions, they would have to wait until the case against [First Architect] was finished before acting in respect of [First Solicitor]. In the meantime [First Solicitor] was free to go about his business, probably "screwing" other clients in a similar manner, and manipulating further conflict of interests situations to his best (financial) advantage.

On 8th June 1992 (File 418) [Second Solicitor] wrote to me, without any vestige of apology:

> *We enclose herewith note by Counsel received today. Please confirm by return whether you wish to attend a consultation in our office with Counsel on Friday 19th June.*

On 12th June 1992 File (420-7) I wrote to [Second Solicitor] saying:

> *I am writing to confirm our discussion in our meeting of the 12th June.*
>
> *As a result of [my Counsel's] Minute of Amendment being rejected you will now write to him requesting him to advise us on the future course of action.*
>
> *Further to us previously sending you copy cheques paid to [First Architect] which were deposited by [the firm he was working for] we ask again that you investigate whether [First Architect] was insured by them.*
>
> *We confirm that all my legal costs will be paid by the opposition over and above the amount awarded.*

On 12th June 1992 (File 420-4) [Second Solicitor] wrote to me as follows:

> *I refer to our consultation today and now enclose a copy of a letter I have today sent to Counsel who met with you here in this office.*

This letter (File 420-5) read as follows:

> *You will recollect your involvement in the above case when unfortunately you were unable to attend the Debate which occurred and which regrettably resulted in the Minute of Amendment you prepared being rejected by the Court. We enclose*

the whole set of papers, including the Minute of Amendment and the judgment of the Sheriff refusing the Minute, together with a manuscript note from The Browns' Advocate who took the case. We have had a consultation with Mr Brown who has asked that you be instructed in the matter. We should be obliged by your perusing the papers and giving as soon as possible a note as to future procedure. We understand an offer of about £5,000 was made at the end of the debate to settle the case and Mr Brown, of course, is not interested in this.

In that the Minute has been rejected, it occurs to us that there is the possibility of a professional negligence claim against [First Solicitor] who previously acted and who should have had the pleadings in better order, having raised the action for Mr Brown in the first place. We look forward to hearing from you just as soon as possible because Mr Brown is getting more than anxious.

On 12ᵗʰ June 1992 (File 420-6) [Second Solicitor] also wrote to [First Architect]'s solicitor:

We refer to previous correspondence and on the subject matter of whether or not your client has a professional indemnity insurance. Mr Brown advises that although he paid [First Architect] the fees charged, these were in fact passed by said architect, and encashed through the company he was employed by at the time. It occurs, therefore, that their Policy should be in force relative to this matter and we should be obliged by your looking into the position before further procedure occurs here.

On 16ᵗʰ June 1992 (File 420-8) [Second Solicitor]'s office wrote to me:

In the absence of [Second Solicitor] from the office, we thank you for your letter of 12ᵗʰ June and confirm this will be placed before [Second Solicitor] on his return to business on 19ᵗʰ June.

On 17th June 1992 (File 420-9-10) the Troubleshooter wrote to me regarding the case against [First Solicitor].

> *Thank you for your letter of 12th instant. I note all you state and look forward to hearing from you in due course.*
>
> *One matter which I would like to remind you of is the importance of instituting proceedings for negligence within the five-year period from when you could, with reasonable diligence, have ascertained that you had sustained a loss by reason of that negligence. That is the test which I think requires to be considered in this particular case to any proceedings you may wish to institute against [First Solicitor] or anyone else.*
>
> *While you are not in a position to identify at this point in time whether you will sustain a loss nor the amount of that loss until the result of the action against the contractual architect has been concluded, I think you should bear in mind the failure which you attribute to [First Solicitor] probably commenced some nine or 10 years ago and essentially related to that period of time. There is therefore in my view a risk that you will be met in the event of your raising proceedings against [First Solicitor] with a defence that any such action is time barred by reason of the quinquennial prescription.*
>
> *At this point in time it is difficult to see what alternative you have other than to argue that you could not know you had sustained a loss until the existing action against the contractual architect is concluded by the decision of the Court in that action.*
>
> *I consider however that this is a matter to which you should give careful consideration at this stage. It may even be that you would feel that it would be appropriate that this matter should be put to a suitable Counsel for his opinion and advice as to whether a writ ought to be raised even at this point in time rather than delaying further. I shall be pleased to hear from you.*

And on 21st July 1992 (File 446-47) the Troubleshooter wrote to the Law Society, as follows:

Many thanks for your letter of 20th instant and as requested by you I write with my comments on the letter of 15th July from Mr Angus Brown to you.

Mr Brown is correct in advising therein that as a result of and following my very long meeting with him and his daughter, I advised him that I thought that he did have a ground of complaint, firstly against his original Solicitor for failure at the earliest point in time to institute proceedings against the contractual architect who was eventually sued. I further advised that his loss would have to be measured by reference to his obtaining earlier whatever his financial entitlements proved to be and possibly also by avoiding the later loss altogether.

Secondly, I advised that when his present Solicitor took over, they also appeared to have delayed progressing adequately the proper adjustment and eventual amendment of the pleadings of his action and as a direct consequence, partly or wholly, the Sheriff in the action has refused to allow what appears to me to be a crucial amendment prepared by the Counsel now instructed which would have much more effectively and relevantly stated the basis of his claim. As a consequence it appears to me that he may lose a part, or indeed the whole, of his claim and therefore his loss, and hence there would appear to be a prima facie basis of claim against [Second Solicitor] also.

I further pointed out to Mr Brown that the quinquennial prescriptive period would affect his right of claim against both Solicitors but that it would be difficult to assess the date from which such prescription would run and that he should take Counsel's advice on that aspect. He responded that he wanted a writ to be raised. I in turn advised that:- he take Counsel's advice in the first place; that the measure of his loss, if any, could not be established, neither could the party(ies) against whom he might have a right of action but that Counsel could advise on these matters also.

On 9th July 1992 (File 424) I wrote to [Second Solicitor]:

> *My daughter advised me in Court on Wednesday 8th July [that]*
> *your representative asked for another continuation of our case*
> ***as the amendment was not ready.*** *I believe a request was made*
> *to the Sheriff for July 30th or September 1st. I want it on July 30th.*
> ***I do not see any reason for another delay.***

On the same day, I also wrote to the Law Society (File 425-6):

> *After your refusal to have a meeting with me per our telephone*
> *conversation of July 3rd I felt it necessary to write to you to clarify*
> *my situation.*
>
> *Both your Troubleshooter and a QC have advised me that both*
> *[First] and now [Second Solicitor] may be negligent with regard*
> *to [First Architect] case. Quoting the Letter: "The Pursuers*
> *could seek recourse from such of their Legal advisors as they*
> *deem to be responsible for failure of their action properly to*
> *reflect their situation."*
>
> *My out of pocket expenses relating to the case against [First*
> *Architect] is £15,000 plus three years of costs still to be invoiced*
> *by [Second Solicitor] since he took over the case three years*
> *ago.*
>
> *Not only do I have to pay more still to finish this 10-year-old case*
> *against [First Architect] but I now have two more further cases*
> *to pursue against the two Solicitors who have been dealing with*
> *the case throughout this time*
>
> ***This is absolutely bizarre.***
>
> *My Troubleshooter has advised me to seek further advice from*
> *Counsel to pursue these matters. To do this I would have to get*
> *a loan.*

Is the system of the law to drain lay people of their savings to the point where they have to quit enabling lawyers not to be accountable for their negligence?

Where do I turn to from here?

This country's legal system has totally drained both our funds and our family. We cannot and will not be forced to quit.

Finally when the Troubleshooter advised me of the issues relating to a time bar possibility relating to my case against [First Solicitor] I was very concerned and hence asked him to serve a writ immediately. He advised me that a letter of intent was more appropriate as the losses could not be determined i.e. until the conclusion of the case against [First Architect]. However he still chose not to issue the letter of intent. I'm not sure why. Please also note the case against [First Architect] has been further delayed.

I must point out these delays are the fault of the Solicitors and the system as has been the case since day one. As an example the Sheriff finally answered the most recent Amendment after four months' delay with his apologies. We were informed by [Second Solicitor] it would only take between four days and two weeks. These delays, throughout the last 10 years, are totally unacceptable but are extremely typical.

I hope my readers will agree that I had been, and still was, going through a very hard time at the hands of a crooked legal system in Scotland.

I had found out to my disadvantage that everyone I had been involved with had completely ignored the rules, i.e. solicitors, Sheriffs, Advocates, Law Society and the Troubleshooter. They had all but destroyed a family, using a crooked system **and they had knowingly done so**, making them the pits of this Earth. They had made it perfectly obvious, by their planned deceitful ways, blaming each other with no intention of following their claims through, that there would always be question marks for their client to handle.

And here is the really vital question for every member of the legal profession involved in my case over the past 10 years: **could it all have been avoided?**

In fact, I do not require an answer to this question. The facts answer it more clearly than any legalistic expressions of mock concern could do in a thousand years. So, to this tawdry profession, I say: I have learned the hard way from you reprehensible creatures. I can never trust your answers. But never mind an answer. Instead let me show your kind how we, the Brown family, had been forced to listen to and obey solicitors, in fear of being dropped by them, for 10 long miserable draining years. Oh to imagine how wonderful it would have been to have found a single decent, honest solicitor. Oh how wonderful to have had on my side a real man, one of integrity and commitment to my cause. A man who, after witnessing the signatures of the contracts in his office in August 1982, being aware that a Completion Certificate should have been awarded six to eight weeks later, had been sufficiently alert to make a simple phone call to the building and Planning Department. That is all it would have taken to immediately see through the mess to the very nub of the issue – the finding of an evasive architect, whose incompetent designs had made the issue of a Completion Certificate impossible. I simply say to my readers and the general public: **Do not trust a legal profession in Scotland operating within the seamy world of self-regulation.**

On 26th July 1992 (File 466) I continued my correspondence with the Law Society:

> *Thank you for your letter of 20th July 1992 We look forward to your more detailed reply to our letter of 9th July and the possibility of a meeting with you.*
>
> *The only confusion that arose from your letter was your reference to a full report to follow from the Troubleshooter. We were unaware of its existence as we thought his letter to you after our meeting contained his full comments.*

a) Can you please send me a copy of this report

b) In a telephone conversation with my daughter the Troubleshooter read the contents of the letter he sent you but we do not have a copy of this. Could you kindly send me this also?

We would very much appreciate a speedy response to the above.

On 30th July 1992 (File 467-8) [Second Solicitor] wrote to me regarding the case against [First Architect]:

Just a note to acknowledge your letter of 24th July the contents of which I have seen. As far as Counsel's Minute of Amendment was concerned, this was probably destined to failure because it came so late in the day and I do not believe it would have been allowed any time after 1987 which was essential when the quinquennium was looked on as having expired.

And who was to blame for that? A good question for my legal team, don't you think?

And here are further questions for my readers to consider: how can one take account of the effect of stress and anxiety on an individual and his family? This is dreadfully difficult to quantify. Could it amount to personal injury, claims for which category of tort have to be raised within three years of the wrong complained of? Accordingly, in my opinion therefore, a claim would have had to have been submitted by 1985. Again, a good question – who was to blame for this planned delay, for planned it was because [First Solicitor] knowingly manipulated this delay to the advantage of both [First Architect] and himself.

With reference to the Minute of Amendment that is now before the Court, the sum being sued for i.e. £30,000, part of that is made up of £3,000 each to yourself and Mrs Brown for what is inconvenience and I think it is going to be too late for that to be included and I am not quite sure why your Advocate has tried to get it in.

I cannot answer all the specific questions you give me because I did not prepare the Minute but [Advocate] did. The Minute could be the subject of further adjustment. There is no doubt that the Advocate would not have dared raise the sum sued for from £30,000 because of the attitude of the previous Sheriff to this particular point in the hope of getting such a new Minute accepted by the Court is strengthened by leaving the sum sued for as the same.

Can I deal now with the last question and the possibility of your taking any action against my firm? All that has happened here is that Counsel prepared a Minute of Amendment which must have been within his anticipation that the Court did not allow because it came too late.

Again I pose the question – who is at fault here?

When asked to deal with the matter further Counsel declined saying he could not help any further. If the matter was to go further, you would need to consider whether you wanted to go in the existing case and also whether you might have a claim against those who were advising you. In saying that he did not distinguish between my firm and [First Solicitor], it is really a matter for you to decide on, and it is not something which I can help you with. As far as I am concerned, I have not been negligent. I know that there has been a lot of delay but that has been caused by various things and I fear the case was already far gone when I inherited it back at the end of 1988.

Your Counsel will not give any further advice, in my opinion, and you really would need another lawyer to advise you independently in any claim against me. I have already advised you that I think you have a claim against [First Solicitor]. The problem is that if you do contemplate a claim against me I cannot carry on with the case and it is on that matter that you need to satisfy yourself first. You are either going to have to be contented with what I have done for you so far, accept the position and let us get on with the case insofar as we can do it but on the written understanding that you do not have any claim against me. If you have difficulty about that you should therefore take legal advice independently of me at his stage before instructing me to go any further. I hope that this is of some help to you and if you have any further queries please do not hesitate to be in touch.

On 14th August 1992 (File 469/70) the Law Society wrote to me:

I thank you for your letter of 26th July and must firstly apologise for the delay in replying.

The Troubleshooter does not provide me with a separate report. He simply provides me with a letter advising me of what has happened and this he has done. I enclose a copy of that letter.

As you will see the Troubleshooter has advised me that he has given you certain advice as to how matters might be pursued. It is for you to consider that advice and, if you feel it appropriate, to instruct the Troubleshooter. I should point out if you do instruct him or indeed any other Solicitor in this matter then such instructions would be on the normal agent and client basis. I would confirm that the cost of your meetings with the Troubleshooter to date have been met by the Law Society.

I think I would wish your comments on what the Troubleshooter has stated before agreeing to meet with you.

I have to say that the difficulty which I have in meeting with you is quite simply that I cannot give you legal advice as to your position or indeed comment upon the matters which are currently before the Court. In your letter of 9th July you have said to me that both your Troubleshooter and the QC have advised you that both [First] and [Second Solicitor] may be negligent. If that is the case then the only place that such negligence can be pursued is through the Courts. The Law Society does not have jurisdiction to claims of negligence.

> *As I have explained to you the Law Society's role in this matter is to consider the Solicitor's professional conduct and also subsequent to 1989 the standard of service offered. However in terms of these fields, the question of negligence cannot be considered by the Society. I would ask you to consider the Troubleshooter's letter and let me have your comments.*

On 18th August 1992 (File 471) I wrote to [Second Solicitor]:

> *I am currently requesting quotes from several QCs for an assessment of the possible negligence of your firm in the (case of myself –v– [First Architect]). As I have stated I very much hope that we find your practice is not negligent so that we can resolve this current claim and thereafter pursue [First Solicitor].*
>
> *In the meantime while I await this information I ask that you make every effort to conclude this case as quickly, and effectively, as possible with as high a financial claim now, legally viable.*

And on the same day – 18th August 1992 (File 472) – I wrote to the Troubleshooter:

> *I am writing to ask for your help on two matters, and also to give you the information you requested.*
>
> *1) Could you please send forms so that I can apply for Legal Aid to enable me to pursue further advice on the negligence of both [First] and [Second Solicitor].*
>
> *2) Could you please send the enclosed letter to Counsel. I would like to pursue Counsel's advice as you suggested. I have attached an extra copy of this letter for your files.*
>
> *3) Please find enclosed the documents retrieved from Town Planning. These documents detail the correspondence that took*

place between [First Architect] and Town Planning regarding their refusal to issue him with a Completion Certificate.

4) *Copies of the Building warrant and Planning permission will cost me £48.00. If you find them absolutely necessary I will get them.*

Also on 18th August 1992 (File 473) I wrote to my Counsel, with whom I'd had a four-hour meeting:

Because [Third Architect], my daughter and myself were all present at the first meeting we had with you, we all felt and agreed that you took the time to listen fully to our case and you responded quickly with your Amendment, unlike the needless delays we have been subjected to throughout the years, as reiterated by the Sheriff and various lawyers. We feel it would be an asset to us if you were further involved.

Can you give us an indication of what you would charge to give us a complete assessment in the case against [First Solicitor] and now it seems possibly [Second Solicitor].

We would supply you with one folder with all the details of negligence of [First Solicitor]. We feel very strongly about our complaints, where you will find the following: Fraud, Malpractice, Defamation of Character, Coercion, Conflict of Interest and obvious Planned delays.

It would be so much easier if [Second Solicitor] was not negligent so that we could conclude the case against [First Architect] through [Second Solicitor] and thereafter pursue [First Solicitor].

However other advisors have indicated that [Second Solicitor] may be negligent and therefore the only sensible thing for us to do at this point in time is to get accurate competent advice.

We appreciate it is not easy for any to be asked an opinion on the negligence of a lawyer. However, as I hope you will understand, innocent people will not give up until justice is done. We ask for your help towards a solution to this incredible stressful situation.

When we meet I would like to cover the time bar issues briefly. We feel very strongly that the evidence shows that the time bar does not apply. However if we are advised it does apply, I would appreciate your comment on going to the European Courts of Human Rights on the length of time this case has taken and will continue to take.

I thank you in anticipation of your cooperation in this matter

The 18th August 1992 was a busy day of correspondence for me. I also wrote as follows to Law Society (File 497):

To keep you up-to-date with matters please find enclosed my recent letters to my Counsel, my Troubleshooter and [Second Solicitor].

I welcome any comments you may have.

The replies began to come back to me. On 21st August 1992 (File 499) [Second Solicitor] wrote to me:

Thank you for your letter of 18th August 1992. This coincides with our receipt of the decision from the Sheriff who regretfully turned down the Minute of Amendment. I have written to your Advocate about this. It is clear that a Minute of Amendment of sorts will be allowed by the Sheriff, reading between the lines of his note. I enclose a copy of the note so that you can see this and I will be in touch as soon as your Advocate comes back to me. I frankly don't think it's worth appealing. I think we should just get another Minute of Amendment done and quickly.

> *In the meantime I note what course you are following, on the question of negligence against my firm. I shall continue to act in the meantime.*

On 26th August 1992 (File 500) [Second Solicitor] again wrote to me:

> *We refer to your daughter's telephone call to this office and now enclose herewith copy Note from [Sheriff] which was omitted from our letter of 21st August. We apologise for any inconvenience caused to you.*

The Sheriff's note recorded his findings on 30th/31st July 1992 (File 501/2), refusing our Minute of Amendment. The above letter was dated 26th August. This is significant because, by keeping the Sheriff's findings from me for almost a whole month he left me with no chance for any appeal, as is shown below:

The following reflects the Sheriff's finding:

> *I have now had the opportunity to study in detail the terms of the proposed Minute of Amendment, and to compare it with the Minute of Amendment which was refused on 1st June 1992. Undoubtedly parts of the new minute would be allowable. I refer to the parts which specify in greater detail matters which are already on record; but, in my opinion, the minute goes much further than this, for it seeks to introduce certain matters which have not been raised before, all of which ought to have been well within the knowledge of the Pursuers since the raising of the action a very long time ago. The proposed Minute of Amendment is certainly an improvement on its abortive predecessor; but I am satisfied that several of the comments made by the Sheriff in the Note attached to the interlocutor dated 1st June 1992 apply equally well to what is now proposed.*

On 31st August 1992 (File 503/4) I wrote to [Second Solicitor]:

The reason I visited your office on Friday 28th August was to pick up a copy of the first page of the building contract between [Contractor] and myself. You had advised me two weeks previous certain pages were missing. As there are many different types of contracts I required the first page to identify the edition to enable me to source a full copy of this type of contract. I apologise for any inconvenience I may have caused your secretary. However I was unable to obtain the copy at that time. I would appreciate a copy of this to enable me to assist you.

Regarding our chance meeting on that day and the 5 minute discussion that followed I am sure you observed my obvious distress due to the content of that meeting which was the last Minute of Amendment heard in Court on 30th July 1992 had been rejected. You confirmed this in your correspondence on 26th August. My request to you on Friday when we met was to appeal immediately and your reply was that my Advocate had also made that request. The answer you gave both of us was we were too late and the costs to date for the rejection of the Amendments would be in the region of £1,800.

What I cannot figure out is the following: the date of the Court hearing was 30th July 1992. We heard the Sheriff say he would make his decision that afternoon and we would hear the next day 31st July. We heard nothing for three weeks until your letter of 26th August 1992 stating that the Amendment had been refused. You further commented to me on Friday that the reason for being too late to appeal was the unfortunate situation of the Sheriff's father passing away.

To add to the confusion when we finally received the Sheriff's findings in your letter of 2nd August 1992 we noted the date of the Sheriff's correspondence and findings, the 31st July, the day after the hearing, which would have given us ample time to appeal.

Queries

1) *I would appreciate if you could comment on the above points.*

2) *Could you advise me as to whether we will recover the £1,800 cost of the amendments plus the previous £750 paid on 21ˢᵗ April over and above the sum sued for.*

3) *Could you also in fact advise me the total cost to date of the case.*

4) *Of this total how much will be reclaimable from the Defender over and above the sum sued for?*

5) *What do you estimate the future cost to conclude this case?*

6) *Of these future costs how much will be reclaimable from the Defender over and above the sum sued for?*

7) *Before the next Minute of Amendment is submitted to anyone I would like a copy for my perusal.*

8) *Could you please ask [Advocate] to provide me with a breakdown of exact amendment?*

9) *Finally can you please confirm the result of your enquiries regarding my repeated question to you on the two copy cheques I sent you previously suggesting [First Architect] may be covered by insurance [of the company he was hired for as chief architect].*

Thank you in anticipation of your cooperation

You can see from this letter to [Second Solicitor] I was asking quite a number of questions, and further questioning his unnecessary delays, which were important for an appeal against the most recent amendment.

[Second Solicitor] was alert to the fact that I was requesting advice and assistance from a QC regarding the possibility of a claim against his firm. Was he now getting annoyed with all my queries, which I was perfectly entitled to raise, regarding all the continued hearings and debates, together with his incompetence in dealing with the same? He should have been looking after his client's interests at all times, never forgetting who was paying for his services.

What I now bring to the story at this time concerns the significance of one **small** word. And yet it is a word with hugely significant meaning as far complainers/complainants dealing with the legal profession are concerned. The important word is quite simply "**notes**."

Not a single member of the legal profession with whom I have ever had meetings, perhaps with the exception of one – the QC – ever took notes. [First] and [Second Solicitor]s, and the Troubleshooter himself, never took notes. Could we be finding another cause for all the delays I experienced at the hands of the complaints process concerning the legal profession? I would say with confidence, and from bitter personal experience, that lack of note-taking is a major contributory factor to legal delays.

[First Solicitor], in his answer regarding my complaint against him, corresponded with the Law Society informing them that he'd had numerous meetings and discussions with me. Yet, would you believe it – throughout all these meetings he never once had a pen/pencil in his hands? Could this be a contributory factor for all my troubles to date? I have no doubt about it. Combine a lack of note-taking as a technique to perpetuate corruption and what do you find – an ideal environment to absolve oneself of responsibility and to milk clients for every penny you can get. An example may be of help here. Remember [First Solicitor]? He still owed me £2,000 because of his corrupt ways. And the Law Society did nothing about it.

Back to my story! I was now getting involved with the Faculty of Advocates in Edinburgh, trying to find a who could possibly advise me in raising an action against [First Solicitor], and possibly [Second Solicitor]. I knew I was facing a task whereby it might well have been easier to scale Mt Everest, especially given the corruption within parts of a self-regulated legal profession. But I had came this far, and resolved only to soldier on.

On 31st August 1992 (File 502/1) the Law Society wrote to me:

> *Thank you for your letter of 18th August together with the copy correspondence, which you have enclosed.*
>
> *I have read it with interest and note you appear to be seeking to instruct your Troubleshooter in this matter.*
>
> *I do not consider it would be appropriate for me to comment upon the various letters you have sent as it is for the Troubleshooter, if he so chooses, to take your instructions and thereafter take the appropriate action.*

On the same day – 31st August 1992 – (File 506/7) the Troubleshooter also wrote to me:

> *Thank you for your letter of 18th instant together with papers herewith which I have only now had an opportunity of perusing. Having considered the papers, it is clear that there is no information when (if at all) the Certificate of Completion was issued by the Local Authority. I assume it has still not been issued.*
>
> *However by July 1983 it appears to me that it should have been apparent to your then legal advisors that the alteration work by [First Architect] and [Contractor] was in serious difficulties;*

and therefore, that proceedings might reasonably have been contemplated from that point in time onwards. It follows that the consequence of delaying in raising such proceedings and obtaining decree on a satisfactory basis might reasonably be calculated in terms of damages from 1983 until decree is obtained (and that at its true value base rather than the likely limited basis which the existing proceedings may achieve by reason of that delay).

You have asked me to pass your letter to your Counsel for his consideration. (I do not know why you have asked me to do this.) However, it does seem to me that that consideration would be premature, as you are seeking his opinion at the time wishing Legal Aid for the purpose of that advice.

It is therefore only sensible for you to complete Legal Aid forms and apply for Legal Aid first, if you intend that the cost of these instructions will be covered by Legal Aid.

I accordingly return your letter to your Counsel together with a Legal Aid form for advice and assistance only, which you will require to complete together with anyone else who may have a financial interest in your property (such as Mrs Brown).

Please therefore return the completed signed Legal Aid form(s) to this office with your further instructions.

On 15th September 1992 (File 510) the Faculty of Advocates wrote to me:

Further to your letter of 11th September 1992 regarding the instruction of your Counsel I'm afraid that Counsel has indicated that he regrettably cannot accept instructions from you as he has previously been instructed in the case (Brown –v– [First Architect]) by one of the firms you apparently may have to consider suing.

2nd October 1992 (File 522) I responded to the Faculty of Advocates:

It has been suggested to me that I may have a case of negligence against two Solicitors representing me in a recent Court action.

In an attempt to source a QC to evaluate the case I contacted the Law Society who in turn intimated that you would be able to recommend one or more QCs who have proven track records in successfully raising actions against Solicitors.

I very much hope you can supply me with such information and thank you in anticipation of your cooperation.

The Faculty of Advocates replied thus (File 522-1):

I refer to your letter dated 2nd October 1992.

Unfortunately you are not permitted to instruct a QC direct.

In these circumstances you should obtain the services of a Solicitor who will be able to make the necessary arrangements for you to obtain an opinion from a QC.

If you have any difficulty in obtaining the services of a Solicitor please come back to me and I will arrange for this through the Law Society.

To which I duly responded on 12th October 1992 (File 523):

Thank you for your response to my letter of 2nd October regarding my request for a list of Solicitors who have successfully sued Solicitors. I fully appreciate that I must go through a Solicitor, which I intend doing once I have sourced an appropriate.

When I contacted the Law Society they advised me that you would be able to supply such a list. I still require this information, which is of great importance and would appreciate your assistance.

I eagerly await your speedy response and thank you in anticipation of your cooperation.

What then followed was utterly disgusting in legal terms, in fact in any terms. So much so, that I have reservations about revealing or even printing it because I could not believe this was actually happening in Scotland, the beautiful country that I love so much.

As my readers will by now know I had been subjected to unending turmoil, pressures and ill health in my desire to get access to justice.

To achieve the full impact of what I am about to reveal, I regret that I must take you back to 11th August 1987 – the date on which [First Solicitor] lodged in Court the initial writ against [First Architect], and then sisted the same. [First Solicitor] left it at that.

Now please come forward to August 1989, to [Second Solicitor] and my meeting with him. He was now going to take the case forward against [First Architect]. In his possession was the complete file of all previous work done by [First Solicitor], which included all the details of the case against [Contractor], and [First Architect].

And now return to the present – 9th January 1991. This particular date is important because it is when [Second Solicitor] recalled the sist (File 511). The interlocutor sheet shows the details:

> *The Sheriff on Pursuers motion No 6 of Process of consent recalls sist of 9th September 1987 appoints defences to be lodged within 14 day from today's date and continues the cause to the adjustment roll of 6th February 1991.*

I'm sure my readers will have spotted the fact that it had taken [Second Solicitor] from August 1989 until 9th January 1991, a delay of 16 months, just to recall the sist!

I wonder what ruling that would give rise to under the Law Society – possibly unprofessional conduct, lack of care and attention, misleading the client, or unnecessary delays? But that was just the beginning!

From the interlocutor sheet mentioned above (File 511) there had been a total of 11 interlocutor sheets through to interlocutor sheet (File 521) spanning a total of 25 different dates from the 9th January 1991 through to October 1992. I had, in short, agonised my way through 22 months of hearings, debates, continuances or what ever else they call them. I know what I would call them, but I must remain civil!

The point which comes to the forefront here, which I would like the readers to note, is that no other profession, not even one, other than the one I was so unfortunate to be involved with, would be willing to waste so much unnecessary time. Otherwise such a profession would be out of business in six months.

Please visualise this – friendly readers and possibly less friendly members of the legal profession alike – join me in my invitation to let your mind picture a scene encompassing 22 months, and covering 25 different hearings in Court rooms. And answer this question – do you really think that I, and a multitude of others in a similar position, would ever believe that these professional people, all dressed up acting the part and addressing each other grandly across a bench, are really abiding by all of our rules of law and natural justice? If any one deigns to answer "yes, quite reasonable", then there is only response I can fairly make! I know that there are many others, like me, who would give a great deal to know how so-called professional people could have taken so long to complete a simple action, and remain of clear conscience.

And may I paint another picture? Visualise instead a similar number of dedicated people with integrity and common sense. Now train them for six months in legal matters, forgetting the pomposities and airs, and ask them to do the same job. I would predict that satisfactory outcomes would emerge in less than half the time it takes our self-important, prolix legal fraternity.

If all this comes across as being insulting, I simply invite you to recap, take a little time and go over the details once again. Then tell me if I have captured a true reflection of how the Scottish legal system works. And if you agree with me, is it not time that we changed our self-regulated system? Only then will these people, the individuals who have happily drifted through the last 22 months of debates, supposed professionals acting in a supposedly professional manner, become accountable and, God willing, begin to show some vestige of compassion for their clients and what they are putting them through.

I hope that members of the legal profession who may be reading this story, and who recognise their loathsome contribution to its corrupt system, now take a good hard look at themselves and admit that they are bringing our legal system into disrepute. That same legal system is undermining the Scottish people by insulting their intelligence, common sense and decency. What could have prevented 25 continuances in 22 months, an utter nonsense that should never have been seen as acceptable for such a simple case? I would like to have thought – conscience and integrity could played a small part. Instead, all the people who were involved should be ashamed of themselves for allowing innocent people to suffer for such long periods of time, **unnecessarily**. I had to pay expenses on five of these hearings.

Back to the flood of correspondence! I set myself to work with a series of letters, the first of which was on 13th October 1992 (File 524) when I wrote to my Troubleshooter:

> *It is now over two and a half years since I approached the Law Society regarding charges against [First Solicitor].*
>
> *I was told by the Law Society then, they would investigate my charges and evidence supplied, and they would seek the answers to the questions that I failed to get after repeatedly asking [First Solicitor].*
>
> *I was informed by the Law Society if the answers were forthcoming it would be for the Law Society files only and they could not be passed to me. My answer was that secrecy creates illegality.*

If you recall our first meeting I reiterated that conversation and your reply was that you had never heard of such a situation and you would get the answers for me. You kindly sent me something but unfortunately I never received a list of direct answers to the list of direct (numbered) questions that I had asked of [First Solicitor].

In addition the Law Society also informed that I would have to wait until I had completed my litigation against [First Architect] before anything could be done.

In our meeting with yourself you also made the same observation i.e. wait for the conclusion of your current case against [First Architect].

If I continue this waiting game, the time bar, that both you and the Law Society have mentioned, may come into play. The reason I say this is it could be another two and a half years before the conclusion of the case against [First Architect].

If we do a recap on the delays that I have suffered we will discover that I had been extremely patient. I was with [First Solicitor] for seven years, three years with [Second Solicitor] two and a half years with the Law Society and now nine months since we first met.

I have followed all the rules and regulations and done everything according to the letter of the law and so far, after 10 long years, it has got me nowhere in fact it has done the opposite; it has destroyed me and my family.

The attached quotations, taken from local and national newspapers over the last six months…highlight what we have been subjected to over the last 10 years. I bring your attention to Lord Mackay's report.

*I do not intend to wait one day longer for the conclusion of the case against [First Architect]. I am now looking for a firm of Solicitors who can take our files and evidence and act accordingly, i.e. with **speed and accuracy and no unnecessary delays.***

I am putting together a libel case to the amount of 1.25 million pounds. I have written to the dean of faculty requesting a list of who have a proven track record in taking Solicitors to Court. I am waiting their reply.

I have been advised that I need to go through a Solicitor in dealing with a QC and my question to you is will you take that role?

If the answer is no, I would appreciate the return of all the documents. If the answer is yes, I will issue you with an updated file which details the sequence of events in greater depth, to avoid any confusion for anyone involved in the future.

Here are the quotes taken from the local and national newspapers mentioned above, which were sent to my Troubleshooter:

18ᵗʰ May 1992 – quote from local newspaper:

Some lawyers are guilty of failing to get all the information they should from their clients according to an Aberdeen University legal expert.

Jessica Burns, chairwoman of the Scottish Client Counselling Committee, said in most other countries there was an obligation on Solicitors to upgrade their skills.

*It is a significant problem; many of the complaints the Law Society receive concern Solicitors not running their practices properly, **not keeping proper notes** of conversations and not recording properly what is said.*

2ⁿᵈ June 1992 – quotes from local newspaper:

The legal system stood today of being inefficient by a furious Aberdeen man: "Public confidence in the legal system was at an all time low partly due to the miscarriages of justice" but he added "I believe this lack of confidence stems equally from the apparent inefficiency of the system. The Courts are there to serve the public and not their own interests".

"The Scottish legal profession is causing clients unnecessary delays, worry and expense," a report by the ombudsman said.

Crooked Solicitors are swindling millions from clients, banks and building societies every year.

A top Scottish legal watchdog warned lawyers to pull their socks up.

In his report, Scottish legal services ombudsman says "There is clear pressure from the public for higher standards at all stages."

He has recommended urgent steps to set up a conciliation procedure to probe customer dissatisfaction, and to advise speedy redress. He also recommends a written guide giving details of Solicitors' charges.

28th July 1992 – quote from national newspaper:

Lord Mackay suggests that with their fancy fees and creaking methods lawyers are failing the general public – and he is right!

Lack of competition is the key. It is this cosy legal circle which bumps up the bill for clients as well as the taxpayers.

The virtual closed shop prevents the system becoming more efficient and user-friendly.

On 16th October 1992 (File 529) I wrote to my Advocate:

In a discussion with [Second Solicitor] yesterday he advised me that you could give me an independent opinion on the negligence of both [First and Second Solicitors].

I had already corresponded with Counsel on this matter but he said he could not assist us as he had already been involved in the case through our second Solicitor.

Can you confirm to me that you can give an independent view, with total confidentiality? Please also confirm what you would charge to give this opinion.

If your response is positive and the cost is acceptable, I will send you some typed notes that will help in your assessment.

Next, on 21st October 1992 (File 530), I wrote to [Second Solicitor]:

Please find enclosed a letter that I have sent to my Advocate. I also enclosed some documents to him. The reason for me doing this is all self-explanatory in his letter attached.

And also on 21st October 1992 (File 531) I wrote again to my Advocate:

[Second Solicitor] informed me that within six to eight weeks you are meeting with [First Architect]'s Solicitor to negotiate an amendment which is fair to both sides.

I would like to clarify something very important.

In the last hearing in Aberdeen on October 16th and in many hearings previously to this [First Architect] has argued that there would be great prejudice in introducing any new information 13 years after the event. No one who has represented me has ever clarified with the Sheriff that this 13 years is inaccurate.

You will find in your files and attached copies of correspondence from [First Architect] in 1983, when once again he was supposed to supply our Completion Certificate, and further correspondence in 1986 when he withheld for six weeks the drawings and warrants when they were urgently required to remove the enforcement order. Therefore [First Architect] does not need to recall 13 years but in fact only six. These documents also highlight the coercing that was going on.

You already have the complete story regarding the sequence of events but I think it would be of great benefit for you to read the attached documents before you negotiate on our behalf.

There were also arguments about in the hearing that he would be unable to locate witnesses with this time lapse. As you know he does not have any witnesses to find.

As always due to past history I am concerned that the Brown family get short-changed in the debate and I trust this will assist in a fairer representation.

On 19th October 1992 (File 552) the Troubleshooter responded to my letter of 13th October:

Firstly can I draw your attention to the fact you have not responded to my letter of 31st August to you wherein I drew your attention to a number of things, including the question of the matter of the Certificate of Completion and on the matter of Legal Aid.

As I indicated to you in that letter I was willing to assist you in the submission of a memorial to Counsel for Counsel's opinion. On the prospects of successfully recovering damages from the previous legal firms you have used, I note you intend to fund that yourself and intend to provide me with the appropriate matters, which you wish Counsel to advise on.

You refer for the first time to a libel case, which is the first suggestion I have heard of that and do not understand the relevance to what we have previously discussed.

I note you want to use a specific QC but I think you must be a little more specific about what you wish to do and pass on all the information before I can be expected to prepare for the consideration.

I replied immediately – on 22nd October 1992 (File 553-4):

Thank you for your letter I received today.

In response to the points you raised. I did not respond to your letter of 31st August in writing but if you remember I spoke to you on the telephone on Wednesday September 9th 1992. The questions that I asked you on the phone were as follows:-

Can we go to a QC without going to a Solicitor? Your answer was yes.

Do we have to pay anything to go through a Solicitor? Your answer was yes.

Can we go to the Counsel we used before or do you have a QC that you prefer us to go to? Your answer was that we could go to our previous Counsel.

How long would Legal Aid take? Your answer was that it could take a long time.

We wrote to our previous Counsel and he replied by saying he could not give an opinion on the negligence of the Solicitors. He had previously been involved in the case through [Second Solicitor]. It was after that refusal that I contacted the dean of faculty for help.

The reason we decided to finance the initial assessment of our case was two-fold. One to avoid Legal Aid delays and two we have been advised of the rates for a senior QC to initially assess cases and we felt we could finance this initial opinion to allow us to understand quickly how things are looking. I do not expect you to understand the strain that further delays and the unknowns cause our family. As I said I will be applying for full Legal Aid after the receipt of the opinion.

You asked me to be a lot more specific about what I wish to do which I will now be.

I would like to get Counsel's opinion on the cases by him reading the enclosed documents.

To ensure the rate that I was quoted from different sources very recently are accurate I would like Counsel to give me a written quotation of his fee for assessment of this information prior to him commencing the work.

If it is absolutely necessary for me to go through you to have you prepare this memorial that you mentioned then I would like a written quotation for this service prior to you commencing this work.

If Counsel can assess the case quickly and effectively from the in-depth story attached without a memorial thus saving me further costs, then of course I would like this (after all we have paid out for 10 long years and got nothing in return).

We would expect the assessment of the case at this senior level to mean that the areas that we have undoubtedly missed, as lay people, will be highlighted by more qualified Solicitors like yourselves, thus presenting a stronger case where appropriate.

On receipt of the above information I can instruct you further.

With regard the libel charge, if this is inaccurate then that will come out of the assessment once everything has been analysed in full. Until then I think it is pointless discussing it further.

Finally I would like to ask you directly, if we are going to get a long-term relationship to bring out the truth in full, you ensure true justice is done, do you genuinely feel you can put the Brown family's interests in all areas absolutely to the forefront and do whatever it's going to take to attack the failures of the people involved and in the system? To do this I think it is vital that both you and the QC try to imagine and really empathise in considering what this would be like if you were in our shoes. We are looking for your sincere help with this matter not a confrontation.

The Troubleshooter's response, dated 27th October 1992 (File 578) was, not surprisingly – given the closed ranks of a tawdry profession – not far short of blunt:

Thank you for your letter of 22nd instant, with the papers therewith. I have read carefully what you intend to do and you ask me whether it is necessary for you to go through me to instruct Counsel. The answer to that is very simple – it is not and therefore there is no purpose in incurring further costs to myself in relation to that aspect. I therefore return all the papers to you and recommend that you take the matter up with Counsel, as apparently the dean of faculty invited you to do. This will at least limit the costs which you are faced with and avoid the necessity of me seeking to obtain further clarification of what you are truly seeking, as I still do not fully understand the point to "LIBEL".

I hope that Counsel is able to assist you in providing the necessary opinion.

On 2nd November 1992 (File 600) the Law Society wrote to me:

Complaint against [First Solicitor]

I refer to previous correspondence relating to the above and have heard from the Troubleshooter, to the effect that you have now decided to instruct Counsel direct and that at the present time your Troubleshooter is not to be further involved.

I would be grateful if you would keep me advised as to the progress of the matter so that I may assess, in due course, at what stage the society may require to be further involved.

On 3rd November 1992 (File 601) I heard again from the Troubleshooter:

I have received a telephone call from faculty services limited in respect of your request to instruct Counsel direct, indicating that Faculty Services Ltd consider that in the particular circumstances they are not prepared to accept those instructions direct from you but that you will require to go through a Solicitor. The matter appears to be one within the discretion of the Senior Bar or their clerks so far as I can ascertain.

As I have indicated to you I am not prepared to instruct Counsel on your behalf without having the papers in the appropriate form and without having appropriate funding. The decision must therefore remain very clearly with yourself as to how you wish to proceed further in this matter.

On 6th November 1992 File (602) [Second Solicitor] wrote to me:

We refer to your telephone conversation [with Second Solicitor] *today and confirm that a consultation has been arranged within my offices at 4pm. on Monday 9th November 1992 with your Advocate. Please ensure your personal attendance.*

My readers will have now got a good impression of the extent to which I had striven, through all factions of the legal profession, to get my side of the case understood, and fairly represented in the legal proceedings. You will also have seen the extent of misrepresentation, from all of my legal agents, unbelievable in the degree of detail exposed! They had cleverly sidestepped all the evidence I provided, and had used double standards and planned delays, knowingly walking me into a time bar situation, starting with [First Solicitor] back in 1983. The obvious question that comes to mind: who is protecting whom? And who has suffered most from their so-called "legal ways" under self-regulation? It occurred to me at the time that I had grown wise all too long after the event. But no longer! I resolved then to challenge all the incompetent legal agents who represented me, and would continue to do so until justice prevailed. I would challenge my incompetent Advocate. I would write to the dean of faculty to **try** to get important questions answered. Notice that I use the word *try*.

On 10th November 1992 (File 603/4/5) [Second Solicitor] wrote to me:

> *I refer to our meeting with Counsel yesterday, attended by your daughter, and to the discussions I had with you both last night and her this morning.*
>
> *I am trying to summarise briefly the advice that you have been given by your Advocate, which I endorse. It is to the effect that an offer is available to settle [First Architect]'s case in the sum of £5,000 plus a certain amount of Court expenses, the amount of which has not yet been confirmed but is likely to include recovery by you of some of the professional fees that you have paid other than legal fees, provided that these professional fees are directly related to the Court action. Otherwise we would expect to recover our expenses and the expenses of Counsel.*
>
> *So that you may consider the acceptability, or otherwise, of that offer your Advocate advised you his views as to the problems you have with the case at the moment. There is an appeal due to be heard tomorrow by the Sheriff principal on the refusal by the previous Sheriff to allow an amendment, to the existing pleadings. It is acknowledged that the existing pleadings require amendment but, given that the previous Sheriff refused the minute that was lodged and that this is a discretionary matter, it is more than likely that the Sheriff principal will adhere to that decision although there is some prospect of arguing that he should allow that Amendment or at least some amendment.*
>
> *There is no doubt that the case as it stands requires amendment. If the Minute of Amendment is refused, we have the option of*

going back and trying to amend again, but each time this is done, the chances of having the amendment allowed will be less. Accordingly if we are left with the position whereby the case as it stands cannot be amended then there is a very strong chance that the Defender's plea to the relevance of the case will be sustained. In other words they are gong to argue that even if we were to prove everything we have set down in the case so far we would not be entitled to succeed in recovering damages because of the way the case has been pled. I think it is probable that some form of Amendment will be allowed but it is not likely to increase the sum that your Advocate feels you could recover in the event of total success in the action against [First Architect]. He put that at a figure of £12,500 plus some figures for loss of business while the premises were shut.

What therefore has to be considered is the prospects of your succeeding in the amendment procedure, and in the ultimate action against [First Architect] if it went on, as against the prospects of losing. In the event that you lose completely against [First Architect] you will be found liable for the whole expenses of the case. The expenses on his side are likely to be about £5,000 and your own legal expenses about £3,000. The downside therefore is the possibility that you pay £8,000 on top of what you have already paid and recover nothing from [First Architect]. Against that is the offer of £5,000 plus relief from your own Solicitors' expenses and recovery of some professional fees. On the balance your Advocate takes the view that the dangers of proceeding with your case against [First Architect] are outweighed by the benefits of accepting this offer. His advice, which I endorse, is that you accept the offer.

As part and parcel of our discussion we went on to consider what happens after this case is settled by way of a possible claim for professional negligence against your previous legal advisors [First Solicitor]. There are clear difficulties with that case in

Law because the basis of the attack would be dilatory behaviour which might be actionable in failure to prosecute the case timeously and failure to draw the pleadings in a form which preserved your remedy given that the negligence was in 1985 and that the case was hardly underway by the end of 1989. Your Advocate has confirmed that he is prepared to process such a case and I have confirmed to support it too. You are concerned that by accepting the offer you will somehow invalidate your case against [First Solicitor]. It is difficult to give a definitive statement on that because he would certainly attempt to plead that that was the position but before settlement I would intend to tell him that we were taking this step and that the reason the £5,000 was being accepted was that we had no choice but to do this in the light of what is regarded as his negligence in preparing pleadings which do not support our going any further and which really demanded that to minimise our loss we accepted the offer on hand. Whether the action succeeds in the end of the day against [First Solicitor] is something that no one can forecast.

I hope that this sufficiently outlines the position as explained and advised by your Advocate and endorsed by myself. The clear recommendation is that settlement should be made and your instructions are needed by return.

To my readers, the legal profession, and to the general public, I wish to make it clear that the purpose of this book is to tell a True Story and to expose the crooked systems used by the legal profession in Scotland, particularly in relation to complaints against solicitors whereby all complaints are handled by a dubious self-regulated Law Society.

This is an allegation I am prepared to justify. Let us begin with the most recent letter, above. [Second Solicitor] had endorsed my Advocate's advice, both men agreeing that I had two simple choices to make. The above letter is most interesting, in many different ways. It shows the true colours of the "legal eagles", supposedly batting hard to support me in my cause! It exposes how they operate – crooked ways that insult the Scottish people's intelligence. Without the comfort of self-regulation, is it possible that the decisions of these same "legal eagles" would result in their proudly standing on the bottom rung of the ladder of intelligence? Of course not – they would have acted with more conscience if they had known that the hand of accountability was about to fall upon their shoulders. They are not stupid, simply individuals blinded by their own arrogance operating safely in their own world of crookedness.

Let us look again at this detailed letter, three full pages written the day after we'd had a meeting. Note the alacrity! If [Second Solicitor] had applied the same focus back in 1989, when we first met, i.e. if he had taken proper **notes** then, when we had plenty of time, and had written three pages with as much detail then **(1989)**, maybe – just maybe – I would not have been forced into the position that I now faced.

Oh how quickly they now wished to close off this case, under the duplicitous guise of acting in my own best interests! And therein lies their true colours, as the saying goes. Are they really feeling sorry for me, their poor client, demoralised after years of hell?

They told me that they concurred with each other about the raising of a possible claim against [First Solicitor]. After all I'd been through, that was an insult to my intelligence. Did they really think I was going to take this on board and truly believe they would raise an action against [First Solicitor]?

And now a point for my readers only. The legal eagles do not have to be told because they are all part of what is going on and are fully aware of the fact:

I had been corresponding with the Law Society, my Troubleshooter, and the Faculty of Advocates where I had asked the question: will you supply me with a list of Counsels including Advocates who have successfully taken a solicitor to Court? I had never received an answer to that question.

I now had [Second Solicitor] and my Advocate expecting me to believe they would make a claim for professional negligence against [First Solicitor]. Why suggest a course of action where there would not be a chance of winning? Why suggest such a course of action, in one breath, having advised, in another breath moments before, that I accept a settlement in respect of the case of [First Architect] that was ludicrously paltry? What was going on? Were they knowingly intent on screwing more money out of me without a chance of my winning?

They knew, just as I now did, that the Law Society and the Troubleshooter were well versed in what was going on, namely that because of this possible claim against [First Solicitor] they were forcing me to inadvertently make a decision that would cover up their own incompetence, and the fact that they had knowingly broken their own rules – to put a client's interests ahead of their own. They had made it clear to me, in the above letter, that the opposition could tear apart any details of my case as far back as the original writ. That suggestion, to my way of thinking, came across as an accusation that someone in the legal profession had been culpable for this whole legal mess. And it exposed how crooked the self-regulated system was, for how can one suggest that a fellow lawyer is culpable and not have in place a system that allows a lay person such as myself to use the legal profession to find redress? Where had a lay person ever used a lawyer to successfully sue a lawyer? Remember, I had never been given an answer to that question.

It is now my turn to tear apart the legal system under self-regulation. Allow me to reveal additional details of this legal mess. These involve Legal Aid and the original writ. The original writ was sisted by [First Solicitor], supposedly pending my application for Legal Aid, normally a six–to–eight–week process, if managed properly, with honesty and integrity. My Legal Aid application followed the same dreary road as my case – a corrupt and never-ending process.

It is already well documented that [Second Solicitor] took over the case against [First Architect] in August/September 1989. At that time I asked him to follow through with the Legal Aid. Here, now, are two examples of incompetence and negligence:

1) **Nine months later** [Second Solicitor], in answering a letter from [First Architect]'s solicitor, states *Our instructions are to proceed with the action against your client* [First Architect].

2) I wrote to [Second Solicitor] on the 14th February 1990 asking for an update on my Legal Aid situation. He gave me the answer **seven months later** (18th September 1990) enclosing forms for me to fill in, and which I hand-delivered two days later.

Does the above reflect speed and efficiency?

By November 1982, we were nearing the end of my case against [First Architect]. After innumerable phone calls to [Second Solicitor], he had failed to follow through with my Legal Aid. If that wasn't enough, I was now going through similar problems with my Troubleshooter who, incidentally, had confirmed further evidence of incompetence against [Second Solicitor] by revealing to me the fact that Legal Aid was itself only available when a Court action had been or was to be raised. As [Second Solicitor] had known for many months that a Court action was to be raised, why had he not assiduously pursued the issue of Legal Aid?

After the conclusion of the above case against [First Architect] there was only one conclusion that I could possibly have arrived at in relation to the performance of the people who represented me throughout that case – I had been dealing with people who were the very pits of this Earth, people with arrogance compounded by incompetence.

It was not until 29th November 1992 (File 610-11-12-13) that I felt able to respond to [Second Solicitor]'s letter:

I now feel I have recovered sufficiently, from the meeting on 9th November, to follow up my letter to you dated 13th November 1992.

Prior to our meeting on 9th November, my daughter and I saw you at the last hearing in the Aberdeen Court on 16th October.

At that hearing the defendant's agent again emphasised the point of the case going back 13 years to 1979 and therefore new pleadings would prejudice the defendant.

After the hearing, I asked the same question I have repeatedly asked: if the opposition keep going back to 1979 and you have always had the proof of [First Architect] being employed and paid for returning 1985/86 to [the guest house] for the purpose of getting a Completion Certificate, plus the letters of coercion between him and [First Solicitor] in 1986 for the retrieval of the drawings, then my question was how can we not get that in, i.e. only 6 years. This comment was once again ignored by you. Furthermore your comment was we should write direct to [Advocate] and ask him the question and also ask him about negligence against [your firm].

You also stated we have plenty of time because you were arranging a meeting between my Advocate and the agent for [First Architect] in Edinburgh to discuss an amendment which would be acceptable to both parties to bring the case closer to an end. You said it would take about 6/8 weeks.

We duly wrote to [Advocate] direct on 21st October (copy to yourself) with an eight-page summary of events detailing the case and a further 12 pages of confirmed evidence against [First Architect] with copies of coercion letters with [First Solicitor] which were all copies of documents which were already in your files.

This was all to help [Advocate] in his discussions with [First Architect]'s agent over the 6/8 week period. I was surprised to find that there was a hearing called for 11th November.

The next time we heard from you was when a meeting was called as per your letter of Friday 6th November which we received Saturday morning 7th November to inform me of a forthcoming meeting on Monday 9th November at 4pm.

Present at the meeting was yourself, [Advocate], my daughter and myself.

Before I go into my summation of that meeting on 9th November and the eventual outcome of that meeting which my daughter and I showed we were under a lot of pressure, and obviously very distressed because of the content of that meeting and the way it was handled, I will say here and now no one, I repeat no one, I don't care who it is, will be allowed to put us through that situation again. My interpretation of the meeting is as follows:-

The first part was the discussion of negligence of both [First Solicitor] and [your own firm], which was in answer to my letter of 16th October.

It was obvious to us that it wouldn't have mattered what [your firm] had done, [Advocate] would have said there was no negligence on your behalf. At one point he was arguing that even nine months wouldn't be enough time for a reasonable Solicitor to get to grips with the case.

Note: This is outrageous. Before making the above statement, my Advocate had had the audacity to represent me in Court after getting the files from [Second Solicitor] only the night before the Court hearing. How could any lawyer effectively represent a client in Court with such little time to prepare and so much information and evidence to absorb?

[Advocate] also tried to argue that perhaps it wasn't until [Third Architect]'s report was submitted to you that you got the full picture. As you well know [Third Architect]'s report just reiterated [Second Architect]'s report dated 1986. Obviously [Advocate] is once again showing his ignorance, unaware of the true facts. Furthermore when you took out the file my Advocate said "just look at how much documentation there is to get to grips with". Again his ignorance comes to the fore. Who made the case complicated?

If you took my correspondence and had it in a lever arch file in date order, you would see clearly that both [Second and Third Architects'] reports, and the City of Aberdeen Building and Planning Department's evidence. There is nothing complicated. However, [Advocate] categorically stated [your firm] was not guilty of negligence, and as far as the negligence against [First Solicitor] is concerned, your letter to me, dated 9th November is self-explanatory.

*The second part of the meeting was about the amendment and our forthcoming hearing, and how [First Architect]'s Counsel could, as [Advocate] put it, **rip apart** any amendment and in fact the **Initial writ**. This was a complete shock to us. It was the first time anyone **had ever mentioned** to us that there was now a prospect of us actually losing. What was the point of all the amendments?*

Previous discussions with you and everyone else had been on whether we would get £30,000 plus interest since 1987 or £100,000, then back to £30,000 but with a potential to build on that.

All of a sudden we are being told, we have little or no chance. It was recommended that we take the out-of-Court offer of £5,000 plus costs and furthermore, you needed a decision by the morning [it was now 6.00pm].

It was then I raised the question about coercion and the six years as opposed to 13. This seemed to upset my Advocate and he seemed very reluctant to try and get this in on the Wednesday hearing. This is when he threatened to withdraw from the case – in other words if I push to keep the case going on the Wednesday he was withdrawing. I felt there was absolutely no consideration, and the recommendation meant that I have to find £15,000 to £20,000 now to fix [First Architect]'s errors...

...As a lay person I thought it was most unprofessional for an Advocate to stand up and threaten his departure and thereafter to repeatedly look at his watch telling us our time was up.

We were under enough strain as it was, being railroaded into accepting a yes or a no and having to answer within an 18-hour period. Furthermore how could I answer for my wife, when...we are living apart.

On 16th November 1992 (File 607-8) [Second Solicitor] wrote to me:

I refer to your case which settled in Sheriff's Court on Wednesday of last week. I did not appreciate that you would not be coming to the Court, since the matter had not been finally settled. You were aware that all we had was an indication of a preparedness to settle at £4,500 to £5,000 and that we were going to try and get expenses over and above this.

As it transpired we ended up with two hours of argument during which time I tried to contact you but you had gone off to Ballater it would seem. I could not get hold of your daughter and your wife naturally enough did not want to take responsibility. They would not pay anything more than a total of £6,500, which was £5,000 to you and £1,500 towards expenses. The documents you have sent to me therefore cannot be relevantly related to the figure we have got because quite frankly the £1,500 does not even cover the legal expenses but for [Advocate]'s part and my own we have agreed to restrict our fee so that you still get the £5,000.

[First Architect] through Counsel insisted that he was not in a position to pay the £6,500. He wanted to pay £2,000 right away and the balance over a period of some nine months. We told him we had no authority to accept this and could not do so. Various other avenues were attempted and we made it clear that as far as we were concerned either the appeal would have to go on or agreement reached that the money would be paid within the usual four-week period allowed when a case is settled.

At the end of the day [First Architect] went off to phone his bankers. It would seem in the result a settlement was reached in the terms of the enclosed joint minute from which you will see that we get the first part of the money within a month and you have a decree confirming that.

I shall be in touch with you about the implications of this as soon as possible. As far as your case against [First Solicitor] is concerned if we now want to deal with this you will need to come and fill in Legal Aid application forms. I am going on holiday on Thursday for about three weeks but the secretary can get these forms completed. The submission to Legal Aid will need to wait my return anyway. I think you probably made an appointment to see me before I go but I thought it best to get this down in paper.

On 29th November 1992 (File 614) I wrote to my Troubleshooter:

Please find enclosed, for Legal Aid purposes, three years accounts, the current bank statement, and the Legal Aid form you sent me, which I have signed.

In the event that you need details of the case for Legal Aid, I have enclosed the full summary of events, and the sheets detailing the Solicitor's negligence. [First Architect]'s case has come to a pathetic conclusion, which is self-explanatory in the final correspondence attached to the summary of events (see pages 15-20 attached.)

If you do not require this for Legal Aid, please retain it for Counsel and once Legal Aid is in place I would like him to receive this for his opinion of my cases.

You will note the summary of events has document numbers referred throughout. I am not sending all these documents at this stage as I think this full story is enough for Counsel to give his opinion. When you feel it is appropriate, I will send the documents which are simply an update of the folder you already have.

I look forward to a mutual understanding in all matters now, and in the future.

On 3rd December 1992 (File 616) [Second Solicitor] acknowledged my letter dated 29th November, which would receive his attention when he returned to business from holiday on 11th December.

On 7th December 1992 (File 617-18) my Troubleshooter responded to my letter of 29th November:

In the first instance I will apply for cover for you under the legal advice and assistance scheme that enables me to properly peruse the papers forwarded and advise you on future steps. That application is made on the pink form I sent you, which you have signed.

In order to complete that form, I need to know the following:-

He then listed nine different queries for me to complete and then told me that he needed more financial information before he could apply for advice and assistance, for example:

Did I live with my wife?
Did my children stay with me and how old were they?
What was my financial position as of 1st December 1992?
Did I receive Income Support, Family Credit?

I was beginning to get suspicious of this Troubleshooter's actions. I reminded him that I had not been required to do this in the case against [Contractor]. I also reminded him of a case in the newspapers regarding a client receiving millions in Legal Aid whilst he was earning hundreds of thousands of pounds a year as a salary. Again I reminded him that the rich did not have to go through what he was putting me through for them to get Legal Aid. I felt that I had already provided him with sufficient information (three years of accounts and my current bank statement) and I was convinced that this was simply another delaying ploy following the footsteps of my first two solicitors who had not succeeded in obtaining Legal Aid for me in the case of [First Architect].

On 21st December 1992 (File 619-1) my Troubleshooter wrote to me:

> *I refer to your letter dated 15th December 1992.*
>
> *Having considered the position, I do not see how you would qualify for legal advice and assistance or Legal Aid on the basis of the figures you have given me.*

1993

On 5th January 1993 (File 620) I responded as follows:

> *Thank you for your letter of 21st December 1992.*
>
> *I would appreciate your full cooperation in sending both the financial details (including the three years' accounts) and the details of our case to the Legal Aid department for their full consideration.*
>
> *Please copy me on all correspondence between the Legal Aid department and yourselves.*

On 20th January 1993 (File 621) the Troubleshooter responded somewhat starchily:

I refer to your letter of 5th January 1993.

As I said in my letter of 21st December, on the basis of the financial information which you have provided me with, I cannot see how you qualify for either legal advice and assistance or Legal Aid. I have not therefore submitted any application to the Legal Aid Board.

*If I am to do anything else, then as previously advised you will need **to put me in funds.***

His last statement immediately made me wonder if he had been made aware that I had received a cheque for £5,000, under cover of a letter dated 24th December 1992 from [Second Solicitor]:

We enclose herewith cheque for £5,000 being first instalment received from [First Architect's Solicitors]. Perhaps you would be kind enough to acknowledge safe receipt.

Note: Is it right that a settlement of money from a previous case should be reason for refusing Legal Aid in a future action? This hardly reflects a balanced and fair system. In fact, is it not reprehensible that the Troubleshooter, after refusing to support my application for Legal Aid, then he asks me to put him *in funds*. I leave my readers to form their own opinion as to the mentality that leads a profession to justify such arrogance. Readers of this True Story and any future complainers/complainants can see from this latest correspondence between me and my Troubleshooter how the legal profession extract the information from you regarding your financial position and then act in their own interests. Does this not expose a lack of morality?

Is it possible they all keep in touch with each other and through the Law Society gain access to any information to assist them in destroying any claimant/complainer who is contemplating action against one of their kind – fellow buddies/solicitors.

On 1st February 1993 (File 622) I wrote to the Troubleshooter regarding the Legal Aid application:

> *I have just been informed by Mrs Brown that our bank account now stands at £800. All other monies have been allocated to alter the unauthorised works at the rear of the guest house.*
>
> *In addition, Mrs Brown is arranging a loan to cover the balance of the alterations and mortgage repayments during the six to eight weeks closure necessary during construction.*
>
> *Because of this change in circumstances, I hope this will help in my application for Legal Aid.*

On 11th February 1993 (File 629) the Troubleshooter responded:

> *I refer to your letter of 1st February 1993 and your subsequent telephone conversation with my assistant.*
>
> *The difficulty we have here is the absence of precise figures. It is necessary to accurately and truthfully state your income and capital in any legal advice application form. Please state precisely what income you receive each week, and also let me have a more detailed explanation of the change of your capital position from £7,353.71 to £800 in a couple of weeks. Clearly I have to be satisfied about all these factors before lodging an application.*

Meanwhile I received a letter from the Law Society, dated 18th January 1993 (File 623) regarding my complaint against [First Solicitor]:

> *I refer to previous correspondence and your telephone call on the 9th November and would be most grateful if you could advise me whether you have been able to make further progress in this matter as you had hoped.*

My readers will by now be familiar with this type of correspondence. The Law Society was continuing to use their favourite tactic of asking me for details of what was going on. As if they didn't already know!

On 18th February 1993 (File 636) the Troubleshooter wrote to me:

Thank you for your letter of 15th inst. which I have just seen. I am even more confused than I was before you wrote to me. So far as I can judge, what you are telling me is that of the bank balance of £7,353.17 per your letter of 15th December 1992, you consider only £800 now remains in your bank account the balance, whatever that is, being now allocated for works at [guest house].

You appear to be expending £230.00-£240.00 per month on rented accommodation which is, say, £60.00 per week and that you have £42.00 left to live on per week, which would indicate an income of approximately £102.00 per week. The position, therefore, is that you now have only £800.00 capital and approximately £102.00 per week of an income from all sources. Please confirm.

Please also confirm that the balance of some £6,553.71 has actually been expended on the works at the guest house or retained for that purpose.

I replied on 21st February 1993 (File 637):

Thank you for your letter of 18th instant, which I confirm all of the contents and details in that letter for my application for Legal Aid. Can you please confirm receipt of the enclosures with my letter to you of 15th February, i.e. correspondence numbered 614, 615, 619, 620, 622.

I am very concerned about the time scale, and any forthcoming changes in the Legal Aid system. I would appreciate all urgencies in these matters. Thanking you. Please advise by return.

On 23rd February 1993 (File 638) the Troubleshooter responded as follows:

> *I thank you for your letter dated 21st February and now enclose legal advice and assistance application form.*
>
> *I have filled in what information I have but could you please complete your date of birth and also the answers to the questions in "Part 111". If you are then satisfied please sign Part 1V where shown and also add the date. Please return the form to me and I will submit it to the Legal Aid Board.*
>
> *You will see that if legal advice and assistance is granted on this basis, you will require to pay me a contribution of £32.00.*

On 24th February 1993 (File 639) I returned the legal advice and assistance application form, duly completed and signed, and sent the letter by recorded delivery, also saying:

> *I think I am correct in saying that it is important that the Solicitor acting on behalf of his client puts forth a precise, honest and accurate report and assessment to support my application for the Board to grant my Legal Aid.*
>
> *I feel sure, after being recommended by the Law Society and with all of the information we have detailed and passed to you, from February 1992 plus the two lengthy meetings in your office in Glasgow, I am sure this will present no problems to you.*
>
> *Thanking you for your help in this and all other matters.*

On 25th February 1993 (File 641-2) the Law Society wrote to me:

> *I thank you for your letter of the 8th February and would firstly apologise for the delay in replying. The reason for this is that I have been considering fully the letter, which you have sent together with the enclosed documentation.*

As I have said to you previously on the phone, I do not in any way underestimate the difficulties these matters have caused you but the Law Society's role is a limited one and as I explained to you in my letter of 14th June 1990, the Law Society did not have power in relation to this matter to pay compensation.

In addition, as I have also explained in that letter, where a case of negligence is to be pursued, the Law Society's policy is that any consideration of the Solicitor's conduct will follow on either the conclusion of the Court matter, or on intimation that the negligence claim is not being pursued. My understanding of your complaint throughout this matter has been that because of the actings of Solicitors you believe you have suffered loss. If that is the case then your recourse really lies through the Courts.

I have checked my file on the matter and would advise you that following the intimation of your complaint to [First Solicitor] in March of 1990, a reply was received dated 22nd March which was copied to you with my letter of 28th March.

A further response was received dated 9th April and copied to you with my letter dated the 18th of April. Thereafter it became clear that you were pursuing the Court action against [First Architect] and considering a negligence claim against [First Solicitor]. Having looked at the correspondence from that time it is quite clear to me that I advised you fully as to the Law Society's position. Indeed I note from a telephone call file note that in a conversation which I had with you on the 6th of February 1991 I confirmed the question of professional conduct could be looked at once the various Court actions had been dealt with. I believe, on considering the file, that I have never suggested to you that the question of the consideration of [First Solicitor]'s conduct would be forgotten and indeed I think that I have made it clear in various telephone conversations which I have had with you that that is the case.

I regret to say that I cannot comment upon the availability of Legal Aid and, if Legal Aid is not available, then I regret to say that you will have to consider whether you wish to pursue the negligence question. As I think you are already aware, the Law Society has in terms of the Troubleshooter scheme paid for the first two meetings you had with the Troubleshooter and the other preparatory work which he did. I made it clear to you at that time that that was the extent of the Society's financial involvement.

It is clear to me in terms of the correspondence which you have sent to me that you appear to wish to make a complaint about the actings of [Second Solicitor].

As far as I am aware, this complaint would relate to their conduct and service.

I assume that at the present time you are not contemplating any other steps in relation to their actings and if that is the case then I would be happy to intimate a complaint to them. It appears to me that your letter of 29th November sets out your concerns. Do you wish me to me to intimate a complaint to them?

I would ask you to consider the terms of this letter and let me have your comments.

Correspondence between the Troubleshooter and myself continued regarding the issue of Legal Aid. On 1st March 1991 (File 646) the Troubleshooter wrote:

I acknowledge receipt of your letter enclosing completed legal advice and assistance form.

I asked you specifically to give me a note of the precise subject matter for which you wanted me to obtain Legal Aid. Please confirm this to me by return.

I responded on 3rd March 1993 (File 647):

In response to your letter of 1ˢᵗ instant, I must reiterate my explanation in my previous correspondence.

As I have not been trained in the legal profession it would be impossible for me to put forward the best possible precise subject matter to enhance my application for legal advice and assistance.

I am sure you will appreciate that I don't want to prejudice my application in any form.

On 23ʳᵈ March 1993 (File 648) the Troubleshooter confirmed that the application for legal advice and assistance had been submitted. He added:

...but I want to know from you what you want me to get advice and assistance on. What are the precise points? Please put them out nice and simple in letter form to me and I will then apply for an increase in cover when I have this information from you.

How was I to know what was required? On 7ᵗʰ April 1993 (File 649) I responded, as follows:

Reference your letter of 23ʳᵈ March 1993.

As I have already indicated to you in the past, I have not been trained in the finer points of the law. I cannot, and will not, put down the precise points because I don't know what the precise points are.

I don't want to jeopardise my position until I receive proper legal advice on all of the information at hand. All I am asking for, once again, is a meeting with Counsel to assess the precise points you mentioned.

Please advise if the legal advice and assistance covers this meeting with Counsel.

My request was neatly parried. On 13th April 1993 (File 650) the Troubleshooter wrote:

> *Thank you for your letter of 7th instant.*
>
> *As I have indicated to you several times, I cannot apply for legal advice and assistance increase for Counsel's opinion without giving an indication of what the advice is being sought on. I am asking what you want that to be and if you cannot tell me, I cannot do it. If you want to come in and see me about it, that is another matter, but there is no point in continuing this correspondence unless you let me have the information required.*

At least the Law Society appeared to be sympathetic. In their correspondence dated 16th April 1993 (File 651) they wrote regarding my complaint against [First Solicitor]:

> *I thank you for your letter received in this office on 7th April together with the papers which you enclosed.*
>
> *I am sorry to read that you have not been in the best of health of late.*
>
> *I think at this stage that the best course of action for me to take is to look at your file together with the copy documentation which you have sent to see if I have any detailed and appropriate comment to make at this stage.*
>
> *I will endeavour to do this within the next couple of weeks and hope that you will bear with me.*

On 22nd April 1993 (File 652-3) I continued to put my case to the Troubleshooter:

> *As I am sure you will understand, I am the last person in the world trying to delay the progression of my case. You are aware of the history of my situation through my case folders and our meetings.*

I am looking for you, the professional, to advise me, the layman, as to how I progress from here to a successful conclusion. I was always under the impression that the Solicitor's duty was to advise the client and not the reverse.

All I can say is what you already know, that throughout this saga, I have been advised by [Second Solicitor and Advocate] that [First Solicitor] has been negligent and further you yourself and my Counsel both said that [First and Second Solicitors] may be responsible for not presenting my claim properly, and in fact there may be negligence, identified elsewhere, after a full accurate assessment is carried out by Counsel, and it is to clarify all of the above that I need advice and assistance and full Legal Aid.

Your advice on the above would be most welcome. I would also appreciate your clear unambiguous advice and understanding as the professional at all times, rather than this continuous confrontation that causes us unnecessary delays and frustrations, as my health has been seriously affected.

This seemed to have some positive effect. On 4th May 1993 (File 654) the Troubleshooter requested a meeting to clarify the situation:

Thank you for your letter of 22nd April. I am sorry but I cannot frame the necessary section of the Legal Aid application on the basis of the information you have given me. Please arrange to see me when it is most convenient and this matter will simply have to wait until you meet with me.

We duly met! On 26th May 1993 (File 655) the Troubleshooter wrote as follows, confirming that he had, at last, acted in my interests:

Further to our meeting on Monday afternoon, I have prepared the Legal Aid form for increased expenditure and enclose a copy thereof. I would be grateful if you would telephone and confirm that it meets with your approval before I forward it to the Scottish Legal Aid Board.

Meanwhile, on 26th May 1993 (File 656), the Law Society submitted a detailed letter regarding my complaints against [First] and [Second Solicitors]. Under the guise of concern for my well-being, the message was uncompromisingly gloomy:

> *I refer to your letter, which was received in this office on 7th April and your subsequent conversation with me on 14th May, and must firstly apologise to you for the fact that I have not been able to write to you sooner regarding the documentation that you have sent to me.*
>
> *As I hope you will appreciate, I have a number of different matters to deal with and regrettably, have not been able to get to your file as quickly as I had hoped to when I wrote to you on 6th April.*
>
> *I have now taken the opportunity of reading the file from cover to cover, as it stands, and I have to say that I must again remind you of the position with the Law Society.*
>
> *Your whole complaint relates to the fact that by actings of one person or another you have, in effect, lost significant sums of money. I am not able to say who is responsible for those losses. There has been a Court action involving [Contractor] and also one involving [First Architect]. Those actions are for the Courts to decide on the evidence available to them.*
>
> *The only matter which the Law Society can consider in relation to [First Solicitor] would be his professional conduct and, possibly, the service provided. This aspect of the matter, however, is not straightforward because the Society only gained power to consider the question of service from January 1989 and you instructed your [First Solicitor] in these various matters, some time prior to that.*
>
> *However, whatever action the Law Society may take, this would not bring you financial compensation for your losses. The only way that you might achieve these would be through taking an action for negligence. That is the reason why, last year, ollowing your requests,*

However, whatever action the Law Society may take, this would not bring you financial compensation for your losses. The only way that you might achieve these would be through taking an action for negligence. That is the reason why, last year, following your requests, and indeed following the difficulties that you had with [Second Solicitor], I considered it appropriate for you to discuss matters with a Troubleshooter and looking at the file and the reports I have received from your Troubleshooter, it did appear that he had taken matters forward.

The Law Society complaints procedure, however, is not a Court of law. It is not for the Law Society to consider specific questions of proof in the matter. If your action of negligence was to go ahead and if during the course of that action, it was shown that [First Solicitor] **had in some way misled you**, *then that certainly would be a matter which I could consider. In your letter to me, you mentioned the fact that [First Solicitor] appeared to have ignored your evidence in the matter. From the responses which [First Solicitor] provided at an early stage of the complaint, I would say simply that they dispute your version of events. The question of proof would be a matter for the Courts. As I also mentioned to you in my letter of 25th February, it does appear to me that you may wish to complain in regard to the involvement of [Second Solicitor].*

I hope you do not mind, but I have retained the copy correspondence which you sent to me, and which may, in due course, be of assistance to me in this matter. I think that it would not be reasonable for me, however, to comment on the contents of the correspondence at this time. The reason that I say that quite simply is that whilst I accept that this correspondence has been extracted from your own files in this matter, clearly, if I am to consider the complaint in due course, I would also require to look at the files of [First Solicitor]. As you know, at the outset of the complaint I did look at these files very briefly. I feel that I would need to look at these files again, before I could come to any view of the matter.

*I know well, both from your correspondence and our telephone
discussions, that this matter troubles you greatly and, indeed,
has led to considerable frustrations and anxieties for you,
However, as I have previously explained, my remit in the matter
is relatively narrow.*

*The only small thing that I may be able to say at this stage to
encourage you is that if, at the end of the day, because of financial
constraints or whatever, you feel unable to take an action against
[First Solicitor] for negligence, then I would seek to reassure you
that I am prepared to look at their professional conduct and also,
possibly, the question of service. However, I must make it absolutely
clear to you that that, in itself, will not in any way bring you
compensation for the losses which you believe you have suffered.*

*I look forward to hearing from you in due course, once you have
decided how to take matters forward.*

So now I had several issues to deal with, with copious correspondence
between myself and the Troubleshooter and also the Law Society.
Remember, I was not in the best of health, but I was determined not to be
the cause of any delay. On 4th June 1993 (File 657) I responded, by fax,
to the Troubleshooter:

*Thank you for your letter of 26th May 1993 and the copy of the
Legal Aid form. There is only one part I would like to change,
that is where you state that [Second Architect] criticised [First
Architect]. I would prefer to state we have full documented proof
for failure in respect of his professional work.*

*With reference to your remark about the £100,000, we have
already spent £20,000 of our own money it will cost another
£12,000 for the unauthorised works. We will lose on resale and if
the additional bedrooms had been completed a future sale would
very much be enhanced. This does not cover everything when
Counsel reads the complete file.*

I have enclosed the documents you requested at our meeting in Glasgow on the 24th May. I have added a few more you might find of interest, I would appreciate five minutes of your time in reading them.

On 2nd June 1993 (File 658) the Troubleshooter responded:

Thank you for your letter sending me the red-backed file. I assume these are all the papers you wish sent to Counsel. Whilst you indicated that you incurred costs of £20,000 and a further £12,000 for the unauthorised works, what I need from you is the total figure. Is the total figure of £32,000 the figure which I should be indicating is the level of damages you are seeking or is the level higher than that? Please indicate the total figure you anticipate seeking for damages so that I can get this letter off to the Legal Aid Board.

On 4th June 1993 (File 660) I responded, saying:

I have sent you under separate cover (Royal Mail Parcel Force) two large files, marked Volume 1 and 2 which are both self-explanatory. Volume 1 has correspondence through pages 1 to 280 and Volume 2 from 281 to 654. These are the files I want sent to Counsel.

In reference to your letter dated 2nd June and the letter you prepared for Legal Aid, which I agreed with except the small change about the Architect and the documents available.

As far as the point you made about the £100,000, that figure was prepared by Counsel. I was only making a point on two items of expense which just came to my mind at the time.

The letter you prepared should go to Legal Aid. Thanking you for your assistance.

On 4th June 1993 (File 661) the Troubleshooter responded, saying:

> *I thank you for your letter received today and note the position regarding the large files etc, and that you wish those sent to Counsel.*
>
> *Turning to the matter with which I am primarily concerned, I require to know from you what your losses have been, not down to the nearest pound but in round terms. I cannot put a figure of £100,000 into the Legal Aid advice note if I do not know how that is made up. It is no use to tell me that your Counsel indicated that figure to you. You have given me an indication of £32,000; are there any further sums of which you are aware which can be added to that figure of £32,000?*
>
> *Please write to me by return as we really must get on with this matter of sending the note off to the Legal Aid.*

I immediately responded by fax on 7th June 1993 (File 659), thanking the Troubleshooter for his letter and saying:

> *I am very sorry I can't send you the detailed figures that make up the £100,000 you requested as they were all passed to Counsel when we met in Aberdeen.*

On 11th June 1993 (File 662) the Troubleshooter repeated his request:

> *What is the figure I am supposed to indicate to the Legal Aid on your behalf for the likely damages you will be seeking; is it £100,000 or is it £32,000 or is it something in between? If it is something in between, please tell me what figure it is. I cannot dream it up for you.*

On 14th June 1993 (File 663) I responded, once again by fax.

> *Thank you for your letter of the 11th instant the query in your letter regarding the figure to be indicated to Legal Aid is £100,000.*

Our correspondence was becoming somewhat circular! On 15ᵗʰ June 1993 (File 664) my Troubleshooter continued his somewhat determined attempt to put on to my shoulders what he could quite easily have done himself – simply contact Counsel for the information he needed! After all, his offices were close to those of the Counsel. Instead he persisted with me:

Thank you for your letter of 14ᵗʰ June. I now understand that you want me to indicate to the Legal Aid Board that the level of your damages is £100,000. I have details up to £32,000. Can you advise me very generally what the remaining £68,000 relates to. I say very generally; I do no want it in any detail whatsoever.

On 17ᵗʰ June 1993 (File 665) I could only respond in the same vein myself. Remember, I had been informed that I could not speak to Counsel directly, and I simply did not have the information. However, it is worth noting here, for my readers' clarity, that I was yet again experiencing delays! I remained firm but polite, saying:

Thank you for your letter of 15ᵗʰ instant.

I am very sorry I cannot advise you very generally what the remaining figures of the £68,000 relates to even in general terms. All the information you require is held by Counsel both in general and detail form.

It would be quite impossible for me to remember even in general terms how the £68,000 is made up, at this point in time. I would require to see the papers held by Counsel.

On 14ᵗʰ July 1993 (File 666) I reiterated this point to the Troubleshooter, using recorded delivery:

Thank you for your letter of 21ˢᵗ June 1993. With reference to your question of me obtaining the information from Counsel regarding the balance of £68,000, this is not possible. As I have already been instructed previously I cannot write directly to a QC.

These instructions came from you personally, and from Faculty Services Ltd. May I remind you that all the information which was passed to Counsel is in the files in your possession in volumes 1 and 2.

You also have a copy of the summary of events, which is indexed to quickly find the necessary information.

With reference to the delay in applying for Legal Aid, I would like to draw your attention to your letter of 26ᵗʰ May 1993 which included a copy of the letter you were sending to the Legal Aid Board on my behalf and asking for my approval. I only asked for one change in that letter, and that was to replace one paragraph about [First Architect].

I have asked you on many occasions in the past for your cooperation, not a confrontation. It seems you prefer the latter because of your lack of cooperation.

Why now after three lengthy meetings in your office, countless letters and seven months of wasted time, are you now asking for details of the £100,000? Why wait till now? Why didn't you ask these questions at the last meeting in your office? All the previous information we sent you, prior to that meeting, was to help before the meeting took place, and at the actual meeting we produced copies of what we already sent you.

*Your attitude then was deplorable, as you told both my daughter and I, in your own words, **"to shut up and close our files".** Mr Troubleshooter, neither you or any other Solicitor has any right to tell his client to shut up under these circumstances.*

I would expect you as an honourable man to give me and my daughter a written apology, especially after the distressed state my daughter left your office. Before she left she attempted to open the files again as the questions you were asking had already been answered previously, and as far as the meeting was concerned it was just a waste of time and money.

I feel that all of the firms of Solicitors who have been involved in this case have systematically delayed and frustrated the Brown family to a point, where they have been mentally and physically drained.

I also feel these same Solicitors have knowingly and effectively created the psychological problems that have risen in the Brown family today and hold them directly responsible.

In an attempt to stop any further delays, you have the necessary powers to get all of the information you require for my application for Legal Aid. All of the professional people involved in my case have been paid in full for that information. I reiterate what I said in previous correspondence: I have sent you all the information I have in the files I sent you.

I require from you your charges and costs to date and also the amount you applied for on my behalf on my first application for Legal Aid.

On 15th July 1993 (File 667) the Troubleshooter's office informed me that my letter would be dealt with on the Troubleshooter's return from holiday. On 4th August 1993 (File 668), he duly responded:

Thank you for your recent letter, which I have just seen on my return to business.

So far as the matter from your Counsel is concerned, that of course can be obtained by you requesting it from the Solicitors whom you instructed to instruct Counsel. I cannot find the information from the papers within my control and, as you know, I consider that I need this information in relation to Legal Aid. I have proceeded

> *with the Legal Aid application on your behalf having prepared it in the best way that I feel able to do so.*
>
> *Returning to the separate matter of the last meeting with yourself and your daughter, your recollection I consider is both inaccurate and highly selective. So far as your daughter is concerned, I understand her condition related to her own personal health problems and no doubt the stress of this matter on both yourself and her in all the circumstances. I am bound to comment that your letter indicates to me that you are still continuing to be under great stress.*
>
> *I can only assure you that I will do the best I can to advance the matter with the benefit of Legal Aid.*

Doesn't this letter have all the appearance of solicitude and concern for my position? Of course it does! But let me now pose a question – what could possibly lie behind this display of solicitude if it were known that this Troubleshooter never had any intention of taking [First Solicitor] to Court? A crazy hypothesis? I have an amazing revelation to bring to light that makes this hypothesis utterly plausible. Meanwhile, I ask my readers to be patient. Let the story unfold.

With growing concern, I responded with the following letter (again using recorded delivery), dated 12th August 1993 (File 669):

> *With reference to your comments regarding my letter to you dated 14th July 1993, recorded delivery, I stand by every word in that letter. The three of us at that last meeting know full well exactly what happened, and what was said, and if you still prefer not to be honourable, maybe it is just possible you will have the decency to answer the questions in the last paragraph of my letter dated 14th July 1993, which you have conveniently ignored.*

On 16th August 1993 (File 670), I received further bad news from the Troubleshooter:

> *I have today received notification from the Scottish Legal Aid Board that they have refused the request for an increase in authorised expenditure to instruct Counsel in relation to this matter.*
>
> *I am considering the prospect of an appeal against this refusal and will write you further shortly.*

The Troubleshooter's response to my letter dated 12th August 1993 was not long in coming! On 17th August 1993 (File 671) he wrote:

> *I have just received your letter of 12th August.*
>
> *I am not at all prepared to accept a letter written in those terms to me against the background of the considerable effort which I have made to try to accommodate your wishes and instructions in this matter.*
>
> *I have just received notification of refusal of my request on your behalf for authorised increase in Legal Aid cover for the instruction of Counsel. I enclose herewith a copy of the Legal Aid documentation and the refusal to facilitate any appeal which you may wish to make through new Solicitors. I shall make the documents available to those new Solicitors when you advise me who they are and upon settlement of my firm's business account in the usual way.*

The man was in a huff! Or was he? Hindsight shows that he had been looking for an opportunity to ditch me as his client, proof of which follows very soon. Meanwhile, back to the story. On 29th October 1993 (File 672) I wrote to the Troubleshooter, keeping calm whilst allowing my deep concern to be voiced:

I am very sorry I have taken so long to answer your letter of 17th August 1993, but I have been deeply concerned, and shocked, that you have taken the attitude not to continue with my Legal Aid application and further represent me.

As you are now fully aware with all of the facts in my case, for me to consult with another Solicitor would be quite horrendous to say the least.

I would like you for the moment to put yourself in a position where you have hired a firm to install carpets in your home, and a firm to install new windows.

If the standards of both these firms weren't up to your liking, and you were upset at the end result, you would, like myself, be entitled to both criticise and withhold payment from both these firms unless they completed the job to your complete satisfaction.

The serious point I wished to make to the man was that very few business folk have the luxury of mistreating their clients and happily walking away from them without any apology or sense of accountability for their own actions.

Not unexpectedly, the Troubleshooter's response, dated 2nd November 1993 (File 673), was in keeping with his latest behaviour:

Thank you for your letter of 29th October.

I have considered carefully everything you have said but see no reason to depart from the decision which I made on 17th August 1993 following upon receipt of your letter of 12th August.

So, my readers can see, from the above File 673, that the Troubleshooter had decided to discontinue representing me as from 17th August 1993.

Now is the time for me to expose what I have discovered to my cost over years of hell. For those who still wish to offer a cynical eye to my words, may I simply say that I have received innumerable similar anecdotes from other ordinary folk who have been through the same mill as myself. In the decade that followed this dreadful experience, I have become a focus for many demoralised individuals crushed by the machine that is our legal profession. We have in our midst a highly organised legal system in Scotland, one that is powerful and unaccountable, one that is able to take control of any complainer/complainant, or anyone contemplating an action against any member of the legal profession.

Take, for example, my Troubleshooter, a man who was supposed to assist me in my action against [First Solicitor]. The Law Society had been fully aware of all the evidence against [First Solicitor], and the gentleman I was dealing with at the Law Society was conversant with all of the details of my case throughout, from the very beginning where he persisted in telling me that the Law Society could not and would not look at my complaint of negligence against [First Solicitor], instead telling me to go through the Courts. And I had kept asking him the same question – how do I get to Court? The Troubleshooter was my only hope.

Imagine that the connections between all factions of the legal profession are like a large circle with tentacles stretching from the centre/core and reaching out to the various departments in public offices. Nothing is left out, i.e. Parliament, Legal Aid, Scottish Consumer Council, Faculty of Advocates, and of course **the holders of the master insurance policy** that cover all lawyers for professional negligence. In all of the above you will find members of the legal profession in control. Is it possible that these members are mutually supporting? Is it possible that they readily close ranks against anyone who has made derogatory remarks against a member of their close and privileged circle? What happens to a person who has had the temerity to challenge any representative from within this circle? What happens when that person requires the services of a lawyer in the future? Their lives are made hell! How?

The answer is that all those within the tight circle keep in touch with each other, through the Law Society, through phone calls, correspondence, even secret meetings. They inform and keep each other up to date with clients' details and in particular, most importantly, **their financial details**. They have the ability to agitate, delay and frustrate. Then, if they have not succeeded, they will resort to character assassination, such as suggesting a client is violent, or unhinged, or difficult to deal with. These are the kind of tactics they stoop to, especially when they know that they can provoke hostile responses from ordinary folk driven to the ends of their tethers. I am fortunate that I have always been able to remain composed during my interactions with this profession. I have been humiliated and shocked into silence but I have never lost my temper or taken the bait and resorted to violence. For that is precisely the reaction that they seek, one that gives them perfect grounds to get rid of, even destroy, difficult clients.

Let me now tie together some of these accusations and postulations, using my "kindly" Troubleshooter, and his behaviour, as a working example:

1) The man gave every outward impression that he was working assiduously in my interest.

2) His letters were couched in solicitude, and yet they unremittingly failed to move my application for Legal Aid forward. Instead I was asked to provide ever more information.

3) The man engineered a meeting in his offices, the one at which my daughter and I attended at some expense given the distance between Aberdeen and Glasgow.

4) The man rudely humiliated us, telling us to close our files and shut up! Had either my daughter or myself reacted violently, or simply lost our tempers, we would have walked straight into his trap. Fortunately we did not!

5) The man could not bring himself to apologise for his outrageous behaviour. Instead he used my polite, if firm, written reprimand as his excuse to ditch his client, knowing that it would be impossible for us to find another solicitor.

6) And for those of you who still think that he had been batting fairly and assiduously on my behalf, seeking Legal Aid in the best interests of his client, consider this:

   a) A solicitor who is intent on taking out an action for negligence against a fellow solicitor is duty-bound to inform the **holders of the master insurance policy** for professional indemnity.

   b) My Troubleshooter **never** informed the holders of the master insurance policy. I know this because subsequent research by me, including paying a fee to the insurers to obtain information regarding my case, resulted in me being informed that no notification of intent to take action was ever submitted.

   c) The Troubleshooter had always told me that he was acting in my best interests. In fact he even feigned hurt feelings when he eventually withdrew from my case. How can he justify his position? Had he knowingly **not** informed the insurers because he had **never intended to take action**?

Note: It is essential that readers are made aware of the fact that the Law Society receives annual bonuses from the holders of the master insurance policy every time they get rid of complainers/complainants like me.

I have to give you, my readers, the above details, so that you fully understand my confrontation with the Troubleshooter. I am told by The Law Society that there are a total of 40 Troubleshooters throughout Scotland. Imagine that my Troubleshooter is typical of a wider system that seeks to fool and con complainers/complainants, and the general public? Now we see the rationale of the Law Society offering to pay for the first two meetings with a Troubleshooter. What a wonderful tactic! For therein lies the con: after the first two meetings, when the Troubleshooter has elicited all the information from his client, he can report his findings to the Law Society. The further con is then to make clients think their interests are being looked after. Instead, through devious and endless correspondence, giving every pretence of moving things forward, they are in fact planning delays.

Take my own Troubleshooter. I had contacted him through the Law Society and his first correspondence was received on 26th February 1992 (File 367). Prior to that I had had a meeting with him in Glasgow the week before. His last letter to me was dated 2nd November 1993, a time span of 22 months during which I had attended three four-hour meetings in his office. And, believe it or not, at no time had the man ever taken **notes**. It was as if, like other lawyers with whom I had been dealing, this Troubleshooter did not know what a pen or pencil could be used for. Throughout those 22 months he had never once written, or referred to, a single note.

I was not alone in having this experience! Unbeknown to both the Law Society and my Troubleshooter, I had made personal contact with members of the Scottish Consumer Council and had met with other complainers/complainants, only to discover that other complainers had gone through exactly the same experience, in each case with different Troubleshooters. The same disastrous results showed that there was an insidious cancer at work. Please bear this in mind as you read on.

My Troubleshooter, and now the Law Society as is evident from their next correspondence, were both waiting for me to seek another solicitor to take up my action.

On 1st September 1993 (File 674-1-2) the Law Society wrote to me:

I thank you for your letter received in this office on 16th August and must firstly apologise for the delay in responding to you.

Since receiving your letter I have received a further letter from [Troubleshooter] who has indicated that he feels, regrettably, that he cannot act further for you. My understanding of the position is that you have been refused Legal Aid for him to carry out further work on your behalf and although an appeal may have some prospect of success, as he is not prepared to act further for you, you would require to draw this aspect of the matter to the attention of any other Solicitor you are going to instruct.

Whilst it may not always have come across in correspondence to you, I do understand the frustrations that you have experienced in this matter. However, the fact of the matter is that the remit of the client relations and complaints department is restricted to consideration of the service provided by a Solicitor and the Solicitor's professional conduct.

In your letter you set out in simple terms your understanding of the legal position of the difficulties which you had with the case against [First Architect] and the involvement of [First Solicitor]. As I have already explained I am not in a position to adjudicate on the legal issues. The clear suggestion in your letter is that [First Solicitor] should have pressed this matter forward in 1985 or 86. If they did not do so and you have suffered loss as a result of what you consider to be their failure to act in your best interests, then that is a matter which in my view requires advice as to whether there has been negligence. That is not something that I can adjudicate upon.

The only place where negligence can be determined is in the Courts and I appreciate from your correspondence that you have particular views of the Court system.

As I have always endeavoured to make clear, I am prepared to consider the complaint you have made into [First Solicitor]'s professional conduct, but any investigation which I make will not result in your losses being made good. It is simply not within the remit of this office to make such an award.

I have taken the opportunity of reviewing the file further, and I have to say that I do believe that I have made it clear that I am prepared to look at this aspect of the matter if you decide not to pursue the question of negligence, or once that aspect of the matter has been completed.

If you are not at this stage going to pursue further the question of negligence, then I am happy to look at the question of the Solicitor's conduct, but the indication from your letter is that you wish to continue to pursue the question of your losses which you believe you have suffered as the result of the actings of one or more people.

I am to be on leave from the office from the date of this letter until late September. I would welcome any further comments you have to make, and if you feel it would help to discuss matters with me by telephone, then I would be happy to do so on my return.

On 18th November 1993 (File 675-1-2) I replied to the Law Society, thanking them for their letter of 1st September 1993 and saying:

Since receiving your letter, I have further corresponded with my Troubleshooter, copies enclosed, dated 29th October 1993 and his reply 2nd November 1993, both self-explanatory.

In page two of your letter 1st September, paragraph one, "The only place where negligence can be determined is in the Courts".

The only answer I can give to that is, how do you get to Court?

My first correspondence with the Troubleshooter was in February 1992. His last correspondence was 2nd November 1993, one year and 10 months later.

My first correspondence with the Troubleshooter was in February 1992. His last correspondence was 2nd November 1993, one year and 10 months later.

My Troubleshooter had three meetings with me, each lasting four hours. The last meeting was called by him, in his correspondence to me dated 4th May 1993, which he stated that the only way this case could move ahead, was to have a further meeting in Glasgow, with which I complied. That was in May 1993.

After all the relevant files, containing the facts and detailed information, which had been sent to the Troubleshooter before the last meeting in May, and after 12 hours of dialogue, he continued to delay matters through unnecessary repetitive correspondence after three meetings. That's when I reached the breaking point.

I felt after the last meeting, and the way it was conducted, and the continuous delays, I was completely justified in my complaints and criticism against my Troubleshooter, irrespective of his replies. If our Counsel can travel to Aberdeen, have a round table discussion for four hours and assess the whole situation, then I am justified in complaining against my Troubleshooter after one year and 10 months plus three, four-hour meetings.

I would think any Solicitor would put his client's interests at heart first, knowing full well this particular client had already gone through excessive delays in the past, and the extreme pressure he was under, both mentally, physically and financially. Any criticism or complaints should have been graciously accepted, especially when you read the last 12 months of correspondence.

As I stated to my Troubleshooter in my letter dated 29th October 1993 I was deeply shocked and concerned that he had taken the attitude not to continue with my case. I feel quite justified in my complaint against him.

With reference to our telephone conversation of last week, I wrote to the dean of faculty complaining of my Advocate. I have sent him a copy of my last correspondence to [Second Solicitor] which you have a copy dated 29th November, where I have stated complaints against both [Second Solicitor] and [Advocate].

I assume after our discussion on the phone you have actioned this complaint.

In closing, I feel after many conversations with you and years of correspondence, surely even the Law Society must agree there has got to be something radically wrong with our system after I went through 22 continuances in the Courts. Once again I could go on, and on. But it's always the innocent that suffer, and the guilty seem to go unpunished. I have enclosed correspondence between [Third Architect] and [Second Solicitor] i.e. files 266 to 272 inclusive, 279, 280, 292 and 296 which highlights just some of the many delays, which have been most distressing over the years, and is now being experienced through the so-called Troubleshooter scheme.

On 22nd November 1993 (File 676) I followed the above letter to the Law Society with another:

Further to my letter of last week 18th November, paragraphs 2,and 3, I have enclosed four additional letters, numbered 141, 148, 210 and 254 respectfully. These are just four more additional queries: how do you get to Court?

If I am not working against a closed shop, then I don't know what is,

1994

On 10th January 1994 (File 677) the Law Society responded:

I refer to your letter of 22ⁿᵈ November 1993, which was passed to my colleague, who is dealing with one of your other complaints.

I note however from that letter you have raised certain matters again in connection with [First Solicitor].

I have again reviewed the correspondence and I feel that I should again make my position clear to you.

You have for some time now indicated that you propose to pursue action against [First Solicitor] in relation to alleged negligence.

I have explained to you in correspondence on several occasions that if that is the case, then the normal practice of the Law Society is to hold consideration of the complaint in relation to professional conduct in abeyance, until any negligence action is completed.

I explained this again to you in my letter of 1ˢᵗ September and would again advise you that if you consider, because of [First Solicitor]'s actions, that you have lost money, then that is a matter outwith the remit of this office to consider. I am quite content at this stage to hold the file open until either the question of negligence has been concluded or you decide that you are not going to pursue the matter.

In your letter of 22ⁿᵈ November you asked the question – how do you get to Court?

The position, quite simply, is that I feel you require to find a Solicitor who is prepared to act on your behalf.

The Law Society is not in a position to either appoint or instruct a Solicitor. As you are already well aware a Troubleshooter was appointed to try to assist you, and it is regrettable that that did not, perhaps bring matters to the conclusion, which might have been hoped.

I know that you have made a complaint against your Troubleshooter and that will be considered separately.

> *The only positive thing, which I feel I could do at this stage, would be to give you names of firms in perhaps Edinburgh whom you might be able to consult. I do not know however whether these firms would be prepared to take the business on. Clearly any Solicitor looking at your case has to consider evidence which is available and form a view upon whether there has been negligence or not, and if so to what extent you may have suffered loss.*

> *I would like to be able to assist you, in this matter, but I am simply not able to, other than to offer you names of Solicitors.*

On 15th February 1994 (File 678) the Law Society wrote to me regarding the complaint against [First Solicitor].

> *I wrote to you on the 10th January 1994, advising you to seek legal advice in relation to the possibility of you pursuing an action for negligence against [First Solicitor]. I would be grateful if you could advise me as to whether or not such a decision has been reached.*

At the end of my tether, I replied on 14th March 1994 (File 679-1-2):

> *Thank you for your letter of 15th February 1994. I am sorry I haven't replied earlier, but the meeting with another Solicitor has been delayed until Wednesday 16th March 1994 and with the other various complaints has added additional pressures I could well do without.*

> *With reference to my complaints against [First Solicitor] I have enclosed further documents for your perusal. I would appreciate your full cooperation into a thorough and precise investigation into [Contractor]'s case, and how the Sheriff found that [First Architect] was not supervising when the evidence at the Sheriff's disposal clearly points to the contrary, and how [First Solicitor] did not immediately appeal that decision, as he must have known that this decision would be very damaging to my future litigation against [First Architect].*

As you will see from the enclosures, the writ against [First Architect] was issued two months prior to our counter claim against [Contractor] which the Sheriff allowed five days to produce the necessary papers and evidence relating to the counter claim.

Part of the evidence produced by [Contractor] was the "minor works contract" which was suggested by [First Architect] at the start of the contract and mentioned by the Sheriff, which clearly states in five pages of the contract "The Architect/Supervising Officer".

The other evidence was a letter from [Contractor] to [First Architect] asking for an extension of time to the contract due to the additional unauthorised works outwith the contract drawings and subject to an enforcement order.

According to the Sheriff's findings [First Architect] was only hired to produce drawings and building warrants. If that is the case how the hell can he be a good witness? This is incredible with the evidence in front of him.

This, in layman's terms, is very suspicious with no appeal and when you read the contents of the writ it's even more suspicious.

Here I am paying [First Solicitor] to protect my interests at all times and he has omitted to mention anything in the counter claim regarding supervision of unauthorised works, £4,000 additional works outwith the contract. This is all criminal and unlawful.

No legal representative has the right to withhold evidence which is crucial to a case to help others, and create further losses to his client, then have the audacity to ask for further monies from that client.

*In a letter from my Troubleshooter he said "I was extremely puzzled that the Sheriff had found that [First Architect] **(wasn't supervising),** and I remain of the view that the omission of anything which would amount to evidence in that respect comes close to negligence in the circumstances of your dispute with [First Architect]".*

The question that must be asked of [First Solicitor] is why didn't you produce the evidence you had from the beginning? Why didn't you appeal immediately and inform The Browns accordingly?

[Mr Deputy Secretary of the Law Society] both you and I know full well, from the information I have already passed to you, all of the answers to the above.

I appeal to the Law Society to question both [First Solicitor] and the Solicitors representing [First Architect], why they have put us through this harrowing experience when a phone call from both Solicitors to the Aberdeen Building and Planning Department would have given them all the evidence that [First Architect] was lying and acted accordingly. I have been frustrated beyond belief that innocent people have to suffer from this crooked legal system. I sincerely hope a full detailed investigation will follow. I think it has been criminal throughout, and would be more criminal if there was no full investigation.

In the hands of the legal experts going through the Courts, i.e. in the hands of both [First and Second Solicitors], we had Court costs awarded against us.

As you have told me in all of our correspondence, the Law Society has its guidelines and I fully understand.

All I want is for the Law Society to understand and come out and tell us where is the so-called justice.

> *I have appreciated your help in the past, and will appreciate it in the future. The meeting on Wednesday 16th March I feel will be fruitless. I would appreciate if you would continue with my complaints against [First Solicitor] as my funds can't further support another Solicitor. I await your comments and investigations.*

On 24th February 1994 (File 680) the Law Society wrote:

> *Complaint against your Troubleshooter*
>
> *Please find enclosed a letter of reply, which I have received from your Troubleshooter. I would be grateful if you would read through this and let me have any comments you wish to make.*

The enclosed letter was dated 20th January 1994 (File 681-2-3) – note the time lapse between both letters – and stated:

> *Thank you for your letter of 17th instant.*
>
> *I note that you consider from the fresh correspondence which you received from Mr Brown that the complaint relates to delay and repetitive meetings and correspondence.*
>
> *Firstly, let me say that I am having difficulty following the photocopy clearly. So far as the matter of delay is concerned, I enclose a copy of my full correspondence with Mr Brown and at the same time I have enclosed the correspondence which I had with the other Deputy Secretary as this of course was a client who was referred to me under the Troubleshooter scheme, and for whom I endeavoured to continue to act in his complaint against a variety of persons including an architect, [First Solicitor]s, [Second Solicitor], and Counsel instructed by the latter. As is apparent, I have now been added to the list.*
>
> *My concerns were to try to assist Mr Brown in identifying precisely whether and against whom he might have a ground of action. I*

believe I identified two such grounds of action both based essentially on negligence (1) by his [First Solicitor], and (2) by his second Solicitor. Both these grounds were, however, quite separate and unrelated, the first in failing to take proceedings against [First Architect], and the second in failing to amend pleadings and conduct a case which had been raised on his behalf adequately as a consequence of which the case was lost.

To a large extent my efforts were initially and for some time concerned with extracting from Mr Brown adequate information and documentation to identify both such claims and it is an understatement to say that this was difficult and time consuming.

Mr Brown has some chronic medical problem which may have resulted from a nervous breakdown and which certainly appeared to me to be ongoing and he was, on a number of occasionas, accompanied by his daughter who confirmed both he and she had been under stress for some considerable period but not, I believe, solely due to the problems on which he consulted me. The combination of father and daughter made the job of extracting information more difficult rather than less difficult as the daughter had clearly been affected by having to concern herself with her father, his problems and his condition, while she herself was undoubtedly and admittedly unwell herself. From start to finish the role for me under the Troubleshooter scheme was a very difficult one, with a very difficult client, who felt he had been badly treated by a variety of professional people, and that he must therefore have a right to compensation. The job of identifying all the information for this was still incomplete at the point in time when I sought Legal Aid at his instruction for the purpose of instructing a new Counsel to institute whatever proceedings Counsel considered might be best raised. I could not obtain details of his losses. It is interesting to me to note that in the copy letter of 29th April 1991 from Mr Brown's second Solicitor to Mr Brown's third architect which you copied to me and, which I had not previously seen, that that was part at least of the information then being sought by that firm also.

I was unable, as you will see from my correspondence, to obtain this information and had to lodge Legal Aid papers as best I could. It was therefore perhaps not too surprising that Legal Aid was refused.

In short, I do not consider that I have delayed in any respect in this matter. If there have been delays judged by some criteria of which I am not aware, then the delays in my view clearly lie at the door of the client.

So far as being repetitive is concerned, I would accept that I certainly continued to press for information and documentation which I considered was essential for the furtherance of both the understanding of all possible grounds of action and for the furtherance of obtaining Legal Aid for the purpose requested by Mr Brown. In these circumstances I reject firmly the criticism, which he has now elected to direct at myself now in this matter.

I would of course be pleased to provide answers to any further points which you wish to raise in relation to this matter and have not sought to deal with the matters on which I have been instructed in detail, as I cannot see at the moment that there is any beneficial purpose in doing so. However, if you wish fuller or further information. I shall be pleased to provide that.

On 28th February 1994 (File 682) I wrote as follows to the Law Society, responding to the above letter from the Troubleshooter (File 681-2-3):

Thank you for your correspondence of 24th February 1994 along with the copy of the Troubleshooter's letter dated 20th January 1994.

In answer to said letter, I think it would be to the advantage of everyone concerned if we were all to meet at the Law Society's offices in Edinburgh in order to discuss in full, the complaints and counter claims. This would certainly speed up the proceedings and eliminate several weeks, or months, of delays which may come about as a result of lengthy written communication.

I would be more than pleased to travel to Edinburgh, if you could possibly set a date suitable to all others concerned. I await your early response.

On 14th March 1994 (File 683) the Law Society responded:

I do not feel a meeting would be beneficial in relation to your complaint. All I wish from you is your written comments as to the terms of the letter which I have received from your Troubleshooter. Once I have these I will be in a position to make a decision as to how to deal with your complaint. If you feel you cannot deal with this matter by way of written correspondence, you can meet with the complaints investigator. He can be contacted at the number above.

Chapter 6

The Law Society – Complaints Procedure

I thank my readers for giving all this correspondence your close attention and now ask you to draw breath! Then consider the following:

Through all the correspondence I have had with the legal profession, little did I realise the benefits I would gain from what was an otherwise draining experience. But there is a gain, and one that pleases me more than I could possibly have imagined at the time. It is this: the more I have corresponded with the legal profession, the more I am now able to expose their corrupt ways. Quite incredible when you give this a second thought! Through that correspondence, often highly repetitive correspondence, I was slowly unearthing their ploys and deceptions.

I now invite my readers to join me on a journey of imagination. Visualise, along with me for a moment, this image:

The offices of our friends, the legal eagles, are lined with filing cabinets, like pigeon-holes in the wall. All are carefully numbered for identification. Now visualise what is going on in these offices – lines of staff pouring over complainers' letters, thousands upon thousands of letters, each one a story of misery and despair. How does the staff handle this litany of human suffering? What is the look on their faces? Do they show concern for a public, shoddily treated by a brotherhood of lawyers? Do they talk about finding justice for the ordinary, innocent man, driven to financial ruin and ill health? Move closer in. Look at their faces again and listen to what they are saying. This is what you hear:

"What template letter did we send to this awkward customer last time? Aha, 42B. Well now, that means 45C should do the trick nicely this time, with just enough repetition of previous arguments and a suitable sprinkling of mawkish concern to show we care! Next time we'll adopt letter type 51D, but not yet. Let's spin this one out a little longer, make him respond in detail, put him through the mill and squeeze just enough to elicit an angry response. Then we can hit him with a real dose of 'my hands are tied – you're on your own chum!' As for what is rotten within this state of lawyerdom, let's leave that one well alone. Don't let's derail our gravy train with too much change."

What a simple way to delay a complaint and create further agitation.

Now turn your imagination to the moment the complainant opens letter 45C, his face nervous with hopeful anticipation that his hours of effort taken to produce detailed pages of information, including perfectly documented concrete evidence, may at last be bearing fruit. And, after waiting for two months, he slips out a paltry piece of paper and reads those cruelly crafted words: "Thank you for your letter, the contents of which have been noted!"

I now offer you a prime example of information I gained from my continued correspondence or maybe, because of the recent experiences, I should use the word "confrontation"! The example I refer to is the letter I received from the Troubleshooter via the Law Society on 20th January 1994 (File 681-2-3).

After going over that letter in detail I simply could not believe that any solicitor would stoop as low as my Troubleshooter had done in trying to cover up his incompetent ways, with the help of his buddies at the Law Society. Even before seeking their help he delves deeply into the realm of character assassination by adopting the pretence, often used by the legal profession, that I was a "difficult client". He stoops even lower, like a bullyboy in school, by insinuating that his client had health problems.

Another attempt to cover his tracks!

BUT, and it is a big **BUT**, the above letter also has the potential to backfire. For here the Troubleshooter's story takes a twist. In the same letter, it appears that the Troubleshooter requested the Law Society to search through my file and extract details of evidence of me causing delays for other members of the legal profession in the past, by making it difficult for them to extract information from me.

Visualise again the image of the Law Society's office. This time the staff are searching through a myriad of files hoping to find evidence to support the incompetent Troubleshooter. Their intention is clear – how can we quash this difficult client, Mr Brown?

And they alight upon a letter! Would you believe it? They are convinced they have found just the thing to send to the Troubleshooter to support his request. Unfortunately, they make a crucial mistake. They choose the wrong letter (File 292). Why?

If both the Troubleshooter, in going through the two large index files I had sent him, and the staff at the Law Society had studied this same letter they would have discovered that a duplicate copy of that same document had been sent to them **by me** as an attachment to my letter dated 18th November 1993. And the reason I had sent it (as stated on page three) was to demonstrate just some of the many delays that had been distressing **me** over the years. The same sort of delays that I was now experiencing through the so-called Troubleshooter scheme.

With the letter, I enclosed partial documentation between [Third Architect] and [Second Solicitor]. Had either the Law Society staff or my Troubleshooter more carefully studied that particular letter, they would have discovered that [Second Solicitor], in a letter to [Third Architect], dated **29th April 1991)**, begins with the words: *I refer to previous correspondence (**your letter of 27th August 1990).***

So my Troubleshooter, in seeking evidence concerning **my** inability to provide information, has only managed to prove the very opposite. Just look at the above dates. It had taken [Second Solicitor] a full eight months to respond to a letter! Proof indeed that delays in the system did exist, but delays by the legal profession, not by other decent folk, such as [Third Architect] trying his best to do a good job.

Look at the tenor of the words in this correspondence between [Third Architect] and [Second Solicitor], in respect of the case against [First Architect] (File 279/80):

> *You may recollect our telephone conversation of **some weeks ago**, when I enquired as to the current status of the litigation between Angus Brown and [First Architect]...I recall that you undertook to investigate the current situation, and advise accordingly.*
>
> ***As I have not heard from you**, I would now confirm the specific nature of my concerns, as these may ultimately have some bearing on the litigation in hand...estimated costs...were forwarded to you **some four months ago**.*
>
> *From our mutual client's point of view, there would seem to be a real necessity to satisfactorily resolve the litigation.*

In conclusion, therefore, not only have we uncovered an attempt at deception (to blame me for delays), but we have unearthed a lie. The Troubleshooter's letter, which he sent to the Law Society, acknowledges to the Law Society that he had not seen the letter before. And yet, in two meticulously indexed files, there it sat! How could this man have the audacity to tell the Law Society that he rejects firmly my criticisms? The above [Third Architect]'s letter to [Second Solicitor] shows exactly how the legal profession are prepared to conspire against a complainant. But ignorance, complemented by arrogance and compounded by incompetence, serves only one end – to make them look stupid and unprofessional.

Further evidence against my Troubleshooter is found in the application he sent to Legal Aid for advice and assistance. In his letter he informed them, in his own words: "Mr Brown has got **two large meticulously indexed files** to support his claims." So here we see him acknowledging that these files exist!

It is interesting to note at this time, as stated above in correspondence from the Law Society, that my request for legal advice and assistance had been refused. Why? I could never find an answer because the legal profession don't, and won't, give any reason for refusal. Yet they share information with each other, for obvious reasons. What has happened to openness and democracy?

In much of the correspondence recorded between myself and the Law Society, my readers will have noted repeated references to one word, namely **negligence**.

It is possible that this word is introduced into conversations and written communications with two sinister intentions. For we have already seen that writs in respect of cases of negligence become reasons in themselves to postpone the moment when the Law Society is obliged to investigate complaints concerning professional misconduct. It has also been shown that **negligence** can become a means by which the Law Society is paid an annual bonus by the holders of the master policy who are all too willing to see off claims by complainers/complainants.

Therefore, it is not outwith the realms of possibility that a complaint that is not related to negligence, for example delays, professional misconduct, not taking notes, or not following the rules, could be tarnished with the word *negligence* and manipulated out of existence. What can you do about it? Nothing!

Then there is the **big con**. The Law Society, through your lawyer, will know your financial position. They will also know what it will cost you to take an action through Court. Remember now who controls Legal Aid

– **lawyers**. What more perfect a means of control could exist to block unwanted actions? As stated earlier, the President of the Law Society, during a speech to lawyers on the subject of Legal Aid is on record as having stated: *Even I could not afford going through Court without Legal Aid, so what hope do ordinary people have?*

On 16th March 1994 (File 684) I wrote to the Law Society (Deputy Secretary):

> *Further to my letter of 14th March 1994 regarding complaints against [First Solicitor] when I sent you copies of my correspondence to [First Solicitor] dated 14th March 1990 (File 213 through to 219).*
>
> *I am puzzled you didn't act on my complaints then, against [First Solicitor] as there was no legal action being taken then against [First Solicitor]. All legal action was against [First Architect].*
>
> *Correct me if I am wrong, but the answer I got from you was I had to wait until the completion of the action against [First Architect], to verify my losses, before action can be taken against [First Solicitor].*
>
> *I am completely puzzled and confused as, in the correspondence received from my Troubleshooter, he states that [First Solicitor] was correct to raise a writ before the completion of the action against [Contractor]. Apart from the fact we wouldn't know what the outcome would be and what losses would be sustained.*
>
> *My Troubleshooter also states the writ could be easily be amended accordingly. I have asked the question many times – why wasn't a writ issued against [First Solicitor] and amended accordingly?*
>
> *It has been stated by all legal parties representing me in the past that [First Solicitor] appears to be negligent*

Details of the above are already in your possession. I would appreciate your clarification in these matters.

The Deputy Secretary responded on 31st March 1994 (File 685-1-2):

I thank you for your letters of 14th and 16th March 1994, the contents of which I have duly noted.

Throughout the correspondence which I have had with you in this matter I think that I have made it clear that I am quite happy to consider your complaint in relation to [First Solicitor] in relation to his professional conduct and, indeed, the service offered. I have also made it clear, however, that my considerations in this respect, could not proceed until the question of your possible negligence action had been dealt with. Where a complainer is contemplating or is, indeed, pursuing, a Solicitor in relation to negligence, the Law Society will not investigate a complaint until that process has been completed.

I accept in terms of your letter of 16th March, no actual action had been raised against [First Solicitor], but it was in contemplation and, indeed, you certainly took advice from Solicitors regarding pursuing the matter. I would point out to you that you have not been prejudiced in any way, so far as the complaint is concerned, by the time that has passed.

In your letter of 14th March you refer, in particular, to the decision made by the Sheriff in the case involving [Contractor]. The Law Society, and the complaints procedure, is not able to look at the decision of the Sheriff, or what took place in Court. So far as the question of an appeal is concerned, I would simply ask you one question, namely: did [First Solicitor] inform you specifically of the decision and did you then give them specific instructions to lodge an appeal?

As far as the involvement of [First Architect's Solicitor] is concerned, I do not consider that I am in a position to investigate their actings. They were entitled to act on behalf of [First Architect], to look after his interests and to take such steps as they saw fit. Whilst I appreciate the comments you have made in regard to the quote from the Troubleshooter, I am afraid that I simply cannot comment upon that.

I do appreciate your wish to find justice in this whole matter, but I must again point out to you that any action that this office may take, in relation to [First Solicitor] will not result in any of the cases involving [Contractor] or [First Architect] being brought to Court or, indeed, prosecution of a negligence action on your behalf. That is simply outwith the remit of the Law Society.

I think I should also make it clear that I am not in a position to comment upon either [Troubleshooter]'s or [First Solicitor]'s professional judgement and this appears to be what you refer to in your letter of 16th March.

Whilst I note what you write in regard to the views expressed about the actings of [First Solicitor] in relation to negligence, I am simply not in a position to investigate this, as I have explained before. In your letter of 14th March, you indicate that you do not have the funds to pursue this matter further with another Solicitor and, that being the case, I am happy to take forward your complaint in relation to the conduct and service. I will do that if you simply respond to the question I have posed earlier in this letter, and that at that stage I will see where matters may go.

On 21st April 1994 (File 686) I responded to the Law Society (Deputy Secretary):

Thank you for your letter of 14th March 1994.

As you suggested I contacted the complaints investigator by phone, and requested we meet in Aberdeen to fully discuss the complaints against my Troubleshooter. Unfortunately, it is not possible for him to travel to Aberdeen. I asked him while he was on the phone, if he could investigate certain questions asked of my Troubleshooter which have remained unanswered.

I will list these questions plus others on a separate sheet, when I conclude my response to my Troubleshooter's letter, which you copied me in your letter of 24th February 1994.

Before I conclude my response, I would appreciate your help in answering the question: why the copy of [Second Solicitor]'s letter dated 29th April 1991 to [Third Architect], which is mentioned in page 2 of the Troubleshooter's letter dated 20th January 1994, was sent to my Troubleshooter and for what reason?

I would thank you for your help in these, and all other matters.

On 25th April 1994 (File 687) the Deputy Secretary wrote as follows regarding the complaint against my Troubleshooter:

I refer to previous correspondence and in particular your telephone conversation with the complaints investigator of 28th March in which you indicated that you wished to know what the cost incurred in dealing with your business was and how much he had asked the Legal Aid for by way of assistance.

In relation to your action for negligence, your Troubleshooter was paid under the Troubleshooter scheme, by the Law Society, for the work which he did. No cost will be incurred by yourself in this regard. With regard to continuing your potential claim for negligence, [Troubleshooter] applied for legal advice and assistance on your behalf. The initial figure for cover which was given, was £150. [Troubleshooter] has prepared a draft account, which extends to £144 although the work exceeds this figure. In relation to the application for legal advice and assistance, you were assessed as having to pay a £32 contribution.

*With regard to the appeal the Troubleshooter has not charged,
and does not intend to charge any fees in connection with this.*

*In order that I can deal with your complaint, if you wish to
continue with your complaint against the Troubleshooter may
I please have your written comments on the terms of his letter
which I forwarded to you on 14th March, in the next 14 days.*

On 17th May 1994 (File 688) I wrote to Law Society requesting a response
to my letter dated 21st April 1994 (File 686):

I would appreciate an early response to the last paragraph.

At this point, my readers may well be thinking: *here we go again – more
letters bouncing around like ping pong balls back and forth across the
barren expanse of a table.* Is all this correspondence leading anywhere? Or
are we seeing the power held by members of the legal profession, sitting
comfortably in their headquarters, whilst manipulating circumstances and
situations at will. Yet again you can see the legal profession at work,
demonstrating to us, the general public, the wonderful art of turning a
simple situation into something unutterably **complex**. Imagine if our
health services acted in the same way towards our legal brethren? They
would very quickly be hopping around like irate birds, squawking their
outrage at a dangerously inefficient world!

**Note: Please take particular note of the next six to nine letters from the
Law Society, in respect of their search for *the two large files* required
to continue their research into my claims against [First Solicitor].**

May I now suggest a simple alternative approach? Please bear this in
mind as you read what follows. If the Deputy Secretary I had been
corresponding with at the Law Society, or for that matter anyone with
common sense at the Law Society, had simply called [First Solicitor] and
instructed him, not tamely asked him, to send his files to the Deputy
Secretary who was dealing with my complaint against him, **he would**

have been duty bound to conform. The files and papers would have taken **one day to arrive**! Instead it had taken from 20th May 1994 through to 18th October 1994.

I am quite happy to describe these people at the Law Society, along with the incompetent solicitors they are connected with, as **incompetent control freaks**. And, can you believe, they are paid for being exactly that? I know these are strong words. I am content to use them now, knowing that I no longer carry any malice. I once felt malice! But no longer. I now simply wish to describe what I perceive as a true reflection of a sorry state of affairs.

Let's get back to the game of correspondence ping pong!

On 20th May 1994 (File 689) the Deputy Secretary wrote to me apologising for the delay in response and saying:

> *I would confirm that I have now written to [First Solicitor] setting out your complaint in some detail and, once I hear from him, I will be in touch with you further.*
>
> *Having perused the papers at length, I do know that according to [First Solicitor], they did hand over to you some time ago [two files], one of them being the one relating to the action involving [First Architect].*
>
> *Could you please make [these files] available to me, for my consideration.*

On 9th June 1994 (File 690) the Deputy Secretary wrote to me as follows:

> *I thank you for your letter of 17th May and note what you write.* ***It is my practice to copy all correspondence to complainers and Solicitors alike****, and this is what was done in these circumstances. I was given no indication that you did not wish this particular letter copied.*

> *If you wish to continue with your complaint, can you please let me have your further comments.*

On 15th June 1994 (File 691) the Deputy Secretary wrote to me. Note the contradiction in the approach!

> *I thank you for your letter of 23rd May and apologise for the delay in replying. With respect, **I do not think it is appropriate for me to copy the correspondence which I have had directly with [First Solicitor] to you**.*
>
> *Suffice to say that you should be aware that the complaint was intimated to them on 9th March 1990 and that on 28th March I acknowledged their response on 18th April. I acknowledge a further letter from them, and then on 11th May 1990 I indicated that I was not considering the matter further at this stage given an action was still ongoing against [First Architect].*
>
> *By that time, they had sent (their files) and the closed record to me on 11th May and I returned to you.*
>
> *I am sorry if my letter of 20th May may have led to some misunderstanding.*
>
> *My understanding of the position was that whilst [First Solicitor] might still hold [certain files], given that you had instructed [Second Solicitor] to pursue matters in relation to [First Architect], I understood that you had sought [the files] of [First Solicitor] to hand over to him.*
>
> *If I am mistaken in relation to the papers actually being handed over to other agents, then I must apologise.*
>
> *I am about to be absent from the office on a period of leave, but I hope on my return, that the [files] from [First Solicitor] will be at hand and I will then be in a position to consider how to take matters forward, hopefully to a conclusion. I will be in touch with you at that stage.*

On 8th July 1994 (File 692) the Deputy Secretary wrote to me:

> *I refer to previous correspondence and write to advise you that during my absence on leave [First Solicitor] delivered [the files] in this matter to this office with a covering letter.*
>
> *I attach simply for your information a copy of the covering letter and would advise you that I will try in the next two to three weeks to look through [the files] and contact you in regard to any further information or clarification which I feel I may need.*

I wonder if my readers are beginning to see how the cycle of corruption works? The details of the covering letter, mentioned in the above letter, from my First Solicitor to the Law Society will give you a strong clue! In correspondence between each other, i.e. between solicitors and the Law Society, I always found it interesting to note that, on some occasions, one receives copies of their correspondence, without even requesting such, and on other occasions when one does request copies, there is not even the remotest likelihood that this will happen.

My years of dealing with a self-regulated crooked legal system, and many more years of correspondence with other sufferers, confirms how the profession colludes through meetings, phone calls, and correspondence.

So, here are the details of the corruption in the copy letter referred to (dated 14th June) from [First Solicitor] to the Law Society. I am sure you will find it of great interest to note the comments I make regarding this letter and its tawdry contents:

> *We thank you for your letter of 20th May and note all you write. We enclose herewith our box of papers relative to the matter. Following on the issue of the Sheriff's judgement in the case against [Contractor], we went over at length the judgement with Mr Brown and advised him in response to his query there was no good grounds for an appeal.*

A hearing on expenses took place on 18th October 1989 whereby the Sheriff found no expenses due to or by either party and we were then instructed to pay over the monies on deposit receipt to the Solicitors for the receiver.

We did not fail to carry out Mr Brown's specific instruction to appeal the case against [Contractor]. No such instruction was given. We understand by this time Mr Brown had already consulted [Second Solicitor] and indeed their letter to us in November 1989 seems to indicate that Mr Brown accepts the position. We trust the matter can now be resolved.

Readers and complainers/complainants may wonder why the Law Society sent me a copy of this particular letter. As you can see from the above letter from [First Solicitor] to the Law Society, he sent a box of papers, or should I say (files), to the Law Society. They at last had everything they needed to deal with my complaint against [First Solicitor]. Or so it would seem.

That self-same letter filled me with concern and conjecture. It made my mind whirl:

1) [First Solicitor] had stated that he *noted all* that the Law Society had written (to him). Was it possible that he had been told that I had written to the Law Society with crucial evidence against both him and the Sheriff, in respect of the case against [Contractor]? Why then had nothing happened, i.e. why had the Law Society not followed through with action against [First Solicitor] in the face of such compelling evidence? This led me to believe that the Law Society was protecting [First Solicitor], even if only by delaying my complaint against him and by giving me a hard time regarding the files.

2) Was the Law Society further protecting [First Solicitor] by informing me that they could do nothing about the Sheriff and his

judgement that [First Architect] was **not** supervising? Whereas I could clearly accept that the Law Society was powerless to overturn the Sheriff's ruling, surely they could have seen the obvious incompetence of [First Solicitor] in failing to properly present my case, resulting in the Sheriff coming to the wrong conclusion? In the face of such incompetence and unprofessional conduct by [First Solicitor], the Law Society should surely have very strongly taken the man to task.

3) Was it possible that the Law Society, to further protect [First Solicitor], had seen the possibility of completely undermining my position by surreptitiously making me aware of the fact that [First Solicitor] was denying that I had ever instructed him to lodge an appeal? This knowledge was designed to fill me with doubt, even though I knew with absolute certainty that I had advised him to appeal the judgement.

Note: Irrespective of whether or not I had instructed [First Solicitor] to lodge an appeal, there is still no excuse for the man to not protect his client. He should have followed the rules and automatically appealed the Sheriff's judgement. For the judgement was based on a poorly presented case and was absolutely fundamental to any prosecution I could have taken in the future, namely that [First Architect] was supervising. Even my Troubleshooter, in his correspondence, had made it clear that [First Solicitor] and the Sheriff had destroyed the possibility of any further action against [First Architect].

4) Even though there had always been good grounds for an appeal, even [Second Solicitor] had suggested it was a waste of time to appeal. In the last paragraph of his letter, [First Solicitor] called on the support of a fellow solicitor [Second Solicitor's letter] to support his case. In fact in the letter referred to, [Second Solicitor] told me I had to accept the decision, adding further that there was nothing I could do about it because it would be *a waste of time*, a

statement I cannot contest. In fact, I could add to it by asserting that the whole legal profession under self-regulation is a waste of time.

In conclusion I hope that my readers, and complainers/complainants will find interesting my comments in relation to the copy letter. Is it possible that the same copy letter was selected for use by the complaints committee? Hardly surprising therefore that the committee found in favour of [First Solicitor].

On 29th July1994 (File 693) the Deputy Secretary wrote to me:

> *I refer to previous correspondence and am pleased to report that I have now had an opportunity of considering this matter and the papers sent to me by both yourself and the Solicitors.*
>
> *When you originally met with the complaints investigator in March 1990 your concerns at that stage appeared to be the delay and failure by [First Solicitor] to progress an action against [First Architect].*
>
> *The difficulty which I now have is that whilst [First Solicitor] have been able to provide me with their file and papers for the action involving [Contractor], I was advised by them in March 1990 that you had in fact taken possession of the [two other files], one of which was [the file] for the action relating to [First Architect].*
>
> *At that stage my understanding of the position was that you were consulting another Solicitor in connection with the possibility of pursuing [First Architect].*
>
> *In order to complete a full and thorough investigation of your complaint against [First Solicitor] I am of the view that I now need to see in addition to the papers that they have sent to me, the [actual file] which you uplifted from them at the time you went to consult [Second Solicitor] about an action against [First Architect].*

If you do not hold the papers in relation to [First Architect] and these are with another Solicitor, please let me know and provide me with authority to approach the Solicitors so that that I may get the papers for consideration.

I am sorry this lengthens the process in this matter but as I am sure you will understand I do require to put to the reporting member all the relevant papers and clearly [the file] relating to your potential action against [First Architect] is relevant. I look forward to hearing from you.

I responded on 3rd August 1994 (File 694):

Thank you for you letter of 29th July 1994 (File 693), regarding the files relating to the action against [First Architect], I am afraid you have been misinformed. The files were never uplifted from [First Solicitor]. My daughter, with the help of one of the secretaries in [First Solicitor]'s office, copied the complete file and then the secretary stamped each copy with [First Solicitor]'s stamp.

These copies were then delivered to [Second Solicitor]'s office in September 1989. If you want these copies from [Second Solicitor], you have my permission to request them from [Second Solicitor].

I think it's [First Solicitor]'s duty to send you [these files]. In doing so, I hope this will give you all of the information you require to put to the reporting member.

At this point I ask my readers to think about a certain sort of person – one who lies and cheats his way through life. I am sure we have all met these types of people. Some are worse than others. They become compulsive liars. These people can never change. In fact their lives become a continuous string of lies, a tangled web that is woven into a fabric of illusion from which there is no escape, forming a tapestry of events that become ever more difficult to maintain as time passes and contradictions multiply. I am talking about [First Architect]. His world of lies was partly shielded with the help of the legal profession and its own dubious ways. However, protection is always limited. The truth tends to come out, partly because compulsive liars can seldom remember what they have said in the past. The truth to them is an unknown quantity.

In the early part of this True Story you will have read how [First Architect] lied and cheated, with the help of an incompetent legal profession. However his true character could not be hidden for ever. My wife, with the help of [Third Architect], complained to RIBA, because she too was weary of his unbelievable actions and reprehensible behaviour. [First Architect] responded to the charges, as can be seen in the following correspondence to his governing body, dated 6th August 1994 (File 694-1):

Note: I have numbered the paragraphs for ease of identification. The numbers will be used to link my comments to each of his statements.

1) *I am in receipt of the notification of the complaint against me by [Mrs Brown]. I refute these allegations absolutely.*

2) *I am however, happy to cooperate fully with the Council in this matter as I feel I do not have a case to answer. In brief the circumstances are as follows:*

3) *The works carried out at [The Browns' guest house] were undertaken by Mrs Brown's estranged husband Mr Angus Brown, in the mid 70s when I was newly qualified. You will perhaps forgive me as I must now rely upon memory as these circumstances occurred almost 20 years ago.*

4) *I was originally contacted by a building contractor* [name withheld] *to prepare drawings for the enlargement of the guest house. Subsequent to this, and after receiving tenders for the work, which included* [name withheld], *Mr Brown appointed a contractor [Contractor] who was not invited*

to tender. This contractor was known by me to be of very poor quality. Following Mr Brown's appointment of [Contractor] I did not wish to be involved in site inspections. I utterly reject the allegations contained within the complaint. They relate to problems which occurred due to poor site practices and workmanship of the builder. Mr Brown rejected the list of competent contractors and opted for a cheap job, and that is exactly what he got. I therefore do not accept any liability for Mr Brown appointing a contractor of whom I did not approve.

5) Subsequent to my obtaining all the necessary planning and building warrant consents I made an application to the Scottish Tourist Board for grant assistance. The STB did not award a grant due to Mr Brown not meeting the necessary financial criteria. I recall that Mr Brown did not then proceed with the works for several years. In the meantime the Planning Department placed the guest house within a newly established conservation area.

6) I understand that the department contacted Mr Brown offering a grant if the design was altered. This was duly done and re-submitted to the department. As Mr Brown had by this time appointed a builder he wished to proceed with haste due to an impending let of the guest house to an oil company. He proceeded with the works without revised planning consent but with the blessing of the department. I understand that the Planning Department lost the revised application, but the building, as executed, complies with their design requirements. As a result of the loss of the application and Mr Brown commencing work before the revised application was determined the conservation grant was refused.

7) Following the bankruptcy of the contractor Mr Brown, at one and the same time, sued me for negligence and required

me to appear as a witness in his defence for non-payment
of monies due to the receiver. I need not say that I found
this situation somewhat unusual. Mr Brown then dropped his
case against me.

8) Several years after the settlement of the above Court
case Mr Brown changed solicitors and again sued me
for compensation, initially for £20,000 and subsequently
for £110,000. Following numerous Court hearings, over
several years, all of which I won, I was advised by my
Council to offer a modest out-of-Court settlement of two or
three thousand pounds. My Council felt, given the complex
nature of the case and almost 20 years lapse of time, he did
not wish to place me in a position of proof. The offer was
made without admission of any liability, and accepted by
Mr Brown.

9) After such a long time I am saddened and distressed to learn
of this complaint. I am inclined to feel that it is prompted
more by way of malice than for any other reason, given that
Mr Brown has failed on two separate occasions to sue me.
I am also somewhat surprised to note that the complaint is
from Mrs Brown, with whom I have had no dealings.

10) I utterly reject these allegations and I would ask Council
to dismiss them forthwith. Given the past circumstances,
the complexities and most of all the time factor of the case
I will be referring your letter to my solicitor, and as such
this letter will be received by you without prejudice to my
rights in law.

Given the facts laid out in this book, I am sure my readers will have some
understanding of my feelings towards this so-called architect. Prior to
his entry into my life, I had never met a human being who could be so
corrupt, evil, and uncaring.

A great deal of learning comes through reading correspondence, which enables one to focus on the mind behind the words and, even after many years, to appreciate a sense of character behind the letter. The above letter does just that. It also gave me a tremendous amount of learning of things I was quite ignorant about. It is ironic that, in his efforts to boost his own ego, and to cover up his incompetence and put himself above the law, he plummets, in my opinion, into the very pits of this earth. Allow me now to expose, paragraph by paragraph, the true character of the person who caused my family years of pain.

Paragraph 3

He states the works at our guest house were undertaken in the mid 70s when he was newly qualified. He asks for the cloak of 20 years to excuse him having to resort to memory!

My response:

Why resort to memory? Surely a competent professional would have effectively archived material indicating, as he well knows, that works started in 1982 when he signed the contract in [First Solicitor]'s office. Just like his qualifications, his arithmetic is way off.

Paragraph 4

His lies are at work again. He was not contacted by any contractor to prepare drawings for the works at our guest house.

His lies continue, stating [Contractor] I had chosen was not invited to tender. Also, because I had chosen this particular contractor, he states that he did not wish to be involved in site inspections. All this is a fabrication.

He then goes on to say that I had opted for a cheap job. That is an interesting comment. The contractor who he claims contacted him originally was the same contractor who was going to do **both** the **conversion and extension** for the same price as the contractor I had chosen for doing the **conversion only.** How low can one stoop in trying to pull the wool over the eyes of RIBA? If RIBA was to check into the full details, it would see that it would have made no difference whoever the contractor was because the Architect had not been competent enough at the outset to draw up simple plans. And **that** is the main reason for his failure to obtain a Completion Certificate and is the reason for all my troubles. I can see now, years later, the reason why my contractor called him a Mickey Mouse architect.

Paragraph 5

After the contractor I had chosen discovered the incompetent [First Architect]'s mistakes in relation to the location of the water tanks, so began this whole mess – the necessity to relocate the water tanks, plus other changes which added £4,000 to the contract and making [First Architect]'s planning and building warrants useless. When he made applications for new permissions, they were refused because he had been warned two years previously that the guest house was a listed building in a conservation area and applications would have to follow the same route as the original application.

In the last sentence in paragraph 5 he lies again about the Planning Department placing our guest house within a newly established conservation area. This is untrue. Just how far will this crook go? The rope is getting longer, and the noose ever tighter!

Paragraph 6

More lies! Ever more lies! He states that I had an impending let with an oil company and I wanted to proceed with haste and had instructed my chosen contractor to start the works without revised planning consent. He has omitted to tell RIBA that he signed a contract in [First Solicitor]'s office, along with [Contractor] and myself, in which it stated the contract for the conversion will start on a certain date and complete on a certain date. He then confirmed in writing to the building and Planning Department these same dates as per the contract. In reference to the revised planning consent, how could there be a revised planning consent when the drastic errors were discovered by my contractor after the start of the contract? This incompetent architect is getting desperate, now having the audacity to blame the building and Planning Department for losing the revised application. That was a gamble indeed, blaming the department so overtly, in writing! On top of that he further blames me for starting the contract ahead of time, and he claims that these were the reasons for the refusal of the grant. What kind of person can cook up a story about the Planning Department losing the revised application and me starting the contract without permission?

He forgets to mention to RIBA that no Completion Certificate was ever issued due to the unauthorised works and the impending enforcement order. He also fails to mention his continued refusals to hand over the drawings to [Second Architect], to help [Second Architect] get rid of both the unauthorised works and the enforcement order, both of which were the real blocks to me being allowed the grant. He just keeps on lying.

Paragraph 7

This is where the conflict of interest really comes out, i.e. the point at which he and [First Solicitor] conceived the scam that would protect [First Architect] as the price for acting as our witness in [Contractor]'s case. I have already made it clear earlier in the story that I had told [First Solicitor], in no uncertain terms, I did not want or need this Mickey Mouse architect as a witness. Nor can they have it both ways. If [First Architect] genuinely had not been a **supervising** architect (which we know is untrue, but assume his assertion is correct for just a moment), then how could he have ever been a good witness?

In the last sentence in this paragraph [First Architect] states that I had dropped the case against him. That is patently a lie. In fact it is the very essence of this story – that I was striving ceaselessly to obtain justice for all the harm he had inflicted upon me.

Paragraph 8

This must really have impressed RIBA. Yet it is all lies. I never accepted a penny in any form of settlement.

Paragraph 9

He is behaving like a little boy at school, stating that my wife's complaint was by way of malice. But what is worse is that he appears to think that I have sued him twice. News to me!

Paragraph 10

He utterly rejects the allegations and asks RIBA to dismiss them. Given the tissue of lies, with no counterbalancing arguments to refute them, RIBA could only dismiss the charges. And, just like the legal profession, they would be only too eager to protect one of their own, nor would they wish to lose this member's annual contribution of fees!

How different things would have been if RIBA had asked me to give my version of events, supported by files of evidence. It would have given me great pleasure to sit opposite [First Architect] in front of his governing body and give them the real True Story.

On 22nd August 1994 (File 695) the Deputy Secretary replied to my letter dated 3rd August 1994 (File 694):

> *I thank you for your letter of 3rd August. Following my telephone discussion with you I am grateful to you for providing me with authorisation to obtain [the file] specifically in relation to the action against [First Architect]. I do note your comments that [First Solicitor] still in fact hold the [original file].*
>
> *In order to expedite matters I have written to both [First] and [Second Solicitor]. I will confirm to you as soon as I receive the necessary [paperwork].*

On 21st September 1994 (File 696) the Deputy Secretary wrote again:

> *I refer to previous correspondence in relation to the above and write to advise that I have heard from [Second Solicitor] in connection with the question of [your file] in the original action against [First Architect].*
>
> *As you will be aware, my colleague is dealing with your complaint against [Second Solicitor]. I understand that she has recently sent a [box of files] received from [Second Solicitor] to a member of her committee for a report. I am advised by [Second Solicitor] that he sent all of his papers to my colleague and therefore [First Architect]'s file is probably in that box.*
>
> *I do not think I can take matters forward until my colleague receives the papers back from the reporting member of her committee.*
>
> *You have my assurance however that when she does I will endeavour to get the papers and take matters forward.*
>
> *As I am sure you will understand this particular delay in matters is outwith my control.*

On 18th October 1994 (File 697) the Deputy Secretary wrote:

> *I refer to previous correspondence and my discussion with you on 3rd October.*
>
> *I would confirm that I have now recovered the [further file], which was passed to [Second Solicitor] by [First Solicitor] and have sent this together with other papers submitted by [First Solicitor] to a member of my complaints committee for a report.*
>
> *As I indicated when I spoke with you, under normal circumstances a report from a member of my committee takes around one month. Given the complexity of this matter however, I think it may be that the report will take a little longer.*

On 29th November 1994 (File 698) the Deputy Secretary wrote again, this time in reference to my complaint against the Troubleshooter:

> *I refer to my letters of 25th April and 9th June and note that I have not received your further comments in this matter.*
>
> *If I do not hear from you within the next 14 days, I shall assume that you no longer wish me to maintain an interest in your complaint and shall close my file.*

On 12th December 1994 (File 699-1-2-3) I responded with the following lengthy and detailed letter:

> *In response to your last correspondence of 29th November 1994 regarding further comments in my complaints against my Troubleshooter, my further comments are in response to the Troubleshooter's letter dated 20th January 1994 which you sent me on 24th February 1994.*
>
> *My response refers to each relevant page and paragraph.*
>
> *Page 1 I have no comments*
>
> *Page 2 Paragraph 1*
> *'extracting adequate information and documentation'*
>
> *Comments: I refer you to the letter my Troubleshooter sent to Legal Aid in which I have underlined a particular sentence in page 2 paragraph 2:- This work will involve careful consideration of two files of meticulously indexed papers.*
>
> *Page 2 Paragraph 2*
>
> *Comments: the contents of this whole paragraph have been written to confuse the whole issue. Starting with the first sentence, I would like to see [Troubleshooter]'s medical degree to confirm his diagnosis on both my daughter's and my own health.*

He has also decided to dictate who caused the problems. The combination of father/daughter was very simple. The dates of both four-hour-long meetings in the Troubleshooter's office, which she attended, were made to coincide with two of her business trips to Glasgow. She was also willing to help out by driving me, thus saving my expenses travelling by train and taxi plus meals and the additional problem of carrying the two large [files] copies of which were and still in the Troubleshooter's possession including the information on losses (which he stated he could not get).

My daughter and I both tried very hard to focus him on the complete file of information which contains every piece of information he needed, but he was adamant about not consulting the files including the 'summary of events' and told us on two occasions to 'shut up and shut the files'.

We were absolutely amazed to get this kind of treatment from a professional Solicitor in the Troubleshooter scheme.

Because of our unbelievable difficulties with our previous Solicitors, as mentioned by the Troubleshooter himself, we felt we were coming to the end of the line and felt rather vulnerable at the time and chose to obey his instructions in closing the files. We felt totally degraded to be manipulated like this. This severely unprofessional behaviour from the Troubleshooter should be challenged, and there are two witnesses to verify his unacceptable tactics. In his letter the Troubleshooter mentions the scheme in which he is a member. I find that he has been most inadequate in relation to the scheme and myself. He never mentioned any difficulties to me about getting information or about us being awkward until I questioned him about his ability and lack of progress. How could we have trouble with information? He was in possession of the full summary of events and the losses in his office and, in addition to that, if I had been asked I would be delighted to give more information – anything to progress our case.

Furthermore it is common sense that before a case goes as far as the Troubleshooter scheme it will by nature be more difficult. That is surely why it's been taken that far, and the Troubleshooter should be qualified to deal with this and should not have the easy cop out of dropping the case due to his client's criticism, otherwise the whole scheme is a farce, and the client is at a complete loss to find redress against his/her negligent Solicitors.

Therefore I challenge the Troubleshooter if he states it was difficult due to lack of documentation or information. The truth of the matter is anyone who takes the proper amount of time to digest all the facts in the file and those who use effective questioning, and more importantly listening skills, have no trouble in understanding all of the events and losses. Those who try to cut corners do not take the time required. They tell their clients to [shut up and close the file] and have little chance of understanding the truth.

With reference to the copy letter that the Troubleshooter refers to, dated 29th April from [Second Solicitor] to [Third Architect] I just can't believe that he is attempting to find excuses, through another Solicitor's letter. The contents of that letter does not overcome the fact that my Troubleshooter had the full losses detailed in the file in his possession. The fact that he states that he had not seen that letter confirms even further that he did not read the file. If he had he would have seen mention of that letter in the 'summary of events' at the front of the file with a full copy to refer to under volume 1/section 16/page 292. These files are on one hand quoted by my Troubleshooter as the 'meticulously indexed papers' yet he argues in his defence that there was lack of information.

Surely, with such contradictions, the Law Society must ask him why he is using this as an excuse, when there is no getting away from the fact that he had the information on losses in his possession.

In reference to [Second Solicitor]'s letter dated 29th April (File 292) this should also be understood, in full, by the Troubleshooter and the Law Society, and the only way to do that is to read it in context by reading pages 266/279/280 and 292 which shows [Second Solicitor] receiving information from [Third Architect] on behalf of Mr Brown whereby for nine months, although the letter was received, nothing was progressed which forced [Third Architect] to send a reminder to [Second Solicitor] (page 279/280 of the file) which [Second Solicitor] forgot to mention and to further refute my Troubleshooter's statement regarding [Second Solicitor]'s letter, i.e. 29th April. I enclose page 317-1 and 340 for your perusal.

To enable you and I to assess the Troubleshooter's performance fairly and fully, I require him to send to the Law Society the concise details as to why Legal Aid was refused, along with the correspondence to and from Legal Aid. When I receive a copy, I will be able to fairly complete my final comments in my complaints against my Troubleshooter.

To further my complaints against my Troubleshooter, I would like to draw your attention to a letter from the Troubleshooter to the Law Society (page 446/447) where it mentions a writ against [First Solicitor] which I had asked him to raise. He stated that I could not proceed with action against [First Solicitor] until the case against [First Architect] was concluded to quantify my losses.

Yet previous to this he contradicts his own statement on page 407-7 where he states that it was correct for [First Solicitor] to raise a writ against [First Architect] before the conclusion of the case against [Contactor] without knowing the losses as it could always be amended. Why couldn't we apply the same logic to raise a writ against [First Solicitor]?

With the above information at hand I would like the Law Society to investigate the reason why my Troubleshooter in his quest to get a total figure from me, a figure which was always contained within his files along with a breakdown of its calculations, wasted so much time, as you will see from the correspondence he sent to you, to get at the total figure. After years of incompetent, negligent Solicitors, its incredible that even at the Troubleshooter stage after three four-hour meetings and us taking the trouble to meticulously copy him on the file it is outrageous that we should have to accept this time-wasting correspondence. We find this unacceptable, exhausting, and frustrating to say the least.

The Troubleshooter failed in his duty to simply read the file and furthermore he could have verified our financial claim by requesting, from the Sheriff clerk's office, the files on both contractor's and [First Architect]'s cases. If he had followed this through, he would have seen the losses were indicated in both cases. You will never begin to imagine how stressful it is for us to listen to these pathetic excuses from a supposed professional who gives up on a case because it's supposedly difficult and I am awkward.

The reality is, this Troubleshooter made it difficult by not taking the time to listen or read the facts. To conclude on the Troubleshooter's letter to the Law Society where he states that the quinquennial prescription period would affect my right of claim against both Solicitors. If you cross-reference that letter dated 21st July 1992 with a letter I received from [Second Solicitor] through the Law Society dated 21st June 1993, one year later, I quote [Second Solicitor] from that letter: "We have of course, discussed the question of whether a claim may be processed against [First Solicitor] and that is of course still a possibility, if you wish to pursue it."

There is absolutely no doubt whatsoever in my mind where the difficulties arose from and who has made these difficulties throughout. Each Solicitor is happy to blame the other, and a full investigation shows that they have all contributed, including my Troubleshooter.

Questions to be answered by the Law Society, re: expenses.

*Please confirm that your letter to me, dated 25th April 1994, supersedes the three following letters **enclosed**.*

1) Law Society to Mr Brown 11th December 1991 – 4th paragraph – page 347 of file

2) Troubleshooter to Mr Brown 26th May 1992 – page 414 of file – last sentence re expenses

3) Troubleshooter to Mr Brown dated 17th August 1993

On 29th December 1994 (File 698-1) the Law Society wrote to me as follows, enclosing the schedule of findings by the Reporter investigating my complaint against [Second Solicitor]:

I attach a schedule setting out the complaints, the circumstances as considered by my committee and the decision of that committee.

As you will see the Solicitors have been ordered to pay to you the sum of £1,000 in compensation. I should advise you that the Solicitors have a period of 21 days in which to appeal against this decision to the Scottish Solicitors' Discipline Tribunal. If I receive notification of such an appeal I will let you know. If, after a period of 28 days, you have heard from neither the Solicitors direct with the cheque nor from me then please contact this office and I will let you know at that stage if there has been any further procedure.

As you will see the committee have reached a decision on the service which was provided to you and have ordered the maximum award of compensation be paid to you. They have however continued the question of [Second Solicitor]'s conduct for further representations, and I will report to you further in that matter in due course.

SCHEDULE

Complaint by Angus Brown against

[Second Solicitor]

The reporter recommended to committee that they find (other than the conduct issue which is still to be addressed) [Second Solicitor]'s delays, failure to prepare adequately, and failure to follow instructions amount to an inadequate professional service. He recommended to the committee that the fees be left unabated but the firm of [Second Solicitor] should be directed to pay Mr Brown the sum of £1,000 by way of compensation. The bulk of the complaint refers to work carried out after 3rd June 1991.

The committee considered firstly the question of fee abatement and took into account the reporter's view that it was clear that the Solicitors had already had their fees considerably reduced having regard to the amount of work done and therefore agreed with the reporter that no further reduction was appropriate. The committee decided however to make a formal notice ordering the Solicitors to charge no further fees.

In relation to the question of compensation the committee agreed with the reporter's view that the maximum amount of compensation should be awarded to Mr Brown to compensate not only for any loss, which he had suffered but for the extreme distress and anxiety which had been caused to him by the conduct of this case.

Committee's decision

The committee agreed that the delay, failure to prepare adequately and failure to follow instructions by the firm of [Second Solicitor] amounted to the provision of an inadequate professional service and firstly in terms of section 42A(2)(a) (ii) of the Solicitors (Scotland) Act 1980 as amended ordered the Solicitors to charge no further fee and secondly, in terms of Section 42A(2)(d) of the Act ordered to pay to Mr Brown the sum of £1,000 in compensation.

The committee continued consideration of [Second Solicitor]'s conduct in respect of the allegation that he accepted a settlement without instructions.

1995

On 5th January 1995 (File 700) the Deputy Secretary responded to my letter dated 12th December 1994 (File 699-1-2-3):

Complaint against [Troubleshooter]

I thank you for your letter of 12th December 1994 and note what you write. I have asked your Troubleshooter to comment on the terms of your letter and in particular the further grounds of complaint, raised by yourself. Insofar as my letter of 25th April 1994 is concerned, at that time the letter was correct. I have noted the information on file to suggest that that letter is no longer correct, and that letter postdates those referred to by yourself. No 1 to 3 in the last page of your letter I will be in touch with you, when I hear further from your Troubleshooter.

On 2nd February 1995 (File 701) the Deputy Secretary followed up her previous letter with the following:

Complaint against [Troubleshooter]

I enclose herewith a copy of a letter, which I have received from your Troubleshooter. As his letter does not contain any new information and is simply a denial of the points of complaint from yourself I have asked him for the file of correspondence. Once I have that, I will be in a position to conclude my investigation.

On 3rd February 1995 (File 702) I wrote to the Deputy Secretary:

In response to my Troubleshooter's letter dated 16th January 1995, which you were kind enough to enclose with yours of 2nd February 1995, I don't feel there is any point at this time to comment on the total contents, as they will all be answered in due course, when you receive the [complete file] from the Troubleshooter.

If it is at all possible I would appreciate a copy of that file.

There is one point in the Troubleshooter's letter I would like to highlight at this time; i.e., the last paragraph, first page, subject: Legal Aid refusal.

I would appreciate your help by requesting my Troubleshooter to write to the Legal Aid Board, with a simple request asking why Legal Aid was refused. I am sure they will comply and give him the precise details why the refusal.

As it is standard practice when an application is received for increase in cover, and refused, the reason is not given.

It is also standard practice if the acting Solicitor request the concise details of that refusal, the Legal Aid Board comply with that request.

In the event that my Troubleshooter declines with this request, I would appreciate your further help in either the Law Society, if it's within the law to go direct to the board, or give me the authorization to write direct to the Legal Aid Board.

If I am correct, I understand that only the acting Solicitor can get this information.

I hope this matter can be expedited with the least possible delay.

On 14th February 1995 (File 703) the Deputy Secretary wrote to me regarding the complaint against [First Solicitor]:

I refer to previous correspondence and confirm that the matter will be put to the committee at its meeting in March and I hope to revert to you thereafter.

On 14th February 1995 (File 704) I also wrote to the Law Society on the same issue, following up on a telephone conversation I had had the previous week with the Deputy Secretary:

Further to our telecon of last week, regarding complaints against [First Solicitor] I would appreciate your cooperation on the format of the coming weeks or months regarding the complaints committee.

In the past it has been mentioned that if a Solicitor misleads a client, it is seriously considered by the Law Society and for this reason [in the event it was not in [First Solicitor]'s files] I enclose File numbers 113 and 116 for your consideration as misleading.

I would again, also bring your attention to File 184/185 (in your possession) which is very misleading, intimidating and to say the least very disturbing.

I have a very strong opinion of this letter and its contents.

As I have said to you in the past, this particular letter was placed through my mail box on a Saturday afternoon, hand-delivered...

...the contents of this letter is very misleading throughout...I am sure that any person reading File 184, with the prior knowledge of all previous correspondence relating to the indisputable evidence which was gathered from various sources and passed to [First Solicitor] without any reply or acknowledgement or confirmation that he had passed this evidence to [First Architect]'s Solicitors.

This can be confirmed by reading the correspondence between [First Solicitor] and [First Architect]'s Solicitor.

It is very nauseating for me to refer to the abovementioned letter, and when I go over the eight paragraphs in that letter which have detailed contradictions, already in your possession. I sincerely hope the Law Society will exercise all its powers and resources in getting to the crux of this particular devious letter.

I feel if I had been weak of mind and body, and succumbed to the intimidations in the said letter, at the time, I am sure I would have faced another £2,000 legal bill from [First Solicitor]. I thank you for your awareness of our problem.

On 17th February 1995 (File 705) the Deputy Secretary wrote as follows:

Complaint against [First Solicitor]

I refer to previous correspondence, which I have had with you and indeed discussions which we had by telephone.

I understand that on 16th February you spoke with another Deputy Secretary about the way this matter has been handled.

The position is that a report has now been received from the reporting member. The matter will therefore go to the committee in March for consideration.

I understand that you raised with the other Deputy Secretary the fact that in another complaint dealt with by another Deputy Secretary you have received a copy of the facts and circumstances before the matter went to the committee. This does not happen in every instance. In the case of your complaint against [First Solicitor] the matter at issue is one of professional conduct of the Solicitors and, in that situation it is not the Law Society's practice to send details of the facts and circumstances to both parties for comment before the committee considers the matter.

In your complaint against [Second Solicitor] the matter specifically at issue was the service provided and in that instance it was normal procedure to let you have the details of facts and circumstances for consideration. I have previously indicated I believe that the majority of matters raised by you occurred before January 1989 which was the first time that the Law Society could consider service issues.

I have discussed this matter with you at some length, over some considerable time, and you well know the reason that the investigation of your complaint has taken so long is the fact at one stage, you sought advice in relation to negligence. Indeed you received the assistance of the Law Society Troubleshooter in this connection.

The matter will go to the committee in March and depending on the committee's view you will then be advised as to the position.

I understand that you indicated to [the other Deputy Secretary] that you will be referring the matter to the ombudsman, and to your Member of Parliament. That is your prerogative.

However, I must point out to you that your complaint was lodged prior to 3rd June 1991, the date of creation of the office of the ombudsman. In that situation the ombudsman may not have jurisdiction to deal with your complaint, as his office was not in existence at the time it was made.

I understand that you indicated to my colleague that you did not wish this matter put to the committee in March. The position is quite clear. The investigation has been concluded, correspondence has been copied between yourselves and [First Solicitor] and the report has now been received from the reporter. The normal procedure following receipt of that report is for the matter to go to the committee and that is what is now happening.

If you do not wish the matter to go to the committee, then I would ask you to advise me in writing why you feel the committee should not consider the matter at this stage.

I would emphasise to you again that this is a complaint specifically involving a conduct matter. The appropriate procedures are being followed, which means in this case that the schedule containing the facts and circumstances are not copied by either party before the committee considers matters.

On 20th February 1995 (File 706) I responded to Deputy Secretary:

Thank you for your letter of 17th February 1995. The connotations in your letter have annoyed and upset me, to say the least.

May I remind you the difference between innocent and guilty and the object of this whole exercise.

If you are upset at the time this whole mess has taken, then you are only fractionally aware of the cost, in every term mentionable, to The Brown family.

Your last letter to me in my file, prior to your letter of 17th February 1995 is dated 18th October 1994, where you mentioned there would be a delay, longer than normal, from receiving a reply from your reporter but you would keep me informed.

I waited until mid-January 1995 before contacting you by phone for an update. I felt I had been more than patient waiting for a progress report, because of no further correspondence from yourself. If you recall our mid-January telecon it was mentioned you would write to the reporter to ask if he had completed his report.

The next correspondence I received from the Law Society regarding my complaints against [First Solicitor] was from your colleague Miss [Deputy Secretary] dated 14th February 1995, which surprised me as I had no knowledge of her involvement.

To make matters abundantly clear, regarding the telephone conversation between [her] and myself and the reason I called her was:

First to find out to whom I was to be corresponding with, in the future, regarding complaints against [First Solicitor]. It was clarified it would be her.

Second to inform her that I had just mailed a letter to you with enclosures, and who would be answering said letter. It was confirmed you would be answering. We continued the discussion in relation to the question I had asked in the letter to you, i.e. the format in future progress about the details going to the committee.

To make sure there is no more misunderstanding, my complaints against [Contractor] concluded in 1989 where we found that we had been seriously misled by [First Solicitor] throughout, and his correspondence immediately following that verified his unprofessional conduct, which has been highlighted in detail to the Law Society, through you Mr [Deputy Secretary] and you only.

In the last five years of exhaustive efforts to get some form of justice through the legal system and the people I turned to for help have let us down badly. It's because of this, in the event we have our lines crossed that I have asked for a copy of your personal investigations and conclusions, from all of the facts I have sent you, and the representations you sent to the reporter.

I am gravely concerned Mr [Deputy Secretary], because no one is infallible. Even you can make mistakes. Therefore I feel it would be a mistake for me not to have access to these representations before any judgement is passed relative to its contents.

I feel it would be in violation of my rights, because I cannot appeal the committee's decision.

You will recall my complaints and charges against [First Solicitor] are quite serious. If my request is refused then I am confirming here and now that the report should be put on hold, and not sent to the committee.

I would require written confirmation that my recent enclosures sent to you last week, and the enclosures I am sending you now, are included in the report that will eventually be sent to the full committee.

In reference to paragraph 5 of your letter, I disagree the presentations at issue included unprofessional conduct, apart from services provided. Paragraph 6, as you have decided to mention the assistance of a Law Society Troubleshooter I feel it requires a response.

All of the facts have been well documented in relation to my experience with the Troubleshooter, which is in the hands of the Law Society. If you recall in his statement to you, in one of his letters, that I wanted a writ issued against [First Solicitor] but confirmed I could not proceed with this action until the action against [First Architect] was concluded to verify my losses. You have previously been sent all of the details in relation to this, including the details why a writ was not issued against [First Solicitor].

From the above documented facts and after you have had the time to fully digest them, is it possible you could come up with the same answer I did, i.e. what the hell is going on?

You will now appreciate why the files are so big, and why I am so angry.

Do Solicitors corrupt the system or does the system corrupt Solicitors?

1)   [First Solicitor] conveniently delayed

2)   [Second Solicitor] conveniently delayed

3)   [Troubleshooter] conveniently delayed

The Brown family have been, and still are, very aware of what's been going on through the last 12 years. We don't need any intellectual to tell us who is guilty. We know the answer...

The letter continued for a further four pages! Is it possible that my readers will have seen the answer? After all, the Law Society had an incredible list of detail of corruption, lies, deceit, and evidence which I had submitted. In fact, with all these details, it would take only a child's intellect to find that [First Solicitor] was guilty of all the charges that had been listed.

On 24ᵗʰ February 1995 (File 707), the Deputy Secretary's reply duly arrived:

I thank you for your letter of 20ᵗʰ February 1995 addressed to myself together with the same letter, which you sent to my colleague Miss [Deputy Secretary].

I am sorry if my letter of 17ᵗʰ February has upset you in any way. The purpose of my letter was simply to set out the factual position as far as this office is concerned.

When I spoke with you in October and indeed when I wrote to you in October I believe that I made it quite clear that it would take the reporter some time to produce a report and indeed as I indicated to you in telephone conversations, subsequent to that I was in touch with the reporter who was in the process of considering the papers and producing the report. I accept that I said that I would keep you informed, but there was simply nothing to report until such time as the report was received.

With respect I do not think that your recollection of our mid-January telephone conversation is correct in that I indicated to you in that conversation that I had in fact spoken with the reporter in relation to the report.

I am sorry if the fact that both myself and my colleague have been dealing with this matter has caused you any difficulty.

I note from the second page of your letter, you are of the view that the conduct of [First Solicitor] was unprofessional. I note that you believe this has been accepted by [First Solicitor]. With respect that is a decision for the committee to reach. The role of both myself and my colleague in this matter is not to express a view.

The job, which we have undertaken, is to carry out and complete the investigation and obtain a report from a reporter from the committee in relation to that investigation. I should say further that even were you in a position to refer the matter to the ombudsman that would not, in effect, be an appeal. The ombudsman's role would be to consider whether the Law Society have handled the complaint in an appropriate manner. I accept however that your circumstances, because of the length of time which has passed, the ombudsman does not have jurisdiction in this matter.

In the circumstances, when the committee next meets therefore, I am prepared to ask them to agree on this occasion that both yourself and the Solicitors involved should have an opportunity of commenting upon the facts and circumstances as ascertained by the reporter, before a final decision in the matter is reached and, indeed I am prepared at the same time to ask the reporter to consider your subsequent correspondence to see if it is considered that it adds anything to the complaint which you have made.

I am aware that you have made complaints against both [Second Solicitor] and [Troubleshooter]. These are not matters which this investigation is dealing with.

It is not within the remit of this office to comment upon the question of negligence or whether prescription may apply or to advise you in that regard.

I trust that this clarifies matters, and I will confirm the committee's view in relation to the question of circulating the facts and circumstances once it has met in early March.

On 27th February 1995 (File 708) I responded to the Deputy Secretary:

Thank you for your correspondence of 24th instant to which the contents have been noted.

As I have indicated to you in past correspondence regarding [First Solicitor]'s inference of credibility between myself and [First Architect] and to whose evidence is most credible.

The question that now arises is the credibility of [First Solicitor] and in particular the action in regards the finances that were paid to him, in relation to both [Contractor] and [First Architect], details of which I passed to you in my most recent correspondence, except for one more item which is now enclosed, i.e. the building society account.

When all the financial details are correlated, you will find a balance of £4,000 plus interest that has to be accounted for. I find this to be quite alarming and concerning. My views have been fully addressed regarding the representations.

With reference to my prerogatives, which have previously been discussed, I will be exhausting every avenue that is open to me, not only in regards to [First Solicitor], but to all factions of the legal system.

I have never asked for any confrontations with the Law Society of Scotland. I don't need them. I have had enough with the three firms of Solicitors that were supposed to protect us.

On 3rd March 1995 (File 709) the Deputy Secretary wrote:

Complaint against your Troubleshooter

I thank you for your letter of 3rd February 1995. As you know I have been considering the complaint made by you against the above named. I have now passed the papers to a member of my committee for a report. When I receive the report, I will be in touch.

On 7th March 1995 (File 710) the Deputy Secretary also continued her correspondence with me regarding my complaint against [First Solicitor]:

I thank you for your letter of 27th February 1995 with enclosures. I can confirm that at its recent meeting the committee agreed in this particular instance that the matter be continued to enable the facts and circumstances of the report by the reporting member to be copied to both parties for their comments. This I will now do and look forward to hearing from you after which I will copy your recent correspondence to the reporter together with your comments before the matter goes again to the committee.

On 11th March (File 711) I replied to the Deputy Secretary, on the matter of my complaint against the Troubleshooter:

With reference to our telecon of last week please find enclosed the details, of our discussion regarding the Troubleshooter and the faculty of Advocates.

Further to our discussion, I mentioned in my letter to you dated 3rd February 1995 certain items I asked you for help in getting the answers.

Your answer to me dated 3rd March 1995 was to only tell me you had received my letter, period.

I would appreciate your help in getting these answers as soon as possible.

I will be interested to receive a copy of the report as mentioned in your letter of 3rd March.

And on 14th March 1995 (File 712) I wrote to the Deputy Secretary, this time in regard to my complaint against [First Solicitor]:

Thank you for your letter of 7th March 1995 and the copy of the report by the reporting member.

The contents of this report has, along with the tedious and ever demanding conflict with the legal profession, put tremendous pressure and strain on my health.

It would not be in my best interests to attempt to answer this report until my health improves, to give it the necessary attention that it requires.

From our telecon, of today's date, I have noted the date of the next committee meeting.

It was also agreed, that I should send my next correspondence with my full report to yourself with a copy to the Deputy Secretary.

It is now very clear, why Mr [Deputy Secretary] was so reluctant to send the report to me before going to the main committee. It has left serious doubts in my mind.

The Law Society's responses continued to come in, speed of response now having all the appearance of a cricketer playing a straight bat against uncomfortable spin bowling. Remember, lawyers thrive on the world of manipulative correspondence. This finds them in their element. On 21st

March 1995 (File 713) the Deputy Secretary replied to me regarding my complaint against the Troubleshooter:

> *I thank you for your letter of 11th March, and acknowledge receipt of the page from **The Legal System of Scotland, Cases and Materials, Third Edition**. I write to advise that I have investigated the matter, and have spoken with the author of the book. The book to which you refer was published in 1983 and is now out of date. The position is that no such an arrangement applies in relation to opinion from Counsel. I therefore cannot criticise your Troubleshooter for not having advised you of the system.*
>
> *In relation to your query about Legal Aid, as I have explained I do not have the file of correspondence in my possession at present, and will require to raise the matter with [Troubleshooter] when the file is returned to me.*

And on 28th March 1995 (File 714) the Deputy Secretary responded as follows regarding my complaint against [First Solicitor]:

> *I thank you for your letter of 14th March addressed to my colleague Miss [Deputy Secretary] and note that you feel that you are not in a position to respond at this stage to the terms of the report because of your health. I can understand this.*
>
> *If you are not able to reply quickly then the matter can certainly be held over for a future meeting.*
>
> *I have to say that I am a little concerned by the comment in your final paragraph in regard to my reluctance to send a copy of the report to you.*
>
> *As I have previously explained to you in correspondence, the matter being considered in relation to [First Solicitor] is a conduct matter. It is not the Law Society's normal practice in a*

conduct matter, to send the facts and circumstances contained in a report to the parties for comment. That does certainly happen in complaints where there is an allegation of an inadequate professional service, but as has previously been explained to you in this particular matter, the actings of [First Solicitor] occurred before the inception of that part of the Solicitors Scotland Act.

I can assure you that there was no desire on my part to be anything other than open and fair with you.

I look forward to hearing from you with your comments in due course.

On 21st April 1995 (File 715) the Deputy Secretary continued writing on the subject of the Troubleshooter:

As you know, I have been considering the terms of your complaint against [Troubleshooter] and attach hereto a copy of the report which I have received from the reporting member. The reporting member had access to the Solicitor's files in preparing his report.

You will note that the reporter is of the opinion that you were given an adequate professional service and that no further action is appropriate.

With regard to Legal Aid, the application which your Troubleshooter was making on your behalf, was for "legal advice and assistance" This is not a full application for Legal Aid, as a Legal Aid application relates to a Court action. The legal advice and assistance cover simply means that you are to obtain the opinion from Counsel if this is sanctioned and to obtain the necessary information to prove to the Legal Aid Board that you ought to be receiving Legal Aid to raise a Court action. In order to get Legal Aid you need to show the Legal Aid Board that you do have a good case in law. When the Legal Aid Board refused to increase the limit to which the Solicitor will be paid to obtain the necessary information to make an application, they do not give reasons. It is then for the Solicitor to establish from you whether you wish to appeal that, and if you do, then the Solicitor will write to the Legal Aid Board asking for reasons for refusal. I note your Troubleshooter declined to act for you before that stage was reached. I do not believe therefore it would be appropriate to ask the Troubleshooter to obtain the reasons from the Legal Aid Board as to why they refused the award of legal advice and assistance. It is however open to you to consult another Solicitor who can make a fresh application for legal advice and assistance and try to establish your case for Legal Aid.

In the circumstances, as the reporter has recommended that there has been no inadequate professional service, I intend to close my file at this time.

If you do not think that the Law Society has handled your complaint properly, you may write to the Scottish legal services ombudsman who is an independent person, not a lawyer, who is appointed by the Secretary of State for Scotland to examine the handling of complaints. The ombudsman may criticise the manner in which the Law Society has investigated and considered your complaint and can make recommendation about this to them, but the ombudsman does not have power to alter the decision.

On 1st June 1995 (File 716) the Deputy Secretary continued her correspondence regarding my complaint against [First Solicitor]:

I refer to your telephone conversation with me on 26th May 1995 in which you advised me the reason that you had not replied to Mr [Deputy Secretary]'s letter of 28th March was that you were similarly awaiting [First Solicitor]'s reaction to your letters of 20th and 27th February in particular with regard to the allegations that the sum of £4,000 still required to be accounted for. Once I have [First Solicitor]'s final comments I will send you a copy so that you can respond to Mr [Deputy Secretary]'s previous letter.

Three weeks later (23rd June 1995, File 717) the Deputy Secretary followed this with:

> *I refer to my telephone conversation with you on 21st June and as requested now enclose copy of a letter from [First Solicitor] dated 16th June. I look forward to hearing from you to confirm which particular points you wish raised with [First Solicitor] again.*

On 18th July 1995 (File 718) I summoned up my limited resources and composed the following response:

> *I write further to our telephone conversation of last week regarding my waiting for an answer to my correspondence relating to the £4,000 discrepancies between [First Solicitor] and Mr and Mrs Brown, and the Law Society's waiting for an answer to the reporting member's facts and circumstances, which you attached to your letter dated 7th March 1995.*
>
> *From the resulting telephone conversation, it was agreed that you would further investigate the £4,000 discrepancies, because of the poor response from [First Solicitor], which you were good enough to send to me.*
>
> *I in turn was to complete my investigation regarding the reporting member's facts and circumstances report.*
>
> *Once again I have correlated all the information required to give you the answer to that report.*
>
> *In the first instance I have sectioned off the report paragraph by paragraph and answered them accordingly.*
>
> *In the second instance I have compiled all the relevant and pertinent information along with the concrete evidence in a red folder, which has been sectioned off, and the details itemised for ease of clarification.*

To help and aid the Law Society to identify with ease all the facts and circumstances relating to not just a single incidence of incompetence, negligence, unrealistic and avoidable delays, but an appalling catalogue of wholly unacceptable, unprofessional criminal actions by a firm of Solicitors.

[First Solicitor] has elected, through this entire action, to protect [First Architect] rather than his own clients.

As you will see by all the documentation in the Law Society's files, and the red folder enclosed he, i.e. [First Solicitor], continued to accept monies from Mr and Mrs Brown under false pretences for [First Architect]'s case with no intention of honestly taking [First Architect] to Court, as you will see from the documentation.

As late as 1990/91 [First Solicitor] corresponded with the Law Society, still protecting [First Architect]. He stated that [First Architect] was correct in choosing a particular contractor. I should have, according to [First Solicitor], chosen the cheapest contractor i.e. £7,500. I suggest the reporting member has access to this letter.

Again what [First Solicitor] failed to understand, or again he was protecting [First Architect] by ignoring the fact, irrespective who the contractor was on the job, does not detract from the catalogue of errors created by [First Architect]:

1) Unauthorised works.

2) Enforcement order.

3) Refusal of Planning Department to issue a Completion Certificate.

4) Adding an additional £4,000 to the contract without advising Mr and Mrs Brown and outwith the contract drawings.

5) Refusing to extend the contract time because of the additions, putting pressure on [Contractor] because of the liquidated damages clause.

I would ask the Law Society, in the interests of true justice pay particular attention to how [First Solicitor] protected Mr and Mrs Brown's interests in the case against [Contractor], and the so-called protective writ as stated by the reporting member.

I bring your attention to the contents of this writ, File Nos 150/151, which includes supervision.

Mr and Mrs Brown were never advised of this writ, or its contents. This writ was issued two months prior to [Contractor]'s Court hearing. It was most vital if this so-called "protective writ" was going to be actioned at a later date that the Sheriff in the case against [Contractor] "finds in fact" that [First Architect] was found to be supervising.

The details in the red folder clearly defines the opposite. The so-called protective writ was obsolete and non-protective.

You will find as you progress through the files, complete gross negligence on the part of [First Solicitor], and how they have handled our affairs throughout.

I sincerely hope the Law Society will give our circumstances, and the information supplied, a complete and full investigation, and advise us accordingly before any decision is taken by the committee, and give us the answers to the many questions that to date have never been answered.

*We have been the innocent victims throughout both in [Contractor]'s case and [First Architect]'s case. Due to complete negligence, we have had to pay Court costs. **Is this justice?***

I would like the Law Society, I hope, in their full investigation before the meeting of the full committee, to look into the hand-delivered File No 184 and its contents, which have been well documented.

As stated before, I have very strong views on this letter, and the gross intimidations contained in this letter. I would appreciate an early response to both letters and the red folder.

On 7th August 1995 (File 719) I received my reply:

> *I refer to previous correspondence, and our telephone conversation on 1st August, and write to acknowledge receipt of your file together with your accompanying letter of 18th July 1995. I must apologise that at the outset of our telephone discussion I did not know your letter of 18th July and your file had been received. Clearly that did get our conversation on the wrong foot. For that I must apologise.*
>
> *I would confirm that I am quite prepared to meet with you to go over the facts and circumstances and your comments on the various questions which you seem to be raising. I am however only prepared to do this in the context of the complaint about [First Solicitor]'s conduct and will not comment specifically in relation to his actings, which may form part of his professional judgement and might more properly be considered in relation to possible negligence. I understand fully your concerns about what you see as £4,000 discrepancies and before I meet with you I propose to obtain from [First Solicitor] copies of their ledger card in relation to dealings with you so that these are available for consideration when we meet. As I indicated to you I am prepared to meet with you during the course of August but I cannot thereafter promise that the matter will be immediately concluded given other commitments which I presently have.*
>
> *At the present time the only dates which I would be available to meet with you would be during the week commencing 21st August on either Tuesday, Wednesday or Thursday afternoon. If these dates are inconvenient I would be happy to meet with you in September, but I simply cannot commit myself at this stage on any other dates during August. If you would care to telephone me on receipt of this letter I would be happy to try and arrange matters with you.*

I phoned the Deputy Secretary as soon as I received the above letter, arranging to visit his offices on Tuesday 22nd August 1995 at 2.15pm. In a letter dated 15th August 1995 (File 720) he confirmed our appointment and added:

> *In order to aid our discussions I attach for your information a copy of a further letter I have received from [First Solicitor] together with their various ledger cards.*
>
> *As you will see they are of the view that they have properly accounted to you for various sums of money.*
>
> *Perhaps you would care to consider their ledger cards and comments so that we may discuss this aspect of the matter when we meet.*

At this point I would like to thank my readers for ploughing through a mass of correspondence between the legal profession and myself, and apologise for subjecting you all to what may appear mind-numbing details. Please bear with me and understand the point I am endeavouring to make:

As a trained mechanical engineer, the concept of the legal profession, and how the legal system works in regards to complaints against solicitors, had been completely foreign to me. It had never occurred to me, and I had never been given a reason to believe or even suspect, that in this beautiful country of ours we harboured a profession that used guile, cunning, and fraudulent, illicit tactics, all within the protective embrace of a supportive system in Scotland – namely self-regulation. Within the comfort of this system we find enshrined every faction of the legal profession, including members of the public working in conjunction with the profession and who can easily be influenced to concur with their way of thinking. Small wonder therefore that they find little difficulty in getting rid of genuine complainants/complainers!

Bear in mind that anyone who is absorbed within this crooked self-regulated profession becomes what I term an "enshrined unfortunate".

They have no choice but to accept the state of affairs in which they find themselves, for how else could they continue to practise law? And once a state of affairs exists for long enough, how easy it becomes for a mind to be won over and accept that a state of affairs is even desirable? It happens all the time. Look around at the world. Like hostages in a kidnapping, the victim is soon empathising with the persecutor. It is called the "Stockholm Syndrome". How much easier can this principle apply in more innocuous, if no less insidious situations such as a profession holding sway over its own kind? Self-regulation is a form of dictatorship, whereby lack of ultimate accountability results in poor standards and even harm to those who seek redress. It eats away at our very culture, undermining so much of what we are proud to call our British way and our sense of fair play.

So what happens? Lawyers become automatons, losing sight of their ultimate purpose. The system becomes everything, and ordinary people shrivel into inconsequential units of monetary gain. Time ceases to matter. One must just accept that the process is tortuous and draining, at least for the victims – the ordinary decent folk who seek justice. As for the others – the lawyers? All you have to do is watch the legal eagles in Court, in their offices and in their lives. They live without inspiration. Their work is gut-wrenchingly repetitive. Their world of multiple correspondences must bore them to tears. Where does their inspiration come from? It is hard to see, beyond the lucrative nature of the work. Could I suggest that some pleasure has to be derived from destroying people's lives? From growing fat on the bones of human misery? From manipulating out of existence the irritation of complainers/ complainants? From collecting their annual bonus from the holders of the master policy? And of course we can never fail to mention their extortionate fees.

All my beliefs about the legal profession had been to hold lawyers in the highest esteem. That was until 1982/3 when the Brown family had the dream of building and increasing their business for a brighter future.

Those hopes and dreams had been shattered. But what makes this state of affairs utterly unacceptable is that I was not the unfortunate exception. Thousands of others in Scotland, and many, so many more thousands in England find themselves going through a similar hellish experience.

Returning now to my latest correspondence. The onus was on the Law Society. Since 1990 I had been in continuous contact with this same Deputy Secretary. At last I had been granted a meeting in Edinburgh, at the office of the Law Society, hoping to personally air all my grievances with this same Deputy Secretary.

The past five years of correspondence had only served to annoy and upset me as I became ever more aware of how the insidious system of self-regulation worked towards a single end – to protect incompetent solicitors. Now I was coming to the point where the Law Society would be making their final decisions in response to my complaints against [First Solicitor], [Second Solicitor] and my Troubleshooter. It would be interesting to see if they upheld my detailed complaints against them. I'm sure my readers know what is coming!

But first, here is some information about the complaints process. The Law Society requires that, before any decisions are considered by the complaints committee all correspondence, from both the complainer/client and the solicitor who is complained against, is collected by the Deputy Secretary's office. It is collated before being passed on to what the Law Society call their "Reporter". This person could either be a lay person or a solicitor. He/she assesses the information/evidence gathered and prepares the finished report which is eventually presented to the complaints committee.

As mentioned in previous correspondence I had objected strongly to this process, the reason being that the person making the final report had in front of him, **supposedly**, all the correspondence and concrete evidence. Yet there I was placing all my trust in an unseen stranger – most probably a solicitor – who himself has only been able to work with screened, and possibly highly selective, information. That is why I had insisted on seeing the report which he had produced and which would form the basis of the brief placed before the committee. My readers will recall that the Deputy Secretary had, very reluctantly, acceded to this request. He had had a rethink and sent to both [First Solicitor] and myself copies of the report.

One final significant update for my readers: when I asked the Law Society for the name of the Reporter, and information as to his status – solicitor or lay person, I got the answer I expected, namely that the information would not be forthcoming.

I was now looking forward to my meeting in Edinburgh, when I hoped to get all of my questions answered. The Deputy Secretary, after making changes to the date of the meeting, finally set it up for 5th September in Edinburgh at the offices of the Law Society at 2.15pm.

At the appointed time, the Deputy Secretary started the meeting by thanking me for coming down and mentioned that the purpose of the meeting was to discuss my complaints against [First Solicitor]. He then said that he had in his possession the red folder which I had sent down with a number of documents. He confirmed that I also held a copy of the same folder.

I was now streetwise. I realised that, after years of fruitless correspondence with members of his profession, and also often attending meetings at which no notes had ever been taken, it was possible that different versions of this meeting could very well be on the cards, depending on whose perspective was being sought. So I obtained permission to tape-record our meeting.

Here is the transcript of the salient points of our meeting. I have placed my words in bold text, leaving plain text to reflect the Deputy Secretary's own words:

The purpose of this afternoon's meeting is that I want to talk to you about one or two aspects of your complaint. I think I should say to you quite clearly at this stage that the purpose of this meeting is really an information-gathering one. There are certain points which I feel I have to put across to you, and I am also interested to hear certain things which you have to say. Once this has been done and the interview has been noted, the papers will all go back to the reporting member who has previously looked at this matter, including the files from [First Solicitor]. The reporter will then produce in effect a final report which will go to the complaints committee. Now, in reality that report will not go to the committee in September as the time scale is too short. It may go in October, depending on whether the reporter has had an opportunity to consider the comments you wish to make, and produce the report by that time or, at worst, it may be November. I cannot give you a more definite time scale simply because much depends on what is discussed today and the fact the reporter will obviously need to look at this red file documentation which you have provided. And, to be fair to the reporter, I am sure you will understand that will take time.

The difficulty is, we like to say that reports and complaints will be completed within a month; in reality, in a simple and straightforward one that can be dealt with. But where the reporter is having to look at a number of files, for example, and various evidence, it is something that can take longer. I wouldn't want to say to you that, indeed, we've been through this at an earlier stage and you would agree, that your reporter is going to produce the report within three weeks, four weeks, or five weeks. What I can say to you is that the reporter will do the best he can to produce the report as quickly as he can. I can't be any more definite than that and I hope you will take it on board.

What I would like to do, with your permission, is to go to what is described as Section 6 in your red folder, at the start of the folder, starting with page 569 and headed "Questions Regarding [First Solicitor]'s Negligence".

I would like to start there because you raise some 27 questions in regard to matters and I think it's quite important at this stage that I make clear to you exactly what the Law Society's role in this matter is, in regard, in particular, to a number of these questions which you have asked because they seem to me to be very much central to the concerns which you are expressing.

You headed it up "Questions Regarding [First Solicitor]'s Negligence". I hope you would agree that, at an early stage of the complaint, given the concerns you had about alleged negligence, you were provided with a Troubleshooter.

Now I am aware that obviously things with the Troubleshooter did not work out and I think I am correct in saying that you made a separate complaint in that regard.

Yes, that's right.

Note: This was my first opportunity to utter a single word! It must appear to any of my readers that this opening speech, its length and the time it took, could only give the impression that the man was nervous. Could this be because he feared what was to come, particularly the questions that he knew I would be putting to him?

I don't want to discuss with you what the Troubleshooter said or not said. That is a separate matter. But what I do want to talk to you about initially is the question of what the Law Society's remit in this matter is, and in particular the fact that where you are raising questions in regard to what you call negligence, those are not necessarily matters which is a complaint in relation to a Solicitor's conduct the Law Society will specifically look at. Now there is a reason for that. The reason for that is basically two-fold. Firstly, when the Solicitor acting for you will give you, for example, certain advice; you may or may not agree with that advice. Thereafter, whatever happens, you instruct the Solicitors.

Now when we look at the Solicitor's professional code of conduct, then we are not necessarily looking at the sort of quality of advice that you have possibly been given. We are not looking at "did the Solicitor choose the right road to take? Have they taken the wrong road? Should they have done it a different way?" If that is your concern, and clearly in some of these questions it is, you are asking why they did or didn't do certain things. Now, in my view, that is a question which will require to be dealt with in an Action of Negligence because, at the end of day, in an action of negligence a Court would require to decide whether or not the Solicitor acted in a way a normally competent Solicitor would do.

Now that is, I appreciate, having read through your file of various correspondence over a long period of time, a matter which has been of considerable concern to you. Because I know you feel that [First Solicitor] have not looked after your best interests, they have not pressed for example in [First Architect]'s matter, pressed home as they might have done to your advantage. But at the end of the day, the way they have chosen, if you like, to run the case would be a matter for a negligence action. It is not a matter which impinges on the Solicitor's professional conduct as such. So obviously I hope you will understand, I accept you may not accept but you will understand, there are a number of issues within here and specific questions as to how they ran and raised the Court case which will not formally be considered by us. However, within that, there are certain elements which undoubtedly do fall to be considered by us and which has been well canvassed within your correspondence.

These relate, for example, to their failure to properly communicate with you. Now when you have a client relationship, that relationship is clearly founded on communication. It has to be founded on the idea of a Solicitor pursuing matters for you, advising you, taking your instructions and advising you for example what the other side are saying.

Now, as I have already said, what is actually within those communications, the advice which is given, the instructions which follow and the action which may or may not be taken, are outwith what we may look at. But the question of communication is something which we can look at, not as I say in relation to the actual advice but into whether communication took place or not, and whether for example the Solicitor did certain things, or as you suggest sought to do certain things, without, for example, coming back to you when you feel they might have done so, even if it was only a copy letter. That is something we can look at, if it falls into the area of a Solicitor's professional conduct and, as I explained to you and I know from our conversations, you understand that because of the timing of this matter, we have not been in a position whereby we can make any financial reward to you. So far as the Law Society's inadequate professional services are concerned, the power to award compensation only came on 3rd June 1991. Now, by that time, [First Solicitor], had long ceased acting for you, and the power which came in on 3rd June 1991 is not retrospective. It means we cannot apply to events which took place before that time.

Therefore, regrettably, what we are going to be looking at here is to consider whether the Solicitor has acted either unprofessionally or has acted in such a way that it might constitute professional misconduct. What that basically means is that, at the end of the day, if your complaint is upheld there would be a disciplinary finding. Now I think I would be right in saying that in many ways, whilst you have always wanted in this pattern to pursue justice, you have always pursued it on a point of principle. You feel that the Solicitors didn't serve your interests properly and you are entitled to see that recognised. What I am saying to you is that, if your complaint is upheld, that may well be recognised. The problem is it will not have any financial benefit to you.

Now I know I have spoken to you on the telephone about that and I think you understand it, but I think however it is worthwhile putting it on record.

What you have recently done is raise with me the question of certain accountings which [First Solicitor] produced and you have made an allegation that they have not accounted to you properly. Since you made that allegation you should have received further correspondence from me with the copy of their ledger accounts. I think I am right in saying, so far as that issue is concerned, clearly we would have concern at the suggestion that a Solicitor had disappeared with money belonging to a client. The position with [First Solicitor] seems to be that when you went to [Second Solicitor] who was your next Solicitor, when they handed over the papers etc, they provided him with a full accounting. Now I know you also made a complaint against [Second Solicitor]. I do not know whether the question of the accounting formed part of that complaint or whether after the accounting was given to [Second Solicitor] you ever raised with him the question that you thought that all that should have been there was not there. Did you raise that with him?

Well the accounting I received from [Second Solicitor] was not the accounting that you sent me. The accounting you sent me is the very first accounting I ever had from [First Solicitor] regarding all the details of the case against [Contractor] and the monies paid to Court.

That's an error right now, of [First Solicitor]'s communication with Mr and Mrs Brown. He never let me see that...

Well, with respect I am not prepared to go that far...

No...

I must state that their position clearly is that they passed papers over to [Second Solicitor], as they would have been required to....

May I just interject here? First of all let us say the date is 5ᵗʰ September, right? Meeting set up at 2.15 at Drumsheugh Gardens?

Yes.

In respect to the papers passed to [Second Solicitor] from [First Solicitor], these papers were passed as far as I am concerned, as a result of being picked up by my daughter.

I already, in correspondence, informed you that this is exactly what happened. The girl in [First Solicitor]'s office copied everything. The file was never in the hands of my daughter. It never left the Solicitor's office – that's very important. It's very important to us, as far as we are concerned. After copying, the girl replaced the file and my daughter left the office.

So you are saying basically that what your daughter got was a complete file which was a copy of the original.

Yes!

Right! What I would say to you, Mr Brown, is that I think in addition after those files were delivered there was correspondence between both [First and Second Solicitors].

Yes. I asked for details from you as I couldn't get them. I paid all the fees to both Solicitors but I still couldn't get the information I paid for. This I cannot understand. As I have said to you on many occasions in our correspondence, secrecy creates illegality. Now, if I pay a Solicitor to act for me, I expect every piece of correspondence to be handed to me.

Let me say to you first, in that respect, if you go to a Solicitor and pay the Solicitor's fee, the Solicitor should certainly hand the file over to you, but not the whole file is your property, and there is an opinion which the Law Society have taken in 1982, which indicates that such things as notes of telephone calls, internal memorandum, and notes of meetings remain the property of the Solicitor.

Why?

In terms of the law, that is the opinion of Counsel and in that situation the Solicitor is entitled to retain these.

I honestly can't believe you are telling me what you are telling me. Is that decided by the Law Society Committee?

No, that bit is decided by...

No it is decided by...?

Opinion was sought from Counsel, that is an Advocate at Parliament House, in regards to what is the Solicitor's property and what was his client's property in a file held by Solicitor for a client.

Now, not to waste too much time on this point as it is irrelevant at this moment, but I would say a Solicitor acting for a client at any given time, whether it be a phone call, a letter, a discussion in an office, if it's relevant to that client then that information should be passed to that client. There is no two ways about it...

That is the view you take. I take your point. Can I just simply say that this view is taken that it is open to, for example, you, as for you here today after a telephone call with your own Solicitor, you would be entitled to keep your own notes. It's arguable if it was a meeting, or a note of a telephone call, it would be just an aide memoire as to what took place, and it is open to both sides in that situation. I merely say that to you, so that you are aware of the position. Can I also make it clear at this stage, from the point of view of the recording that you are taping, that I will certainly undertake to check the files that I have from [Second Solicitor] over the question of the accounting that you have never had. I am happy to do that as it does occur to me that it is a matter that clearly does require clarification. Not that we are going to say whether the accounting is right or wrong but I do accept that you should have had that, and I can't say at this stage why you haven't. I am quite happy to make investigations into that for you.

Thank you.

Moving on. If we could go to Section 1 of your folder, you have taken the report from the reporter and produced a schedule setting out what you regard as factual inaccuracies. Now, can I say in regard to this, I would ask you to bear in mind the comments which I made earlier in regard to precisely what the Law Society is going to look at and not look at. The reason that I say that is two-fold. Firstly, it is entirely clear from your correspondence that you felt there were certain actings or non-actings on your behalf from [First Solicitor] and which have prejudiced you, and as I have explained already that is something which falls outwith what we can look at, and which falls properly, if you like, within the pocket of negligence.

The fact of the circumstances and the statement of schedule, which has been put together by the reporter, sets out facts and circumstances gleaned from the correspondence and the files that are available. That includes all of your correspondence, also the Solicitor's and their files, and we give both yourself and the Solicitor the opportunity to comment. Clearly, you have now produced this, which the reporter will of course see and have the opportunity of considering and, on the basis of that, it is entirely possible that the reporter may amend the schedule of facts and circumstances. But I can't say whether the reporter will or not, as he will have to take into account and consider paperwork previously considered. But what I can say to you is that the schedule of facts and circumstances, and your comments on its accuracy and your concerns, will certainly be considered, and that is something which I am sure you will understand is left to the reporter because it is not myself that produced that schedule, and this is a fact that is one of the things which is very important to point out, as in the roles of myself and the other Deputy Secretary, which if she was here in this matter, are, if you like, as information gatherers, pulling things together.

At the end of the day it is not my decision as to what happens. It is the decision in this case of the reporter and his reports and the complaints committee. The committee will make a decision, which is under the auspices of the Council of the Law Society, which is the Law Society's Government Body. A complaints committee is made up from both lay people and qualified Solicitors. In addition to the actual schedule and comments and other correspondence, if the reporter thinks it appropriate, these will be put forward before the committee for consideration.

Does the reporter consider all the facts irrespective of the dates of the facts? Does he take into account all the facts in these files?

Well, the position is that the reporter looks at the heads of complaint, which are set out in the schedule....

As I notice in the schedule he goes back to 1982.

Yes, well the reason the reporter does that of course is whilst the original complaint against [First Solicitor] started at a later date, you will agree that when everything set off, everything appeared to be satisfactory, but the reason he does that is so both you and the Solicitors and the committee when they look at it, have a full picture.

Ok, so then I can just say then that in my case, he will have access to my summary of events.

Yes. Can I just confirm with you, the summary of events which you have set out, I think in your red folder, section 7, page 555 on the copy which I have.

Yes. Will he have access to that?

Yes. And I will be honest and say to you that I think that it is an extremely helpful summary, and I think it is perhaps unfortunate that the form it is in wasn't available earlier.

> *It was! I can give you the date it was sent to you. It was a long*
> *time back. All of the above was sent on 5th April 1993, including*
> *555.*

> *Let me have a look. 5th April 1993. Now, I think with respect what*
> *may have happened here...yes 555...that comes with your letter*
> *received on 7th April (1993) here.*

> *That's always been on the file, OK? He will have access to all*
> *of that?*

> *Yes. He will have access to all of that. Let me check, just for*
> *the record, as far as that was concerned there, it was on the*
> *file. What, however, I propose to do, and I consider it entirely*
> *reasonable for me to do, is to draw the reporter's attention*
> *specifically to that, and ask the reporter to actually look at*
> *that.*

Note: For my readers, I must now point out that the legal profession
makes use of the term "negligence". You will already have seen that
this has been a cause of some confusion in the past. So let me now,
instead, use the word "incompetence" to describe the efficiency of
the Law Society in its ability to handle complaints. For here we
have proof of them at first denying the existence of a vital 17-page
document – *Summary of Events* (File 555-571) – that I had given to
them some three years previously and which the Deputy Secretary
now acknowledged, somewhat shamefacedly, to have found in his red
folder – the very same folder that he agreed at the start of the meeting
was in the possession of both of us. Small wonder that I should lack
confidence in the ability of the Law Society to effectively brief the
Reporter!

> *Now can I just say something whilst it is on my mind. We have*
> *been talking about negligence quite a number of times.*

> *Yes.*

I have looked up negligence quite a number of times. I have looked up negligence in a number of dictionaries and it comes across here from the dictionary as "lack of proper care and attention".

Yes.

And it also means carelessness.

Yes, that is negligence in the form of English – but the legal definition of negligence is slightly different…

OK?

When it comes to Solicitors' actings, if you are to prove that there is negligence on the part of the Solicitor, you basically have to prove that he deals with the matter, in simple terms, in the way that a reasonably competent Solicitor would not have dealt with it. I think that may be slightly confusing. If I can perhaps explain it in a slightly different way – the test of the duty of care is that your Solicitor acts in a reasonably competent fashion. Now in a case, the actual test to be applied is that competence of care may be: if you are to pursue something like a negligence case then, under normal circumstances, it may be that you need to get an opinion from someone, say an Advocate, in relation as to whether the Solicitor had acted in a reasonably competent manner. But the difficulty insofar as our discussion as to the Law Society's consideration of your complaint is considered, is that it is a matter over which the Law Society has no jurisdiction.

Note: The man was clearly rambling. My questions seemed to unsettle him!

I was making the point that negligence is lack of care and attention, and carelessness. That is what we are going over here, as well – not negligence, we are talking of lack of care and attention.

Yes. But…

But as far as the Law Society is concerned negligence is different. OK?

What I would say to you is this, that until January 1989 the Law Society's function was to solely consider a Solicitor's professional conduct and, at that stage, the concept of an inadequate professional service is what might be described as shoddy, careless work. The difficulty is, that it is an entirely separate matter, if you follow me, from a Solicitor's professional conduct. A Solicitor could be, for example, careless by not providing you with an adequate service. That does not necessarily mean that they have acted unprofessionally or that they are guilty of professional misconduct.

What about misleading a client?

Misleading a client is certainly a matter of professional conduct.

Right. What about delays of a year and four months?

That may or may not amount to unprofessional conduct or misconduct.

OK. What about suppression of evidence?

Could you explain to me what you mean by "suppression of evidence"?

At [Contractor]'s Court case, [First Solicitor] was fully aware that [First Architect] was paid to supervise the contracts throughout from day one.

Yes?

He had issued a writ to that effect. [First Architect] was paid and in [Contractor]'s Court case it was judged by the Sheriff that [First Architect] was not supervising. Now the evidence was in the hands of my Solicitor acting for me in that Court case.

Now the answer to that, I understand what you mean by suppression of evidence. The Law Society when looking at a complaint will not look at what takes place in the Court, and the reason for that is that when a Solicitor is presenting a Court case, whether it be a criminal matter or a civil matter, the Solicitor is entitled to look at the way the case is going and to consider the evidence which is available to them and to decide how, when, or indeed if, he reviews to bring forward that evidence. It is a matter of the Solicitor's professional judgement. If a Solicitor errs so badly, that he is unwilling to bring forward a piece of evidence, that might amount to negligence.

What if he has evidence and already issues a writ with the information that he was supervising? And he knows full well the importance of the Sheriff judging that [First Architect] is supervising. It is very important that this Sheriff particularly does judge that he was supervising, because when they go to Court against the Architect on the writ written two months before the Court case, it is important that has been judged that he has been supervising because the writ would be useless.

I could not, Mr Brown, go so far as to say, as for example, that the Solicitor acting in that way would be guilty of professional misconduct.

I can say he was.

Oh yes, you can say he was. But what I am saying to you, and I want to make it quite clear what I am saying to you, is that the Law Society when considering any complaint, will not consider anything that took place within the Courtroom.

But you will look at suppression of evidence?

With respect, you are saying here that what took place in the contractor's case was that [First Solicitor] who was not willing or did not bring forward the evidence that [First Architect] was the supervising party, with respect, whether or not that evidence was in [First Solicitor]'s view appropriate and relevant to the case, is a matter for his professional judgement and not a matter which we can be adjudicating on. It is a matter of judgement. As I have said to you, the only way that matter could be challenged possibly would be if there was an argument in the negligence case, which we have already previously discussed.

But if he suppressed that evidence for reason unbeknown to me, or his other reasons whatever they might be ...

If I can interrupt for just a second, Mr Brown, the fact of the matter is, when you have given a Solicitor a list of instructions to pursue a Court case, that Solicitor is entitled, in pursuing that case in Court, to use their judgement precisely in how they run that case, the evidence they lead, the witnesses they bring in, the questions they ask.

May I say that in the instruction I gave to Court, I did not want, I did not need, [First Architect] as a witness. I didn't need him.

As I say, that is not your decision.

With respect, the lawyer must listen to the client.

With respect, the Solicitor is certainly to listen to the client. I entirely agree with that. But if the client instructs the Solicitor to pursue the Court case, the Solicitor has to be entitled to use his professional judgement in the way he progresses it for his client's best interests. Now you may well have been of the view, for example, [First Architect] was not a witness you would have wished called. [First Solicitor] is entitled to listen to you saying that and to consider that, but if he is of the view that in fact [First Architect] could help your case, in my view he is entitled to use his judgement and to call [First Architect] as a witness.

OK – I'm not accepting that. What I want to say now is another Solicitor has stated that it was important that the Sheriff judged that [First Architect] was supervising and he was amazed, and this is in writing, he was amazed that that happened.

Can I just say to you at this point that this emphasises what I just previously said to you, which is that if a Solicitor does not fulfil their duty of care and act in a reasonably competent manner, then that may be something which may amount, and I have to use the word **may**...

You are coming back to negligence.

Yes.

I know you are coming back to negligence which cannot be discussed here.

Yes.

I know what you are going to tell me again. Yes, I understand that. But now I am going to show you a letter from RIBA where [First Architect] (it's not in your files) but [First Architect] clearly stated that he was amazed that he was being used as a witness. The architect himself! Now, to bear up my facts against [First Solicitor] for his poor service, not listening to his client, lack of communication, after being paid £2,000 to act for me, ahead of time, which was never used. Now, if [First Architect] states himself that he was quite taken aback to be used as a witness...

Well, the difficulty I have with that is [First Architect] may well have been taken aback to have been used as a witness...

To be sued afterwards...

But that was a matter for [First Solicitor]'s judgement.

Now, if I go to any Solicitor today and I would like him to sue an architect, he is going to say to me – Mr Brown, it's very important but we need him right now even though we are going to sue him later on – then I would say the Architect's not going to be in my favour if I'm going to be suing him so I don't want to use him. I would tell my Solicitor that if I'm suing my architect, then there is no way he is going to help me if I'm going to sue him. He would be detrimental to my case.

Well, can I simply say before you go on, I entirely understand what you are saying and the logic of what you are saying so far.

Right, OK. It was very important on the same case that he found to be supervising because the amount of information that was to be passed to [First Solicitor] from various people, number one – the building and Planning Department, number two – [Second Architect], number three – myself. That's three different people passed concrete evidence, and evidence from [First Architect] himself, that he was paid to supervise from day one. Now they knew this from the day we signed the contract in [First Solicitor]'s office, that [First Architect] was paid to supervise because the most important thing in this complete project was to get the Completion Certificate to enter back into the house.

Well, I can understand that.

Now, that is understandable from everyone's point of view. So you sit in the lawyer's office, [Contractor], [First Architect] and yourself, and all the papers are signed, and it is understood he is the supervising architect, he is the contractor – you will build this contract which is a conversion and an extension, you will build this according to these drawings. Now, if there are any changes to these drawings, the RIBA book of – I forget the name right now – the book of contract, clearly states the Architect supervising officer to stage 'H' where he must, if there are any changes, get changes to these drawings, the RIBA book of – I forget the name right now – the book of contract, clearly states the Architect supervising officer to stage 'H' where he must, if there are any changes, get quotations, must inform their clients and give the contractor time, if there are big enough changes. No 1 – [First Architect] did not inform Mr And Mrs Brown of the changes, he added £4,000 to the contract, he built a conversion and was about to do an extension outwith these contract drawings. Now, all this information was passed to [First Solicitor]. Now, this case could have been a simple case of getting [Contractor] and [First Architect] back on the job and finished it at the same contract price – around about that price. That's when my Solicitor should have acted on my instructions, but he chose to take another road.

Well, that brings us back, with respect, Mr Brown, to the point I made in the very early stage of our discussion this afternoon, which is the remit of the Law Society and the question of negligence. I know we have been through this and I know you understand precisely what I am saying. I have no difficulty with that, but I think I am sorry to bring it up again, but the bottom line is the Law Society cannot within its complaints procedure judge the merits or otherwise of your case, either against [Contractor] or against [First Architect]. Nor can we specifically comment upon the way in which [First Solicitor] has chosen to pursue matters for you using his judgement and I simply say that now – and again, I know you understand negligence, but I think I must make it quite clear to you what you are saying to me seems at least to fall into that category, and that gives me a problem in relation as to how to deal with it. Can I just also add – What I would like to do, with your permission, is that once I get a copy of your tape recording from this, it does seem to me appropriate that it should go to the reporter, because I think it would be useful for the reporter to hear exactly what you have to say and where you are coming from. If you have no objection to that, I think it would be helpful too.

> *I have no objections at all. I have nothing to hide, Mr [Deputy Secretary]. I never have.*
>
> *But it would have been wrong of me to give it to the reporter without your permission. I am sure you understand.*

Tape turned over.

End of discussion on side one, which was simply in regard to noting Section 1 of Mr Brown's files in relation to the schedule by the Reporter for Mr Brown's comments to be considered by the Reporter.

> *In the interim I have simply confirmed to Mr Brown that I have no objection at all to the tape recording of the meeting, the only rider being that the recording is used for Mr Brown's purposes and my purposes. Indeed I think it is appropriate for the reporter to hear what has been said and Mr Brown has agreed to that.*
>
> *Moving on. In the red folder, Section 2, this has a section with heading "Formal complaint regarding the professional incompetence of [First Architect]" that I think might be interesting from the point of view of the background to the complaint. I don't think it can be any more than that. The one question that has occurred to me, and perhaps I should already know this, did you ever make a complaint about [First Architect] to his professional body?*
>
> *I have not. My wife has... I will be.*
>
> *You intend to? Can I simply ask – did your wife's complaint succeed?*
>
> *I don't know what the complete answer to that is. I can't possibly answer that.*
>
> *Right. But what you were saying is that you certainly propose to be complaining.*
>
> *Absolutely!*

Right. Moving on to Section 3 – this is a section for various copy documents, including Court proceedings, various notes. This comes about, I think, simply in relation to [Contractor]'s case and I am quite sure, having looked at it and some of the numbering on it, that – Mr Brown – you have copied various of these things to us before?

Yes.

Not in this format but with various of your letters. And from that point of view, again this will be available to the reporter for consideration. It may, in fact, make it easier for the reporter to consider from the point of view of the way it is put together.

The main reason this was sent to the Law Society reporter and the Law Society was to show exactly what happened in the contractor's case, and what happened between [First Architect] and [Contractor], which was always unknown to Mr And Mrs Brown. We did not know what was going on because [First Architect] was paid to supervise. In other words, he takes over the whole contract, and it's between him, the Planning Department – the building department, rather – and [Contractor] himself. We stepped away from everything – that is the contract.

The evidence in this contractor's case – it shows us that on page 1 (marked Py2), it states there that "Defenders said architect issued instructions for additional work". He failed to deal with the application from [Contractor] for extension of time. Now he is telling everyone that he did the work but never gave extension of time. Now the actual cost of the additional work was £4,000. The original contract was for £14,500. That's quite a considerable amount to add to the contract – now the additional time, I shall just make this point.

Sure.

He did not inform Mr And Mrs Brown of this. What I am showing here is what type of person the Architect is. He had lied constantly throughout, constantly from day one – he has lied. I have proof of all the lies which have been passed to [First Solicitor], without any shadow of a doubt.

Well, again I would say that will certainly be available to the reporter, whilst it appears to me that it may in fact relate more properly to the merits of the case as to what took place in Court. But it's for the reporter, I think, to look at and consider the relevance of it to the issues which the Law Society is considering.

Now for the reporter to consider that the unauthorised works...

Can I just stop you there for one second, Mr Brown? I must make it clear as I did, I think, during the first side of the tape that whilst the reporter will consider the documentation, he is not going to consider the actual evidence and merits of the case.

No. What we are saying here – the merits of the case – I don't want him to look at the merits of the case if that is not the point. The point I am trying to make here is all the lies that come into it. Where people are deceived and the Solicitor has deceived his own clients. In that respect, what I mean there is, in the same case where you say it is the duty of the lawyer to use his authority and his knowledge for my benefit, to state in Court, not to mention [First Architect] was supervising. You are saying that is the road he decided to take, that it was the best way?

Yes.

He also admitted the unauthorised work, which was in the writ against [First Architect]. Now, if there were unauthorised works with an order from the Aberdeen Planning and Building Department, if there was an order placed on Mr and Mrs

Brown to alter these unauthorised works at the cost of – we don't know – these unauthorised works were never mentioned in the case that [First Architect] and [Contractor] together had gone outwith the contract drawings. Now, for a minute, picture yourself in the Court as a client and the Solicitor acting on your behalf, and he never mentions to the Sheriff that this contractor sitting here and this architect sitting here, both connived to build unauthorised works without permission and also added £4,000 in additional costs without permission.

The only comment I am prepared to make on that is – I hear what you are saying and it is for the reporter to consider on the information you are providing and to decide whether or not it merits action.

Well, I am stating this – whatever you decide, or whatever the reporter decides, right, regarding your decisions, I can't change that. What I am looking for, again, I must emphasise Mr [Deputy Secretary], my whole purpose is to get justice. I want somebody to listen to what I have gone through and nobody has heard it in the Courtroom. And I paid a Solicitor to put this information into a Courtroom. I paid two Solicitors to put it in a Courtroom. I was paying a third Solicitor to put it in a Courtroom and not one Solicitor has put this information in a Courtroom.

Well, Mr Brown, as I have said to you earlier, the Law Society's remit is limited. But you know that.

Yes, yes.

I think you also know that I have, throughout this matter, and it has gone on a long time. I think, with respect, the Law Society has listened to you, whatever our view of your complaint may be. I do understand what you are saying. I understand what you mean when you say you are pursuing justice. I understand that entirely now. I simply make the comment that what you are looking for, or what you may be looking for, may not be something you are going to get as a result of this investigation.

I can only put my points to you.

Of course you can.

You have no objections to that?

None at all. All I am saying to you is, I understand where you are coming from. I think I understand what you are looking for. All I feel I have to say to you is, irrespective of what action, if any, the Law Society decides to take, I am not sure at the end of the day whether or not you will see that as justice, or justice on your terms. I think it would be wrong of me not to say that. We have had, indeed we are having, a full and frank discussion and I have no difficulty with that. The only slight concern I have is that what we may be able to do, or the view which we might take if the complaint is upheld – and once again I have to say "if" as once again I cannot say if it will or will not be upheld – is whether, even if it is upheld, the view we will take will actually bring you as what you see as justice.

We obviously have difference of opinion here. What I am trying to do here, because of all the files I have been sending to the Law Society regarding all the Solicitors, all the details I have been writing to them continuously, it doesn't seem to me that the Sheriff, the lawyers, the judges, nobody has heard the case. Nobody has heard the true facts of this case...

Well, can I raise another question with you which I think is relevant. The contractor's case was decided...it was not in your favour

No.

Did you ask [First Solicitor], or have you asked any other Solicitor since, what is the prospect of appealing that decision?

Yes. [Second Solicitor] said there was no point in appealing. It's in his letters to you. You have the copy there. [First Solicitor] said there was three to four days of exhaustive debate, which I thought was despicable.

Well, can we just come back for a moment. When you refer to [Second Solicitor], I assume – and I simply mention this for clarification – his letter about that is on this file, rather than with the file which registers your complaint.

I can't remember which file – [Second Solicitor] said it was too late to appeal. Now, as you have told me in many correspondence, the remit of the Law Society, and I fully understand that – you can go (if I can use the phraseology) from, say, A to B but you can't go past B.

Right.

What I want the Law Society, and yourself in particular because I have been dealing with yourself, to understand when I am sitting in a Court room and I know there are unauthorised works to the tune of £10,000 to £12,000, say ...

Can I just interrupt for a second? It is just, so it's clear on the point you are making – I do understand what you are getting at. So far as the contractor's case was concerned, your real concern is – you sat there in the Court room, you had given your Solicitor certain information which in your view disproved the case being taken against you ...

He suppressed evidence – that's basically what it is. My Solicitor suppressed unbelievable concrete evidence, that's what I am saying.

Can I say to you that I understand what you say in relation to suppression of evidence. Simply for the record, can I make it clear that my understanding of that in my terms ...

In your terms.

...is that evidence was available to [First Solicitor] which, for whatever reason, he chose not to use. Now, I think that is a slightly different interpretation of the matter.

No. I would say there that you are actually speaking for [First Solicitor] as a Solicitor yourself. You are stating [First Solicitor] omitted this evidence for reason known only to him.

What I am saying is, as we said on the first side of the tape, that when a matter goes into Court, a Solicitor is entitled to use his professional judgement as to how to take the matter forward.

I want the Law Society to take these facts to judge that Solicitor on his judgement.

That is not the role of the Law Society.

OK, that is not the role of the Law Society.

And it brings us back to where we were before.

So basically you are saying that any Solicitor in the future, no matter who he is and in any client in the future who has a case against an architect or a contractor whatsoever, you are saying that any Solicitor can go into a Court of law and not put in evidence he has been given by a client, even though a client is going to suffer. It's up to a Solicitor to protect his client at all costs. I have been told that already by the Law Society – he must protect his client.

Let me make it clear to you, Mr Brown. I understand entirely where you are coming from. What I am saying to you is this – when the matter goes beyond the doors of the Court into the Courtroom, the Law Society cannot interfere in that process, cannot look at the question of how the case is presented to the Court. It is arguable, as I have said to you earlier on this tape, that if the Solicitor has acted in such a way as to have obviously ignored the duty owed to you, that might amount to negligence but that is not something the Law Society can determine. The issue which could possibly look at is the question whether the Solicitor prepared properly but...

OK.

...from what you were to me saying, the evidence was in his hands. It was in his hands when he went to Court...

Yes.

He then chooses, once he gets into Court, to present the case in a particular way, to follow a particular route, a line of questioning, a line of witnesses.

OK. I could present to you a client/Solicitor relationship which is very important, very important. I am taking a client into Court, and I am representing that client. Two weeks before I went into that Court I am sitting with the client and I am telling him what I am going to do for him, and this is what we are going to discuss – here's a rough format of what we are going in with. I have a chance to say to the Solicitor – that is excellent. But I question this. Why are you doing that? I don't wait for the day of the Court for a Court lawyer to say it because, once it's said in that Court, then that lawyer should have given me the chance to tell me that I will not be telling the Court all ...

Right. Can we qualify something, because I think it is useful? Is it your position that, before you went into Court for the Court case, [First Solicitor] did not meet with you to discuss the case, the evidence which was going to be led, or the people who were going to be called?

He told me who was going to be called as witnesses.

He told you who was going to be called?

Yes, and I objected, strongly objected to [First Architect].

Right. That having been said, if he told you that, as I said to you earlier on, whilst I appreciated that you objected to [First Architect]...

But he never mentioned the writ which was already written against [First Architect]. I did not know about that, as you already know. I passed this information to you earlier.

Can I ask you a question about that which I think is very relevant? Are you then saying that you did not give him instructions to draft a writ against [First Architect]?

Did I give instructions to issue a writ, to draft a writ?

Yes. Let's get this entirely right. Did you give him instructions to pursue [First Architect]?

Well, yes. Right. I was after [First Architect] since 1982. It was up to the Solicitor to advise me what he was going to do.

So you said to [First Solicitor] that you wanted to pursue [First Architect]?

"...if we don't get the Completion Certificate, then there is something wrong, Mr [First Solicitor]. We brought back [First Architect] back in against...the figure of £371. I was bringing him back to pay £371. I was bringing him back to get the Completion Certificate. He was paid for that. I am concerned that we don't have the Completion Certificate, Mr [First Solicitor], we don't have the Completion Certificate and it's very important..."

Did you ever give written instructions to [First Solicitor] saying "Raise an action against [First Architect]"?

I can't remember giving him written instructions. That I can't remember, but let me just check something.

Certainly. Can I perhaps go on whilst you are checking that? What I am trying to get at here is whether Mr Brown gave written, or indeed even if he can recall – verbal instructions – to [First Solicitor] to raise an action against [First Architect] and, if he did, whether at that stage [First Solicitor] had advised him not to issue the writ, and if at that stage Mr Brown accepted the advice.

I consider this important because, whilst I understand Mr Brown's concern in wanting to pursue [First Architect], I think it is important to ascertain precisely whether formal instructions were given, or not.

There were three dates in 1986 where [First Solicitor] writes to [First Architect]'s Solicitors and states: "we are under extreme pressure from our client to (I don't know the exact words) take [First Architect] to Court".

I understand that was then, but the question that I am asking is a step further, which is – were instructions given for the action to be raised?

I would say they have to be, if he is saying in the letter "we are under extreme pressure from the client..."

But in that situation, what may have happened is you are saying to him: "Look, I want to get on with this", whilst he is saying: "Let me have another go". What I am trying to tie down, and I appreciate it may not be possible to do this, as to whether there is a stage where you specifically said to him either what you said verbally from your records or in a letter "Mr [First Solicitor] I have had enough. Raise an action against [First Architect]."

The general consensus of opinion between us both was – if we can't get a Completion Certificate, then we would have to issue a writ against [First Architect].

Right. I can understand that. The question which I am asking is, given that there was clearly correspondence with [First Architect]'s agents, which I think we agreed there was, did the time ever come when you said to [First Solicitor] "Enough is enough – raise the action."

Yes, I think he issued instructions to [First Architect]'s agents. He raised the writ and [First Architect]'s agents replied they would be defending strenuously.

Right – OK… He writes to…who I assume are [First Architect]'s Solicitors. He comes back and says "Raise the writ and put it to the defendant strongly." At that stage did you recall actually saying: "Raise the writ."

No…no.

You didn't? I think that is quite important because, if you are talking about your specific instruction, then if you go to a Solicitor on the other side and say "Look, our client is really minded to raise the writ" and they come back and say "We will defend it strenuously"…

I gave the facts to [First Solicitor], right? I say "Mr [First Solicitor] I have got a letter from the town, there is a newspaper article, which you have a copy"…

Indeed, yes.

…and I hit the roof. They are blaming me – blaming me for all this what happened in (guest house), and I don't know the first thing about it! What were they proposing to do? Were they proposing to get rid of the unauthorised works? What were they doing about [First Architect]? If I went to a shoemaker and said to the shoemaker "I have a pair of shoes – which are the best way to repair them?" and he would tell me because he is the expert. If I went to a Solicitor for advice, he advises me. I don't advise him.

No. You're quite right. But the point I am trying to get at here is that you speak to your Solicitor. Your Solicitor gives you your advice. You write a letter on your instruction and a letter comes back from the other side's Solicitors saying if you raise an action they will defend it strenuously, then you were obviously made aware of that letter.

Yes. I would say yes.

At that stage it would seem to me you are either faced with a choice – what way to pursue it, or raise a writ. But at that stage, all [First Solicitor] has done is to signal an intention to the other side who said "Fine; you raise it, we'll defend it". At that stage, if that writ is then going to be raised, to my mind there may well be the question of whether specific instructions were given to raise the writ.

We had no other choice.

I can understand you saying you had no other choice. But what is concerning me, given what you previously said, is whether at that stage you said to [First Solicitor]...

I think it was before that I said to [First Solicitor] to raise a writ. I think well before that.

Right. Even after that exchange of correspondence the difficulty I've got of trying to put this together. You get this back. [First Solicitor] comes to you and says "Here is the letter – they're going to defend". Do you say to him: "Right, don't care, let's get on with it."?

Yes.

And that's if, and I appreciate it is difficult trying to do it here...

I have been pursuing [First Architect] since 1983. Pursued [First Architect] first to get the Completion Certificate. Then I pursued [First Architect] for the letter that appeared in the newspapers. I was furious. Then I said to [First Solicitor] "I want you to get [First Architect] in Court. As I was pursuing [First Architect], if I had known that was coming up I would have had the correspondence with me.

Well, what I can say is I can understand that. Obviously, if you can take that home and look through your records and pinpoint it, it would undoubtedly be very helpful.

Yes.

What I would like to say now is, if I can just move you forward slightly?

If I can just ask a question?

Of course you can.

The Aberdeen Planning and Building Department issued an order against Mr and Mrs. Brown – to change the works back – it must be changed. No two ways about it. 1985.

Yes, that's right. There are various bits and pieces of documentation in this regard which, if you take what is described in Section 4 of the folder.

Yes. That's right.

And again that is something important for the reporter to see and indeed consider.

<Long pause – looking through the documents>

Now perhaps, can I move you forward briefly because, in Section 5 of the folder you have given me, you have raised a very interesting question, which I think does bear some consideration. There is a copy of the initial writ raised against [First Architect] whom you are suing for the sum of £30,000.

Right.

Now, I assume before this writ was served there was a discussion with yourself and [First Solicitor]?

<At this point Mr Brown shakes his head>

No. I am saying no.

Right. Can I therefore clarify something in relation to this? This writ was drawn up by [First Solicitor]. Mr Brown was unaware, as I understand it – (a) of the existence of this writ, (b) all the actual set down in the writ about the amount of money (£30,000) specified in it.

Is it your position, Mr Brown, within this regard, whilst you were aware that you wanted to sue [First Architect], you were not consulted about the writ, the details in it, or indeed the amount that was being claimed?

There is no correspondence of any kind regarding this particular document – 150, 151 – no documentation at all from [First Solicitor] or myself.

Can I therefore ask another question which comes from this? There is then a letter from [First Solicitor's agent], to [First Solicitor], dated 10th September 1987. Is it your position, Mr Brown, that at this time you were aware that the writ was actually in Court?

No.

You were not aware that it was in Court and am I right in saying you were not aware of anything that took place in Court?

None whatsoever. Regards 154, I was completely ignorant, myself and Mrs. Brown were completely ignorant.

Can I, at this stage, make a point about what is being apparent during our discussion which in relation to this matter involving [First Architect]. I do consider that there are certain further questions which may well need to be put to [First Solicitor] before we can draw this matter to a conclusion. It seems to me that, in relation to the complaint against [First Architect], the complaints specifically are, firstly the writ in this matter was put into Court without Mr Brown's knowledge. Thereafter, the first that he knew the writ had been in Court was the letter dated 10th September 1987 from [First Solicitor's agent] which indicated that action had sisted pending an application for Legal Aid. I am now going to ask Mr Brown the simple question – at this stage he had been asked to complete the Legal Aid application?

<Mr Brown shakes his head to indicate 'No'>

So what you are saying is, when [First Architect]'s action started off, your position was basically you had not applied for Legal Aid, you were unaware that the writ had been drawn, you were unaware that the writ had been put into Court and you were entirely unaware of what was happening?

<Mr Brown nods>

Yes. That is correct.

There is a complete contradiction of this from [First Solicitor] himself. You are aware of that – I wrote and told you of this before. [First Solicitor] contradicts this letter from [his agent] about 154. It's a contradiction. [First Solicitor] states they did not apply for Legal Aid, yet this states here – client's Legal Aid – there's your answer there.

Right. I think this particular aspect is certainly something that may well bear further investigation.

We then move on to what is described as Section 184. This is the letter of 23rd August 1989.

Now, in this he says – the writ was sisted. There's a contradiction right there.

It was agreed that the action would be sisted because of [First Architect]'s evidence. There's a contradiction in terms here – in this letter of 23rd August 1989 [First Solicitor] is indicating that the action against [First Architect] was to be sisted because of the evidence he would be giving, whereas other correspondence, and particularly the letter from [First Solicitor's agent], is indicating that the action has to be sisted to enable an application for Legal Aid. Those two letters appear to contradict each other.

Exactly. There is one observation here – that the date of that letter (184) is 23ʳᵈ August 1989 addressed to Mr A Brown. I have looked through the papers for this. An initial writ has been served. This is the first indication to Mr and Mrs Brown that there had been a writ served.

I have noted that comment, and I have noted that on the letter Mr Brown has marked "never agreed" at the end of the first paragraph.

If you look at the evidence which has been produced all the way through, and I sure hope you will look at the evidence regards [First Architect] which I passed to [First Solicitor], I would like you to look at paragraph 3 – the bottom of the last two sentences:

"[Second Architect]'s opinion came subsequently. The core of the case appears to rely on the evidence of you and [First Architect], and in relation to these matters – at whose evidence would be most credible".

Now the credibility of [First Architect] which I have shown where he has lied continuously. And they talk about credibility! As indicated previously, onus of proof in showing professional negligence, is very high especially particularly when there seems to be particular doubt as to whether [First Architect] was responsible for supervising the work.

This is, of course, a point you made earlier.

No, I am going back to 150 and 151 – the writ. Here is where a professional Solicitor advises the Courts that the writ has been issued, stating that [First Architect] was paid to supervise works. That was in 1987 – August. In August 1989, he tells me that as to whether [First Architect] was responsible for supervising the work, then I suspect there would be difficulties in showing that [First Architect] was professionally negligent. Now, if that is not misleading a client, I don't know what is!

The only comment that I would make is that, when any Solicitor looks at evidence, they are entitled to look at that, consider it and come to a view of it. Now that view of it may not, on many occasions, correspond with the view of the client and as I have said to you previously so far as the Law Society's considerations are concerned, I think I should make it clear – we will not look at the quality of the interpretation of the evidence that may be available. That is a matter, if there is going to be anything done, which may fall again to the question of professional negligence.

I want to bring your attention again to the Sheet 184. I mentioned just before that the reference DC/AC, which has never appeared on any other correspondence. It might mean little to the Law Society, but the reason I bring this to the attention of the Law Society is that, at the very top of this page, you will see marked "hand-delivered".

This is the last paragraph of 184: "I would like to point out finally that not only have we raised an action in [First Architect]'s case and not charged any fee but, over the years, I have given various advice in relation to various matters and so far not charged any fee. We have bent over backwards to try to accommodate you and give your case sympathetic approach. I leave you to decide whether you wish to further the matter."

Now, he has already raised a writ, and sisted the writ, and if you cross-reference this 184 and 150/151, can you also cross-reference with my letter to [First Solicitor], ref 201 and 206 and – yes 206.

May I repeat the last paragraph: "not only have we raised an action…and not charged any fee". I bring your attention to File 206, Section 7: "Further to your statement regarding a no-fee charge for [First Architect] see copy of my letter dated 11th October 1986 in which you will see that certain payments have been received and you suggested that further payments of between £50 and £100 per month would be a realistic figure. My files highlights payments as follows: September 1986 – £200, October – £200.

If I can stop you there. I can see that Mr Brown and I can see what you are driving at...

There are six payments of £200 on a weekly basis. That was in 1986 and in 1989 [First Solicitor] is telling me he never charged me any fee. What I am trying to highlight here – on many occasions [First Solicitor], I have found them to be unprofessional.

Yes. Can I simply make the comment at this stage for information – that £200 payments made by Mr Brown and referred to in his letter are shown in [First Solicitor]'s ledger card as having been received and further payment to accounts of £250 in January 1987. I am just simply making that for the record.

What I would like to say, Mr Brown, I would like to draw this towards a conclusion and I think there are a certain number of questions that I have to ask [First Solicitor]. I think I can quite reasonably ask for clarification as clearly you have pointed out – there are contradictions in certain letters which have been received. There is no doubt about that and I understand your point in that regard.

I think it would be helpful, from my point of view, if you would be able to pinpoint your own records and any reference specifically to giving any instructions to raise the writ, and as I said previously, I will look into the files, and indeed the file in relation to [Second Solicitor] in relation to the question of the accounting. The final section within your file, which is No. 7, is basically setting out your position in this matter from start to finish, and giving a very useful historical background as to what has taken place. I will confirm it to the reporter, even though I am sure he has seen that, but will bring his attention to it again. I don't think we have terribly much more to add. We have been speaking now – we started just after 2 o'clock and the time by my watch is just quarter to four.

We started at 2.15 – it's been one hour and forty minutes.

In fact I think it's now five to four as I think my watch is slow. Can I say for the record – I have found it to be an extremely useful and helpful meeting. It has certainly highlighted certain issues which I think are worthy of consideration. And, as I have said at the outset – obviously I would like to get this matter to a conclusion for everybody's sake as quickly as possible. I cannot put a time limit on that because of the further enquiries and checks I may be made to make, and indeed any information that the reporter might need clarification of, but I will certainly try to deal with matters as quickly as I can.

I would like to add here that the Law Society should check into the Legal Aid applications number one, the dates they were applied for, the reason they were refused, the exact dates they were applied for.

I would simply make the comment that whilst I would be prepared to consider doing that...

Yes.

*...I think that there may be, and I simply say there **may** be, a problem given the length of time that has passed. I don't know how long the Legal Aid Board keep their Legal Aid applications.*

Well, I have been checking into that and I am sure that the Law Society knows about that. Can I say right now that this particular case between me and you, Mr [Deputy Secretary] that I am not naïve enough to know that the Law Society and the Solicitors, who are all part of the Law Society, and the Legal Aid, do not contact each other regarding clients and complaints, etc. etc.

Well, can I interrupt you, Mr Brown, and say quite clearly to you for the avoidance of any doubt – the Scottish Legal Aid Board and the Law Society are two entirely separate organisations.

The Law Society did, at one stage, do Legal Aid, but does not do so now. If any complaint where there is an issue raised in relation to Legal Aid, it is open to the Law Society to approach the Legal Aid Board for information, and that is something that does take place.

Yes, but I also know that the Law Society is in constant touch with Solicitors regarding new clients. They have to be, naturally. There was a complaint against a Solicitor and some other Solicitors consulted all the details of the past. I am not naïve enough to misunderstand that, but what I object to is monopolies. I don't think it is professional. I can't express my views strongly enough – but the monopolies which the Law Society carries on, and the legal profession, against the general public...

With respect, Mr Brown – it is not a question of a monopoly. If you are referring, for example, to the way complaints are handled – that is a statutory duty which is imposed on the Law Society by Parliament. The only way anybody else could consider complaints is if there a change in the law.

Yes. I am hoping that we can do that and make these changes in the future because...

If I can respectfully also point out to you – as a statutory obligation, the Law Society, unlike some other organisations, do not make any formal charge in regard to investigating the complaint...

End of second tape.

Side 3:

...Mr Brown's concerns about the Law Society dealing with complaints and what Mr Brown describes as a "monopoly" – as I have already explained, it is the statute which empowers the

Law Society to consider complaints being serviced, of considering complaints being justified, or not, is a free service. That is not the case in all bodies such as the Law Society in considering complainants who may require a deposit which may be non-refundable. The Law Society, however, takes very seriously its duties to the public and endeavours to look at complaints fairly and impartially. That is one of the reasons why complaints committees are made up of Solicitors and non-Solicitors.

But I must also add, Mr [Deputy Secretary], which I think is very important, that I think that we could call it a partnership between the Law Society and the public because it's the clients who take the lawyers to the Law Society at their cost. I would like to point out, right now, that the cost that my family has incurred, forget financial costs – that doesn't come into it—

What I would say, Mr, Brown, as far as that is concerned, as I explained to you at the very outset of this interview, the Government in 1989, then in 1991, gave the Law Society powers to consider inadequate professional services. I think you are already aware, in connection with one of the complaints you lodged against [Second Solicitor], the Law Society operated these powers, and I think I am correct in saying that you received a payment in compensation in your favour from [Second Solicitor].

Well, you call it compensation, right?

Yes.

The amount of compensation, as I said to [your colleague] – all he has to do is send 50 letters to his clients, he has got his money back.

Can I simply make the point on top of that – the limit of £1,000 compensation is a figure, not one set by the Law Society; it is a figure set by statute, by Parliament.

OK.

Can I also add one final thing which I think is important? That anyone who doesn't feel the Law Society has considered their complaint properly, fairly and thoroughly, has the right to go to somebody called the Scottish Legal Services Ombudsman. Now the ombudsman is appointed by the Secretary of State for Scotland. The ombudsman is not a Solicitor but he is in power to consider the way the Law Society handles complaints, and to consider if they handled them properly. Otherwise they can make recommendations in regard to specific complaints, and the way they have been handled. I raise this simply because, Mr Brown, you originally made this complaint in 1990. The office of the ombudsman was not created until 3rd June 1991. Prior to that the ombudsman had a different title – the lay observer. At the time of bringing the ombudsman into creation, the Government of the day did not have any transitional provisions introduced. What that basically meant – the office of the lay ombudsman finished on 2nd June 1991 and the office of the ombudsman commenced on 3rd June 1991, and it means for someone like you who made their complaint in 1990, if at the end of the day you refer them on to the ombudsman, it is entirely likely that the ombudsman will say to you that he does not have the jurisdiction to consider that as the complaint was made before the creation of his office. I think I should make it clear to you that, when this difficulty became apparent some two-and-a-half years ago, the Law Society did make representations in regard to the matter because we did not think it reasonable that a particular number of people should be disqualified, in effect, from going to the ombudsman because of error in legislation. Regrettably, in my view, the Government did not take that on board and did not take any action. The Law Society has nothing to fear with anyone going to the ombudsman.

Well, if you want my opinion about the ombudsman, I have no fears about going to the ombudsman. I would say that every government has failures, every government has successes. I don't care what country you belong to – there are ministers who are poor. The ombudsman who has been appointed by the Secretary of State is a figurehead. He is not even a lawyer so for a non-lawyer to compete with a professional body, as far as I am concerned! I have been in touch with [First Ombudsman], and I have talked for many hours with [him]. I have been in touch with [Second Ombudsman], and I personally think I am wasting my time. That's my personal view.

Can I simply say – you are entitled to your personal view, Mr Brown. Can I say – I have found this afternoon useful. I hope you have, and that we have been able to sort out any misunderstandings that we may have had in the past on the telephone, and I will do what I can to draw this complaint to a satisfactory conclusion.

I have been very upset. I haven't concluded this that I have brought down. I thought we would have had a longer time, but obviously we don't. There are certain letters that you wrote to me that I have made comments on, hoping to go over, but as you say – time is concluded. I would like to say that I would like more time to go over with you these details. One of them was [First Solicitor] in 1991 writing to you saying that Mr Brown chose the cheapest contractor. If you recall, he was defending [First Architect] once again, and I think the reporter should have access to this. I asked you to give that to the reporter...

But the reporter has had access to the whole file.

But he could make mistakes. Everybody is prone to make mistakes.

It's not my job to tell the reporter precisely what facts to put into a report.

No, but you could present them. Doesn't the Law Society write out a report before it goes to the reporter?

No – that is not my function.

Well, I have been totally misled. I always thought the deputy who the client deals with takes all the information from the client and puts a report to the reporter.

That is not the case. The position is that the Deputy Secretary, or whoever might be dealing with your file, collates the information, gathers the information from you and the Solicitor, considers it with the Solicitor's files, and passes the papers to the reporter for the report – information which would be given to the reporter in the case, [is what] heads the complaint.

Don't you think its fair that he should have access to all the information that I have just been telling you about?

But the reporter does have.

Right! He has the letter from [First Solicitor]?

He has everything that is on that file – the yellow file. He has everything that is in the red file, and he will have [First Solicitor]'s files.

I am sure that you have detected by now that I trust no one. I have become that type of person – I trust no one.

Sceptical, I think. I'm sorry you feel that way.

I am sorry too, but I was never like that.

I can assure you that the full file of correspondence, your red file and the Solicitor's file...

So you're telling me I can accept that Mr [Committee Member Reporter], has access to every letter? So that's very good. I would expect him to go through everything I have just mentioned, and I would hope he would come up with...

Right. Thank you, Mr Brown for coming down, and I wish you a safe trip back home.

Thank you. I couldn't believe what you said in your last letter, but...meeting is now concluded.

Yes.

After the meeting at the Law Society's office in Edinburgh it was as if nothing had changed and correspondence continued to flow back and forth.

On 20th September 1995 (File 722) the Deputy Secretary wrote:

I refer to our meeting on 5th September 1995 which I found to be useful and indeed, very helpful.

I look forward to receiving from you a copy of your tape of the interview. I would confirm that I do propose at this stage to take the following action:-

1)   Check the position in relation to the accounting, and

2)   Check the position in regard to the Legal Aid applications.

I think it is only fair to remind you that this may take some time and the timescale originally mentioned to you for concluding this matter may lengthen as a direct result. I will however try to deal with matters as quickly as I am able to.

On 26th September 1995 (File 723) I replied, as follows:

Thank you for your letter of 20th September 1995 and its contents regarding the meeting.

The copy of the tapes in relation to the interview, which you mention, have been sent, under separate cover, in a jiffy bag, recorded delivery. I hope you and the reporting member find them helpful.

In relation to the accounting and the Legal Aid applications, I have further details in my files, which appears you don't have but should have been in [First Solicitor's files]. I am sure they will be of interest to you, with the actions you are taking which you mentioned in your last letter.

I thank you again for the interesting meeting. I was a little disappointed that we didn't have longer to discuss the complete contents of the red file. The further details mentioned above, I will mail you in the next three or four days.

The affable nature of this correspondence belied my growing concern that I was getting nowhere. I did not truly believe that the Deputy Secretary would follow through, to my advantage, on the two issues he said he would pursue. But I remained polite, knowing that no purpose would be served by venting my frustration through anger.

Note: Some vital information that was known to the Deputy Secretary during our Edinburgh meeting had not been passed on to me at the time. This I did not discover until the following year – that [First Solicitor] was being investigated by the Law Society for another case. Can you imagine how the meeting would have been conducted if I had known of this other investigation? How would the outcome have differed? Secrecy and cunning continued to play their insidious part in the Law Society's approach to my complaint. As it transpired, [First Solicitor] was eventually fined £5,000 (for conflict of interest) in the other case that was running in tandem with mine. Oh that I had known at the time!

After many years of correspondence with the Deputy Secretary of the Law Society in regard to my complaint against [First Solicitor], I felt I was back against a brick wall. It was becoming clear that they were going through motions only, but would eventually ignore all of my **concrete evidence** against [First Solicitor], and even clear him of all of my complaints. I now regard this behaviour as tantamount to criminal. With regards to appeal rights, they were effectively non-existent, allowing only an appeal to the legal Ombudsman, **who has no jurisdiction over the complaints committee's decisions.**

Remember too that I had not lodged just a single complaint. Both prior to and after the meeting in Edinburgh I was involved with the Law Society in regards to complaints against [Second Solicitor], the Advocate, and the Troubleshooter. I hope you the readers will bear with me, and my precarious position. Further incompetence and planned delays were looming! Take a look at the following correspondence

1996, 1997, 1998

On 16th February 1996 (File 723-1) the Law Society wrote to me regarding my complaint against [First Solicitor]:

> *I refer to my recent letter to you in respect of this matter and now attach for your attention a copy of the letter received from the Legal Aid Board.*
>
> *As you will see, despite the request which has been made the board are unable to assist in providing information to progress this matter.*
>
> *Before I put this matter to the reporting member for a completion of the report, I consider that the letter from the board, and your letter of 12th December, raise issues, which I should reasonably put to the Solicitors.*

> *I will be in touch once I have their further comments, which I consider are important to obtain given a number of the allegations you are making.*

I responded on 11th March 1996 (File 724):

> *Thank you for your letter of 16th February 1996 and the copy of the letter from the Scottish Legal Aid Board.*
>
> *I am very disappointed that no information was to be found, regarding Legal Aid applications.*
>
> *I am also very angry to say the least, at the time it has taken you...to write to the board back in November 7th and then wait till January 10th before you send a reminder.*
>
> *I will remind you the meeting in your office was 5th September 1995. At that time the notes you were taking included writing to the Board.*
>
> *Two months to send a letter across the street, to the Legal Aid Board, and a further month to send a reminder. Then you tell me in our last telephone conversation you didn't write to [First Solicitor] until 16th February 1996 regarding the contents of my letter to you dated 12th December 1995.*

On 28th March 1996 (File 725) the Law Society wrote again regarding my complaint against [First Solicitor]:

> *I refer to previous correspondence in respect of the above and my brief discussion with you on 20th March.*
>
> *I attach hereto a copy of a letter received from [First Solicitor] together with a statement of accounting which they have now produced.*

Whilst I am passing the papers in this matter to a member of the complaints committee for a report at this stage, I have kept a copy of the statement of accounting and if you have specific questions to raise regarding this, perhaps you could write to me.

I should say that I believe it will take the reporter 4-6 weeks to consider the matter, He will clearly need to look again at the files of [First Solicitor], and listen to the tape recording of our meeting. That will clearly take some time.

On 1st April 1996 (File 726) I wrote again to the Law Society:

Thank you for your letter of 16th February and the copy of the reply from the Scottish Legal Aid Board, which you enclosed.

I have found certain papers, which I am sure will be of help in regards to those Legal Aid applications. I have enclosed them for your perusal, and for the reporting member.

I have gone over them carefully and find it appalling that any professional Solicitor can behave in this way. The timing, with the full knowledge of all the relevant facts at hand, speaks for itself.

I am also in receipt of your letter of 28th March 1996, with copy of the letter from [First Solicitor] attached.

If [First Solicitor] thinks that I am going to waste my time going over different sheets years after the issues, then they are mistaken. I have already answered, in my letter to the Law Society dated 12th December 1995.

[First Solicitor]'s letter to me (which I have enclosed) dated 14th October 1986 is a prime example how to keep a client up to date with his financial affairs. At that particular point in time, he tells me that this full statement of accounting goes back a long way,

*(close to **five years**), but his opening statement is classic. You will have received copies of our letters getting the ball rolling.*

*But, better still to come, apart from the above comments [First Solicitor] corresponds with Mr Brown way back in 21ˢᵗ March 1985. The classic statement then is "It surprises me that this matter has been going on for such a long period of time, without anybody taking the **bull by the horns** and getting the matter solved." Note a time span (of one year and seven months), and a further three years to get to Court.*

This is what you call professional communication at its best.

As far as I am aware the Law Society now have all the details of my complaints against [First Solicitor], which I believe are about to be put to the reporting member.

As stated in your letter it will take 4 to 6 weeks, by then I should be in receipt of a copy of his report. Should you require any additional information please advise.

The Law Society responded to my letter on 11ᵗʰ April 1996 (File 727):

I refer to your letter of 1ˢᵗ April 1996, and enclosures, and write to confirm that I am sending these to the reporter for consideration.

As I believe I have already made it clear to you the issue which the Law Society is considering in connection with [First Solicitor]'s actings relates solely to his professional conduct during the time he actually acted for you. May I also point out that I will certainly confirm to you once I have received the report from the reporter. As I believe has previously been made clear in correspondence, the committee will consider this matter on the basis of the reporter's report. I would, however, say that whilst I am prepared to copy the basis of that report to you it is not the case that you would have a further opportunity to make representations at this time. Precisely the same applies to [First Solicitor].

I wonder if my readers are feeling a sense of heaviness and dread? It has now been six months since the September 1995 meeting with the Law Society. Are things moving forward? Remember, I had been corresponding with he same Deputy Secretary for the last five years. What do you think?

I was upset five years earlier. After returning home and listening, a number of times, to the tape recording of our September 1995 meeting, I felt ever more upset. And now, six months later, I was close to despair. Promises were made in writing prior to the meeting. Where was the follow through? Listening to this corrupt official repeatedly coming up with the same excuses to protect [First Solicitor] – namely his exploitation of that notorious word **negligence**, with its different meaning in a legal context as opposed to the public definition – I was being blocked with all the suave nicety of a clever and complacent professional. I was being edged out of the picture, as have so many complainers/complainants. And how easily the Law Society achieved this end!

Here is another piece of advice to those who may be in the same position as me. Do not, even inadvertently, refer to your lawyer's negligence unless, of course, you really do mean negligence in all its legal grandeur! Talk about **inefficiency**, even **incompetence** or **conflict of interest**, but do not let slip those words **negligent** or **negligence**! You will be opening the door of opportunity to a profession whose very success depends upon loopholes and unethical manipulation of true fairness.

Using the word **negligence**, always to their advantage, opens the way for the legal profession to exploit that well known tactic – **delays**. **Delay** saps the life out of a complainer's/complainant's endeavours.

And do not forget, when you turn to the Law Society for help, you will be required to feed them everything about your case, opening yourself up to delays and the possibility of criticism that you are not being honest enough to allow them to know they can act on your behalf. A bottomless pit opens up, demanding to be fed and filled, long after the simplest of common sense would indicate that your case is a fair one.

Be warned. You must follow through with their perpetual requests, yet again leading to energy sapping delays. With all of the information you send them, they take their time in checking each and every detail, whether you are a high or low risk complainer. And if you are a high risk, rest assured you will be led inexorably into the **negligence** trap. Look again at the transcript of the taped meeting in Edinburgh and check how many times that very issue came up. Just as often as their other ploy – the ultra vires tactic, limiting their powers to help you by only following the prescribed remit of the Law Society. Of course this has its place in the world, but let my readers ask this question: at what point, irrespective of their remit, does it become apparent that they are dealing with a decidedly incompetent solicitor? And what do they do when this happens? Do they ignore a blight on the name of their profession simply because action would mean going beyond their remit? Or do they understand that a human's misery lies behind the story and lean over backwards to work their remit in favour of the complainer/complainant? Of course they do not follow the latter route. But what would happen in a non-self-regulated world?

I say all this to my readers in the spirit of "fore-warned is fore-armed". So when you first hear the Law Society apologise, saying you must go through a Court action if your solicitor is negligent, no matter what term **you** choose to use, be prepared to nip that tactic in the bud because, unless of course you are qualified for a civil action against your solicitor, then you will need the services of a qualified registered solicitor to act for you. And in my case, I have without success asked from the highest authorities to name a solicitor who has taken another solicitor to Court in a civil action. Thus you will be walking into a dead end. In all my research through various sources, including the Scottish Consumer Council, I have been refused this information – no one will give me the name of a solicitor who successfully challenged another solicitor in Court in a civil action.

In the moment you first ask the same question, you may think that my advice is incorrect. For just a moment, and I mean just one moment, the Law Society in their wisdom (and for their own benefit only), will appear to find for you, if you are having trouble finding one yourself, a solicitor. When this wonderful gesture is made, remember that they are in complete control at all times, and know exactly what is going on. You will be given the name of one of their fold, one prepared to communicate with all the others such that they will miss nothing.

The Law Society will find you a Troubleshooter (solicitor) and, not only that, they will help you (only because they are helping themselves first and foremost) by paying for the first two meetings with that particular Troubleshooter. How very kind of them! Or is it not another one of their ploys? For, if you have not passed all of the information in correspondence regarding your complaint against your solicitor to the Law Society, and if there is any doubt at all, your Troubleshooter will eradicate those doubts. Where do you think any missing information will be passed?

If you are fortunate, or should I say unfortunate, enough to get a Troubleshooter, be prepared for a long and time-consuming journey. These people are well trained, to destroy complainers by various methods, the most classic one of all being our old friend – **delays**.

It is extremely important for my readers, and future complainers/complainants to get to grips with what I am now able to expose regarding negligence, and the Troubleshooter scheme.

In following through in my quest for justice, I have discovered the following regarding Troubleshooters and the Law Society:

1) When I claimed deception by [First Solicitor] whereby he misappropriated my own funds in the amount of £2,000, held by him (this part of the story has already been told), I was informed by the Law Society to go to the legal ombudsman and then the

police. Why? Because the Law Society would not look at criminal deception. Does that mean, even with the knowledge of likely deception, they do nothing but sit on their hands?

2) In my research to find a complainer/complainant who had been successful in a civil Court action regarding a negligence complaint against their solicitor, with the use of a Troubleshooter (solicitor), my research proved negative. Out of the 40 Troubleshooters in Scotland I could not find one. I tried through the Law Society, with the help of the Scottish Consumer Council, to find one who could obviously help me with my case. As you have already seen in this story, my Troubleshooter used a contrived reason as an excuse to get rid of me. He used the same ploy as others of the profession constantly use – to goad a client into anger and then drop him/her as being unreasonable.

I invite my readers to review this crooked system once again:

1) All complaints against solicitors go through The Law Society, and they are always in charge. There is nothing you can do about it. They control everything – their members, our Government, Legal Aid, Scottish Consumer Council and any other government departments you may want to check.

2) Do you have any right of appeal against the Law Society's decision regarding your complaint if the decision is against you? **No**! But don't despair – they will help you. How? Advise you to go to the ombudsman. But the ombudsman can do nothing for you. He cannot change the decision of the ruling committee of the Law Society. And, in some cases where he has been able to help a complainer, the most he can award is a pitiful £1,000. Imagine how insulting £1,000 is to someone whose life has been ruined, whose life savings have been lost, whose health has been all but destroyed and who has already spent thousands of pounds dragging his way through the mire of the legal process. Having

twice been forced to go to the ombudsman (details to follow later in the story) I can confirm all of the above. The ombudsman is simply an extension of the Law Society and a waste of the taxpayers' money.

3) The Law Society, as represented by the particular Deputy Secretary I have described in this story, are endowed with professionals well trained in legal matters who know how to outwit those who come before them knowing nothing about the legal profession. When you follow the tape-recorded details of my meeting in Edinburgh, you begin to appreciate how, in his attitude and mannerisms, that the Deputy Secretary was suavely able to maintain complete control and, in so doing, make a mockery of democracy and accountability.

4) Now, if you were to add to paragraph (3) above the details of my confrontation (there is no better word to describe that episode) with my Troubleshooter, my readers may have at last come to grips with some idea as to how the whole legal complaints system works – it is basically crooked.

I ask my readers to believe me when I say – there is a lot more to come later in this story. I implore you to bear with me. First of all, please consider whether the following record of correspondence is something that engenders confidence in a genuine complainer/complainant, when all that person really needs is support and confirmation that their own painful and unnecessary experience merits recognition, at least at the human level:

Between the end of 1995 through to 5th February 1998 the correspondence between myself and the same Deputy Secretary of the Law Society consisted of 14 letters:

1) Seven were written in 1996 (between 31st May through to 22nd December).

2) Five were written in 1997 (between 13th January through to 30th April).

3) All were essentially repetitive, and some contained details that reinforce my message above regarding negligence.

4) In only a couple of instances does the Deputy Secretary offer an apology for the delays. Then he explains the reason for these delays (well worth noting!). He basically blames me, because he states I went down the negligence route! Oh for the benefit of hindsight! Remember who lured me down this path, and into the hands of the dreaded Troubleshooter, working hand-in-hand with his fellow lawyers to use this easy way to get rid of complainers.

I challenge anyone in the legal profession to prove me wrong in this accusation.

This part of the True Story relates to the meeting with the Deputy Secretary in Edinburgh, where I complained to him that I wasn't given enough time to go over all the files I had brought down with me and obtain answers to further important questions. For example – did he find in [First Solicitor]'s files details of any meetings, followed up with correspondence in regards to the contents of these meetings? In his correspondence [First Solicitor] claimed he had numerous meetings with me. Now, if I had met him so often, I would have asked some very important questions. After all, any decent solicitor looking after his client's interests, who has raised a writ into Court, would and should have meetings with his client, a necessary and sensible action to any fair-thinking person, especially in relation to this particular writ (suing [First Architect] for £30,000). One cannot dream up £30,000 just like that. One needs justification. All the details would have to be put in writing to the client to verify to the client that the figures are in order. And finally, surely, they would have to be sanctioned by the client? In this case I would have rejected the above amount outright. So where did this figure come from, and why was I never consulted about it? Is it not possible that this was a perfect figure for a conflict of interest situation?

As I have previously informed my readers when, I was sitting opposite this Deputy Secretary in Edinburgh I was unaware that [First Solicitor] was being investigated in another case in which he was eventually found guilty of – wait for it – conflict of interest! Now anyone going over my case, with the evidence I had passed to the Law Society, would come to the obvious conclusion – even a nincompoop would have seen – yes, another case of conflict of interest! The Deputy Secretary had gathered all the evidence I gave him before passing it to the Reporter for his investigation. Two great minds would have seen the same evidence. If both of these so-called professionals could not, with the detailed concrete evidence in front of them, detect an obvious conflict of interest, then God help us all! Are they really incapable of doing a professional job in reference to complaints against solicitors, or is there something altogether more sinister at work here? I charge them with incompetence, double dealing, and perverting the course of justice.

What I would like to do now is replay a story. I am going to see the world through the eyes of [First Solicitor], starting at the time when I first went to see him – when the contracts were signed in his office in 1982. I will now enact this solicitor's role, and show my readers, and future complainers, exactly how double standards are applied. I am going to take over from him – play his part. I will act in the same incompetent manner but also show how a decent honest solicitor could have acted otherwise to better protect his client's interests.

I will start in "my" office with the signing of the contract which clearly states both the start and completion dates, with the supervising architect in charge up to the awarding of the Completion Certificate.

Mr Brown then asks me the question – what does the signing of the contract do for him in the event of any invalidation of the contract? Now, as the solicitor in charge it is my responsibility to communicate accurately to my client, so I tell him – it is to ensure things are progressing as per the signed contract and to offer a line of remedy in the event that things go badly.

After the contract starts, I visit the site just to have a look, and things seem to be going well. Then Mr Brown becomes suspicious because it is getting near the completion date and there seems to be no likelihood of a Completion Certificate being issued after all. Mr Brown informs my office of his concerns in December 1982. As his solicitor, it would have been quite simple for me to contact [First Architect], my friend, or better still make a simple phone call to the proper authorities – the department of planning – to find out what was going on. That way, I could ascertain the disturbing details of the incorrect design and the resulting mess. I know that Mr Brown obviously trusts both his solicitor and his architect. After all, that was what he was paying us for.

My friend [First Architect] is obviously in a panic and is desperate to delay the moment when his incompetence is revealed to the world. He needs to delay this moment of truth, and perhaps colludes with the authorities regarding his inept drawings. I get in touch with him, asking him to return to the guest house to do a snagging list for the Completion Certificate. But I suggest to him not to do any more work until he has confirmed in writing, to me, that he requires further payments. I offer to write to Mr Brown informing him of this request. Now that should help with our plan – to further delay matters. You, Mr Architect, can always take your time with the snagging list. Also, don't worry about the grant or the authorities. I will take care of them.

We are doing quite well with our "delaying" programme. But I think the authorities are getting restless because of the delays. I discover, with the help of a newspaper article in 1985, my client's unfortunate situation over unauthorised works at his guest house. I know the person responsible for this whole mess. As if I didn't already know. But I originally recommended this architect to Mr Brown when he told me previously what he intended doing to increase his business.

Remember too, I once acted as his factor in relation to the letting of his country home, so I know his financial details.

The information that comes my way is incredible. I find out from the building and Planning Department that The Browns' guest house is a listed protected building in a conservation area. The unauthorised works that were carried out without planning permission will therefore result in a severe penalty to those responsible – possibly even a prison sentence!

I also discover from the law administration department that the £3,000 grant promised to Mr Brown prior to the start of the works will be withheld. I will obviously pass all this valuable information to my friend, [First Architect].

What possible reason could I have for doing that? Well, I can't find myself in a better position. I now have two clients, both ignorant of many of the facts I now hold in my files. What about the rule book, where it states categorically that, if there is the slightest chance of a conflict of interest, I must inform either one or both of my clients of the situation? But to all appearances I am not in that situation.

I act immediately to protect [First Architect]. I arrange a meeting with the law administration department where I deploy a very clever tactic, i.e. I suggest my friend, [First Architect], does not attend the meeting. That way he will avoid having to answer any awkward questions regarding the unauthorised works. I also advise Mr Brown to find another architect, knowing full well he will have difficulties with such a task.

Mr Brown seems to be under the impression I am doing quite well so far! Excellent. As I thought, he was having difficulty finding another architect, so I manage to find one for him. They arranged a meeting and sign a contract, i.e. one between Mr Brown and [Second Architect].

The readers are all fully aware of what happens next. We move into a phase whereby there is much correspondence between the Architects, all in relation to [Second Architect]'s need to get the drawings from [First Architect].

I know, as a solicitor, that wrongfully taking funds from my client is risky. But fortunately Mr Brown is ignorant of the law, and my friend [First Architect] knows well enough the extent to which I have already protected him thus far. Whatever goes on between [First Architect] and me is our business. The further protection I give him is incredible. I drive to his house, 17 miles from Aberdeen, meet with him to discuss certain things now that we are just prior to the case against [Contractor]. The details of that meeting have already been told.

When I issue the writ against my friend [First Architect] I had a plan that was well conceived so that the Law Society could do nothing about it. The methods used would protect both me and [First Architect], because of the way I present them to the Law Society who, in their wisdom, will protect me anyway. After all, I am one of their fold.

I also tell the Law Society that I had many meetings with my client, Mr Brown, regarding his complaints. But there is nothing in the files relating to the writ or any correspondence relating to same. I keep that information to myself. The Law Society will have no way of knowing that I did not tell Mr Brown about the writ. I leave the perfect impression that we have communicated constantly and completely. My well-thought-out plan is as follows: after putting the writ into Court, I will immediately sist it, using as my first reason the fact that I have to apply for Legal Aid. This, of course, is never done. In fact, Mr Brown did not sign any forms for Legal Aid simply because I never sent him the forms. Obviously I could not. I needed to delay and cover up my inaction with regard to suing [First Architect] – all part of our discussions in the man's home. However, if I leave the writ sisted in Court I can always recall it at any time – further protection for me, should the need arise. It can be made to look as though I have been assiduous on Mr Brown's behalf all the time! This keeps me nicely in control. The second excuse? Well I can always say I needed Mr Brown's [First Architect] as a witness. He was rather well paid for that too!

Now you can see, from Mr Brown's meeting with Mr Deputy Secretary and all that followed, that my plan worked out rather well. The Deputy Secretary is doing what exactly what I thought he would – protecting me, using all his guile and ploys to get rid of Mr Brown, the complainer. But, having been found out in a previous conflict of interest case, I have already been exposed as an incompetent solicitor. So I must be careful – the Law Society are already having trouble with me. My carefulness seems to pay off, however. The case against [Contractor] goes well from my perspective – I am saving my friend, Mr Brown's [First Architect]. Even the Sheriff rules in [First Architect]'s favour and Mr Brown can do nothing about it! To top it all, the Law Society can do nothing about it either – they have already told Mr Brown that the road I choose to go down, and any witnesses I choose to use in the Court room, have to be accepted by Mr Brown, in the case against [Contractor]. I also know that Mr Brown can do nothing against the Sheriff's decision. I made sure he couldn't, in my correspondence with him advising against an appeal. The Sheriff ruled that my friend [First Architect] was not supervising. I must say, however, I would not like to be put on the stand in a Courtroom and be asked if I had anything to do with the Sheriff's decision. I also think that if the Sheriff was put on the stand, he too would have difficulty in justifying his decision, given all the concrete crucial evidence that Mr Brown could produce to prove him wrong.

I was always confident the Law Society would rule in my favour. They had no choice because of my perfect plan and well-managed conflict of interest.

Now I will end the pretence and hope you my readers understood what I was trying to demonstrate. One important consideration – I don't have the ability to prove monies passed between [First Solicitor] and [First Architect], supporting a conflict of interest charge. Other complete concrete evidence substantiates that fact. I defy anyone to tell me otherwise.

I am not acting as a solicitor now. I am back to my normal self! How refreshing it seems not to be inhabiting the corporeal presence of that odious man. As my normal self, I would now like to ask my readers to imagine what our system of law is like if what I have demonstrated is not an isolated case, but more a common occurrence – solicitors getting away with what [First Solicitor] got away with, and all because of an incompetent Law Society who took eight, long years to inform me they have dismissed my complaint.

If the Law Society allow him to keep on practicing like that, what kind of signals are they sending out to other solicitors, or even the whole legal profession? Maybe it is possible, in our total ignorance, that this is common practice. Are we now rife with incompetent solicitors under an incompetent self-regulated system? Is this possibly the reason why there is such a marked increase in complaints against solicitors.

I have found it very difficult to come to terms with what the Law Society has accepted from a solicitor and what they have let him get away with given all the crucial detailed evidence in their possession. And what they have allowed to be inflicted upon the Brown family, beggars description!

The Law Society has repeatedly confirmed to me I could go to the legal Ombudsman, and even to the police. More of that later.

Meanwhile, moving into 1998, I wrote to the Law Society, on 5th February (File 734), regarding my seemingly endless ongoing complaint against [First Solicitor], trying to make sense of, and respond to, the plethora of issues raised by the Deputy Secretary's previous correspondence to me, including many enclosures, the essence of which are shown below:

Heading	Schedule
Page 1	*Heads of Complaint*
	Facts and Circumstances
	Reporter's Considerations
Page 2, 3 and 4	*Reporter's Further Considerations*
Page 5	*Committee's Considerations*
	Committee's Decisions
Pages 6, 7 and 8	*Facts and Circumstances*

I was devastated by the committee's findings. My letters reflect the anger and turmoil of a man who has been driven to the limits of his physical and mental resources by years of blockages, setbacks, incompetence, ploys and heartlessness. Here is what I said. I have included the words of my letters verbatim, even though they are not in perfectly constructed English. I do so to capture the flavour of authenticity, and to give my readers some insight into the torment I was going through. I am proud that, during my entire experience at the hands of individuals of dubious integrity, I have never resorted to physical abuse, or to foul language. However, when you read what follows, please understand that you are hearing the words of a basically decent, yet incredibly troubled man. Please bear with me:

> *With regard to the abovementioned complaint and subject, you were advised in my previous correspondence, and telephone conversations, I would use all the avenues open to me if I was to be excluded from the committee's decision-making meeting in regards to my written complaints against [First Solicitor]. The fears I expressed then have now been clearly verified by the enclosures.*
>
> *You have been informed of my involvement with the legal ombudsman. This has been time-consuming. I also required an extended holiday because of the legal pressures and frustrations I had to endure, because of the inconceivable crooked falsified*

report, and consequent finding, attached to your letter of 30th April 1997Hence the delay in answering said letter.

I want to make it abundantly clear that in past correspondence I stated that the Law Society had no right to jeopardise, or deny

me, access to justice by holding a committee meeting to determine the outcome of a complaint by me against [First Solicitor] on the basis of a report by a reporting member where the complainer has no right of appeal. The complainer has a right to know the written evidence contained in his various complaints have been acknowledged, entered into the records, and answered in sequence with the committee's findings, so that the records will show exactly what written evidence was produced from the files by the reporting member. Where the committee draw their conclusions and make their final decision, as stated, with no appeal rights, this decision which I am told, would be based on a unbiased fair and open conclusion without any fear of the records being falsified.

Once again, I find it incomprehensible, that the written concrete evidence produced and forwarded to the Law Society in support of my complaint have been completely excluded from the enclosures except for one item.

After many promises from the Law Society of Scotland through Mr [Deputy Secretary] of being fair, open, and unbiased, and many assurances that my complete files and written evidence would be passed to the reporting member, I now find myself in a position of complete mental strain, and finding it very difficult trying to compose myself to answer the contents of these enclosures.

Before I start making any accusations, I will for the record first, then you Mr [Deputy Secretary], then the reporting member, whoever he or she is, and finally the committee, whoever they are (I believe eight Solicitors and four lay members) pass on written information I received from the Law Society in relation to my complaint.

Here are the facts (information)

1) *Will consider matters on the basis of written evidence provided.*

2) *Will look at the professional conduct during the time [First Solicitor] acted for you.*

3) *Will look at suppression of evidence, Withholding evidence, failing to follow instructions*

4) *Will look at service provided and service offered*

5) *Will look at request for monies that already had been paid*

6) *Will be fair and open*

All of the above have been completely ignored

The contents of this letter, which will contain remarks and accusations, will be taken as being very offensive, derogatory, destructive and so on, but they are all without malice, and founded on written evidence. In my continued fight to retain my sanity, because of this crooked mental torture tactics programme, forced on me and others by the legal profession, I have managed to refrain from using physical retaliation. This would fall right in with the [legal parasite's] plans. [This is just one of the ploys that are used to undermine the client or complainer]

My daughter and I as previously stated, were told by a so-called professional Solicitor i.e. Troubleshooter not to be quiet, but shouted at on two occasions to **shut up,** *both within a 10 minute period. Needless to say, disappointment for this particular Solicitor – the ploy did not work.*

Observations and conclusions taken from the enclosures:

The reporting member, in my view, because of facts 1 through 6 is incompetent, is lacking knowledge, his or her qualifications are questionable.

These views are taken on the information received from the Law Society through you Mr [Deputy Secretary], that my complete file, which contained the concrete written evidence, was passed to the reporting member along with that of [First Solicitor].

You will see, by comparing both the reporter's considerations, and the facts mentioned above i.e. 1 through 6 and the written evidence, comparisons between the two is non-existent.

I accuse the reporter of false, crooked, biased reporting, where he based some of his findings on assumptions rather than written. He has related to certain Court case documents and ignored others. He has also lied to cloud the issues. It has become very clear the written evidence he did extract from [First Solicitor]'s files was purely for his protection, and his protection only. Reference the writ and the correspondence relating to the difficulty of taking an architect to Court.

In normal circumstances this would be agreed, but this particular architect by his own hand and his own actions, after signing a contract and cashing a cheque for supervision of the contract, made unbelievable errors outwith the normal practice of that of a professional architect, applying three times for a Completion Certificate, refusing to extend the contract, requested by [Contractor] because of the additional works costing an additional £4,000 to the original price of the contract, unknown to Mr and Mrs Brown. The list of evidence is endless, all in the hands of the Law Society.

I further accuse the reporting member of further clouding the issue. He refers to correspondence from [First Solicitor] to myself warning the difficulties of action against an architect. This is standard procedure between Solicitors and their clients. This is obviously to protect the Solicitor in this report to undermine the complainer. How low can you stoop? With reference to the writ File 150/151 [First Solicitor] clearly confirms, and is detailed in the writ that [First Architect] was supervising.

The reporting member, in his continued efforts to cloud the issue, relates to a Court room decision taken by a Sheriff in 1989. Doesn't change the fact that records will show where [First Architect]'s duties, in relation to the contract between him and Mr and Mrs Brown, were signed and sealed seven years previous to supervise the contract throughout.

The case of [Contractor] –v– Mr and Mrs Brown was for monies due them for a contract to carry out works at The Browns' guest house. This case was to decide whether we owed monies to them against a counter claim, nothing to do with [First Architect]'s contractual hired position.

Further observations and conclusions Ref. Witness.

To say we needed [First Architect] as a witness is a joke. We were against using him as a witness and have continually verified this. He is clouding the issues. We had expert witnesses in [Second Architect], our quantity surveyor and the Aberdeen Building and Planning Department.

Further to the report i.e. assumptions by the reporting member – very clever. He has assumed, prior to the writ being issued in 1987, that there was telephone contact with his agent in Stonehaven prior to the issuing and relevant to the writ against [First Architect]. You won't have to assume it was done by telephone. You will find in [First Solicitor]'s files correspondence between him and his agent in Stonehaven prior to the issuing and relevant to the writ against [First Architect]. Further to the date of the writ, a month later, File 154 10ᵗʰ Sept to [First Solicitor] from his agent in Stonehaven "We write to advise you when the case was called in Court, we tabled it on your behalf, and thereafter moved that the action be sisted pending consideration of your client's application for Legal Aid." You will find this is contradictory to [First Solicitor]'s other reason for sisting.

(What category does that come under?)

May I also bring to your attention File 117 from [First Architect] to [First Solicitor] where he makes a demand and a threat, dated 3rd February 1986. This is what I described as coercion between them both.

***Written concrete evidence.** File 184/185 dated August 1989 trying to extort monies already paid. Files 243/244/257 ** dated 11th April and 19th April 1990 respectfully*

** No date statement of accounting

With reference to our past correspondence regarding the account and financial documents, I already pointed out to you that the correspondence between [First] and [Second Solicitor], Files 243 and 244, amounted to financial criminal deception on the part of [First Solicitor].

File 244 Heading Mr and Mrs Angus M Brown –v– [First Architect], [First Solicitor] is confirming to [Second Solicitor] he has paid £2,000 in this connection.

The deception and the mockery is incredible. Files 184/185 extortion claims along with files 201 to 206 and 213 to 219 are in the hands of [Second Solicitor]. He [First Solicitor] is convincing [Second Solicitor] that he has paid me back for the monies in connection with [First Architect]'s case, because of the extortion claims. He further distorts the situation with a so-called accounting sheet, with other items he had already been paid for.

I find it very difficult, and can't comprehend, how these very important facts were completely left out of the report, completely ignored, where my correspondence dated 20th February 1995 included all of the above written facts, where they were identified, and was later promised that the committee would look into the complaint.

Further observations, conclusions and accusations

Mr [Deputy Secretary] I find you are guilty of deception, misleading a complainer, years of unnecessary delays, perverting the course of justice. You are part of a fictitious, crooked, incomplete, falsified document. The facts and the evidence will verify these accusations.

[First Solicitor] states to [Second Solicitor] that he has repaid £2,000 to Mr and Mrs Brown in connection with Mr and Mrs Brown –v– [First Architect].

These written facts become the subject of a payment that is due to Mr and Mrs Brown none other than the remainder of the balance of the outcome of the contractor's case. I believe in the region of £2,700 plus interest. You can't claim you're making two payments when in effect you have only made one. **What category does that come under?**

To the crooked reporting member

As you have decided to extract certain items from the files, always in the favour of [First Solicitor], apart from one small item, in contrast to the others, it's become quite obvious my accusations are well founded, provided the complete written evidence, in the hands of Mr [Deputy Secretary] whom I have been dealing with was passed to you. I find that if you had gone through these files and made a thorough and detailed investigation, you would have found I was **not** *trying very hard to reopen the contractor's case. I was trying very hard to show how all the concrete evidence passed to [First Solicitor] from various professional people was completely ignored, including the contents of the writ before the case against [Contractor]. Once again you are trying to cloud the issues. Your statements are untrue, lacking in content and misleading. You have lied and distorted the facts.*

[First Solicitor]'s duty, already stated, was to protect his clients Mr and Mrs Brown at all times. He failed with his unprofessional, crooked devious methods.

The so-called protective writ was a farce. [First Solicitor] was accepting monies from Mr and Mrs Brown under false pretences, and if you are too stupid or ignorant or can't comprehend what crooked [First Solicitor] was doing, then I suggest you are not, and weren't qualified to make any report, as far as my complaint was concerned. If I had been informed earlier that this was going to be one of the basis of your report you would have got the same answers.

Reference, you mentioned **counter claims.**

Again these were farcical, failed by ignoring: the conservation grant, additions to the contract and unauthorised works, and additional six weeks closure, failed to get a Completion Certificate, additional costs for other architect's completion date over ran for 12 weeks, additional lost revenue £4,200

[First Architect] was protected from all these costs [Why?]. [First Solicitor] could have, in a professional manner and protecting his clients, counter claimed, for all of the above resulting in the following.

Conservation grant	*£3,000*
Unauthorised additions to contract	*£4,000*
Closure for second time loss of income	*£4,000*
Enforcement alterations	*£10,000*
Additional architects fees	*£2,000*
Plus the above	*£4,200*
And others, etc., etc., etc.?	*£££££*

To further prevent me from getting access to justice, you have deviously inserted a statement regarding my accusations about a conspiracy, involving [First Architect], [First Solicitor] and the Sheriff who officiated at the contractor's case. Are you making sure that all the legal profession know about these accusations, that any further attempts by me, to further this conspiracy will be blocked, because of [First Solicitor]'s manipulation of the law? If this is your obvious intention, if this can happen within legal circles, then it's my duty along with others to make sure the public are aware this legal corruption, allowed to go on un-checked, could happen to them, where their money along with the tax payers', can be misused. If the unsuspecting public are paying their hard working and well earned cash when they forward their complaints to the Law Society regarding the actions of their Solicitors, they are trying to do what the Law Society have failed to do i.e. weed out the crooked ones, you are blocking and protecting them. This is making a mockery of the tax payer. I would like to point out that the contents of this letter, and the enclosures, is in no way aimed at anyone in the legal profession who abides by law and order, who is trustworthy, is a pillar of his profession, who acts with integrity, who is fair and open and protects his clients at all times. The accusations are only aimed at the crooks in the profession.

On separate sheets you will find further observations, conclusions and accusations. These will be headed [to the reporting member], the [committee] and cross reference sheets.

I conclude by stating that the three well known facts, in relation to Solicitors' client relations (delays, lack of communication, and failure to take notes), your peers have stated: "Your outdated, creaking, behind the times system requires updating". I fully agree, and the school for updating Solicitors' skills is, I believe, least attended by Scottish Solicitors as opposed to other countries.

I would require confirmation on receipt of this letter within the next seven days, and what actions are being taken in regards to files 143/244 criminal deception.

> *Cc   Secretary of State for Scotland*
>
> *Sir Robert Smith MP*
>
> *Mr Douglas Mill, Secretary to the Law Society*
>
> *Deputy (Secs) Law Society*
>
> *Legal Ombudsman*
>
> *Others etc*

On 16th February 1998 (File 737) the Law Society responded!

I write to acknowledge receipt of your detailed letter and enclosures dated 5th February 1998 in relation to your complaint against [First Solicitor].

I must again stress to you the fact that your complaint has been dealt with in accordance with the Law Society's standard procedures. No members of the public address a meeting of a complaints committee in relation to their complaint and no Solicitor is able to do so either. The procedure in that regard is fair and even-handed.

The reporter, when considering this matter, had an opportunity of looking at all the Solicitors' files, and the paperwork, which you submitted to this office and before any view was reached you were given an opportunity, as were the Solicitors the opportunity, to make comment upon the reporter's report.

The fact of the matter is the Law Society's complaints procedure operates on the basis of the committee's considering reports from the reporters after having given complainer, and Solicitors the opportunity to make comment. I understand your concern about having "no right of appeal". The fact of the matter is that the currency of your complaint, the office of the lay observer became the office of the legal services ombudsman and the fact that there were no transitional provisions allowing the ombudsman and the fact that there were no transitional provisions allowing the ombudsman to look at complaints made prior to the 3rd June was, arguably, an error in the legislation which the Law Society had no part in.

I have taken the opportunity of looking again at the reporter's report and the evidence, which you have now provided. In my view there is no question of the reporter seeking to protect [First Solicitor]. As I have made it clear to you over the course of the correspondence, what the Law Society cannot look at is the actual case itself, the evidence relating to it or the way that matters turned out. You make clear reference to the actions of [First Architect] in this matter, which lie entirely outwith consideration of this office. The reporter can only look at what has taken place, and cannot reach a view on matters which would properly be determined by the Court.

Let me make it clear, I have no reason to cover up what you describe as the real evidence. I have simply tried to make it clear to you in the correspondence that the number of the issues that you raise fall outwith the remit of this office to determine, in particular, negligence and I would respectfully remind you that during currency of this complaint, you were afforded the services of a Troubleshooter to advise you specifically on negligence.

Turning to the question of the complaints procedures, which you refer to on page 6 of your letter, I would respectfully point out that the Scottish legal services ombudsman considers very carefully the procedures operated by the Law Society. The fact that both a complainer and a Solicitor make written representations is the accepted way to deal with complaints.

You make reference to the change of procedures during the course of your complaint and in particular the fact you were allowed to review the facts and circumstances. It is fair to say that in all complaints where a report is called for, both parties now see the facts and circumstances.

As a matter of fact, the Law Society does not disclose the name of any reporter either to a Solicitor or a complainer. I would confirm however that when your complaint was before the committee that those present were both Solicitors and lay people. I do not consider it appropriate to advise you of the Law Society's method of recruitment for lay complaints committee members I consider that there is nothing further I can usefully add.

On 5th March 1998 (File 739) the Law Society wrote again:

I note you have sent a copy of my letter to the Secretary of State. I have no difficulty with that.

With respect, I do not consider that the issues numbered 1-6 on the second page of your letter of 5th February were not looked at and considered by the reporter. It was explained to you during the currency of the complaint that because of the timing of the actions of [First Solicitor] the Law Society was not in a position to exercise its full powers in relation to inadequate professional service and in particular because [First Solicitor] ceased to act for you prior to June 1991 that, even if your complaint were to be upheld, there was no possibility of the Law Society awarding compensation because it did not have the power to do so.

I entirely accept that you provided evidence in relation to your complaint. The reporter considered that and, as you are well aware, you had the opportunity to comment on the reporter's report so far as the facts and circumstances were concerned before the matter was determined by the committee. I do not intend to go into the individual points which you have raised about evidence relating to your complaint. The reporter was well aware of the issues which you were raising and, as I have endeavoured to explain to you on several occasions, this office is not in a position to look at the actual merits of your case itself.

I note your comments in regard to the question of advising you to go to the police. I believe that it has been clear to you throughout this matter that the remit of the Law Society is limited to consideration of a Solicitor's professional conduct and where appropriate, the standard of service provided.

If you believe that some crime was committed then that is a matter for the Police.

The question of accounting to you was dealt with during the course of your complaint. If you are dissatisfied with the accounting procedures which have taken place, then there may be civil remedy available to you although I appreciate that you might not wish in the circumstances to seek further legal advice. I would respectfully remind you that during the currency of this complaint you have had the benefit of an appointment of a Troubleshooter, paid for by the Law Society of Scotland, and in addition as I understand matters, your complaint made against [Second Solicitor] which is separate to this was upheld.

I note you make a number of accusations against me personally. I would respectfully point out that throughout the course of this complaint I have endeavoured to make it clear to you that the Law Society's remit for looking at matters is limited and does not extend, for example, to negligence. I make no comment over and above that.

You ask for comments in particular to documents 243 and 244 of which you note provide evidence of criminal deception.

If you believe that then I have to advise you that it is for you to report those matters to the appropriate authorities, in this instance the police. The Law Society is not empowered to investigate and to adjudicate upon what might be described as criminal deception.

If at the end of the day, the police investigate and show that there were actions on the part of any Solicitor, which caused them concern, then it is certainly possible that the Law Society might take action. There is nothing further that I can usefully add.

On 13th March 1998 (File 739-1) I responded to the Law Society:

> *I am in receipt of your letter of 5th March 1998 and respond as follows.*
>
> *Reference your past correspondence in relation to the 6/ numbered Facts (circumstances) in my correspondence to you dated (5th and 22nd Feb 1998) as follows.*
>
> *2nd April 1990 (2nd paragraph)*
>
> *"I can assure you that the question of the **professional conduct** of the Solicitors will be looked at."*
>
> *14th June 1990 (last paragraph)*
>
> *"Rest assured that the question of **professional conduct** will be considered."*
>
> *26th May 1993 (paragraph 5)*
>
> *"The only matter which the Law Society can consider, in relation to [First Solicitor], would be the **professional conduct** of [First Solicitor] and **possibly the service provided. The Society only gained power to consider the question of service from January 1989**."*
>
> *31st March 1994 page 1 (2nd paragraph)*
>
> *"Throughout the correspondence which I have had with you in this matter, I think **I have made it clear** that I am quite happy to consider your complaint in relation to [First Solicitor], in relation to his **professional conduct and indeed the service offered**."*
>
> *I have also made it quite clear, however, that my considerations in this respect could not proceed until the question of your possible negligence action had been dealt with. Where a complainer is contemplating or is, indeed, pursuing a Solicitor in relation to*

negligence, the Law Society will not investigate a complaint until that process has been completed.

"I would point out to you that you have not been prejudiced in any way, so far as the complaint is concerned, by the time that has passed."

Page 2 last paragraph

"I am happy to take forward your complaint in relation to the **conduct and service.***"*

17ʰ February 1995 page 1 (3ʳᵈ paragraph – File 705)

"The position is a report has now been received from the reporting member. The matter will therefore go to the committee in March for consideration."

(4ᵗʰ paragraph)

"I understand that you have raised with the other deputy the fact in another complaint dealt with by another Deputy Secretary. You have received a copy of the facts and circumstances before the matter went to the committee. This does not happen in every instance. In the case of your complaint against [First Solicitor] the matter at issue is one of professional conduct of the Solicitor and, in that situation, it is not the Law Society's practice to send details of the facts and circumstances to both parties before the committee considers the matter."

Page 2 (last paragraph)

"I would emphasise to you again that as this is a complaint specifically involving a conduct matter the appropriate procedures are being followed which means in this case that the schedule containing the facts and circumstances are not copied by either party before the committee considers the matter."

11ᵗʰ April 1996 (2ⁿᵈ paragraph – File 727)

"As I believe I have already made it clear to you, the issue which the Law Society is considering in connection with [First Solicitor]'s actings relates solely to his professional conduct during the time that he actually acted for you."

(3rd paragraph)

"May I also point out that I will certainly confirm to you once I have received the report from the reporter. As I believe, as has previously been made clear in correspondence, the committee will consider this matter on the basis of the reporter's report. I would, however, say that while I am prepared to copy the basis of that report to you it is not the case that you would have a further opportunity to make further representations at this time. Precisely the same applies to [First Solicitor]."

11th February 1997 (paragraph 6)

"The second issue which you raise in relation to [First Solicitor] is suppression and withholding concrete evidence. When the Law Society investigates a complaint it is able to call for the Solicitor's files as has been the case here."

(Paragraph 7)

"The Law Society is entitled to consider the complaint and take a view upon the information which is contained in those files. The question of requesting monies which had already been paid, and failing to follow instructions, certainly are issues which fall within the Law Society's remit."

5th March 1997 (paragraph 2)

"This complaint is following the usual procedures in connection with a complaint relating to conduct and service. The Law Society's procedures are such it is for the reporter to consider the evidence available and for the committee to finally determine the matter. The Law Society's practice is to considers matters on the basis of the written evidence provided."

I now bring your attention to a very important factor in relation to why the legal ombudsman should be involved with my complaint. By your own written word, I refer to correspondence dated 31st March 1994 and the following details.

Your correspondence complaints against [First Solicitor]

Dated 20th July 1992

Dated 22nd Aug 1994

Dated 21st Sept 1994

Dated 18th Oct 1994

Dated 14th Feb 1995

Dated 17th Feb 1995

In my correspondence to the legal ombudsman dated the 10th May 1997, I confirmed that all the files relating to my complaint against [First Solicitor] should be fully investigated by the legal ombudsman, on the determination and conclusions by both the reporter and the committee of my complaint against [First Solicitor], which would have included the abovementioned details. I would have expected the full cooperation of both the self-regulating body, namely the Law Society, and the appointed legal ombudsman, to facilitate my request and act accordingly, but obviously these important details have been overlooked. This requires investigating with a full explanation why. In my quest for justice, where I turned to the Law Society for help to gain recognition in my complaint against [First Solicitor] the innuendos have just been horrendous, and still are, as has been found in the latest correspondence received from the Law Society.

I now believe that the reports, the considerations, the findings, have all been done by one and the same person. I, like the Law Society, believe in written evidence provided. I don't have that written evidence to prove otherwise.

Any self-regulating body must act in accordance and within the legal rights pertaining to law and order, and must be governed by same. That's the way I see it.

Simple questions I have asked of the Law Society required simple answers pertaining to my complaint against [First Solicitor] bearing in mind, after all these years, I shouldn't be in this position in the first place if the people involved had legally adhered to and protected my legal rights.

The Law Society, in their investigations into both the Solicitor's and complainer's files, would have discovered that a report by the reporting member "Protective writ to the amount of £30,000" had been issued by [First Solicitor] and also stated that [First Solicitor]" had nothing to gain by concealing this protective writ from his clients. This writ, after being sisted, could be recalled at any time".

One of the questions I put to the Law Society, as a self-regulated body, was did you ask Mr Brown's [First Solicitor]: In your correspondence to Mr Brown dated 17th August 1989 you stated "I will deal with Mr Brown's [First Architect]'s case separately". After prepayment of £2,000 in relation to this case and the issuing of this protective writ, what further action did you take against [First Architect] to protect your clients Mr and Mrs Brown, with the concrete evidence available from various sources which we have received and in our possession, from Mr Brown?

The Law Society received correspondence from Mr Brown's [First Solicitor] in 1990 which contained a statement protecting Mr Brown's [First Architect]'s actions. This letter, along with the statement above, should have triggered off a conflict of interest investigation by the Law Society, but they did nothing.

Any self-regulating body, such as the Law Society, who is supposed to act in an exemplary manner, who asks a complainer for details, evidence in relation to his complaint, has to rely solely on the honesty and integrity of this self-regulating body, who have complete control of the entire situation; i.e., evidence, files, correspondence, where the complainer has no regulative control between the offending Solicitor and the Law Society... I will show where this crooked closed shop system could be used by the Law Society in handling many of their complaints.

In my possession I have certain correspondence from [First Solicitor] which, if used by the reporting member then passed to the committee to be analysed, could be completely misconstrued. If my evidence was ignored or omitted, which could completely contradict this particular letter, I as a complainer have no written guarantee that my civil rights for access to justice, have been or could be violated. This is illegal.

Further to the reporting member and his report, he has now given us the proof, which could now show another situation, where information could be withheld unknown to me, the complainer, but released to the committee to undermine me, the complainer, and my complaints. I refer to Pursuer –v– Defender. If the information received from the offending Solicitor in regards to this situation and read out to the committee and presented in such a manner without any representation from my side, and again, if my evidence was ignored or omitted, my complaint would be misrepresented and deny me my rights to access to justice.

Any self-regulating body who cannot act with fairness, honesty, integrity, openness, who cannot account to a complainer in detail, gives a broad statement, like his complete case was looked into, has got to be replaced and acted upon.

In reference to accounting and your investigations relating to same, which I have been told on many occasions will be done impartially: I now refer you to my correspondence dated 20th February 1995 which contained concise important details to which, after long delays previously, would have been given some kind of priority. Your reply was a simple thank you for the letter, with no mention of the contents.

The contents were related to the accounting, the question then which should have been put to [First Solicitor] immediately by the Law Society to verify payments mentioned in Documents 243, 244 and 257. This would have ensured that the Law Society does investigate a complaint properly. I mentioned to the Law Society that document 257 was not a proper accounting sheet. You will see from your records various different accounting sheets were eventually received from [First Solicitor] where some of the details were in question which resulted in a further delay of three months by [First Solicitor].

As the Law Society are the investigators where a complainer highlights a particular situation, is it not your duty – reference leaflet "Dissatisfied with your Solicitor?" – to act in a professional manner as a self-regulating body, to verify and ask an explanation, i.e. you accepted these accounts where it simply states 6th April To you cheque £2,000. Why didn't you question, and ask for details in relation to these monies? My correspondence to you was dated 20th February 1995 where I stated I had faxed [Second Solicitor] and gave him the details relating to the true nature of the monies. I had to wait until 15th August 1995 before ledgers were sent to me. The questions should have been asked prior to that.

If the Law Society intend to take no further action in reference to my complaint against [First Solicitor] and refuse to answer the questions in previous correspondence, I would like to know the reasons why.

I would also ask for written confirmation that all the information, all the evidence that I had passed to the Law Society in relation to complaint against [First Solicitor], was fully researched and investigated by the reporting member and the committee.

I have searched endlessly to try and make sense out of this whole bizarre situation, where the innocent parties have suffered unbelievably at the hands of all the legal experts that the Brown family turned to for help, to find there is no access to justice through the Scottish legal system.

*Finally, as it seems the Law Society are determined to protect [First Solicitor] I, like the reporting member, can only **assume** that the reasons could be that the offending Solicitor had another case in tandem with mine going through the Law Society's complaints office approximately the same time. Is it possible that the ramifications could present certain problems to the Law Society?*

It is public knowledge and has been mentioned in the press that [First Solicitor] was found guilty of professional misconduct and fined £5,000 by the Scottish Solicitors' Discipline Tribunal in May 1996.

I have asked questions in my previous correspondence, and there are questions in the above that also require to be answered. I would appreciate your full cooperation in replying with the relative answers.

Cc   *The Lord Chancellor*

     Secretary of State for Scotland

     Sir Robert Smith MP

     Mr Douglas Mill, Sec to Law Society

     Legal Ombudsman

     Chairman Scottish Consumer Council

I also included the following additional document with my letter:

To the Reporting Member

Additions to the main **Observations** and **Conclusions**

The reasons for these additions, is to highlight your particular conduct, in relation to your report.

First, your report.

You have tried to vindicate all of [First Solicitor]'s reports by excluding evidence contained in his files to cover up the true nature of this evil, cunning man. You have ignored evidence available in both [First Solicitor]'s and Mr Brown's files.

[First Architect] was not a crucial witness in the main action – see main report. We were aware of the writ and its sisting. You are one hundred percent correct. But only when we picked up copies of the files in [First Solicitor]'s office after very depressing phone calls first with [First Solicitor] regarding an appeal against [Contractor] where he just put the phone down. Then with one of his sidekick's – question: "When are we taking [First Architect] to Court?" Answer: "Why are we taking [First Architect] to Court and for what reason?" We had paid £2,000 plus for that answer. This was in 1989.

With reference to instructions may I remind you the Solicitor takes instructions from his client. Your comment regarding Defender in this action was because of unprofessional crooked action by [First Solicitor].

*If you can't find in your search through the files, or you can't tell the difference between proper legal conduct as opposed to legal misconduct, then you have a problem of proper **honest** investigating and fair open reporting.*

The rest of the further report is concentrating on the Legal Aid issue, with further emphasis on financial details where the phraseology used (i.e. "it appears") on several occasions, tells us a lot but actually tells us nothing. Except for the main issues contained in the main report. I refer you to files 243/244, which you have failed to mention in your report.

Your facts and circumstances have already been answered, and in your possession except for additions to which I didn't have the chance to answer, or were made available to me in past correspondence, you have cleverly introduced new statements that are untrue, to undermine me and my evidence.

Your conduct in relation to the report

You have contrived through your dishonest crooked methods, through your lies, to undermine my whole situation, trying to give a completely false picture where the Solicitors we consulted did everything to help us to further our case and protect us at all times (when in fact they did the opposite).

*As you are nameless and hide behind a crooked closed shop system, you have to be referred to as the reporting member. As your professional credentials remain secret, you want me to assume, like you did in your report, that your credentials are such that you are qualified to make such a report. The Law Society, I am told, are only interested in written evidence. I agree with them. I also require written evidence regarding your qualifications. I have, as stated above in my main report, you're incompetent, you're lacking in knowledge, you have lied in your report. When a person lies, his or her character is undoubtedly in question. For a person in your trusted position, a member of law and order sitting behind a desk, in a matter of days after supposedly investigating all of the evidence in the files ... concoct a devious unreliable report based on **selected evidence** to protect a crooked Solicitor. Are you protecting this particular Solicitor because he has made a mockery out of the Deputy Secretary, and the Law Society, as stated, in my main report?*

How far are you willing to stoop? Your lies and deceit are incredible. How can we look up to these professional people, supposed to be held in high esteem, when an impostor like you (I would bracket with a parasite) has inserted an addition into facts and circumstances to distort and cloud the true facts.

Facts and circumstances

Again your professional credentials come into question along with your integrity. You already know the facts. You have once again tried to cloud the issues. I did not consult with [Second Solicitor] just regarding the outcome of the case against [Contractor]. I consulted with him also in regards my case against [First Architect].

[Second Solicitor] didn't have to ask for the papers from [First Solicitor]. You already know my daughter picked up a complete copy file from his office, and hand-delivered to [Second Solicitor] who advised us it was too late to appeal. Check the files, you have lied again.

Your report and its contents are falsified. Because of the lies and the new insertions, purposely included to further cloud the issues, where I wasn't given a chance to reply to, and the evidence in the files which you completely ignored, your selective report is criminal. You are trying, and have, perverted the course of justice. You have ignored the information that was passed to the Law Society regarding criminal deception. You have allowed [First Solicitor] to misappropriate funds belonging to Mr and Mrs Brown. He is holding these funds under false pretences, that is a criminal offence. This information was passed to the Law Society on 20th February 1995.

Professional conduct *(protecting our interests, details in your files.)*

[First Solicitor] to Mr Brown 21st March 1985: "It surprises me that this matter has been going on for such a long period of time without anyone taking the bull by the horns and getting the matter resolved." (Now that should build a client's confidence).

[First Solicitor] to Mr Brown 14th October 1986: "You will have received copies of our letters getting the ball rolling." My Goodness!! (That really sounds impressive). This is what you call getting sucked into a web of deceit. One year and seven months later, this particular delay is different from that mentioned in my main report.

To you Mr Reporting Member, these are just two items in your files. When you read them will find they are minimal to the others. You have the audacity to pull out a few items from the files, insert a few quotes, add a few assumptions from these, then have it passed through into the records. That's got rid of another complainer, simple, just like that. You can get away with this because you are protected. I refer to fact No 6 in the main report. I have this to say to you, Mr or Mrs Reporter, when you look in the mirror, I mean a good hard look, do you see someone with integrity? Do you see some one who can identify with righteousness, fairness, openness? I hope you get the real truth because you sure as hell have not identified with me. What about our children in the future. Who are they going to look up to, because the Law Society, its members, and the legal profession have railroaded, backed me into a corner after 15 long years, and inflicted this continuous mental torture tactics? And you are doing exactly the same. I accuse, charge you, with the following:

1) Concealing written evidence.

2) Suppression of evidence.

3) Aiding and abetting a crooked Solicitor.

4) Allowing a Solicitor to misappropriate his client's funds and keep said funds.

5) False reporting.

6) Violating my civil rights.

7) Lying to conceal the true facts plus others, etc, etc, etc.

The information contained in the enclosures with this letter have been in your possession for some considerable amount of time. Because you failed to mention these and other, I thought it prudent to remind you.

As you're determined to protect [First Solicitor], I will have to assume you did this for various reasons. I would suggest you look at the correspondence between [First Solicitor] and the (first agent) who took over from [Contractor].

Your crooked report mentions Pursuers and Defenders. Let's assume for the moment [First Solicitor] is really protecting Mr and Mrs Brown's interests and his correspondence with the (first agent) – can we assume he told this agent his chances of success will be minimised because [Contractor] constructed unauthorised works outwith the contract drawings, followed by an enforcement order to remove the unauthorised works, constituting further closures with loss of revenue with the additional £4,000 added to the contract, with additional architect's fees. Any Court would frown in any action being taken under these circumstances. Why would any agent think of pursuing further? But this agent had further information. I suggest you check their correspondence regarding [First Architect], hence the big cover-up. Defender and Pursuer? Check the files, confuse the issues, delay the case, arrange it so we protect [First Architect], cook up various deals, send out more letters to The Browns. Tell a lot but tell them nothing. Conceal the evidence. More money for us the Solicitors.

Because you have to belittle, disparage me in different ways, I can only find one last word for the moment to describe you and your actions – despicable. I would before I close remind you of this beautiful country of ours, and the freedom we enjoy under a democratic Government and a democratic policy, to be enjoyed by all not just a few.

The whole backbone, the basic principles of our society, our very own culture, is being slowly eroded by the legal professional, who have no principles that I can see except greed. I can only feel revulsion when I think of the war years when Mr Churchill, then Prime Minister, paid a glowing tribute to the Royal Air Force in the Battle of Britain (not forgetting all of the other forces who died). His tribute: "Never have so many owed so much to so few."

I have a tribute to pay the crooks in the legal profession:

*Never have so few screwed so many (**Concise English Dictionary** – screwed: squeeze, extort). These people who died during the war would turn in their grave to know even our fundamental rights are being denied.*

Your criminal report, I am demanding to be scrapped because of misrepresentation, lies, deceitful statements, lacking in content, trying to pervert the course of justice.

And finally, I attached the following words for the complaints committee:

To the Decision Making Committee

Ref Complaint by Mr Angus M Brown against [First Solicitor]

*I find it quite intolerable that a group of Solicitors in Scotland, making decisions under the heading **Law Society**, can agree and sanction the action of this particular Solicitor, and the falsified report by the reporting member.*

In 1989 [First Solicitor] went in to Court of law/hearing/proof and committed offences in front of the Sheriff against his own clients, in that he failed to protect them in the full knowledge that the concrete written evidence in his possession from various source, was withheld.

He was paid in advance for this protection. He took money under false pretences. He further committed an act of unprofessional conduct in that he allowed a decision to be taken that would have a lasting, damaging, effect on his client's pursuit on any future claims against [First Architect] with the full knowledge he had been paid in advance for this particular action. He further committed an unpardonable offence still not protecting his clients by refusing an appeal which would have been overwhelmingly accepted with all the concrete evidence in his possession.

*In my letter to the Deputy Secretary and the letter to the reporting member, I have covered all the details. I don't need to repeat them, but I am livid, furious, that my fundamental rights have been violated. This criminal cover-up is just beyond comprehension. You have, by your actions, accepted the fact that this aforementioned Solicitor can go on manipulating your laws to suit himself, to go on taking monies under false pretences, getting away with criminal deceptive letters. In my correspondence with the Law Society, reference was always made to uphold the law. I have done exactly that for 15 long purposely delayed years, and you have sanctioned and gave a permit for a crooked Solicitor to do the opposite. If any future Scottish Government sanctions this so-called **Law** Society under its present system, I don't have to tell you my reactions. By your decisions, in upholding the report, except for Legal Aid, you have committed offences against me, by denying me my rights, of access to justice.*

[First Solicitor]'s character is well tarnished, and I have to keep fighting a crooked system where the more you protect, the more exposed your system becomes. You are like bully boys, playing dirty games in a school playground. You make me sick to my stomach.

I have somewhere in the region of 60/70 pages of articles taken from the newspapers over the last eight years, where the legal profession are really showing the general public their true colours, and you are still at it.

The police are sick of the whole situation trying to maintain a decent society, being completely eroded by the legal profession.

I conclude by demanding the falsified report, and committee's decision be revoked. If not, I will obviously be taking further concrete action.

I think it's important to let you know exactly what you are doing to me, and others. To get these reports done, write letters and try and live a normal life is impossible, as you all know. The intimidations you inflict on us puts so much strain on our health that when I go over the details, the heart starts to thump, the stomach starts to turn, the blood temperature increases to such an extent you have to stop and take walks, then more walks. You are separated from family and friends. The list goes on.

Because my blood pressure is sky high at the moment, to help me reduce this situation and calm myself, I can only say this to you: why don't you crawl back under the rocks from whence you came? Things have got to change. I will close with this well-known saying: "You can fool some of the people some of the time but you cannot fool all of the people all of the time." And if you think that the public are unaware that Solicitors pass conflicting letters to boost their client's morale (more money) and self-protect each other at the same time, in case of complaints, I think you better waken up.

Chapter 7

The Ombudsman and the Scottish Consumer Council

When I received the decision from the Law Society of their findings regarding [First Solicitor], I knew for certain that their clever ploys had come to the forefront. Once again they had succeeded in destroying the case of a complainer. Legal parasites had invented, conspired even to create, these clever ploys starting with the word negligence, continuing with the travesty that is the Troubleshooter scheme, sitting back smugly as a complainer's bank account is depleted, their health failing and their energy levels brought to zero, and finally, of course, to add ineffectiveness to corruption by offering the Ombudsman as a last resort of hope. It is also worth noting that two years prior to this moment, the Law Society had introduced the concept in what was known as the **lay observer** – another waste of time and taxpayer's money.

And there we have it – a system that had been going on for more than 20 years, prior to the Ombudsman's role which was introduced in June 1991 (details of which follow later in this story). Here we have a legal profession operating within a flawed system doing all that it can to quash complaints against fellow solicitors. Surely such a system is illegal? Surely it perverts the course of true justice?

I personally went to two Ombudsman. I am a glutton for punishment! I went to the first one in 1995. The particular complaint I took to him related to the Advocate who was acting for me after receiving the papers from [Second Solicitor], the night before the hearing/debate against [First Architect]. One of my main complaints was the refusal of the dean of faculty to hand over the pages of notes my Advocate was supposed to have taken prior to the case; i.e. the night before.

My correspondence with the Ombudsman regarding the Advocate was short-lived, starting in February 1995 and concluding in April 1995.

On 7th February 1995 (File 701-1) the Ombudsman wrote to me regarding my complaint against the Advocate:

> *Thank you for your letter dated 1st February 1995, following our telephone conversation earlier in the week. With this letter you will find our standard letter which goes out to all complainers following which we will be obtaining the faculty file, preparatory to examining the complaint.*
>
> *I regret that I am not able to give you any advice regarding how to approach the European Court of Civil Rights but I suggest that this is information, which you could obtain either from your present Solicitor, if you have one, or from the Citizens Advice Bureau in Aberdeen.*

He also wrote as follows in an undated letter in April 1995 (File 714-1):

> *My function is to examine allegations concerning a professional organisation's handling of complaints against a legal practitioner, and I operate under general directions laid down by the Secretary of State for Scotland. My objective is to ensure that in dealing with complaints against practitioners, the relevant professional organisations act reasonably, impartially and efficiently. I do not give legal advice and am not required to assess the merits of particular complaints against the practitioner. I am concerned to ascertain whether or not the professional organisation has given each complaint the attention it deserves and has, on the basis of fair and thorough investigation of all the evidence, taken appropriate action. I am unable to criticise the dean's decision not to forward copies of the Advocate's personal notes to the complainer.*

Conclusion

In my opinion, the faculty's investigation of this complainer has been fair and thorough, and I have no recommendations for the faculty.

What could I do about the conclusion? Nothing whatsoever. Maybe he would offer me some prospect of success/help with the details of the Law Society's handling of my complaint against [First Solicitor]?

On 21st February 1997 (File 730) I wrote to the Ombudsman:

Thank you for your letter of 5th February 1997. After reading the contents of your letter I suddenly realised I had omitted, or forgot, to include certain important documents in my previous letter.

These documentations are now enclosed, for your perusal, including a sheet showing the proper sequence of events, which supersedes the original, on page 1 of my previous letter. I apologise for these errors and any confusion it has caused.

When you read through the enclosures, you should now get a clear picture of the basis of my complaint along with many others.

Before any conclusions are drawn or decisions taken, I feel, and think, it is very important you ask the Law Society for the files regarding my complaint against [First Solicitor], ref LSC/90/210/ PYJ/JAS.

The question of the timing, of my complaint, and the involvement of the legal ombudsman, regarding my complaint against [First Solicitor] has now been raised by the Law Society who I am sure has already been in touch with you regarding same.

*The details of the timing, the concrete evidence, the tape recording
of a meeting held at the offices of the Law Society, are all in the
files, to verify the timing and the justification, of my complaints.
Before any decision or course of action is taken this would be fair
to both parties, and ensure proper legal procedure is followed.
I have enclosed a copy of my most recent correspondence to the
Law Society regarding above.*

I was corresponding with the ombudsman on the advice of the Law
Society, who also suggested that I contact the police in my claims of
criminal deception. My readers will see, as I continue with this True
Story, that I was very much involved with various organisations, all
because of the ploys used by the Law Society. So I also contacted the
director of Scottish Courts' administration, regarding my complaint about
the incompetent Sheriff who officiated in my case against [Contractor]
– declaring the Architect was (**not**) supervising. Not unexpectedly, I
received the usual negative response. I wrote to the Aberdeen Police, as
suggested by the Law Society, and I also had communications with the
Scottish Consumer Council (SCC).

The interaction with the police was short-lived! On 11th June 1997 (File
730-2) I wrote to the chief constable of Aberdeenshire:

*I am writing to you for your assistance, to further my fight for
justice, through the Scottish legal system.*

*You will see, from the correspondence enclosed, why I have
contacted the police department.*

*All the pertinent details are on file, and any questions relating to
any accusations can be readily answered.*

*The full cooperation from the Aberdeen Police Department
would be most appreciated.*

I believe, along with everyone else, that justice should be made available to each and every one of us.

Confirmation on receipt of this correspondence would be most appreciated.

I received my reply on 20th June 1997 (File 731):

I acknowledge receipt of your letter 11th June 1997, and accompanying copy letters.

From the information you supplied, it appears that the events to which you refer took place around 1985 or earlier, and that a civil case was heard in Aberdeen in July 1989. As stated in the copy letter from the Scottish Courts' administration, the course of action open to you then was to appeal to the Sheriff principal if you were dissatisfied with the outcome of the case.

Given that many years have passed since this incident took place, and as it appears to be purely a civil matter, I do not intend to take any further action.

Now, back to my correspondence with the Ombudsman. On 9th June 1997 (File 730-1) the Ombudsman wrote to me regarding my complaint against [First Solicitor]:

Further to my letter of 20th May 1997, I am now writing to you in the light of our subsequent telephone conversation. In that conversation you advised me that I was incorrect in suggesting that your complaint against [First Solicitor] was first intimated to the Law Society in 1990, maintaining that at that stage you were simply making enquiries of the Law Society and obtaining pamphlets with a view to understanding the role of the Law Society in complaints matters.

I have examined the correspondence on the Law Society file covering 1990. The file essentially starts with a resume of an interview, which you had with the complaints investigator on March 1990, which is headed up as a statement in connection with a complaint that you wish to make against [First Solicitor]. Enquiries were immediately made of the Solicitors, and the Law Society correspondence is clearly headed as being a complaint against [First Solicitor]. I can see no reference to this being disputed by you. There is considerable correspondence in the course of 1990 between the Law Society and yourself and the Solicitors. I appreciate that you were advised by the Law Society that it could not pursue your complaint while you were pursuing actions against [First Architect] and the Solicitors. But there is nothing in the correspondence in 1990 which would enable me to conclude that a complaint was not intimated to the Law Society in that period.

I appreciate you will be disappointed with my conclusion, but my remit does not allow me to examine a handling complaint made to the Law Society before 3rd June 1991. I very much regret that I cannot assist, and that I have to return your file of papers which are now closed.

On 22nd October 1997 (File 732) I wrote to the Ombudsman:

In response to our meeting on the 9th September 1997 and your recent correspondence regards your jurisdiction over my complaint against [First Solicitor] through the Law Society, I reiterate what I stated in your office, the official complaint did not take effect until late 1991 when it was confirmed at a meeting with the QC.

This was also confirmed by the Law Society; by their statement, that "until the case against [First Architect] was concluded, I had no case against [First Solicitor] or a complaint".

If the Law Society, in their letter heading, mention complaints against Solicitors when corresponding with clients, or the lay person, they should have a signed document stating the date when the complaint originated.

If you still refuse to further my case against the Law Society, you can rest assured my fight to get access to justice will never end.

On 28th October 1997 (File 733) the Ombudsman responded:

Thank you for your further letter of 22nd October 1997 in response to my own letter of 6th October 1997. I note the points that you have made, but I have no doubts with regard to the conclusion that I have reached. The fact that the Law Society defers the investigation of a complaint because of ongoing litigation does not invalidate the original intimation of the complaint.

I am sorry that I am unable to be of assistance.

I was getting nowhere. But I did not give up. On 11th February 1998 (File 734) I wrote to my MP:

On Friday 6th February I mailed you a large brown envelope, containing a file of documents and a letter to the Deputy Secretary of the Law Society who I have been dealing with.

The letter and documents you will find are self-explanatory. I also hope you find them very disturbing to say the least. They are just the tip of the iceberg.

*I have gone through all the avenues in law that have been open to me, and the very people I have turned to, the (**pillars of law**) are like people behind bars, because of the fact they are supposed to be the law and uphold that same law turned against us, and prevented us from our due rights.*

The legal ombudsman refuses to act because he states my complaint was outside the date of the introduction of the legal ombudsman's duties.

I totally disagreed. My complaint did not become live until 1994, (within the realms of the ombudsman) relative to a writ being sisted. The Law Society, by its own actions, held up my complaint due to my ongoing case against [First Architect].

In my correspondence, and phone calls with the ombudsman prior to a meeting in his office in September 1997, he informed me by phone that he had requested the files in relation to my complaint against [First Solicitor] from the Law Society, went through said files, came to his conclusions, and sent the files back to the Law Society. His final comment: I cannot get these files back from the Law Society.

At the meeting in his office in September, I asked if I could tape-record the meeting. After all, there was nothing to hide. He refused. He was surprised when I opened my case to reveal my files in meticulous order. His next remark "most of the complainers come here with little or no papers". He then asked me for my papers. I refused, and stated he already had my files. He then stated that he would get the files returned from the Law Society.

Any person that lies is not to be trusted. Any person that lies to me I will never ever trust.

The question that remains, after you have digested all of the papers I have sent you, is: what can my MP do for me, and others in his constituency, to rid our society of this ongoing crooked closed shop Solicitors' protection racket? We have the concrete written proof to show that our fundamental rights for access to justice is being denied.

I went through this same procedure with the last Government, i.e. the local (Cons) MP and then the Secretary of State at that same time. (Conclusion) they are happy with the way the system works, i.e. The Law Society and the ombudsman. We have been promised in no uncertain terms this present Government will be very open not secretive like the last.

On 12ᵗʰ February 1998 (File 735) I followed up the above letter to my MP with the following to the Secretary of State for Scotland:

On the 24ᵗʰ February of last year I wrote to you, and included a large file, detailing my case history regarding my continued efforts to gain access to justice, continually blocked, by (crooked) Solicitors and a (crooked) Law Society system that dates back to 1798 way behind the times.

You responded on the 24ᵗʰ February, outlining various points. I sent you a thank you response on 4ᵗʰ March. I also stated my case was not isolated and also mentioned...what I would be fighting for.

*It is now one year on. I am still fighting for access to justice, which is still being blocked by the same (crooked) closed shop legal system, and a so-called **Law** Society.*

You will find, when you read the enclosures, this horrendous situation created by crooked Solicitors and a similar Law Society, is beyond belief. That this can happen in this beautiful country of ours Scotland!

I must point out at this particular time, before you investigate the enclosures, that the lay people in Scotland are becoming very aware of all the ploys that are used by the legal profession – how to block, 'pass the buck', frustrate, drain their financial resources.

We are all gathering these ongoing crooked ploys for future reference. The biggest and most damaging ploy: your individual rights, how to enforce these rights – only in a civil Court of civil law? How do you get in to a civil Court?

Questions that have to be answered, openly, truthfully:

1. *How do lay people, after passing their complaints to the Law Society with all the written evidence available, find the way barred for access to a civil Court?*

2. *Find a Solicitor who will realistically take on their case, in a civil Court, against another Solicitor?*

3. *What is the Government going to do about this legal shambles? Are we going to be governed by a bunch of crooks who have no shame, are ruthless, who don't care about what they are doing to the people or the country? They must be singled out as they are a continual threat to the well-being of Scotland.*

4. *I would like to be told simply, how to get a Solicitor into a civil Court, with the services of another Solicitor. It has not been done, or can't be done in Scotland.*

5. *And finally the enclosures. I hope you find them extremely disturbing. If you do I would expect immediate action from a man in your position. I would expect a man of your education, honesty, integrity, and a government of openness, to make sure we can be a nation again ... the citizens and people from other countries will not be dictated to by any crooked legal profession. Our Courts are there for, by, of, all the people, not just a few. We are a democracy and should be governed accordingly.*

If you don't find the details disturbing, I will expect little action and a delay in answering my letter (I am only one in a large growing number).

I sincerely hope your answers are positive with a way forward.

Meanwhile a source of hope lay in the hands of another body. On 2nd March 1998, (File 738) the Scottish Consumer Council issued the following statement regarding their research into the Law Society's complaints procedure.

This year, the Scottish Consumer Council is conducting a study of people who have used the Law Society's complaints procedure. The Law Society is cooperating with the research by sending out questionnaires to recent complainers, but will not see the questionnaires that are completed and sent back. The names and addresses of people being sent the questionnaires will not be known by the SCC.

There has never been a survey of people who have complained to the Law Society of Scotland, and it is very important that we find out what your experiences were really like. The report that we will eventually produce, based on your experiences, will help us to recommend to the Law Society how their system can be improved.

Please be assured that your responses will be kept confidential and we will not be passing individual questionnaires to the Law Society. Since we have not been given your name, there is no way that what you tell us can be linked to your identity.

I would be grateful if you could complete the questionnaire and return it by 31ˢᵗ March. If you would like to find out more about this research or about the SCC please do not hesitate to contact the researcher working on this project.

Naturally, I was keen to take part in the survey! I immediately made contact with the SCC, via a telephone call. On 6ᵗʰ March 1998 (File 740) the chairman of the SCC wrote to me:

Thank you for your telephone call this morning. I hope I was able to dispel some of your anxieties about the research that we are doing into the Law Society's complaints system, though I fully understand the reservations that you have. However, I promised to write and let you have various other pieces of information and I enclose with this letter a copy of our last annual report to give you some background about the Scottish Consumer Council and a copy of our code of practice on openness.

You also asked some specific questions about the research which I will try to answer. Over a number of years the Scottish Consumer Council (SCC) has worked in the area of legal affairs in order to try and improve things for the individual person using the system. This work has ranged, for example, from looking at conveyancing to looking at the operation of the Court system. We were for example, instrumental in bringing the small claims system into the Scottish Courts, which gave people easier and cheaper access to the Courts for claims that were valued at less than £750.

In general terms, we have always stressed the importance of good complaints and redress systems in helping to maintain the quality of any service that is provided. For a number of years now we have been concerned about the system of handling complaints against Solicitors, partly because it is handled internally in the Law Society in contrast to England where the system is more independent. The purpose of the current research is to see what the level of satisfaction/dissatisfaction is with the complaints system run by the Law Society of Scotland from the point of view of those who have taken complaints to the society. From the research we hope to be able to make recommendations, which will improve the system. At this point I should say that (quite properly) the SCC has no powers and can only bring about change through the quality of our research and the skills with which we present our findings to those who are responsible for policy.

There are real practical difficulties in undertaking this research because the first thing you have to find is the people who have complained to the Law Society.

With stirrings of hope, but also with a degree of mistrust given the fact that it was the Law Society that was issuing the survey sheets, I responded on 18th March 1998 (File 742):

Thank you for your correspondence of 6th March 1998 and the return telephone calls you made after hours on Friday 13th (of all days). I was most appreciative of the call and the time taken out of your busy schedule.

I thank you also for a copy of the annual report 96/97 and the additional leaflets.

The questionnaire I received through the Law Society is, to me, incorrect in procedure, as I explained on the telephone. I do not, and will not trust the Law Society.

On principle alone I will not be filling in said questionnaire. To me it is illegal if any survey quantified, or reflected through the Scottish Consumer Council's part in this survey, is only with part control, then it is not valid, whatever the outcome.

My frustrations as you will have gathered, which was quite evident in our telephone conversations, gathers momentum, and reaches heights of anger, which is very worrying, at times, because of the damage to one's health.

From the correspondence between myself, and the Law Society, which I have enclosed for your perusal. They are self-explanatory, and will help explain, just some of the frustrations, that I, and thousands of others, over the years, have had to endure.

I am fully aware of the role of the Scottish Consumer Council and individual complaints to the Law Society are not within your jurisdiction. These enclosures are to show the Council, the relativity between a self-regulating body, the Law Society, a secret society and a closed shop system, more for the protection of Solicitors than the complainers, and may I remind the Council, that after a decision by the Law Society complaints committee – no appeal rights for the complainer.

This is how we show the world how a democracy works, and how the legal rights of the people of Scotland are fully protected.

Why this is allowed to go on is just beyond any form of reasoning, and for the people in power to have the full knowledge of the existence of this crooked illegal system is, in itself, complete moral corruption.

Thank you for your cooperation, and understanding, in these, and all other matters.

The chairman of the SCC responded on 25th March 1998 (File 743):

Thank you for your letter of 18th March, together with the enclosures which I will read at a later date.

Although I understand the position you take in not wishing to complete the questionnaire, I was very glad to have the opportunity of both speaking to you and writing to you in that it has allowed me to tell you something of the roll of the SCC and what we do.

On 7th April 1998 (File 744) I wrote to the Ombudsman regarding my complaint against [First Solicitor]:

I have been corresponding with the Deputy Secretary of the Law Society regarding my complaint against the above, where copies have been sent to various individuals, including you.

The latest correspondence, (copy in your possession) dated 13th March 1998, I outlined various important details that require investigation by the office of the Scottish Legal Ombudsman.

Your proposals, and comments, in relation to said letter, would be most appreciated.

And on 5th May 1998 (File 745) I wrote to the Deputy Secretary of the Law Society regarding my complaint against [First Solicitor]:

In answer to your correspondence, of 24th March 1998, I would like to, or suggest to you, that you take the third paragraph of your letter of 24th March 1998, i.e. "Let me set out for you what I regard as the correct factual position."

Instead of giving me these continuing, repetitive details in all of your correspondence in regards to the Law Society and its powers, I would prefer you spare me the boring details. You don't have to sort out the factual position for me.

The factual written details, evidence, have been clearly defined in my letter to you dated 13th March 1998. Starting with page 1, 3rd paragraph, continued through pages 2 and 3.

These written details are very clear. Instead of going round in circles just give me the factual response that is clearly justified. It is very simple the answers that I require.

All the Law Society have to do is compare the list of details in the correspondence they sent me, in reference to professional conduct, service, and other complaints which have been listed in my correspondence dated 13th March 1998, where it gives the extracts from these correspondence starting with

Page 1.	*2nd April 1990*	*Professional Conduct*
	14th June 1990	*Professional Conduct*
Page 1.	*26th May 1993*	*Professional Conduct and Service*
Page 1.	*31st March 1994*	*Professional Conduct and Service etc. etc.*

If the Law Society were to research through the remaining contents of my correspondence and list the answers to each paragraph with these mentioned above, I would then be convinced my complaint against [First Solicitor] is starting to take on some kind of resemblance to justice.

In your letter of 24th March 1998, you state that [First Solicitor] dealt with only very minor matters of business after 1989. I don't understanding the meaning of this statement.

Is it possible you can clarify this statement in detail along with the others mentioned above. We can then determine exactly what the position is.

I would appreciate no more ploys, no more deviations just straight answers.

Finally, if the Law Society are to take no further action in my complaint against [First Solicitor], I would require a simple YES or NO.

On 19th May 1998 (File 746) the Deputy Secretary of the Law Society responded:

I thank you for your letter of 5th May 1998 and read this together with the previous correspondence.

I am happy to try to directly answer the questions which you posed in your letter of 30th March 1998.

As I believe it has previously been indicated in correspondence, the Law Society has a role to consider complaints of professional conduct against Solicitors and also the adequacy of the service provided to clients. The Law Society only obtained powers through Parliament to consider the question of the adequacy of service provided to a client from late January 1989 and, the power to consider inadequate professional service for a period prior to that was not retrospective.

On looking back and re-reading the report and conclusions in the matter, I am entirely satisfied that the reporter and committee considered the whole question of professional conduct and indeed your complaint about delay in lodging the Legal Aid application between June 1987 and February 1988 was upheld, and it was considered that this was unprofessional conduct to be regretted.

That was the only part of the complaint which the committee considered could be upheld and, given that that delay did not occur after January 1989, the Law Society was not in a position to consider any finding of inadequate professional service in that regard.

I appreciate that there may, in your eyes, be an inconsistency in some of the correspondence in relation to consideration of inadequate service but the position only became entirely clear during the reporter's considerations of matters and what aspect of the claim might be upheld.

The short answer to your final question posed in your letter of 5th May is that the Law Society will be taking no further action in connection with this matter.

I hope my readers understand the significance of this response – you have just witnessed the man showing his true character, with all its limitations. In his letter he uses the Reporter to cover up his own inadequacies. I actually feel sorry for him that he has to behave in such a manner. I wonder what his abilities would be if he had no support. What has happened here is that I have used my sense of determination, and my tenacity, to keep challenging members of the legal profession. As you will by now know, I have challenged an Advocate, a Troubleshooter and now, after dealing with this particular person at the Law Society since 1990, the Deputy Secretary himself. He knew that my complaints/challenges were quantified through honesty, integrity, and openness, and I had the evidence to back it up.

Returning to the subject of the SCC questionnaire, on 23rd November 1998 (File 747) I wrote to the SCC director:

In reference to the above subject, where 1,200 questionnaires were mailed out by the Law Society in Feb/Mar this year, in conjunction with the SCC and where it was requested that these questionnaires be returned by the end of March.

I am sure you will agree with me, this request would give recipients of these questionnaires a confident feeling that the SCC are going to act in complete contrast to how Solicitors act.

It has been found in the past, confirmed and accepted by both the Law Society and the ombudsman, two of the biggest complaints faced by the general public and complainers alike against the legal profession are unjustified delays, and lack of communication, added to this Solicitors do not take notes.

I now find after various requests regarding the outcome of the questionnaire, and the findings of the SCC, that (I am sure you will agree) the confidence which has been instilled in the general public, because of past achievements by the SCC, will start to decline because of the same pattern developing and growing in the SCC, where the general public are growing increasingly annoyed and becoming very impatient in the knowledge these problems are not being addressed in a manner where future complainers will find they will not have to endure, what I and thousands of others have, and are still going through, i.e. horrendous experiences because of a crooked closed shop legal system. Details of proof available.

On 3ʳᵈ December 1998 (File 748) the SCC duly replied:

I write with reference to your fax of 23ʳᵈ November addressed to the director which she has passed to me as I am dealing with this matter.

I can assure you that we at the SCC take this research very seriously indeed, and that a tremendous amount of work has been put into it. As you will appreciate, we are anxious to ensure that the report is as accurate as possible before publication, and the work involved in doing so has taken some considerable time.

I would like to thank you for your interest in this matter, and can advise that the report is likely to be published soon.

Note: This letter was signed by a solicitor in the SCC.

1999

On 12th February 1999 (File 751) I wrote again to the Ombudsman:

I refer to the recently published report from the Scottish Consumer Council, 'Complaints Against Solicitors', which I am sure you are familiar with, and its relative contents.

Through the years, the office of the lay observer, first, then the office of the legal ombudsman, have attempted to find a balance of justice between the consumer/complainer and the Law Society. (Please correct me if I am wrong).

I am sorry, I don't have any details at hand, but could you please provide me with any information whereby there were recommended changes, from both the office of the lay observer in the past, or recently, by the office of the legal services ombudsman, in regards to the handling of a complaint, through the Law Society and the complaints committee, where the complainer has no representation or appeal rights. Your cooperation would be most appreciated.

P.S. I am fully aware of the relative correspondence to the duties of the reporting member. My question relates strictly to representation and appeal rights

On 16th February 1999 (File 752) the Ombudsman responded:

Thank you for your letter dated 12th February 1999.

*As I think you are aware, **I am not the consumer's champion,** my concern over the last four and a half years having been to satisfy*

satisfy myself that the Law Society's investigations have been fair, thorough and impartial. It is my responsibility to identify the concerns that have been raised by a complainer, to consider whether these have been addressed by the Law Society, with explanations having been provided in relation to conclusions reached, and to make recommendations where I believe that a complaint has not been dealt with satisfactorily or in circumstances where the legal body has been dilatory or where there have been administrative failings.

If I understand you correctly, you are asking whether recommendations have been made with regard to providing a complainer with representation or rights of appeal. If I am incorrect in my understanding, then please advise me. I cannot say what recommendations may have been made in the past, but for my part I have never made any recommendations with regards to complainers being represented. I have in the past taken issue with the Law Society's practice of allowing Solicitors to make personal representations before a complaints committee, and my recommendations were accepted. An alternative would have been to allow complainers to make their own representations before a committee, but it seemed to me that that would have created an uneven playing field, as not all complainers have the articulation skills which a Solicitor will be expected to have by the nature of his/her work and experience. It therefore seemed to me that it was right that both parties should be able to make representations in writing and that of course is what now happens when a statement of facts and circumstances have been prepared by a reporter.

With regard to complainers having a right to appeal to some outside body, I have never made any recommendations in that respect, it being a feature of current legislation that the Law Society and the other legal bodies have a statutory responsibility to investigate complaints against their own members.

And there we have it! Statutory responsibility is indeed precisely the main reason why we cannot get any appeal rights or access to justice, why and how the legal profession has totally abused its responsibilities and have set up a foolproof system of denying a complainer any chance of getting into a Court of law to state his case and the strength of that case – namely in front of a jury whereby the crooked legal system would be excluded from the comfort of their unethical bias and control.

The Scottish Legal Ombudsman claims in the above correspondence, he is not *the consumer's champion*. Indeed he is not! I would like to warn my readers about this same Ombudsman, because he has been involved with, and is an integral part of, the legal profession. He has learned the tricks of the trade. It "just happened" that, before retiring, he used a very clever ploy – to get into the press a report/article in the newspapers stating that solicitors who have stepped outwith their rules, and been fined, should be shamed by having their names exposed to the general public. The ploy, on paper, certainly looked good. But do not be fooled. We are beginning to wise up. There is a growing awareness that we are living with a crooked legal system, one that is constantly trying to fool an unsuspecting public. Consider instead the following questions about this man's ostensibly comforting article:

1) Is he promoting his successor for the future?

2) Is he promoting his own future?

To the readers of this book and the general public, would you believe, his ploy actually worked in his favour – he was voted into the Scottish Parliament as standards advisor!

On 7th January 1999 (File 749) the Director of the Scottish Consumer Council wrote to me regarding their *Study of Consumers' Experiences of the Law Society of Scotland's Complaints Procedure*. In his letter he said:

*I am pleased to enclose the Scottish Consumers Council's new report **Complaints Against Solicitors**. This report is based on a postal survey, carried out in the Spring of 1998, into the views of people who had recently used the Law Society of Scotland's complaints procedure to make a complaint about a Solicitor.*

Those taking part were asked about how their Solicitor dealt with the complaint in the first instance, about specific aspects of the Law Society's procedure, and about the outcome and handling of the complaint.

The results of our research show that half of those taking part believed the procedure to be unfair. We have made recommendations based on our research which we believe would considerably improve the present system. However, if consumers are to be confident that the procedures are entirely fair, we believe the research suggests that the way forward should be to establish an independent body to deal with complaints about Solicitors in Scotland.

The report's main recommendation is that the Scottish Parliament should establish a review of the current procedure, with a view to establishing an independent body, to deal with complaints about Solicitors in Scotland.

The report recognises the positive aspects of the way in which the Law Society carries out this function, but also criticises many aspects of the Law Society's current procedure, and makes various recommendations as to how this might be improved. It is also critical of the manner in which many Solicitors deal with complaints, and recommends ways in which they might improve their client care and complaints handling procedures.

I would very much welcome your views as to the issues raised in the report.

Over the years I had gathered a huge amount of anecdotal evidence from a multitude of other people who had suffered similar experiences at the hands of the legal profession, and the Law Society. I needed no convincing that the system was intrinsically wrong, even damaging. What pleased me now, however, was that here at last I had feedback from a formal body, supporting my conclusions. On 14th January 1999 File 750) I faxed the following to the Director of the SCC:

Thank you for your letter of 7th January and the copy of **'Complaints Against Solicitors'***.*

May I congratulate you and the staff of SCC on the contents, and the way the report was written. I feel sure the recipients of this report, like myself, will be inspired by the results.

I will answer your letter in detail once I have scrutinized the report thoroughly. I am sure you will agree, this lengthy report, to give it proper justice, from a layman's point of view, will require more time because of its contents.

I am sure your continued efforts, and the success of those efforts, along with recommendations you have made, not forgetting the unrelenting slog, hard work, frustrations, each one of those unsatisfied complainers have had to endure, with no one to turn to for help, because they were let down by the very ones that were supposed to help them.

If we are to move forward, i.e. removal of self-regulation, as the report recommends, surely any or all obstacles that would hinder this process, should obviously be removed.

Therefore I think it would be imperative, and recommend that all MPs should receive a copy of the report **'Complaints Against Solicitors'** *for obvious reasons, as stated above.*

Finally the general public, and ministers alike, fear the wrath and the consequences of speaking out on their own against lawyers and the legal profession in the event they could require the services of the legal profession at some later date. They could be black listed. Same applies Solicitors –v– Solicitors.

In January 1999, invigorated by the turn of events with the SCC, I decided to do some further investigation, this time with regard to the earlier actions of the Troubleshooter. I resolved to find out whether he had informed the master policy holders of solicitors' professional indemnity insurance that he intended to sue [First Solicitor] for negligence on my behalf. Remember, it is a legal obligation for a solicitor who intends to sue another solicitor, or a solicitor being sued, to immediately inform the master policy holder. I phoned the master policy holder asking if they had on record my name in the context of a law suit against [First Solicitor].

On 1st February 1999 (File 750-1) the master policy holders wrote to me:

> *I refer to your telephone conversations on 28th January with my two colleagues. In order for me to be able to consider properly the nature of your enquiry, and to ascertain whether we are able to assist you, I shall require to have your enquiry in writing.*
>
> *On receipt of your enquiry, I will let you have a response without delay.*

On 4th February 1999 (750-2) I duly responded, by fax:

> *Thank you for your correspondence of the 1st Instant. My initial, i.e. telephone, conversation with your two colleagues was simply to establish if my name was entered into your database list of possible insurance (claims, risks) against the master policy.*
>
> *Correct me if I am wrong, but I believe (you) operate the insurance cover for any possible claims through the Law Society. All I need to know, has my name been registered?*
>
> *I think you will agree my request is minimal and will require little effort on the part of your colleagues to furnish me with the details. Your cooperation would be most appreciated.*

For a month nothing happened, so I again wrote to the associate Director of the master policy holders. On 4th March 1999 (File 756) I said:

> *I refer to your letter of 1st February 1999 where you stated you would require my enquiry in writing before you could consider properly, the nature of that enquiry, and to ascertain whether you were able to assist.*
>
> *The last paragraph of your letter, clearly states: "I will let you have a response without delay".*
>
> *On the 4th of February I faxed your office direct, with the details in writing, of my enquiry.*
>
> *On the 12th February, I again faxed your office direct, asking for a date I could expect a reply to my enquiry.*
>
> *Because there was no response, or acknowledgement, I called your office, last week in February, and was simply told by your colleague, I would be receiving a reply.*
>
> *Proper business acumen, in my experience, in the past, would relate to answering a person's enquiry, if they were asked to put it in writing, and follow this up with an acknowledgement of receipt.*
>
> *In view of the fact you informed me on 1st February, you would let me have a response without delay, and it is now the 4th March, could I possibly have a response to my original written enquiry.*

On 31st March 1999 (File 757) master policy holder's branch executive responded, giving me the information I sought:

> *Data Protection Act 1984*
>
> *Thank you for your letters of 4th and 12th February (fax only) and 4th March addressed to associate director.*

I can advise you that [we] do not hold any personal data concerning you in relation to the insurance cover you refer to in your faxed letter of 4th February.

Please note that although [we] are entitled in terms of the Data Protection Act 1984 to charge a fee, (which is currently £10 per purpose to which the enquiry relates) for confirming whether or not personal data is held by [us], we will not be seeking payment of this fee on this occasion. We reserve the right, however to charge the appropriate fee for any future enquiry.

Armed with this new disclosure – that the Troubleshooter had made no effort to initiate proceedings against [First Solicitor] – on 18th May 1999 (File 757-1) I wrote to the secretary of the Law Society:

On the 15th May 1999 I wrote to you, copy enclosed.

As of today's date I have had no acknowledgement of receipt of said letter. I would appreciate your cooperation, with an answer to my letter of the 15th May and also to my further request as follows.

Ref. Data Protection Act 1984

I require a full disclosure from the Law Society of all references, and their dates, relating to myself as held on your systems, affected by legislation under the Act.

Further to the abovementioned Data Protection Act 1984, I was in correspondence with the associate director of [Master Policy Holder] in Edinburgh, requesting information from their database list because of my involvement with a Legal Aid application to proceed with a writ against a crooked Solicitor. I have now received from [Master Policy Holder] (after a long delay) the information I requested, which is very disturbing.

I am sure you will agree, there have been quite concise, and clear, guidelines issued to all Solicitors in Scotland from the insurers regarding instructions that must be followed when applications for Legal Aid and possible writs issued against offending Solicitors.

I look forward to hearing from you in the very near future, with acknowledgements, and the information requested.

On 2nd June 1999 (File 759) the director responded, under the heading of *Various Complaints*:

I write to acknowledge receipt of your letter of 18th May received during my absence from the office. I note you request a full disclosure from the Law Society detailing all references and dates relating to yourself, held on our systems.

The client relations office keeps a record of all complaints made by members of the public together with their addresses, the firms against whom the complaints have been made, the dates the complaints have been made, and closed, and the outcome of those complaints.

According to the Law Society system you have made three complaints.

The first of these was against [First Solicitor] and was received by the Law Society on 5th March 1990. It was allocated a reference number. The file was closed on 30th April 1997 after consideration of the complaint with no action being taken.

The second complaint which you made was against [Second Solicitor]. This complaint was received on 22nd November 1993 and matters were closed on 28th February 1995. This complaint was upheld with a finding of inadequate professional service being made.

The third complaint which you made was also received on 23rd November 1993 was against [Troubleshooter]. That complaint was concluded on 21st April 1995. That complaint was dismissed.

I trust this information is sufficient for your purposes. If you wish additional information then could you please specify precisely what you seek.

I note also your comments in relation to your correspondence with [Master Policy Holder]. Clearly, I do not know what information you have received from [Master Policy Holder]. I am therefore totally unable to comment on your comment in relation to the information you have received.

On 11th June 1999 (File 760) I wrote to the deputy Director of the Law Society, referencing my correspondence with their chief executive dated 15th April and 18th May and their reply dated 2nd June 1999, regarding records held at the client relations office of the three complaints previously made by myself, against both [First] and [Second Solicitors], and my Troubleshooter:

The answer to your question of the 2nd June 1999, i.e. additional information, is as follows: I require a full disclosure from the Law Society clients relations office, detailing all references and their dates relating to my complaint against the abovementioned Solicitors, which are held in your records under the Data Protection Act 1984.

Your help would be most appreciated, by giving me the records and details held relating to my Troubleshooter in the first instant, followed by [First Solicitor] and then [Second Solicitor].

I would also appreciate a time when I could expect to receive the abovementioned records.

If you require any further information, please do not hesitate to contact me as soon as possible.

On 24th June 1999 (File 761) the director wrote:

Complaints Against Various Solicitors

I refer to previous correspondence and your recent fax to my colleague requesting information from the Law Society in connection with matters held on our database under the Data Protection Act 1984.

I now have the information which you have sought available but, for security reasons, it is my understanding that it is inappropriate to send this information to you.

I would confirm that the information is available at the Law Society's offices and if you would care to call to collect it, and bring suitable identification with you to exhibit before the documentation is handed over to you, then it would be made available.

If you would care to telephone me before you intend to come to the Law Society I will arrange for the information to be left in our reception.

For reasons shown later on, I decided not to accede to his request and make the journey south. However, I did decide to take the matter up with my local MP, which prompted the director to write a further letter on 14th July 1999 (File762):

Complaints against Solicitors, Data Protection Act

I refer to previous correspondence, and a letter I have received from your Member of Parliament. I do appreciate your difficulty in travelling, but at the same time I am sure you will understand the Law Society's concern in relation to making this information available.

Please find enclosed the relevant information held under the Data Protection Act, for your assistance.

So, although it seems as though I have prevailed, it is important to note here that the information submitted with his letter was paltry and all but useless.

On 4th August 1999 (File 763) the Deputy First Minister and First Minister for Justice of the Scottish Parliament, himself a QC, wrote to my MP:

Thank you for your letter of 5th July asking whether there are any proposals to go before the Scottish Parliament to change the self-regulation of the legal profession.

There are currently no plans for the Scottish Parliament to consider changes to the present system of self-regulation

On 15th September 1999 (File764) my MP responded:

I refer to your letter of 4thAugust and our recent conversation on the self-regulation of the legal profession. I cannot be unique in having constituents who feel thwarted when trying to complain about the service they have received from Solicitors and the Law Society. I have also had it pointed out to me that at times members of the profession feel that their interests might be better protected if there was a method of independent scrutiny.

In particular I think it would be worth looking at the proposals made by the Scottish Consumer Council in their report on complaint handling by the Law Society.

On 30th September 1999 (File 765) I wrote to the Scottish Legal Aid Board:

Ref. Refusal of Legal Aid application

Further to our meeting of last week at 44, Drumsheugh Gardens, regarding the above, I have enclosed for your perusal copies taken from the files, details of the application and refusal, but with no explanation why.

My Solicitor, i.e. [Troubleshooter], ceased to act for me after refusal. Therefore reasons for refusal of Legal Aid were never conveyed to me.

I find it very difficult to believe 1) That I was refused Legal Aid in the first place considering the detailed letter supporting the application, and 2) Under a democratic principle and a democratic government, it is my right to have the true reasons why I was refused.

Further reasons why I find it so difficult: I applied for Legal Aid on an earlier application. This application was accepted where I made a partial payment of £413.

The question that now presents itself: What if the papers I have enclosed were to be used for a further application for Legal Aid? Can you please reply with the answers.

On 23rd November 1999 (File 766) the Legal Aid advice and assistance unit responded as follows:

Thank you for your letter of 30th September 1999 and I refer to our recent telephone conversations.

As I confirmed to you over the telephone, I have had one of my colleagues in the legal services department look over the papers you gave me. On the basis of the information that you supplied, if we were to consider this request now it would be refused for the following reason.

"It is not considered that Counsel's involvement is appropriate at this stage and, as this is a case against Solicitors, a report is required from a Solicitor."

It would be useful for you to pass this information on to any Solicitor that is to take this matter forward for you.

Over the past few pages, I have placed on record a series of letters. Before I continue with this True Story, I think it is only fair that my readers are given some context to the correspondence, and are also offered some conclusions that may be of interest, especially if you find yourself in a similar situation. Another reason I am doing this is to show you what type of people I had to deal with, and am still dealing with, or rather, should I say "having to cope with".

The Director of the Law Society who wrote the letter referred to as File 761 is the same person as the Deputy Secretary I had been dealing with since 1990, and with whom I had had a meeting in Edinburgh (see transcript of taped conversation of September 1995). He was promoted in the early part of 1999. Obviously the man disliked me and had every reason to want to make my life difficult. In File 761, he was quite clearly being obstructive, under the "guise" of security, by being unwilling to send the papers I requested by a secure means of post. Instead he wanted me to have to travel down to Edinburgh to pick up these papers and bring along identification. He also informed me that I could collect the papers at the front desk, but, before doing all of this, I had to give him a phone call. In other words, that difficult character Angus Brown was going to have to jump through a few hoops!

Before rushing into action, I decided to calmly think things through. I could see through the man's strategy, but I needed to do some positive thinking. Clearly this incompetent director understood perfectly well what sort of predicament he was putting me into. He knew I was a pensioner, and still he contrived to subject me to a journey of approximately 400 miles, plus costs, just to pick up a few papers. And, before doing all of this, he wanted me to phone him. Let's consider why. Is it possible he was hoping to provoke a reaction – maybe an irate phone call, one that could be recorded without my knowledge? Or was he showing both to his subordinates and his superiors that this newly appointed director was a man of authority and not to be trifled with?

Now look at File 762 again. Notice how he has changed his mind, becoming almost obsequious, as he has the audacity to tell me that he appreciates the difficulty in travelling, as if this is a new revelation – one he has only just appreciated. He then asks me to understand his reasons (security!), insulting my intelligence yet again! And to think he had just been promoted.

Is there any other profession, other than our friends in the legal profession, that promotes people for screwing complainers, draining their finances, sometimes stealing client's monies, and destroying their lives? Everyone in that profession should be ashamed, knowing perfectly well what is going on.

Looking further at File 762, you will see that our incompetent director had received a letter from my MP, with whom I consulted after receiving the original, ludicrous letter, obstructing me under the guise of security. This is an insult to anyone's intelligence. I am sure my readers all had the same thoughts as I did – what about registered mail, or special delivery? The man eventually sent me the papers registered mail which, of course, he could have done in the first place.

This book cannot be all about criticism. At this point I must praise the help I received from my MP and his staff, including his secretary who, over a number of years, have been incredible. Their support has been inspiring and an example to others. When I asked for his help, he and his office responded quickly and efficiently through their inspiring correspondence.

I would ask all MSPs and other MPs to follow his example and his understanding, a perfect example of genuine listening. Here is democracy at work – by listening to constituents and advising accordingly. It is worth adding here that **my MP was not a lawyer**.

After I consulted with my MP, it is clear from the above correspondence that he had followed through by writing to the Law Society. The director must have been disappointed that I not jumped to his tune and, in particular, that I had not followed through with a phone call, giving him the mouthful he had hoped to provoke. Remember, this was the same man who, as Deputy Secretary at the time I was involved with the shambolic Troubleshooter scheme, had been instrumental in subjecting me to delay and stress through his numerous and repetitive letters. He was also the same man who claimed to have helped me so much by setting up two free meetings with the Troubleshooter. And yet, if the Law Society, in their wisdom and through such wondrous generosity towards complainers, had genuinely been able to help complainers, then why had they not been able to convey this message to the world – that the Troubleshooter scheme genuinely helped complainers?

As a result of the SCC research into claims against solicitors in 1989/1990, I decided to do a little research myself, with their help, in finding an example of a Troubleshooter who had genuinely helped a complainer to take action against his offending solicitor in a negligence action through the Courts. After all, if anyone had that information it would be the SCC, with all the feedback from its survey. I corresponded and asked them to ascertain whether there existed any such success stories. This would have enabled me continue with my search for justice.

The question that I asked was a very simple one, surely? Little research would be needed to find an answer, without any complications. After corresponding with the SCC, who in turn corresponded with the Law Society, the answer I got was very disappointing; but having said that, I should have known, or did know the answer would be negative, because of the type of people I was dealing with. Here are the details of the research, and the correspondence.

2001

On 25th January 2001 (File 767), I wrote to the Director of Scottish Consumer Council:

I am writing to confirm other details we discussed in our telecom of yesterday afternoon besides the fax, which I also sent you yesterday.

These are as follows, in our discussion I mentioned some of the facts we had discussed at the meeting held at the offices of the Scottish Consumer Council on 6th November of last year and, in particular, I reiterated to you yesterday the problem complainants come up against in securing legal representation for an action against their offending Solicitor.

In your 1998/1999 survey and report, there was little mention of a Troubleshooter scheme operated by the Law Society, which I am led to believe is to assist the complainer to further their action, or complaint.

You mentioned in our discussion you do receive the annual reports from the Law Society, i.e. 'Complaints Against Solicitors'.

These reports contain the number of complainants who have taken their complaints further, through the Troubleshooter scheme.

In the last three years' reports, it seems quite a considerable number have used the Troubleshooter scheme, and it's with this in mind, and our discussion at the meeting and as mentioned above, our search for legal representation has been fruitless.

Could it be we need to search no further? Surely, it is possible that one of the Troubleshooters, who acted for a complainant, was successful, in a Court action, against another Solicitor, and could we gain access to this Solicitor for our future services.

Your research into our ongoing situation is vital, and we would welcome and appreciate an early reply.

6th February 2001 (File 768), a legal officer writes to the Law Society on behalf of the SCC:

Information on Reporters, Committee Members, and Troubleshooters

We have been contacted by Mr Angus Brown who has made a number of complaints to the Law Society. He is concerned that the society refused to provide the names of the reporter and the committee members who dealt with his complaints.

As you know, we do not pursue individual complaints. However we have an interest in understanding the general policy of the Law Society in this matter. Is it your policy that this information should not be publicly available to anyone, or do you make decisions on a case by case basis?

On a related matter, as you are aware, it can be difficult for complainers who wish to sue a Solicitor for negligence to find another Solicitor who is willing to act for them. This, of course, is the main reason for the existence of the society's Troubleshooter scheme. However, while the society's annual report contains statistics on the number of referrals to Troubleshooters, there is no information on the outcome of these referrals. We would also like to understand if the names of these firms are withheld from all enquirers or not.

19th February 2001 (File 769) the Director of SCC wrote to me:

Thank you for your recent letter, and phone calls to our office. We have undertaken to look into the issue of the confidentiality of the names of those involved as Troubleshooters, reporters and committee members, under the Scottish Law Society complaints scheme.

As we have explained, the Scottish Consumer Council is not able – under its articles of association – to investigate individual complaints or complaints from individuals.

I will undertake to write to you as soon as we have something to report on the matter

26th February 2001 (File 770) the Director of the Law Society wrote to the legal officer of the SCC:

Information on Reporters, Committee Members and Troubleshooters

I write to acknowledge receipt of your letter of 6th February following receipt of correspondence which you have had from Angus Brown.

The question of whether or not the identity of a reporter should be disclosed either to a complainer or a Solicitor is a matter, which has been considered by the Law Society, over a period of time. The Law Society's current policy is that the identity of a reporter is not disclosed either to the complainer or to the Solicitor. The reporter or reporters in any particular case are independent and it is not considered that disclosing the identity of the reporter would assist in the process of considering the complaint. There have been two occasions to my knowledge where in error the identity of a reporter has been disclosed to the parties. The result of that has been efforts by both parties to contact the reporter directly, with a view to trying to influence the reporter's view. That is clearly unhelpful and, given that parties have the opportunity to make written representations both on the reporter's report setting out the facts and circumstances and also on the reporter's opinion, it is considered unnecessary and counter-productive to disclose the identity of the reporters to the parties.

You will be aware that in the Law Society's annual report, details are disclosed each year of the members of each of the individual client relations committees. It is not normal however for us to disclose details of the individual members who might have been present at any particular committee meeting.

As a matter of fact members of committees abide by a convention that they will declare an interest if they know the complainer or Solicitor involved in a complaint or have some direct connection with them.

The Troubleshooter scheme does continue to operate and it seems to me from the comment which you make in your letter that you may not fully appreciate precisely the terms and remit of the scheme. If a member of the public approaches the Law Society in the first instance indicating this they are having difficulty in finding a Solicitor to advise on the question of a possible negligence claim against a Solicitor, then the Law Society will in the first instance provide names of Solicitors whom they may be able to directly approach to assist. The names of Solicitor firms, which are normally provided at this stage, are of firms who are known to be able to deal with matters, such as negligence claims against professionals. If the person making the approach still has a problem, then the Law Society may consider appointing a Troubleshooter, to consider papers and give advice about whether or not the person may have a claim. The Troubleshooter is not obliged to act beyond giving advice about whether a claim exists or not, although in many instances the Troubleshooter may carry on with the case.

The Law Society's involvement with the Troubleshooter is simply to ensure that the Troubleshooter, once appointed, meets with the complainer and gives advice. If the Troubleshooter takes the matter on thereafter there is no requirement on the Troubleshooter to report the progress of the matter or the outcome of the matter to the Law Society because by that stage the Troubleshooter is acting as a Solicitor for the client on an ordinary agent and client basis. The Law Society has no requirement, nor indeed any locus to require a further report from the Troubleshooter or to be advised of the eventual outcome. Indeed it would not be proper for the Law Society to receive such a report.

As a matter of practice, if a request for a Troubleshooter is granted, then the Troubleshooter is approached first, and asked if he or she is prepared to see the individual involved before the identity of the Troubleshooter is disclosed to the complainer.

There are circumstances where a Troubleshooter may decline to see a complainer. For example, the Troubleshooter may have knowledge of the case. Given that the Troubleshooter scheme is voluntary it is considered appropriate that the Troubleshooter is advised of the position before indicating whether or not they are prepared to take the matter on.

2nd March 2001 (File 771), the Director of the SCC wrote to me:

Information on Law Society Reporters, Committee Members and Troubleshooters

I enclose for your information a copy of our letter of 6th February to the Law Society asking for information on the above matters, following our correspondence on these points.

I also enclose a copy of the director of the Law Society's reply dated 26th February. In case you were wondering about the slight delay in forwarding it to you, I have been out of the office until today, and this is the first chance to send it to you.

I note what you write in your fax dated 1st March. I do not recall saying in our telephone conversation that letters from the Law Society could not be copied to you. What I did say was that I would have to see any such letter first before agreeing to copy it to you. This is quite consistent with our policy of openness.

I must interrupt this True Story once again, to inform the readers of vital information, regarding the scope of the legal profession and how they have magnified their incompetence to show us all, everyone, how far they will travel, through their correspondence not only to insult the Scottish people, but to make themselves look so stupid, and insult their own profession. Please take special note of the following.

If you start off by reading my letter above (File 767) 25th January 2001, you will note I never mentioned Law Society Reporters, or committee members, in my search for a Troubleshooter, (solicitor) who had taken another solicitor to Court in a civil action.

If you now look at the letter (File 768) 6th February 2001, the legal officer at the SCC to the director at the Law Society who I have been dealing with, you will see the heading:

Information on Reporters, Committee Members and Troubleshooters

After the above heading she starts talking about names of Reporters and committee members, which is completely against any details described in my letter, dated 25th January 2001. Question: did she have a well-planned telephone conversation with the Director of the Law Society to cover up the simple question I posed regarding information regarding a Troubleshooter?

The well-planned response, (File 770) dated 26th February 2001, where that same director responds to the legal officer at the SCC same heading:

Information on Reporters, Committee Members and Troubleshooters

This particular letter, two pages long, is again very repetitive, boring, and making, as I said before, the Law Society look stupid. Not only that, the reputation of the SCC has been badly affected, in that they have been made to look incompetent by their own correspondence, and it also shows the influence the Law Society has by encompassing the SCC into its corrupt system.

On top of that, if any professional body who is intent on helping complainers to get not only access to justice, but to follow that up with a system that actually gets a complainer into Court in a civil action and gets that same complainer the justice he deserves with the help of a Troubleshooter, you would think that same professional body would make absolutely sure the whole world would know, and hear about this particular, successful, Troubleshooter, especially the Scottish Consumer Council, whereby they could have answered Mr Brown's original simple question.

This is where the Law Society, in conjunction with their legal eagles, have conned the complainers, and the Scottish public, and myself, who took that perilous journey with my Troubleshooter.

To the readers, I think it is very important to go back to the letter from the director at the Law Society and his response to the legal officer at the SCC; any complainers/complainants will see variations in this letter to the point of being untruthful.

It is a known fact that the Law Society will **not** look at complaints where there is a possibility of negligence; they will tell you that is for the Courts, therefore if the Law Society arrange for a Troubleshooter to consult with a complainer regarding a complaint of negligence or vice versa, and the Troubleshooter agrees to take on the case, it will be arranged that the first two meetings between them, as we all know, are paid by the Law Society. This is where the **lies and corruption** take over.

In his correspondence of the 26th February, this Director of the Law Society has the audacity to expect the public, the readers of this book, and all complainers, to believe there is no contact between the Troubleshooter and the Law Society, either in correspondence, telephone or by any other modern means after the Troubleshooter has come up with his findings, i.e. a negligence claim, after consulting with his client, and his conclusions after the two meetings, with the possibility of taking the case further to Court. If that is the situation then both the Law Society and the Troubleshooter are involved with their own rules and instructions relating to the holders of the master insurance policy, therefore to insult the intelligence of the people of Scotland by stating they do not contact each other is disgraceful, and unprofessional to say the least.

Further to that, **if** this Troubleshooter is really going to Court with this complainer, (you will see I started that last sentence with an **IF**) and if he wins this complainer's case, that means there will be a claim against the holders of the master policy who, prior to any solicitor taking an action of negligence to Court, must be informed.

Special note to the readers: I think it's important to let you know that the Law Society are paid bonuses annually by the holders of the master insurance policy for getting rid of complainers, especially high-risk ones. I would also like to show you **similarities** within the legal profession when we ask what we would term as simple questions, but they would term it as being difficult, and damaging. For example, the contents of the letter from the director at the Law Society to the legal officer at the SCC gave them a lot of information, but in actual fact gave them nothing in relation to my simple question. But we have to remember the Law Society is always in complete control, therefore it only takes common sense for us to realise, they will confer with each other before relaying or broadcasting anything that is backward or damaging to members of their profession, and help a high-risk complainer, I refer to the contents of the letter from the lega officer to the Director of the Law Society which gives the director plenty to write about, and gives him every chance to evade the simple **question**. Now, if we were to use our common sense, is it possible they had a clever conversation to use a cover-up, or a ploy, to upset this complainer, by not answering his simple question.

If you look at the headings of both letters, very clever:

Information on Reporters, Committee Members, and Troubleshooters

The main point I must bring out here is, I did **NOT** ask for the above information, the simple details are in my letter dated 25th January 2001 to the SCC.

Chapter 8

The Justice 1 Committee's Major Inquiry and The Public Petitions Committee

I mentioned **similarities** in the previous chapter. I would like you the readers to compare the letter that the Director of the Law Society wrote to the legal officer of the SCC with the following details found in **The Scottish Parliament's Justice 1 Committee's Major Inquiry into the Regulation of the Legal Profession,** held in Edinburgh in 2001.

In this inquiry, certain difficult questions as far as the legal profession is concerned were asked of elite members of the Law Society who were present at this inquiry, namely: the then current President of the Law Society, followed by the vice President, and then the Director of law reform.

The convener of this inquiry reminded everyone present that this was just a briefing to assist in refining the terms of reference and was not formally part of the inquiry.

To the readers: be prepared for a lengthy story; but some parts are interesting, others very revealing.

> **The Convener:** *The 1980 Solicitors (Scotland) Act sets two objectives: the promotion of the interests of the solicitors' profession in Scotland and the promotion of the interests of the public in relation to that profession. Can there be a conflict between those two objectives?*
>
> **The President of the Law Society:** *The Royal Commission on Legal Services that reported before the Solicitors (Scotland) Act 1980 was passed, summed up the position the committee will no doubt refer to*

the commission's report during its inquiry. That report stated: "While therefore we are in no doubt that the interests of solicitors and of the public can from time to time be in conflict we consider that there is undoubted benefit to the public in having the solicitor's professional body under a wider obligation than simply to look after their own membership. Much of value would be lost if the Law Society were to become simply the professional association of trade union of solicitors."

I trust that when we give evidence to the committee we will be able to address that issue. This is a difficult matter for the Law Society to deal with, but it is a privilege, and one that must not be abused.

An MSP: *I believe that negligence is the factor that creates the most problems for you. One problem that seems to arise is that when someone has made a negligence claim against a solicitor, it is extremely difficult to find others to pick up the case and assist the individual in the Courts. What role does the Law Society play in such cases? What do you do, when you cannot find solicitors to take on such cases?*

The President of the Law Society: *That is a difficult problem, which is double-edged. If I said that the Law Society should have a panel of people who would deal with such cases on behalf of consumers, some would accuse us of bringing that into our club and controlling it, so we cannot have such a panel. Instead, we have a Troubleshooter scheme. If someone is toiling to find a solicitor to assist them, the Law Society – at arm's length – will pay for two interviews, the preparation and preparatory work for that person, to see whether they can take the matter further.*

The difficulty with which we constantly toil – members will know this from constituents who will approach them in relation to negligence matters – is that the fact that something is wrong, is not necessarily a result of negligence by a solicitor. Furthermore, if it is established that something is wrong, the value that is put on that by the person who feels aggrieved is not necessarily the same as the value that would be put on it by a Court.

Let me make an analogy: if I had a car accident, the first thing to establish would be who was at fault. Although I have a big bump on the front of my car, it might not have been the other driver who was at fault. Even if the other driver was at fault, if I think that my car is worth £5,000, but an insurance company determines that it is worth £2,000...

The MSP that asked the question in the first place, must have been annoyed. Here is his response: *I think that we have drifted off the point. I recognise that no Court case will be 100% satisfactory – whoever wins will feel good, but whoever loses will feel bad. However, I come back to the point on negligence and how the Law Society addresses the fact, that on occasion, individuals find it difficult to find a solicitor to oppose another solicitor.*

The President of the Law Society: *To be frank, I do not consider that the difficulty would be in finding a solicitor to oppose another solicitor. The difficulty may be in finding a solicitor who would be prepared to take on a case, if there was no merit in the case. That is difficult, because again, it could be said that, that is an example of the profession looking after its own.*

The fact is that the professional indemnity insurance statistics show that, on average, about 600 claims are notified each year. Those claims are notified and dealt with, and solicitors pay premiums to cover that. The typical premium per partner in a firm is £2,500 to £3,000 per annum. If we multiply that by the number of solicitors, the amount of money that is involved becomes clear.

Occasionally, people may feel aggrieved that their case is not being taken forward, but in the majority of cases in which there is a valid claim, the case is being dealt with properly. However, [Mr MSP] makes an interesting point about an issue that we have talked about over the years. We have pulled back from the idea of having a panel of solicitors to deal with such matters, for the reason that I mentioned earlier I suspect that it would not be long before the panel was devalued as a result of people saying that it did not work because the Law Society was looking after its own.

After that long-winded similar type of story, that tells us a lot but again tells us nothing, with the original question still to be answered, **a second MSP answers with the following statement:** *You said that when a client comes to you with a case that clearly involves a matter of **negligence**, you advise them that remedy must be sought in a Court of law as opposed to through the Law Society. The other MSP pointed out that people find it hard to secure the services of a solicitor who is willing to take up such a case. You also mentioned that you operate a Troubleshooting scheme that could help with such situations. Would you tell someone who was having difficulty in finding a solicitor about that scheme?*

The President of the Law Society: *Yes. We have no statistics on that matter, as it is difficult to link together all the incidents, but we know that the majority of cases are dealt with when people go to a solicitor. Solicitors are in business to make money, and, if they can take on a case and fulfil a professional duty for a client, they will do that, regardless of whether the case concerns another solicitor. A solicitor may not want to raise an action against a local solicitor because, apart from anything else, the perception of the client would be affected if he or she saw the two solicitors in the bowling club. In such a situation, a solicitor might refer the case to a solicitor outside the area.*

To the readers, I again refer to **similarities.** What I now refer to is questions asked of a professor when he attended an inquiry of the Justice 1 Committee. This professor declared his status for the record, i.e.: "I am a member of the Law Society Council and I sit on Law Society committees that deal with complaints."

The first question that is asked of the professor is quite interesting. Again, it involves the legal profession. Therefore it is complicated and lengthy, as follows:

MSP to the professor: *Can you give examples of definitions of professional misconduct, unsatisfactory conduct, inadequate professional services?*

His response: *The first thing to say is, if you find these confusing, I wonder what the average member of the public find them, and that was the point I was trying to get across in my evidence. I find these tests to be largely opaque. I don't think they reveal very much to the average member of the public and I don't think they provide very much guidance, to the average practitioner, nor to the client relations committees, not just the lay members of these committees.*

I frankly don't understand how lay members can, of their own volition, come up with an understanding of what competent and reputable solicitors would regard as serious and reprehensible without any further guidance, and the point I was trying to make in my evidence is that they don't get, all too often, that additional guidance and that is what I would like them to have. The way they can get guidance, the primary way to do it, is from the discipline tribunal precedents. The discipline tribunal has given a lot of guidance as to what culpability in all circumstances means.

Rather than go on with the further details in relation to the above statement – i.e. the MSP to the professor – I will save you the boring details. I will finish with one other last question put to the professor by the same **MSP:** *What about remedies for clients and consequences for the solicitors? Are you looking at the penalties, if you like, and the way that clients can be compensated?*

Professor: *Clients are compensated not through unsatisfactory conduct findings, but they are compensated through IPS (inadequate professional service) findings. The test for IPS is professional services which are not in any respect of the quality which could be reasonably expected of the competent solicitor. Now lay people are able to comment on that. But both lay people and lawyers on the*

> *committees, when presented with lay people and lawyers on the committees, when presented with "You can compensate up to £1,000", unless we develop forms of guidance to say what level of compensation is appropriate for what kind of case, then, there is no mechanism to achieve consistency. So it's the same problem that you have with the test of misconduct and unsatisfactory conduct. Unless you look at the guidance, unless the committees are given more guidance than they currently receive and the same for the Council, then there is no mechanism to achieve consistency or result. I think that consistency is very important in a complaints procedure.*

Before I could put any details in writing, I had to make sure that I gathered all my information, especially in respect of the Justice 1 Committee mentioned above. This same committee formally announced the remit of its inquiry on 19th June 2001, identifying key issues and options to be considered by the committee.

Background papers reveal the following note by the clerk:

> *In previous discussions the committee agreed to request the preparation of a summary of individual views in order to aid its consideration of the issues arising from the evidence received as part of the inquiry into the regulation of the legal profession...*

> *...It should be noted that this summary does not cover every point raised, and committee members should refer to the detailed submissions for a complete outline of the issues.*

Regarding the Justice 1 Committee's consultation paper, the committee agreed that it would **not** pursue individual cases or complaints, but that it would examine the main issues arising from the individual cases to explore how the system worked in practice and the difficulties experienced. Therefore, the committee agreed not to call individuals to give oral evidence for this inquiry or to call for the release of further information on individual cases.

2002

I concluded with the Justice 1 Committee through a 15-page letter dated 4th November 2002 to the convener of the Justice 1 Committee, Christine Graham:

MAJOR INQUIRY INTO THE REGULATION OF THE LEGAL PROFESSION

Dear Ms Graham,

On the 23rd June 2002 I wrote to you regarding my research into the above.

I now feel the time has come to give you the details of my continued research and my personal views in relation to the above Inquiry and the papers you sent to me in April setting out The committee's introduction and remit of the inquiry summarised in annexe A.

*After research, viewing and taking notes at the Justice 1 Committee's various meetings with the Law Society, The ombudsman, Scottish Consumer Council, Marsh UK, Professor Alan Paterson, Margaret Ross deputy head of Law school in Aberdeen, members of SACL, my personal involvement with Petition PE361 and a meeting with the petition's committee, I have discovered that The Justice 1 Committee, throughout this so-called major inquiry has, by **prevarication and double standards**, given the Scottish public an insight into what a complainant comes up against when going through the Law Society's complaints procedures. The Justice 1 Committee has itself duplicated exactly the facts and circumstances which are constantly encountered within self-regulation of the legal profession. Sadly, the Justice 1 Committee's irresponsible, unethical and undemocratic behaviour has reflected the following:*

1. *Arrogance, abuse of power, lack of accountability*
2. *Conflict of interest*
3. *Deception, dictatorship, double standards, discrimination*
4. *Falsehood, deception, misrepresentation, fraud*
5. *Inadequate professional service, incompetence, intimidation*
6. *Prefabrication of evidence, pretentious double standards, prevarication*
7. *Manipulation, maladministration, malpractice*
8. *A pretence at openness*
9. *Suppression of evidence, abrogation of responsibility*

I recognise that these are strong words and would ask you to consider my justification for holding these views, outlined in the following sections of this letter.

For your convenience a table of section and page details is summarised at the end of this letter.

Section 1

1) *The concrete evidence relating to the above can be found if ethically researched into Petition PE361 and the various other submissions by members of the public, over 100 of which have been submitted to the Justice 1 Committee. Furthermore over 400 submissions have been made to the Scottish Consumer Council's 1998/9 survey. All this research clearly demonstrates that a great deal of vital information is in the public domain and, even in the face of self-regulation, it is not possible to bury facts and circumstances (evidence).*

2) *Self-regulation is no regulation; it merely creates the illusion of regulation making it impossible for honest, decent lawyers to practise their profession freely and properly.*

3) *It is important to remember that most lawyers and judges are decent and hard working. However, the legal system has been corrupted by a minority of lawyers and politicians who look at the justice system as a means to exploit decent people by taking advantage of a corrupt system that denies any ordinary human being any form of redress.*

4) *You have and still are imposing unnecessary suffering by protecting self-regulation which, in its present form, gives a permit for the legal profession to abuse at will. This also applies to the manipulation of the Scotland (Solicitors) 1980 Act.*

Section 2

1) *May I remind members of the Justice 1 Committee that you are there to serve the public on the basis of the following:*

The Seven Principles of Public Life
Selflessness, Integrity, Objectivity, Accountability, Openness, Honesty, Leadership

2) *In carrying out its inquiry into the self-regulation of the legal profession the Justice 1 Committee is obligated to perform under the above-mentioned seven principles of public life. In making my own study I can reveal to the Scottish public that these are non-existent. Your conduct throughout this inquiry quite simply mirrors what a complainant has to endure at the hands of the Law Society when it follows its own complaints procedure, i.e. I refer again to the nine points of incomprehensible incompetence listed above.*

3) *A poorly run justice system is bad for both lawyers and judges and, in the long run, the whole legal system suffers.*

4) *I would remind these incompetent lawyers and politicians that our Courts and our system, along with lawyers and judges, are here to serve us the Scottish people by helping us to solve our differences as quickly, efficiently, and inexpensively as possible.*

   The Judicial system is here to serve us; not to make lawyers rich. The rights of the people must always take precedence over the profits of lawyers. The ethical integrity of the justice system is of paramount importance.

Section 3

1) *All judges, QCs, barristers and lawyers should be held accountable to the highest of ethical standards. The public should never be given any cause to think that these public servants are crooked. Certainly the public must never believe that this is simply the way it is and that there is nothing can be done about it.*

2) *It is up to our politicians to support their constituents, as complainants, and help them to follow their complaints through to a successful conclusion using a proper, unbiased complaints procedure, free of any intimidation, corruption, or abuse of power by any member of the legal profession or an incompetent Law Society. It is imperative that an independent lay committee, free from any legal influence, is incorporated not only into the complaints procedure as soon as practical and without undue delay, but also into the offices of the Scottish Consumer Council.*

The judicial system is here to serve us; not to make lawyers rich. The rights of the people must always take precedence over the profits of lawyers. The ethical integrity of the justice system is of paramount importance. **Section 3**

3) *The present system is extremely damaging and inflicts serious consequences on the health and well being of complainants and their families. In fact, it causes untold misery.* **An inquiry must be set up by the medical profession** *to assess the mental and physical suffering that has resulted from years of persecution.*

4) *We need urgent changes to save our legal system's worldwide reputation. Although many Court procedures have a long history of tradition, they are not written into law. The judicial system should be actively evolving its traditions to find better ways to serve the public.*

Section 4 – Self-Regulation of the Legal Profession

In the last 22 years, since the introduction of the Solicitors (Scotland) Act 1980, this statute requires:

Part 1 Organisation. The Law Society of Scotland. Establishment and Objects of the Law Society of Scotland

1) *The Law Society of Scotland (referred to in this Act as "the Society") shall continue to exist and shall exercise the functions conferred upon it by this Act.*

2) *The object of the society shall include the promotion of*
   a) *the interests of the solicitors' profession in Scotland and;*
   b) *the interests of the public in relation to that profession.*

3) *The society may do anything that is incidental or conducive to the exercise of these functions or the attainment of these objects.* **Section 4 – Self-Regulation of the Legal Profession**

In the last 22 years, since the introduction of the Solicitors (Scotland) Act 1980, this Statute requires:

Part 1 Organisation. The Law Society of Scotland. Establishment and Objects of the Law Society of Scotland

1) *The Law Society of Scotland (referred to in this Act as "the Society") shall continue to exist and shall exercise the functions conferred upon it by this Act.*

2) *The object of the Society shall include the promotion of*
   a) the interests of the solicitors' profession in Scotland; and
   b) the interests of the public in relation to that profession.

3) *The Society may do anything that is incidental or conducive to the exercise of these functions or the attainment of these objects.*

4) *Schedule 1 shall have effect in relation to the Society.*

The above privilege granted to the legal profession, with an added privilege of self-regulation of that same profession, should have been the basis of a near perfect system for regulating law and order in Scotland, promoting a close bond between the people of Scotland, the legal profession and various public bodies like the office of the ombudsman, Scottish Consumer Council, and Parliament.

Section 5

1) *Under the above statute and self-regulation of the legal profession over the last twenty plus years many questions have been raised about our Scottish culture, including people in heads of Government and the various public bodies which have been formed to help promote (a) and (b) of the statute. Failings exist because the people who are there supposedly to protect us under these privileges are the very people that are themselves ruthlessly destroying, let alone failing to promote, our culture.*

2) *Using statistics (at which the Law Society excels), consider the following:*

> *In 1984 900 complaints were made to the Law Society. In the year 2000 1200 complaints were made. Taking an average of 1000 complaints per year between 1984 and 2000, there must have been some 16,000 complaints. Including complainants families, this means that some 50,000 human beings must have been affected. A total of about 3500 lawyers have taken part in these civil actions, NOT the 10,000 claimed by The Law Society.*

> *Are we to take from these figures, (and a lot more questions need to be asked in relation to them) that the 1980 statute has been promoted and complied with and self-regulation under the present system has been a success?*

> *According to the Law Society it has been a success. The obvious next question is: In whose favour? Who is protecting whom?*

3) *Since the early 1980s and prior, the legal profession has continued to Advocate to members of the profession, through meetings and seminars, including literature such as* **Professional Ethics and Practice for Scottish Solicitors***, the following professional ethics and practices:*

>   *a) A duty of care is owed to clients, and negligence may not only render solicitors liable to compensate the client, but may also be of such a character and be so aggravated as to constitute professional misconduct. Similarly, delay can amount to professional misconduct.*

>   *b) A cardinal principle is that a solicitor should always put his client's interests first ahead of his own.*

>   *c) Solicitors should never allow anyone to act fraudulently towards their clients and must not take improper advantage of the youth, inexperience, lack of education, senility, ill health or unbusinesslike habits of a client.*

4) *In addition The Law Society, in its meetings with the Justice 1 Committee, claims it is still making changes within the system. Taking on more lay people and the Troubleshooter scheme are examples. The Society's assertion that the introduction of more lay people is the salvation that will satisfy all complainants, is simply another ploy – a confidence trick.*

Section 6

1) *(These same practices (outlined above with regard to the legal profession) also apply to the members of the Justice 1 Committee. You have acted with abuse of process and abuse of power against the petitioners who submitted Petition PE361. We demand democracy, equality of rights, and a Government by all the people, free from discrimination.*

2) *Members of the Justice 1 Committee **must** be reminded that it is your duty to follow, **not** to pervert, the true course of justice. Lay members must not be misled or intimidated by members of the legal profession. It is your duty to ensure that the evidence provided by members of the public is properly scrutinized so that all important pertinent questions and answers have been rigorously researched, and asked of the public bodies that appear before the Justice 1 Committee, and that the entire process is carried out openly, without secrecy, and the findings are placed in the public domain.*

3) *The public quite rightly expect a **justice** committee of the Scottish Parliament to act within the realms of a democracy, in line with any statute enacted by parliament to promote **justice**, and to ensure that both LAY and legal members of that committee **separately** and without undue influence interview openly a cross section of complainants (with representation) to ascertain the true facts and circumstances before proceeding with this inquiry. Bearing in mind the seriousness of this issue and the effect on the general public, this must surely be the proper way forward for any committee to conduct itself. The people in Scotland need inspiration; certainly not corruption. This is particularly important for Parliamentary staff.*

4) *It must be obvious to the lay members of the committee, assuming your research and investigations have been of the highest rigorous standards and, in particular, you have studied the details and concrete evidence found in Petition 361, that the evidence contained in the petition clearly shows a distinct advantage in favour of the legal profession. Disadvantages are quite evidently encountered by complainants at the hands of a self-regulated Law*

*Society and now the Justice 1 Committee. I further stress that complainants are **ALWAYS** at a disadvantage having to prepare their evidence and then expose it to the opposition for them to act accordingly. It needs no high level of intellect to see this unfair imbalance, irrespective of how many lay people are involved. This is no reflection on the legal members of the committee who, I am sure, have scrutinized in detail all of the contents of PE361. Fore-warned is fore-armed. You must, however, ask yourselves the question: Why should the complainant always be subject to a disadvantage when it is the self-regulated body that has been incompetent. **We, the complainants are being controlled and discriminated against.***

5) *On the same note, it must further be obvious to the lay members that a complainant ON HIS OWN is at a disadvantage. He/she must give all his/her evidence to the Law Society in writing which is then passed to the incompetent lawyer, leaving the complainant helpless against ALL the legal powers arrayed against him/her engaged in setting up their deterrents, counter actions and ploys. A sole complainant faces a powerful force, alone.*

6) *In giving PE361 to the Justice 1 Committee before the major inquiry into the self-regulation of the legal profession, that same committee has been fore-warned to put into operation a warning code to protect the law society and self-regulation at all costs. This is **conflict of interest**.*

7) *Up to now the Justice 1 Committee has been successful in the use of that code, ignoring democracy, statute of responsibility, suppressing evidence, and enabling abuse of process, abuse of power and prevarication.*

8) *Up to now the Justice 1 Committee has been successful in the use of that code, ignoring democracy, statute of responsibility, suppressing evidence, and enabling abuse of process, abuse of power and prevarication.*

9) *Complainants under self-regulation of the legal profession have no access to democracy. They should not have to forewarn their opponents. They are placing themselves at the mercy of an undemocratic process and could find themselves being harassed, intimidated, and facing unrelenting delaying tactics. There are already thousands of victims under this system all of whom have been, and still are being, controlled and victimised outwith the 1980 Act.*

Section 7

1) *It is imperative that a new system to combat corruption, secrecy, and to prevent continued persecution be adopted and put in place with immediate effect. There must exist a system that can be adopted to help both the complainer and the legal profession. This should be discussed openly without intimidation or arrogance, and involving various public bodies. There should be no restraints on anyone or their credentials, except for the naming of individuals complained against.*

This meeting should not be controlled or chaired by any member of the Law Society or legal profession. This would demonstrate openness, integrity, accountability, and no fear of intimidation.

This new system, with an independent lay committee, will succeed given a proper reasonable time scale. It would not need 22 years. All we need is the cooperation of retired business men/women of good business acumen, honesty and integrity. It could not fail.

2) **Complainants have a right to an effective remedy in law** pursued through a democratic process, namely the right to a fair unbiased hearing, a right to justice through proper representation with financial assistance (i.e. Legal Aid), and without undue delays. An effective remedy should not be blocked by any individual or group of people using unethical methods or deterrents for their own benefit, i.e. financial gain or **promotion** (as is currently the case with self-regulation).

3) **Financial Assistance Through Legal Aid**

Ian Dunbar, then President of the Law Society, stated in his speech to newly-qualified solicitors at Parliament House in Edinburgh: "There are a huge number of members of the public who could not afford to contemplate going to Court without the protection of some form of Legal Aid or other financial contribution. I **know I** couldn't face up to a major proof in the Court of session with the prospect of expenses being awarded against me. How much more for the ordinary man or woman in the street." He then went on to state: "I believe the Government speaks with forked tongue on these issues; it pays lip service to citizens' rights to get to the Court but **effectively puts so many barriers in their way** of a financial nature that it is quite unrealistic for the ordinary man/woman ever to cross the threshold of the Court."

4) "Effectively puts barriers in the way" – quite an interesting quote from Mr Dunbar? What effective barriers and deterrents does the Law Society use against complainants who, incidentally, are HUMAN BEINGS simply trying to get access to justice.

5) *One of the main tactics used as a barrier to combat an effective remedy is to undermine the will and energy of the complainant. Let us call this the **"flea in the jar policy"** i.e. when you place a number of fleas in a jar and put the lid on, you will observe them all jumping like hell until, after a short while, one by one even the strongest will cease to jump or even move. This is what happens to complainants who have no support and are left helpless by the corrupt few and the corrupt Law Society under self-regulation.*

6) *After one has fought for years with undying willpower at one's own cost, which could range from thousands, hundreds of thousands, even millions, the most you can receive in compensation is one thousand pounds from the Law Society. One's next move, they tell you, is to go to Court on your own if you still wish to pursue a negligence action against the offending lawyer (see Section 7(3) above), because the Law Society does not deal with negligence cases. THE OMBUDSMAN THINKS AND STATES 1000 POUNDS COMPENSATION IS REALISTIC. This is truly incredible and, for many, an insult in the face of massive financial loss.*

Section 8

1) *I am sure the committee must have deliberated on the next questions:*

   a) *Where does the complainant go next? What is his/her alternative given that his/her lawyer has been fined for IPS which must be an indication of their incompetence?*

   b) *To whom or to where does the complainant turn? Can the committee provide an answer to how complainants recover their losses which far outweigh the level of compensation? How do they now get to Court with a legal representative?*

2) *If the answer is to use the Law Society's Troubleshooter scheme, that would be an insult to both the complainants and the intelligence of the Scottish public.*

Section 9

1) *I would now refer you to the meeting between Scotland Against Crooked Lawyers (SACL) and the Public Petitions Committee (8th May 2001). Starting with page 9/ Col 1096 through to page 17/, the questions I would ask the committee, especially the lay members, are: How carefully did you examine this petition? Did you take particular note of the various statements of the members of the committee? I will remind you of some:*

2) **Col 1099 Dorothy-Grace Elder;** *"In my 25 years in journalism before I entered Parliament, I found that no other profession brought such a weight of misery to the public, especially when they tried to get redress, which could drive people almost insane. I agree with what Dickens said in "Bleak House" that the law is a beast that feeds on human misery."*

"There is no redress in Scotland and we should not be proud of such a system, which leaves the Law Society sitting in judgement like the devil sitting in judgement on sin".

Col 1103 Dorothy-Grace Elder; *"We should ask the Law Society and the Faculty of Advocates specific questions. We will not get straight answers unless we ask straight questions. We do not want broad-brush answers but specific details." I now pose the questions: Did we get straight answers (**No**). Did we get broad-brush answers? (**Yes**).*

The Convener; *"The bodies involved have to realise that the Scottish Parliament oversees the legal profession now and they must respond to it honestly and openly."*

The Convener; *"The petitioners' evidence shows that **there is a case to answer**".*

Dorothy-Grace Elder; *"We would be doing a most useful job in addressing the issue. This is one of the biggest grass-roots issues, whether the grass roots are in rich areas of Scotland – they rapidly become less rich if there are bad encounters with the law – or with the poorest of the poor. People are living in mental agony for years because of bad legal work."*

*I would like you to now cross reference the above petition details with the meeting between the Law Society and the Justice 1 Committee which, **conveniently**, just happens to be a briefing that is not part of the inquiry.*

3) *Col 2604 Phil Gallie;* *"I believe negligence is the factor that creates most problems for you."*

*Martin McAllister then began a lengthy debate resulting in a **broad-brushed answer including an analogy to a car accident and an insurance company.** (Again an insult to people's intelligence).*

Phil Gallie responded: **"I think we have drifted off the point".**

As we all know, Mr Phil Gallie and the convener, Alasdair Morgan, were conveniently replaced by two members of the legal profession, one of whom happened to come fresh from the Law Society and the other, a QC, who has

*written to me through my MP stating that he has no plans
to change self-regulation. Our then First Minister – Mr
McLeish – and our Justice Minister – Mr Jim Wallace –
have also both written to me stating: "We have no plans
to change self-regulation".*

Section 10

1) *How and why should we, the Scottish public, put up with
this continued corruption and persecution? There must
be a better system – one that can be proved to be better.
The legal profession have had it all their own way for far
too long with the Law Society's complainants procedure,
with disastrous results for the public. Certain members of
the Law Society have gained promotion through design
and manipulation to destroy and get rid of complainants.
They will do anything to hold on to their position and
gain promotion whilst creating misery for others with the
help and collusion of their "buddies". They thus promote
double standards and corruption whilst laughing at
the complainants helpless in the face of their corrupt
systems.*

2) *In a recent parliamentary debate on television a well-
known Tory party member vehemently opposed a fellow
member MSP with a final statement: "You will do
anything to hold on to your job".*

*The obvious question that now arises and which should
be pursued regarding that statement is: Could this be
pertinent to all of the 129 MSPs, which include members
of the Justice 1 Committee?*

Is it possible that strong influence by certain members of Parliament could adversely influence others by perverting the course of justice by using their professional position, and by asking loaded questions such as: "If you were to oppose self-regulation and you were one day to require the services of a lawyer, where would you turn"? There is an obvious inference behind this question. It would need a very strong person not to be influenced by the prospect of losing favour with the legal profession.

Could the Tory party member's final statement be one of the most significant issues in respect of the Justice 1 Committee's MAJOR INQUIRY INTO THE SELF-REGULATION OF THE LEGAL PROFESSION?

Could it even be possible that, being an MSP in a position of power, with a recent significant increase in salary, taking part in a major inquiry in a constant close relationship with members of the legal profession, could affect your personal investigations which, in turn, could sway important decisions affecting our nation? Bearing in mind the Tory party member's statement, I see probability, not just the possibility of this happening.

3) *The public perception of the legal professional throughout the world has been well publicised – unfortunately the masses suffer because of the few. One prominent and destructive feature that is **always** prevalent in the legal profession is a very descriptive word **ARROGANCE** (not necessarily applicable to all lawyers) but found in the upper echelons, amongst those comfortable with power, influence and money. It is a word that has influence on the learning process – people who are arrogant stop learning. And that is when ignorance takes over.*

4) *A perfect example of this was found in the Justice 1 Committee's meetings with the various public bodies where members of the legal profession excelled in showing their arrogance or, should one say, their ignorance. These people are blatant in their complacent assumption they are above the law and somehow untouchable. Indeed, in some cases, they are untouchable and that is against the principles of a democracy. Society would be well rid of this mindset. The people who have this mindset take hundreds of thousands of pounds every year from the taxpayers' money (i.e. Legal Aid) and use this money to compound their arrogance and dictate and control the very people they take the money from. Such details are simply water off a duck's back to these people who are utterly bereft of morals.*

Section 11

1) *There are still a substantial number of searching questions that have not been asked of the various public bodies that were requested to appear in front of the committee. These questions and answers, if properly researched, could very well offer numerous important bearings on the final decisions and outcome of the committee unless, of course, this major inquiry is a puppet exercise and the decisions have already been made.*

2) ***The Dean of Faculty Mr Colin Boyd*** *made a statement to the committee that could be taken as intimidation. He intimated that, if self-regulation were to be removed, the legal profession would be in dire straits. He could possibly be speaking solely out of self-interest as opposed to the public interest.*

Your refusal to allow individuals to give evidence against the various public bodies, including the Faculty of Advocates is contrary to democracy and the European Court of Human Rights. These individuals would have given the committee a cross reference of facts and circumstances similar to the ombudsman where she gave two examples relating to specific cases without naming individuals.

Martin McAllister, President of The Law Society, defending lawyers and the legal profession, had the audacity to bring on a layperson who had supposedly served on committees for five years with the Law Society. The Justice 1 committee allowed this. Again, very convenient for the benefit of whom? Is she the wife of a lawyer? We are entitled to know.

3) *Lay people working on committees in the Law Society complaints section are **specifically** not named. This is a fact verified by the Law Society. Yet this person has been named and brought before the committee in the public domain to state her support for self-regulation. This is obviously the reason she was brought before the committee in the first place. Again this is not democracy; it is double standards and full of pretences. **I will require her full credentials and status.***

Section 12

1) *Refer to Section 10 (2). "Do anything to hold on to your job". The things people will stoop to and how far they will go is beyond comprehension. A recent article by Robert Hare, a world expert on mental disorder who teaches at the University of British Columbia, observes that psychopathic behaviour helps people get to the top in big companies. "Office psychos", he said, "gain promotion*

*because they have no hint of a conscience and have an inflated sense of self. But once they get to the top they can place the giant companies they run in grave danger". He added that office psychos "are deceitful, short tempered and display early behavioural problems that later become anti-social." They are callous, cold-blooded individuals who do not consider that you have feelings. They have no sense of guilt or remorse. "That is why the **manipulative, arrogant,** behaviour of psychopaths often makes them prime candidates for promotion". He further states that police and teachers are screened, so why not also screen people who handle hundreds of millions of pounds.*

2) *Hundreds of millions of pounds is handled through our Court system. (a) Does it work? and (b) Who benefits from our Court system?*

   (a) *According to Judges and Sheriffs, it does not work. Jack McConnell promised reforms to Scotland's Court system as part of a three-pronged thrust to improve justice, law and order. That was in January 2002.*

      *In May 2002 – **Wasted time puts our Court system on trial.** Police are claiming that they have to find £42m every year from their budgets to pay for officers to sit and wait for their cases to start.*

      *In January 2002 – **Ramshackle Court system.** For too long, Scots have borne delays, excessive cost, stress and a needless drain on the time of police, social workers, witnesses, juries, indeed anyone who has the misfortune to encounter the process of law in its current ramshackle state.*

   (b) *Lawyers benefit from our Court system through Legal Aid which has been found to be constantly abused. The legal aid costs are soaring and, in 2003, because of the massive increases proposed, i.e. "Lawyers are about to demand an increase in hourly fees from just over forty pounds to one hundred, and for other one-off fees to be raised from around two hundred to six hundred pounds. The fee for instruction to do work should go up from two hundred and seven to five hundred pounds," says the committee and the charge for adjustment to pleadings should increase from one hundred and eighty two pounds to six hundred pounds under the law Society's plans. All other charges would be increased by at least one hundred percent. Is the system of self-regulation about to be further abused? It would seem that this is already happening.*

3) *August 2002 – It has been reported that a North-East solicitor's "potential dishonesty" could cost a lawyers' compensation fund millions of pounds. Three judges at the Court of session were told that there had been "wholesale breaches" of accounts rules and one client had three point seven million pounds at risk.*

4) *The Scottish Parliament and the Law Society of Scotland have failed the Scottish people. They have allowed a system of corruption under self-regulation to go on for far too long. Our so-called **justice** minister has, and still is, making a mockery of so called **democracy** by continually supporting self-regulation. Complainants have a basic right to an effective remedy of redress. All this could have been in place for the last twenty years. If implemented then, it would have secured a protection for clients before they even approached the services of a lawyer, with further protection when going through The Law Society's complaint system where a further simple effective remedy could also have been implemented.*

No other profession in the world creates and imposes so much misery on so many people continuously, with millions of pounds being wasted and going astray.

5) *The Scottish Parliament, with immediate effect, would be well advised to save face, and force the Law Society and the legal profession to set up a special Court to accommodate and compensate complainants who have been made to suffer persecution under the nine points listed on page one. These same complainants have been through the Troubleshooter scheme and have been judged by temporary Sheriffs and can produce evidence to prove negligence in a Court of law. They have been deprived of justice and discriminated against because of an incompetent legal profession and system. That is why they are now, because of the strength of their complaints and supporting concrete evidence, seeking redress under ECHR and 1980 Act.*

6) *A special group of legal experts, independent of the Law Society, should be set up to represent these complainants with the support of Legal Aid. This would set the records straight, at last confirming that Scotland has both the best Legal Aid and best legal system in the world (if we are to promote such, as we all should wish to do).*

Section 13

1) *All through the contents of these fourteen pages I have tried to show just some or should I say a LITTLE of the misery that I personally and others have gone through in the last twenty years. I think, if you were to go through the documentation again in detail, the Justice 1 Committee might just get a **slight inkling** that our legal system, our*

Law Society and Parliament must make the necessary changes to stop this misery and get rid of corruption once and for all.

2) *I would suggest no more **ploys**, the most recent one being a member of the Justice 1 Committee showing "concern" about increased costs in Legal Aid and ensuring that the public knows about it via an article in the newspapers, dated 22nd September 2002. Could this be double standards?*

3) *We are supposed to be a democracy. Yet you, the Justice 1 Committee, have not kept within the parameters of that said democracy. And if you think you have, then your arrogance and ignorance has again come to the fore. The facts and circumstances will prove same.*

4) *Before I make any accusations and charges against the Justice 1 Committee, I wish to inform the committee members of something very coincidental from three different people who all gave examples and stories relating to car accidents, i.e. Mr Martin McAllister, Mr Gordon Jackson, and Linda Costella Baker when meeting with the committee. I found this interesting but without any relevance to a Major Inquiry. Even so, I now feel that I must also relate to a car incident to show, by analogy, an **effective remedy** involving any of the following: Judge, Sheriff, Lawyer, Barrister, QC.*

*He/She has filled a car with petrol and is making his/her way down one of the main highways. To his/her dismay the car slows down so he/she pulls over to the shoulder and the car eventually stops. "**What do I do now? Who do I turn to? Who is going to help me?**"*

He/she knows nothing about cars and how they work. Fortunately a car pulls up behind and the driver offers assistance, taking him/her to the nearest service station to phone for the AA man or use the services of the service station. He/she has a choice. Within an hour the car is fixed and he/she is on his/her way. **Effective choice/Effective remedy.**

In reference to both of the Justice 1 Committee's legal profession inquiries listed above, it's important to note how they keep control of every given situation, you will see from their inquiries they requested comments from everyone involved, with this information in hand they are in complete control at all times and plan accordingly, they also had in their possession the petition submitted by myself, with a group of complainers. This system is an exact duplication used by the Law Society when a complainer contacts them regarding a complaint against a solicitor.

As I said earlier, all the information I gather is done through my personal involvement, with the help from the clerks of these committees. I formed an excellent relationship through correspondence and meeting with them to sign for letters I personally delivered.

These letters were for each member of the Justice 1 Committee.

They also helped to book my seats for my personal viewing, at first hand, of these committees at work. Prior to all of this I was involved with the petitions committee whereby, I had, along with another group of complainers, submitted a petition to the Scottish Parliament's Public Petitions Committee. The meeting with them was arranged for Tuesday 8th May 2001 in Edinburgh. I think it's important at this point in time to mention a friend who lived in Edinburgh who was a great help to me; he was also a fellow complainer who was also involved with the petition.

Here are just some of the details of the official report of the Public Petitions Committee (8th May 2001):

> **MSP:** *My question is the age-old one, "Who guards the guardians?" There seems to be no tribunals or procedure to question the actions of the Law Society. Is that what you are seeking?*

> **Angus Brown:** *There is a complaints committee, but complainers have to assume that it has looked at all their documents, and all the details, just as we have to assume with the petition. If that committee throws the case out, the complainer cannot appeal. I had a meeting with the ombudsman. Certain changes are supposed to be made, but they are for the benefit not of the complainer, but – as always – of the legal profession.*

> *I ask the public petitions committee, the Parliament, and the Lord Chief Justice to tell me in writing how I can get a lawyer into a Scottish Court of law in a civil action, with proper representation, under the European convention on human rights. That is all that I am asking.*

> **The Convener:** *Self-regulation does not usually get much support in a democratic society. An independent body or person should oversee what any profession is up to.*

> **AB:** *The issue does not affect only people like us; it also affects the morale of the police and the prison services. Two and a half years ago, the papers reported that £9.5 million was wasted by having police sitting in Court rooms waiting to take part in trials that were later abandoned by the lawyers. Today the papers report an attempt to stop such a waste of police time. The issue is important because the Government is trying to cut crime. Having policemen wasting their time sitting in Court rooms, knowing that they are there only because the lawyers want to make hundreds of pounds an hour from the Scottish Legal Aid Board, damages their morale, the Parliament must make note of that.*

The Convener: I accept the point...[and then went on to various items, which included his following comments:]

The petition raises important and wide-ranging issues such as the Lord Advocate's powers, self-regulation the role of the Law Society and so on. The committee will need more information before we can progress the petition, It is suggested that we should agree to seek the views of the Scottish executive, to find out its response to the petition; the Law Society of Scotland and the Faculty of Advocates, who will be able to respond on behalf of the legal profession; The Scottish Legal Services ombudsman, who will be able to comment on the standard of the investigation of complaints by the Law Society; and the Scottish Consumer Council, which has produced a report on complaint handling by the Law Society.

While we await those responses, we should pass the petition to one of the justice committees for information. We could take a decision on whether formally to send the petition to the committee when we have received the responses

One Committee member, an MSP responded: WE should set a deadline because the bodies could delay the matter. We should ask the Law Society and the Faculty of Advocates specific questions not only about the number of complaints, but the type of complaint, which is just as important.

Convener: I am sure that would be possible.

Further response from the same Committee member MSP: We will not get straight answers, unless we ask straight questions and preface those questions with a statement to the effect that we do not want broad-brush answers but specific details. You know who we are dealing with, Convener. We would be doing a most wonderful job in addressing the issue. This is one of the biggest grass-roots issues, whether the grass roots are in rich area of Scotland – they rapidly become less rich if there are bad encounters with the law – or with the poorest of the poor. People are living in mental agony

*for years because of bad legal work. In future, a full inquiry should be
launched by one of the justice committees.*

Further, vital information for the readers: when I booked my seat for the
Justice 1 Committee Meeting that they termed as a briefing, I discovered
later a very disturbing situation regarding the MSP who asked the question
about negligence.

*He upset the legal members of the Justice 1 Committee when he
made the following comment:*

*Every month, we are besieged at the Parliament by a group – I
will not name it – that has a considerable number of complaints
about Solicitors and which, in my view, makes a number of
slanderous statements against them. Given the requirement to
uphold the image of the profession, have you had any contact,
with such groups?*

The Convener: *You missed the early part of the meeting. We are
merely having a briefing, to help us determine the remit of our
inquiry. That question is properly a matter for the inquiry, when the
Law Society will undoubtedly come back to give further evidence.*

The vital information I mentioned above relates to both the convener
and the member of the committee, i.e. the MSP who asked the difficult
questions.

At the end of the meeting, I asked the clerk if I could purchase a video of
the meeting. This I did, and was shocked to find, after viewing it, the part
of the meeting where the MSP asked the difficult questions was not on
the video, and further to that both the convener and the aforementioned
MSP were removed from the committee and replaced by two members of
the legal profession.

I once again warn you the readers, you the past complainers, you the
general public, and yes, you potential future complainers – beware. I

have mentioned before, the legal profession has no boundaries, as far as control is concerned. They will do **anything to maintain that control.** The details above are the perfect example.

To you the readers, and all concerned, I thought the above was a perfect example, but it is superseded by the following:

Top Secret The Law Society of Scotland Internal Memorandum, **Doctored by the Parliament's Lawyers.**

The Scottish Parliament's lawyers struck out the crucial words from this top secret Law Society memo. MSP, leader of the opposition, knows all about this memo and its contents. He describes it as an "explosive" document proving "insider influence" by the Law Society of Scotland on individual insurance claims made by clients against Scottish solicitors!!!

This memo is written by the chief executive of the Law Society, and he proposes arranging a "summit meeting" with (a member of) (holders of the master insurance policy) to discuss a complainer's "several valid claims". This complainer is a big threat to the legal establishment in that he holds a lot of evidence exposing high-level legal corruption – not least, this Law Society internal memo.

The chief executive goes on to describe this complainer as an "intelligent and well organised individual who would come across very well in giving evidence to the Justice 1 Inquiry"!!!

So to crown it all, while the Justice 1 Committee were holding a **major inquiry** into self-regulation of the legal profession, the top executives of the Law Society were again using double standards to undermine complainers and pervert the true course of justice. They are the pits of this Earth.

So, as my readers will by now know, I have been corresponding with the Law Society since 1990, which included deputy secretaries, director, and top executives, asking for access to justice and now in the year 2001. I had to sit composed, listening and watching these same crooked executives from the Law Society giving evidence at the Justice 1 Committee meetings, where they were knowingly, along with the legal members of these committees, perverting the course of true justice.

But at least we can now see, through their own words and actions, how they have more or less exposed the crooked system they work to, whereby they have completely ignored a very important fact. The legal profession is governed by a statute of law; **Solicitors (Scotland) Act 1980** in which it is stated:

1) The Law Society of Scotland (referred to in this Act as "the Society") shall continue to exist and shall exercise the functions conferred upon it by this Act.

2) The object of the Society shall include the promotion of

   a) The interests of the solicitors' profession in Scotland;

   and

   b) The interests of the public in relation to that profession.

3) The Society may do anything that is incidental or conducive to the exercise of these functions or the attainment of those objects.

Just look at these words again! It is my experience that a self-regulated legal profession – which is what we currently have – has looked after its own interests, in perfect accord with 2(a), but has done so at the expense of complainers whose needs have been ignored. Thus the balance offered by 2(b) has been nullified. Add to this the potentially sinister emphasis of the word "anything" in 3.

Now that you have read my True Story, I am certain that you have clearly seen how the legal profession is able to go to "any" lengths whatsoever, to protect its interests. In a purportedly democratic society, this has been the sinister and perhaps inevitable consequence of self-regulation. Certainly, the needs of society have not been met.

I mentioned above **we all know.** What I mean by that is, by their own exposures, i.e. the secret memo and the details of these exposures which were highlighted in the national newspapers, all MSPs, the general public, readers of this book, and all complainers have now been given an insight into the legal profession's crooked method of self-regulation. And because of that method and ignoring the above 1980 Act they are and have been destroying our culture and further ignoring democracy.

Because of my involvement with certain members of the Justice 1 Committee, i.e. through correspondence and personal contact, I have had to sit and listen to the corrupt details of certain members of the committee. Two well-known to me legal members of the committee discussed the matter of "name-calling" – water off a duck's back!! However, as far as these two are concerned, plus all the others, they won't have to worry about name-calling in the future. **We all know the real truth**.

Finally, I mentioned earlier, when I attended the briefing of the Justice 1 Committee meeting, that two MSP lay members were replaced by two members of the legal profession (very convenient) one of whom was granted the position of the convener. I think it is important to note that we can say anything about these two members of the legal profession because of their statement above, given my observations regarding both of them, which clearly came across at various meetings, i.e. displaying ignorance complemented by arrogance. Is it possible that their being involved with both the Scottish Parliament and the legal profession makes them untouchable? This can only serve to demonstrate to the people of Scotland how shallow is the connection between these individuals and democracy and a democratic policy.

I rest my case.

Chapter 9

Conclusion

I am sure all my readers will have a number of different opinions in respect of my correspondence to the convener of the Justice 1 Committee. I am also quite sure there will be a lot of anger throughout Scotland, in the minds of people, even the possibility of angry reactions after reading this True Story. But I would ask you – please do not react adversely and fall for the various ploys the legal profession adopt, all described within this book. Remember, this is exactly what they want you to do.

Instead, I ask you, the British people, to emulate what happened in America 40-50 years ago, when the American public was subjected to the same type of legal corruption. I suggest that we react in the same way as they did, by using a very important concept: **Education**.

In America, defendants have suffered unbelievable losses as a result of plaintiffs embarking on the most minor of claims, even ones as simple as those involving tripping over kerbstones! As reported, Americans grew wise to this. They apparently saw through the motives of the lawyers who were working towards their own ends, and eventually learned how to challenge the behaviour of those who used ostensibly attractive opportunities to conjure up business in a surreptitious and devious manner. We in Britain must learn to do the same. We too must learn to challenge those in the legal profession who use subtle and insidious means, such as delaying tactics and other ploys, to mask their own self-serving ends.

Note: Incidentally, here in Scotland a QC who also happens to be an MSP, according to the newspapers, is suing the Edinburgh Council

for £60,000 for tripping over a kerbstone! Is it possible that the "no win, no fee" policy in the UK mirrors the above American system? Is it possible this QC is promoting business for his own crooked legal profession? Is it also possible that some people could lose their homes or their businesses because of such claims?

Let us now return to that important word **education**. I would ask the Scottish people now, and for the future, to join with me in helping everyone in Scotland to become fully conversant with legal procedures in relation to complaints against solicitors, and make sure that we are not left ignorant by the educational authorities in regard to legal matters. Rather than allow school leavers to enter society naively, it should be our civic responsibility to teach every citizen about legal processes and potential pitfalls. Nobody should be forced into the hands of the legal profession, as I was, naively trusting that all would be well and justice would inevitably prevail.

After reading this, I am sure my readers are quite rightly asking the obvious first question – how do we get started?

The answer could be so simple. After reading this True Story your wisdom will be fortified by the knowledge that the system used by our legal profession has the potential to be crooked. Through a Law Society whose main interest is to support fellow lawyers, as evidenced by their ineffective Troubleshooter scheme, we clearly have an ineffective system to deal with complaints. It is a system that manipulates to its own ends, as witnessed, for example, by their clever use of the word **negligent**. Now, with the considerable concrete evidence in our possession, what would happen if we were to concentrate all our efforts together? We would very quickly find ourselves in a position to challenge the legal profession in Court with proper genuine legal representation. With this additional knowledge, and because of our concentrated efforts, the task of challenging the legal profession would not seem so formidable.

In the meantime, it is extremely important to warn any future complainers to refrain from going to the Law Society with their complaints against solicitors. My suggestion would be for each and every one of us to contact both our local MSP and MP and tell them, after reading this book, that you do not want to follow in the footsteps of previous complainers, because of the possibility of falling into a similar trap leading to potential financial ruin, let alone health and other problems. For Scottish readers, you may be comforted to know that a copy of this book is in the hands of every single MSP (as of May 2010). I have made these copies available to MSPs **free of charge**.

If you are given a difficult time, remind them of their position as your MSP/MP and let them know that you are aware of how the crooked legal system works in respect of complaints against solicitors. Also, let them know you have started a programme to educate yourself of the pitfalls involved in going to the Law Society with complaints. Inform them where you found the details. This will help you protect yourself from unnecessary suffering.

And suffering there may well be. I must inform my readers of what I have had to endure over the years since my involvement with both an incompetent Law Society and a self-serving legal profession:

For years I suffered with angina. Then I faced a double heart by-pass followed by stent insert. Finally, I succumbed to a stroke. Financial ruin pales into insignificance when health is involved.

It will now have become apparent to all concerned why I advise future complainers to avoid going to the Law Society with any complaints against solicitors. Their self-regulated system is crooked. In the future, I strongly advise on the importance of contacting the Scottish Consumer Council. When you do so, remind them of the details of their correspondence, reflected in this book, and follow through by informing them of my True Story. Also, I shall be in touch with the Ombudsman with reference to our tape-recorded meeting and all that is included in this book.

I think it is vitally important my readers remain fully informed, and educated, about all the details found in this True Story regarding complaints handled through the Scottish Law Society. Be aware that this sorry tale is also duplicated in England, through their own system of complaints against solicitors. After approximately five years of correspondence between myself and a group of complainers and individuals in England, vital information has been passed between us. We are able to keep ourselves updated and are completely alert to the fact that duplicate information exists regarding the sufferings and hardships imposed on complainers in both England and Scotland. Sadly, however, the numbers and types of complaint in England are greatly magnified compared to Scotland.

Over and over again I have been thinking – what would be the best way to come to the end of this True Story? I have decided that the best way forward would be to inform the readers of my 25 hair-raising, demanding years. In those years I have been involved with two exceptionally well-known professions in Scotland, namely the legal profession and the medical profession.

My main reason for introducing both these professions at the end of this True Story is very simple. **It is certainly not to complicate matters,** but to highlight the **vast** differences which can be found within these two professional bodies in relation to the health and well-being of the Scottish public. I, along with other complainers with whom I have been in contact, can substantiate these vast differences. And I can assure my readers that other complainers have suffered far more than I have from their experiences at the hands of the law profession.

However, with reference to the medical profession:

Over the past years, I have been personally involved with four different hospitals and a nursing home. In the last eighteen years, I have taken my health problems to my local surgery, local doctors, nurses, and other staff. The treatment I have experienced with all of these professional people has been incredible. I give them my sincere thanks. With these two words – praise and admiration – I pray to God that each and every one of these wonderful people receive the strength, energy, and wisdom to continue their outstanding work

Furthermore, in the last 20 years the medical profession have made incredible progress in the field of medicine and technology, all aimed at advancing the cause of the health and well-being of humankind.

Let us now contrast this with the legal profession. In the same 20-year period I think we can say that they too have progressed! But not in any way designed to **improve** their system of helping complainers to get to Court. Changes have only been introduced to help themselves. Indeed, it would be interesting to invite them to tell us of any kind of progress or improvements they have made within the legal system that is not self serving, bearing in mind the continual and periodic complaints from their own members such as judges, Sheriffs, etc.

I think the best people to be challenged to offer an answer to the question about improvements to their system would be the legal members of Parliament, the Scottish Consumer Council, and the legal Ombudsman. Let us hope we get a **simple truthful answer** – one that does not insult the intelligence of the Scottish people.

Finally to my readers, may I remind you how often, through this True Story, you will have read the often repeated sentence: **What can I do about it? Nothing!** This is very relevant to everyone involved in the legal profession, and in particular the Law Society, where they have the comfort of not having to concern themselves about complainers, nor for that matter the general public, because they know well enough that there is really is **nothing** that complainers can do – the public is powerless, which means of course that democracy is non-existent.

With this in mind, I would like my readers to join with me in placing ourselves in the minds of those members of the Scottish Parliament who hail from the law profession. They too have this knowledge of the complaints system and how complainers **can do nothing about it.** Is it possible these particular MSPs, with the comfort of this knowledge, now use it to such an extent that they take advantage of it. Think how they behave in Parliament, or in public. Think of their look of arrogance. Remember that look. Remind yourself how complacent they are – how sleaze and corruption are now a part of public life – and know that the insidious tendrils have spread to the law profession. I am continually watching MSPs and their behaviour. I am no longer surprised. It makes me ever more determined. Change **will** come. Join me in being a part of that change.

I look to the day when change will take the form of seeing **lay** members of Parliament asking legal members, without fear of reprisal, questions relating to negligence and how to get true justice through the Scottish Court system.

I look to the day when we see true democracy in action within our society, within parliament, and within the legal profession. I ask my readers to take one final leap of imagination. Read the following words, then ask yourself a simple question "How different would Angus Brown's (or my own) story have been in such a world?":

In a true democracy all people listen,

all people care,

all people's needs are important,

all people feel cared for,

all people experience respect,

all people serve,

all people are equal,

all people are free.

In a true democracy there are no demagogues,

there is no violence,

all people are entitled to equal representation,

all systems serve people,

all people are responsible for their actions,

all systems are adequate to meet people's needs,

there are no judgments based upon characteristics,

all people are free.

In a true democracy all people are open to learning,

religion is spiritual, not political,

minds are not controlled by fear and guilt,

all minds are open to explore,

paradigms can be challenged,

children learn by example,

adults model the behaviour they want from their children,

all children and adults are free.

In a true democracy all elected officials serve from a position of caring,

all elected officials lead by following,

all people may trust their leadership,

all people are in control of their lives,

all people are free of self-limiting beliefs,

all people contribute that which they are uniquely designed to contribute,

all people give their lives in service to the principles of democracy,
all people are truly free.

In a true democracy all wisdom is preserved,
all people are known by their true motives,
motives are that which allow relationship,
motives are for the highest good,
there is trust,
there is no fear,
all people can trust their leaders,
all people are truly free.

In a true democracy all people know their purpose and calling,
all people contribute their calling,
all needs are met through people,
all who take also give,
giving and taking are an unbroken circle,
all people believe,
all people are empowered,
all people are truly free.

In a true democracy all people are free to heal,
healing is a birthright.
people know how to access healing power,
power is free,

power is in the people,

power is used only for the highest good,

power flows from the top,

all people are truly free.

In a true democracy all people return to their Source.

The Source is free,

the Source is available to all.

One is not assessed for access to the Source,

all races, genders, ethnicities, and spiritual expressions are equal,

all people value their heritage and that of all others,

differences are regarded as enriching,

all people are truly free.

In a true democracy our acceptance creates unity,

our unity is our strength,

our unity is our power,

all people are empowered,

all people are empowered to serve,

all people also receive,

all people care and are cared for,

all people are truly free.

(From *United We Stand: Reflections on a True Democracy*, copyright 2000, by Sue Kidd Shipe, Ph.D.)